A GREAT DUTY

CARLETON LIBRARY SERIES

The Carleton Library Series, funded by Carleton University under the general editorship of the dean of the School of Graduate Studies and Research, publishes books about Canadian economics, geography, history, politics, society, and related subjects. It includes important new works as well as reprints of classics in the fields. The editorial committee welcomes manuscripts and suggestions, which should be sent to the dean of the School of Graduate Studies and Research, Carleton University.

192 The Blacks in Canada:
A History
(second edition)
Robin Winks

193 A Disciplined Intelligence:
Critical Inquiry and Canadian Thought in the Victorian Era
A.B. McKillop

194 Land, Power, and Economics on the Frontier of Upper Canada
John Clarke

195 The Children of Aataentsic:
A History of the Huron People to 1660
Bruce G. Trigger

196 Silent Surrender:
The Multinational Corporation in Canada
Kari Levitt

197 Cree Narrative: Expressing the Personal Meanings of Events
Richard J. Preston

198 The Dream of Nation:
A Social and Intellectual History of Quebec
Susan Mann

199 A Great Duty: Canadian Responses to Modern Life and Mass Culture, 1939–1967
L.B. Kuffert

A Great Duty

*Canadian Responses to
Modern Life and Mass Culture,
1939–1967*

L.B. KUFFERT

Carleton Library Series 199

McGill-Queen's University Press
Montreal & Kingston · London · Ithaca

© McGill-Queen's University Press 2003

ISBN 0-7735-2600-5 (cloth)
ISBN 0-7735-2601-3 (paper)

Legal deposit fourth quarter 2003
Bibliothèque nationale du Québec

Printed in Canada on acid-free paper.

This book has been published with the help of a grant from the Canadian Federation for the Humanities and Social Sciences, through the Aid to Scholarly Publications Programme, using funds provided by the Social Sciences and Humanities Research Council of Canada.

McGill-Queen's University Press acknowledges the support of the Canada Council for the Arts for its publishing program. It also acknowledges the financial support of the Government of Canada through the Book Publishing Industry Development Program (BPIDP) for its publishing activities.

National Library of Canada Cataloguing in Publication

Kuffert, L.B. (Leonard B.) 1968–
    A great duty: Canadian responses to modern life and mass culture in Canada, 1939–1967 / L.B. Kuffert.

(Carleton Library; 199)
Includes bibliographical references and index.
ISBN 0-7735-2600-5 (bnd)
ISBN 0-7735-2601-3 (pbk)

    1. Popular culture – Canada. 2. Canada – Civilization – 20th century.
I. Title. II. Series.

FC95.4.K83 2003   306'.0971   C2003-902403-2
F1021.2.K83 2003

This book was typeset by Dynagram Inc. in 10/12 Sabon.

Contents

Acknowledgments   vii
Introduction: Cultural Criticism in English Canada   3

PART ONE: WAR AND THE CULTURE OF RECONSTRUCTION, 1939–1945

1 Light from the Crucible of War   29
2 The Culture of Reconstruction   66

PART TWO: POSTWAR REALITIES, SHIFTING PERSPECTIVES, 1945–1957

3 Science and Religion in a Mass Culture   107
4 Cultural Policy, Cultural Pessimism   135

PART THREE: FULL CIRCLE: A BROADENING DEFINITION OF CULTURE, 1957–1967

5 Mass Media, Broadcasting, and Automation   177
6 The Long Long Weekend: Centennial and Expo 67   217

Conclusion: A Secret Understanding   235

Notes   239
Bibliography   319
Index   343

Acknowledgments

This book originated as a dissertation at McMaster University, where it benefited from Michael Gauvreau's generous attention and genuine interest. Thanks also at McMaster to Ruth Frager and Wayne Thorpe and to Ken Cruikshank, who provided helpful comments on the introduction. Brian McKillop provided encouragement and advice on improving the book. Joan McGilvray at McGill-Queen's did the same, and John Parry's careful copy-editing brought clarity.

Archivists also sped things along. Special thanks to: Charles Armour, Linda Baier, Odile Bourbigot, George Brandak, Robert Fisher, Anne Goddard, George Henderson, Ken Puley, Carl Spadoni, and Pat Townsend.

In academic and other ways, many people and organizations helped get this book out the door: Wendy Benedetti, Steve Billinton, Teresa Bochow, Lori Brown, Zoe Chan, Nancy Christie, Anne Clendinning, Darin Currie, Mike Dawson, Antonia Edwards, Gary Evans, the Family Centre of Winnipeg, Gerry Friesen, Natalie Johnson, Russ Johnston, John Kendle, Mary Kinnear, Giles Knox, Ron Love, Bob McDonald, Lisa McKendry, Kevin and Michelle Murison, Derek Neal, Susan Neylan, Marline Otte, David Plaxton, Till van Rahden, Brian Raychaba, Diane Reilly, Dick Rempel, Doug Robertson, Sharon Rudy, David Russo, Greg Smith, the Social Sciences and Humanities Research Council of Canada, St John's College, Geoff Spurr, Lisa Szefel, the University of Manitoba Institute for the Humanities, Mary Vipond, Keith Walden, Dermot Wilson, and Dario and Maria Zoppetti.

Thanks also to my parents, Leo Oswald Kuffert and Ann Darlene Kuffert, and my parents in-law, Olive and Doug Cossar, for everything. My tiny kids Eamon (small e) and Anna (my annie) made this a blissful blur.

Roisin Cossar can see in the dark and hears through silences. This book is for her.

Winnipeg 2002

A GREAT DUTY

Introduction:
Cultural Criticism in English Canada

While introducing their analysis of a wealthy Toronto neighbourhood in the early 1950s, sociologist John Seeley and his colleagues confessed that they wanted to help the community "just as the therapist assumes that the patient will benefit by a clarification of what has actually happened in his life hitherto and is happening now."[1] The authors of *Crestwood Heights* (about Toronto's Forest Hill district) were only three of the numerous English-Canadian commentators who, during the Second World War and for a generation or so afterwards, tried to show their compatriots what was "happening now." Canada found itself less isolated from a world figuratively becoming Marshall McLuhan's "global village," and to many of these self-appointed healers, what had happened "hitherto" seemed plain. Rapid changes to the rhythms of contemporary life, though hardly peculiar to the mid-twentieth century or to Canada, had brought along forms of culture inimical to individuals' personal development and even to Canada's coherence as a nation. This mass culture was inextricable from the turbulent environment of modern life. Surprisingly, attempting to mitigate some of the cultural effects of modernity meant subscribing to one of its basic tenets – that change could and should occur.

Rather than simply declaring that standards of taste were irretrievably in decline and taking refuge in tradition, some outspoken observers of culture worked to draw "ordinary" people into their struggle – to arrest the decline that they perceived by democratizing a critical understanding of the mass society and its cultural products. In 1948, *Saturday Night* magazine's Willson Woodside echoed American commentator Richard Weaver by denouncing the notion that progress in other areas of life meant cultural progress. Woodside reviewed Weaver's *Ideas Have Consequences* most favourably, spending two and a half columns on its importance, and then interjecting breathlessly: "That is only his introduction. I have given it at some length to induce thoughtful people, who have been pondering on where the sensational press, the debased movies, the flood of crime fiction and 'comics,' the abandonment of the classical studies for more 'useful' ones, mass living in the cities, the decline in religious belief, the loss of pride of work or craftsmanship, and other modern trends are carrying us, to get and read this book."[2]

How did cultural critics such as Woodside address those whom he called "thoughtful people"? If we wish to understand Canadian society more fully during the mid-twentieth century, we must appreciate critics' sense of detachment from the forces animating modern life and generating a mass culture. As outsiders, they were fascinated by the processes that had rendered them outsiders, and their sense of frustration was exceeded only by their desire to broadcast or inculcate their own perceptions and standards. Though frequently anti-modernist, nationalist, or elitist in tone, wartime and postwar commentaries on modern life and mass culture in English Canada were not simply attempts to recapture some golden age, distinguish Canadians from other North Americans, or introduce "Culture" to far-flung settlements. Commentators worried that they might be sending such messages and consistently emphasized their democratic intentions and credentials, especially when trying to unmask the commercial entertainments that they believed were disguised as "what the people wanted." Influencing the developing wartime and postwar culture meant marrying an expert-approved "worthwhile" leisure to the ideal of self-determination and often involved more than mourning a lost world. It required commenting on particular works, programs, or cultural practices and, most important, suggesting ways to help the onrushing modern world retain an air of civility. This attempt to question the pre-eminence of the most popular forms of entertainment and leisure constituted a significant interpretation of the concept of cultural democracy.[3]

The postwar years offered consumers abundance and convenience at the supermarket and on the airwaves. Improved living standards provided compelling reasons to think that science and technology would furnish all of life's necessities. Concerned onlookers warned that renewed prosperity and blind faith in progress might make Canadians a dangerously passive lot. A defence of the humanities, often carried on via cautionary tales of a technocratic dystopia, did not dismiss modernity outright but called for balance between spiritual and materialist instincts. In academic journals, magazines, pamphlets, or broadcasts, authors, editors, or inspired citizens seldom missed remarking that aesthetic and interpersonal standards were changing while what they considered human needs remained the same. They asserted their authority as expert-guardians of a middle way between rampant modernity and romantic visions of cultures long ago and/or far away. Over the course of a generation, many of these observers acknowledged the imprecision and permeability of cultural boundaries, widening their definition of acceptable leisure to include entertainments or works falling short of the exclusivity that had been bound up, by the earlier part of the twentieth century, with Shakespeare's plays or self-consciously artistic pursuits. By the mid-1960s, the solution to the "problem" of mass culture appeared to lie in understanding the media and using them effectively rather than in a coercive, highbrow approach that portrayed society's alternative futures as a stark choice between culture and anarchy.

Concern about the potentially harmful effects of developments associated with modern life, just like new educational theories, television, and automation, thus helped shape postwar public discourse and cultural policy in Canada. Critics of the mass society favoured self-improvement, self-awareness, and lively engagement with one's surroundings and thought that a creative sphere that gave prominent roles to amorphous concepts such as taste, nation, community, and tradition was essential to a mature and independent Canadian culture. Increasing economic integration with the United States had long caused alarm, but in the years following the war several observers believed that their warnings about modern life and its cultural dangers would yet sustain the sublime, the genuine, and the demanding against the convenience of new ways of life and an abundant, largely foreign mass culture. Their highly impressionistic assessments, based as much on their prejudices as on their experiences, led to their denunciation of pulp novels, "science-worship," or conformity. Neither did they fully acknowledge the complexity or contingency of culture as we now do almost reflexively since the "linguistic turn". Still, their worries about the ability of modern life and mass culture to affect the individual and society indicate a nascent Canadian orientation towards cultural self-determination, for the evidence shows that, even though such bleak prospects for Canada's cultural future were not widely held, much was done in their name.

I now introduce in turn, first, the context of this book – the historiography of mid-century Canada and my focus on English Canada; second, the cultural critics – their natures and roles, the framework of their analysis, and the ways they categorized culture; and, third, this study itself – the period examined and the contents of this book.

CONTEXT

Historiography

If historians of Canada have all but abandoned the pre-Confederation period, as Allan Greer has suggested,[4] they have not swarmed to study the most recent half-century. As written so far, the history of Canada from the second World War through the 1960s has tended to be one of development, urbanization, dominion over new economic frontiers, growing nationalism, and the updating of old party rivalries.[5] Despite the advent of social-history methods during the 1970s and a more recent interest in cultural history, postwar Canada is only now coming under the gaze of historians working in these fields. Generalists have on occasion nodded in the direction of "everyday experience" or the "arts community," usually by including chapters that seem out of place in relation to the rest of their work. For the most part, however, a journalistic disposition towards the wartime and postwar years – towards reporting the political and economic events with which newspaper readers would have been familiar – has taken precedence over addressing questions of complex social or cultural change. Even the Second World War, one of the century's more cathartic periods, has inspired few studies that look beyond the paper trails left by Ottawa's mandarins or battlefront memoirs to do more than account for a "new maturity" abroad in the land after 1945.[6] The threats of fragmentation via Quebec nationalism or regionalism have combined to provide another powerful theme, which cultural and intellectual historians have more satisfactorily approached. Historians, and more often others interested in prescribing remedies, have revisited the immediate postwar decades in order to unearth the roots of federal discord or the as-yet-unfulfilled promise of harmonious multiculturalism and have had to integrate social and cultural factors with the undeniable influence of high politics.[7]

In attempting to trace the cultural contours of mid-twentieth-century English Canada, a few historians cite state involvement in that field as evidence of broader political trends or of the search for an identity through cultural policy. Efforts to adjust to mass culture have become, in this formulation, functions of an awkward but devout nationalism.[8] The idea of nation certainly has its place. Decades before the Second World War, members of an English-Canadian "elite" began their quest to raise cultural standards and broaden access to what they considered worthy pursuits, frequently yoking such initiatives to the task of cultivating nationhood. Some historical writing on Canadian culture during the early twentieth century is careful to maintain a distinction between these two projects.[9] Monographs on such topics as sport, advertising, war remembrance, exhibitions, shopkeeping and the interplay of religion and leisure have recently illuminated popular culture and a public culture of commemoration between the late nineteenth century and the interwar period.[10] On occasion, Canadian historians have brought out works that set up compelling links between philosophy, belief, or ethics and action during those same years.[11]

As for postwar culture, studies of individual thinkers have helpfully examined the lives and thought of some particularly observant Canadians without focusing on Canada's economic or political history.[12] Works on the period have been appearing more consistently over the past decade or so,[13] and some have helped me clarify my interpretation of cultural criticism from 1939 through Canada's Centennial. Most relevant and recent has been Philip Massolin's *Canadian Intellectuals, the Tory Tradition, and the Challenge of Modernity, 1939–1970*. It is a well-organized intellectual history of a group of Canadian academics, united by their toryism and angry at what Massolin calls modernization or modernity. The book provides an exhaustive treatment of the changes affecting Canadian universities, traces a tory "pedigree" from the Victorian era into the second half of the twentieth century, and pays consistent attention to the Canadian political context as well as to ideological shifts. Massolin is concerned with a "main group of critics" and clearly defines his criteria for inclusion. At the expense of not coming up with an "anti-modernist coterie" of "tacit intellectual collaborators"[14] that coheres as tidily, the present study deals primarily with mass culture, admits a broader range of voices, and shows how cultural critics' proposed remedies for mass culture changed over time.

Although her interest extends only to the early 1950s, Maria Tippett argues in *Making Culture* that early-twentieth-century patterns of cultural activism extended through the Second World War period and became state-sponsored. She recognizes that an invigorated culture was a "principal objective of the cultural producers, politicians, and bureaucrats increasingly preoccupied with the task of post-war reconstruction"[15] and that this activity raised culture's public profile after 1950. Tippett concentrates on institutions – particularly museums and associations of artists. Her view of reconstruction as a *preoccupation* divorced from the effort of cultural development seems to deny it cultural significance. However, the wartime and postwar critique of mass culture and modern life drew heavily on the wartime energy surrounding the ideal of reconstruction. Anticipation of a cultural and social leap hardened cultural critics' and activists' determination to bind an idealized national character to high or folk culture – a resolve that gradually softened in time to allow Canada to be respectably marketed to Canadians during the Centennial year. For historians, the chief legacy of this wartime awakening seems to have been the Royal Commission on National Development in the Arts, Letters and Sciences (1949–51). Paul Litt's book on the Massey Commission (as the body was known) is a sensitive portrait of this institution and discusses its distaste for the entertainments to which most Canadians had access.[16] His chapter on liberal humanism outlines a particular kind of cultural ambition. However, he remains most concerned with the politics behind the promotion of high culture and seems to stretch the elitism of Vincent Massey and other officials to over a larger "elite" group, which included some commentators who were more democratic in their outlook. Litt presents a story of influential highbrows at a point when such categorizations were beginning to break down.

It is now more than ten years since Brian McKillop called for "an historical scholarship that is not parochial – one that recognizes that other national experiences can at times provide insights into the structures, dynamics, and contexts of culture that we may find of use in understanding our own cultural circumstance."[17] A few studies that treat "other national experiences" may be profitably held up to Canada for comparison or to supply useful metaphors that can characterize, not reduce, more complex processes. In bringing international theoretical literature to bear on Canada and encouraging us to think differently about culture, Gerald Friesen and Ian McKay have subtly shown that culture has become a field in which there are no disinterested parties. Friesen re-evaluates both the historical and contemporary roles of communications in the development of Canadian identity, asking some of the same questions that Harold Innis asked fifty years ago, but answering them with help from academics and "plain" Canadians. McKay contends that governments, researchers, and people in the tourism business can construct and maintain visions of a folk culture that become accepted as authentic.[18] I have attempted to follow where these scholars have trod by drawing in such useful perspectives as Daniel LeMahieu's work on how democracy altered the cultural playing field in Britain, Michael Kammen's on the social and cultural transformations that mass culture wrought in the twentieth-century United States, and Joan S. Rubin's on the valuable concept of middlebrow culture.[19]

Why English Canada?

Perhaps English-Canadian cultural life itself has been a process of borrowing largely from British and American models and to a lesser extent from other national groups. Certainly the dynamism and wealth of the United States have played increasingly important material and cultural roles in Canada since the Second World War. We must remember, however, that this presence did not go uncontested. Doug Owram discounts – prior to the 1960s – the possibility of lively resistance to continental integration, arguing in his 1996 study of the "baby boom" generation that after the war Canadian society followed in the wake of a prosperous United States and underwent a reorientation towards youth and freedom from tradition.[20] He pays careful attention to the accompanying trends in popular culture and concedes that youths were easily led, even as they worked up to rebellion. Although Owram's domesticated 1950s and angry 1960s sketch the dominant social trends of those years, the obverse side of the reorientation that he noted is worth examining, not by following a generation, but by placing in context evidence left by numerous men and women old enough to compare, from their own experience, the postwar period to other times. Fortunately, the archival and published resources that preserve their reflections are plentiful.

Abundant source material and the variety of themes explored here necessitated research choices. Most obvious to the reader will be my decision to focus on English Canada. Extending my interpretation of postwar cultural criticism to cover French-speaking Canada would have turned this into a comparative study, half of which would then be based on my bad translations. While introducing his second season of "cultural" broadcasts during the war, critic and playwright John Coulter promised that he would listen vigilantly for the "kindling of the spirit to speak of the things of today in terms of today."[21] Historians cannot count on such immediacy, but we can try to bring representative and often contradictory voices to the attention of the reader. I have attempted to listen closely to English Canadians by reading both manuscript collections and published or broadcast works – more specifically: critics' personal or organizational papers, pamphlets, broadcast transcripts, articles, books, and occasionally even advertising. I undertook complete reviews of three periodicals that ran through the entire period from 1939 to 1967: *Canadian Forum*, *Maclean's*, and *Saturday Night*. While the first and last of these were limited in their circulation compared to *Maclean's*, all three consistently included more than descriptive reflections on contemporary issues. American and British periodicals such as *Dissent*, *Partisan Review*, and *Scrutiny* – hotbeds of cultural criticism – certainly had small and faithful readerships in Canada, but their Canadian imitators were generally short lived. Wherever possible, I have mined these smaller publications, as well as university periodicals, for commentary.

The voice of "the people" may seem curiously absent. During the period encompassing the Second World War through the mid-1960s, "ordinary" English Canadians satisfied with their circumstances rarely generated the sort of documented discontent that historians can examine. Documentary sources favour the voices of journalists and academics precisely because making public and sometimes emotional responses to their surroundings was expected of such people. The conditions of modern life affected soldiers, factory workers, or farmers just as profoundly as they did writers and broadcasters, and – depending on their tastes – mass culture joyfully transported or quickly repulsed them just as powerfully, too. These people were, however, less likely to leave behind their views. Some histories can draw upon the experiences of "ordinary" people quite successfully. Jonathan Vance's study of Great War memorialization in Canada benefits from his attention to voices heard in the "less august fora of the small-town newspaper, the smoky Canadian Legion hall, and the IODE meeting" and to the commemorative rituals that "average Canadians" observed year after year.[22] When we look at wartime and post–Second World War commentary on modern life and mass culture, we see that commentators often had no quarrel with these "less august" local institutions. Their own roots and daily associations showed them how vital an involvement in one's own community could be in the face of a culture dominated by what became "popular."

CULTURAL CRITICS

It was difficult for me to conceive of just where to look for popular reactions to modern life and mass culture. The Canadian Institute for Public Opinion took public opinion polls on a range of topics, but a *qualitative* assessment of how Canadians responded to the proliferation of mass culture and the pressures of modern life does not emerge from such data. An auto worker in Windsor may have written to a friend about feeling useless at work after his section of the plant became automated, and a series of such letters or evidence of an automation study group would have rated attention had they turned up. The most compelling reason for my not pursuing the "popular" perspective is the position of the people as an *object* in the critique of mass culture. How can anyone have reflected on the effects of modern life for the average person without professing some distance from that person? Critics believed that they could empower the public by helping its members – often over the radio, yet individually – to recognize their place within a troubling new order. Those who could declare that some forms of culture existed for no other reason than easy reproduction and sale thereby excused themselves from the modern mass, even though they still might choose to attend cowboy movies. Formulating an understanding of how mass culture worked freed them from its grasp. Additionally, the selective reproduction and systematic redistribution of canonical or "authentic" works or practices (i.e., middlebrow culture) also became an acceptable way of transcending one's subjugation to prevailing trends. Reaching beyond the most convenient cultural option was more than half the battle. Certainly many of those who provided the observations that I analyse here used a rather inclusive "we" when they offered strategies for coping with consumerism or remedies for the inanity of the soap opera, but their benevolent and knowing tone of concern often betrayed their sense of separation from the hoodwinked herd.

Despite the lonely nature of a critique in which critics wrote and spoke as if they were a tiny band of the alert toiling in obscurity, it is probably most idiosyncratically Canadian that several of the research trails pursued came to involve the Canadian Broadcasting Corporation (CBC). Whether commentators portrayed it as the salvation of Canada or as a "government monopoly," many expected this organization, which grew by leaps and bounds from the 1940s through the 1960s, to do more than broadcast popular fare, essentially because its early supporters and creators had not intended it to be a creature of the commercial marketplace. From its inception, it defied prevailing economic wisdom by attempting to serve the entire country.[23] Radio, and later television, overcame the time and space separating most Canadians from those centres in which artists and writers had settled. Historian Paddy Scannell notes that "in modern societies radio and television are part of both the background and foreground of our everyday dealings with each other in a common world."[24] Broadcasts, perhaps even more than exhibitions arranged via university extension departments or drama festivals, represented the foundations of an accessible national culture.[25] In the same way that organizations such as the Canadian Association for Adult Education (CAAE) and the Canadian Institute of Public Affairs (CIPA) contained a significant proportion of those interested in broad social and cultural trends, the CBC served as an outlet for opinion on weightier questions, as policy and programming choices for the corporation often reflected the tastes and desires of critics employed by the CBC or appearing regularly on it.

This book is not a collective biography. British author E.M. Forster wrote about the amorphous and eclectic nature of "groups" such as the cultural critics whose commentary forms my evidentiary base, noting: "the aristocrats, the elect, the chosen, The Best People – all the words that describe them are false, and all attempts to organise them fail. Again and again, Authority, seeing their value, has tried to net them and to utilise them as the Egyptian Priesthood or the Christian Church or the Chinese Civil Service or the Group Movement, or some other worthy stunt."[26] Concern, rather than a shared set of credentials, affiliations, or habits, brings together the main agents of a rather wide-ranging critique. The absence of a powerful intellectual establishment in English Canada should not dissuade us from thinking and writing about how Canadians have approached complex themes. As one historian argued over twenty-five years ago, a conception of national identity that allows for "contradiction, diversity and paradox" is more useful to us here than studying only strands of thought originating within Canada and referring only to Canadian experience: "The important activity is the assessment of how those ideas, whatever their origins, are handled within the Canadian context."[27] Australian historian Nicholas Brown observed that one of his journalistic sources called the 1950s a "demoralising decade for those in the commenting business." Regardless of whether the 1950s was as demoralizing or exhilarating for Canada, Brown's identification of his sources as "a diverse grouping, including politicians, academics, advisers, bureaucrats, professionals, public intellectuals and commentators,"[28] serves as an apt description of those whose more profound reflections on contemporary society and its dominant culture I examine here. They were the people living for – and earning a living by – voicing the discomfort that others could not or would not.[29]

Critical Framework

Usually lacking formal frameworks over which they could drape their discontent and doomed to rail at forces largely beyond their control, critical observers none the less threw into sharper relief the anxieties that accompanied the interminable process of becoming modern. Northrop Frye wrote that "the habitually worried and anxious attitude of the more responsible citizen has a significance out of proportion to its frequency."[30] Even though this type of citizen represented an extremely small proportion of the population, eavesdropping on his or her reactions to a rapidly changing wartime and postwar environment provides us with a better sense of how such people – as American cultural historian Jackson Lears put it – "experienced and articulated moral and psychic dilemmas which later became common in the wider society."[31] Listening to what they had to say about some slippery concepts is one of our best opportunities to learn how distinctive Canada's postwar bout of modernization and cultural anxiety was. Andrew Ross, writing about intellectuals and their experience in the realm of adjudicating culture, contended that even histories of popular/mass culture "cannot simply be a history of producers – artists, the culture industries, the impersonal narrative of technological 'progress' – and/or a history of consumers – audiences, taste markets, subcultures." The distilled opinions of a cultural elite are central to histories of cultural difference and hierarchy because such people "define what is popular and legitimate taste, who supervise the passports, the temporary visas, the cultural identities, the threatening 'alien' elements, and the deportation orders, and who occasionally make their own adventurist forays across the border."[32]

Classifying and evaluating contemporary life and culture is a calling that few pursue, and this does not make the results of such work any less complex or elusive. In his work on interwar Britain, Daniel LeMahieu uses the term "cultivated élites" to denote a "deliberately ambiguous, fluid category embracing writers, artists, musicians, academics, and a variety of other educated individuals" whose response to the mass media was at best "an intricate mosaic of shifting opinions among complicated individuals who could not agree among themselves."[33] Whether acting alone, or from within associations whose memberships and fortunes waxed and waned, the "worried and anxious" citizens' approach to the social and cultural implications of modern life (especially mass-produced culture) was decidedly unpopular. It was not derived from the will of "the people," but rather operated on the premise that the vast public was in dire need of guidance. Although commentators generally despaired of such guidance ever originating from within the deluded mass itself, the political temper of mid twentieth-century Canada suggested rather strongly that democracy was the only acceptable foundation on which to build postwar society.

Despite their demonstrated ability to bring culture to the attention of policy-makers, cultural critics could not transform the state's tacit approval of their tastes into immediate or effective authority over public behaviour. They were, to employ Forster again, "an invincible army yet not a victorious one,"[34] consistently on the losing end in the struggle over culture, but always holding the high ground. Antonio Gramsci spoke of intellectuals as "the dominant group's 'deputies' exercising the subaltern functions of social hegemony and political government." However, while the vocal individuals and organizations that populate this study advocated the maintenance of certain cultural standards, they were hardly simple functionaries of the government or even of a ruling class. If anything, their consistent exposure of the contradictions and difficulties imposed on the general public by modern life and mass culture had the potential to undermine the very processes of social conformity and consumer hypnotism that built efficient nations and corporate fortunes.

Certainly they contributed to the more orderly conduct of the Second World War as writers and broadcasters nudging the public towards maintenance of the *status quo* at home, but critics of mass culture and the technocratic society stood for the most part outside what Gramsci referred to as the "prestige (and consequent confidence) which the dominant group enjoys because of its position and function in the world of production."³⁵ They spoke in strident, but ineffectual tones of humanist indignation. They wanted answers to the kind of fundamental questions about mass culture that historian Richard Pells first articulated and film scholar Anna Siomopoulous has since rendered more succinct: whether mass culture "would promote self-government or a passive, conformist citizenry incapable of democracy; whether the aesthetics of mass production would provide a model for collective and cooperative action, or destroy the moral content of experience."³⁶ Author Morley Callaghan advised a panellist on the radio-forum program that he hosted that the purpose of debating public affairs over the radio was to register disappointment at a range of current conditions. "We want to put the idea across," he wrote, "that men of the younger generation today won't be content to let the world drift aimlessly along on the worn-out wheels of the old liberal capitalist bandwagon."³⁷

Our anxious Canadians were far from uniform in their opinions, and it would be difficult to portray them as an elite in quite the same way that Mary Vipond could present the Canadian intelligentsia of the 1920s – as a group containing "not so much social critics as aspiring social leaders and moulders of public opinion."³⁸ They belonged to a cultural elite in that several came from privileged backgrounds with plentiful opportunities to travel or spend time becoming educated. However, they were equally likely to offer innovative responses to new cultural irritants and to join or work with governmental commissions or volunteer organizations to provide the sort of unimpeded access to the arts and community life that most among them considered the unfulfilled promise of democracy. In a few cases, the voices presented here are those of ordinary citizens whose opinions on modern life and mass culture have survived in the documentary record. One playwright and broadcaster maintained that the arts were not the preserve of one economic class or of a group apart from the "common" people but served as the "sensitive antennae of the community, feeling toward the evolutionary path of historic change."³⁹ If this image seems too abrupt a break from an elite model, it might be better to consider artists a kind of democratic clerisy operating "above society's normal activities."⁴⁰ Paul Gorman notes that the subjects of his work on left-liberal critics of U.S. popular culture constituted such a clerisy, for they could be "concerned for the state of the lower classes and ... defend them actively while still maintaining the superiority and universality of their own standards for the arts." In Canada during the war, a new kind of intellectual and cultural elite was emerging – one that, as Gorman put it, "justified its superior standing by its devotion to practicing democracy."⁴¹

"Sensitive antennae" or "democratic clerisy" are names too unwieldy for the people whose complaints appear here. In his study of advertising, Jackson Lears uses the term *cultural critics* to denote a group that "had a tendency to view the United States – and, indeed, the modern world – through the standardizing lens of 'mass society' theory."[42] Ultimately, Lears urges his readers to look beyond such judgments to the connections between advertising and an older vision of abundance, but his term is none the less useful. The term *cultural critics* or simply *critics* operates here not as a job description, but as a way of referring to a proclivity for analysing modern life or mass culture. It suggests a critique not only of cultural forms themselves, but of the environment(s) that shaped those forms. Again, that group of Canadians who, like their foreign counterparts, used terms such as *mass society* relied quite comfortably on the notion that there existed new, complex, and interdependent contexts in need of the thoughtful interpretation that only they could provide. Before proceeding, I would like to offer more concise working definitions for two frequently used terms, while noting that, like the symbols, gestures, and often-unconscious practices that inform and constitute culture, our understandings of the language involved in representing it are contingent and always contestable.

Modern life here means conditions arising from the standardization, commodification, and mechanization of work and leisure that began long before the second World War, as well as the attendant social and cultural norms and pressures that these changes brought to bear. Historians and others have used "modernity" to refer to this state, and in his seminal work, *All That Is Solid Melts into Air*, Marshall Berman draws attention to a paradox in what he calls the "experience of modernity": "People who find themselves in the midst of this maelstrom are apt to feel that they are the first ones, maybe the only ones to be going through it ... however, great and ever increasing numbers of people have been going through it for close to five hundred years."[43] Modern life represents this experience because that term addresses changes in way of life and culture in much the way that contemporary observers did. In 1938, educational activist Edward Anand (Ned) Corbett spoke of the "swiftly changing panorama of modern life," indicating a sense of motion or displacement that had long before become a common way of referring to everyday experience.[44] For men and women such as Corbett, the possibility of autonomy from the rhythms of the city and factory dwindled as living seemed to become what one historian has called "a race against death for achievement."[45]

Modern life connotes a set of conditions in which the social foundations of culture undergo significant and accelerated changes, and culture itself becomes on the whole more uniform, as people in widely separated communities can listen to the same broadcasts or see the same movies. Warren Susman noted that early-twentieth-century critics could perceive this connection, as they recognized "the full consequence of living in a machine age – an age of an industrial civilization in which new technology brought about changes in the material base of society that were altering patterns of social organization and structure." Susman argues that, compounding these shifts in organization and structure, "there was also a growing awareness of subtle changes in the value structure as well, changes in part precipitated by the operations and needs of that very industrial civilization."[46] Mid-century English-Canadian observers' bewilderment, anger, or dismay at their shifting surroundings reflected exactly that sort of awareness. Their approach to modern life as a prerequisite or staging ground for mass culture is crucial. For them, modern life was the state in which the individual suffered while "the masses became recognized as the key constituency, imagined and figured as an often-undifferentiated grouping with putatively common desires and aspirations."[47] In the eyes of cultural critics, attempts to satisfy mass desires seemed particularly at odds with their own fondest hopes for Canada's cultural and national destiny.

An early-1950s attempt by two American anthropologists to classify the various definitions of *culture* and to trace the term's development yielded 164 variants, and since then neither formal nor working definitions have become any simpler. Literary scholar Terry Eagleton sees culture as derived from an even more complex term: *nature*.[48] To compound the problem, pinning down *mass culture* requires an understanding of what (or who) comprises the mass. Still, a quite serviceable definition of mass culture comes from Canadian historian Paul Rutherford, who defines it as "products, services, and practices manufactured by the communications, advertising, education, sports, leisure and recreation industries to serve a huge market of consumers."[49] The key concepts here are manufacture and distribution, which carry rather strong industrial connotations. Rutherford's definition should be qualified with a third element – namely, commerce. The perception that mass culture constituted a segment of the cultural spectrum in which considerations of profit consistently trumped aesthetic choices helped critics differentiate their hopeful visions for a refined Canada from the narrow gaze of the entertainment business. When they responded to what they considered the commercialization of contemporary culture by lending support to centrally organized or local arts initiatives or to the mass distribution of "cultural" programming, they did not do so as entrepreneurs.

Critics' assumptions about mass culture and the audience are central to defining how mass culture operates in this study, so outlining the main conceptual difference between mass and popular culture is also important. Popular culture, according to one widely accepted definition, consists of "beliefs and practices, and objects through which they are organized, that are widely shared among a population."[50] When speaking about culture we often use the terms *mass* and *popular* interchangeably, and we do so in imitation of some distinguished mid-century minds.[51] In doing so, however, we acknowledge the role of the mass media as the now-dominant supplier of common points of reference. The mass media are not, however, the only suppliers that have ever existed. Mass-produced points of reference may have overwhelmed or transformed popular ones that developed prior to or independent of them – the department-store Santa Claus has conquered St Nicholas – but we need to preserve the distinction. It is true that what Rutherford called the "products, services and practices" that comprise mass culture often become widely shared and thereby form part of a popular culture, but they can only ever be a subset of it. Though mass-produced culture may be the source of much that we share, observers have for some time suggested that it cannot be entirely synonymous with the broader range of possibilities that make up the popular – or, as Raymond Williams more aptly calls it – the *common* culture.[52]

Categorizing Culture

During the past two decades, researchers in cultural history and cultural studies have expended considerable energy examining entertainments or practices that have become popular and have often asked how much power or resistance cultural producers and consumers have exerted (or can exert) in the creation or reception of films, novels, broadcasts, or other manifestations of culture.[53] A less frequent question is: What happens when well-meaning cultural "authorities" intervene? I attempt to provide an answer by examining the preconceptions that English-Canadian cultural critics brought to their mid-century interventions – interventions that specifically addressed new modes of living and leisure.[54] As it happened, critics had some means (political and social influence, access to a budding state cultural apparatus) to further their aims. These means ranged in their complexity from single articles in journals with small circulations, through briefs submitted to royal commissions by citizens' groups, to a radio (later radio and television) forum series that would run for more than twenty years. We can study such efforts and the motivations behind them more easily than we can apprehend popular opinion on mass culture, which market researchers polled relatively infrequently and then only in the interest of making a narrow range of cultural products even narrower by making it less offensive.[55]

Historian Lawrence Levine disparages histories that view consumers of "popular culture" (his preferred term) as passive and powerless. He offers an alternative – the image of popular culture as "the folklore of industrial society" – and conceives of it as an "interaction between complex texts that harbor more than monolithic meanings and audiences who embody more than monolithic assemblies of compliant people."[56] Levine offers an image that indicates the impossibility of separating culture from its social context and suggests the folly of presenting audiences as automatons gladly consuming whatever is set in front of them. The empowered consumer can, and does, construct popular culture. Levine admits, however, that critics rarely tried to understand this cultural "give and take" in such sympathetic terms: "it was the critics and scholars who were often incapable of making distinctions, of comprehending that the culture they were examining or critiquing was not all formulaic pablum with no substantive or stylistic distinctions."[57]

Levine's assessment applies reasonably well to Canada during and after the Second World War, even though critics began to adopt a more holistic and inclusive vision of culture. While literary scholar John Carey is wise to point out that "intellectual phobias about the mass are ... circular and self-deluding (for the mass is invented by the intellectual whom the invention gives pain to),"[58] such "delusions" kept critics vigilant and thereby affected the shape of Canada's cultural policy. However unsubtle their readings of a culture in which mass entertainments were becoming insurmountably influential, critics had clout. We must also pay closer attention to the way in which critics represented the sort of culture that they supported (lively local arts scenes, social activism, the creation of community/regional/national mythologies, the cultivation of one's own tastes) as integral to the realization of a Canadian identity. Critics believed that mass culture had become the folklore of industrial society undeservedly – that the passivity, simplicity, and conformity characterizing mass society were by-products of a mentally-taxing modern life. The archetypal mass person may not have existed in Canada, but critics whose authority had been largely circumvented by the mass media still had need to invent him or her.

Even societies that colonial status or geography kept from developing rigidly hierarchical social structures of their own still accord their more literate and learned members a role in categorizing culture. Critics themselves may not have been successful at influencing tastes – they may have been far less influential than the wealthy members of society whose way of life the middle and lower classes emulated – but it was rare to encounter observers who did not subscribe to some variation on the high-low method of categorization, even outside the group whose social identities were served by maintaining it. There existed a sense that Canadians were being deprived of cultural forms either more refined or more relevant to their circumstances than most of the fare supplied by the U.S.-dominated cultural industries. Convinced of the incompatibility of high and low, academic and sometime broadcaster J.M. Ewing declared: "If we are made familiar with bad art – and this is our unhappy plight – we can scarcely be expected to occupy our leisure with any other variety."[59] However, during the postwar period, critics began to promote cultural uplift by blurring the distinction between "highbrow" and "middlebrow" and by advocating tighter regulation of the mass media to protect those cultural forms that they classified as edifying or essential to Canadian cultural autonomy. They hoped to superimpose their own tastes and sense of identity on the common culture – the range of activities and cultural works to which everyone had access.

Although mass culture became a more visible target for criticism, critics' assumptions also reflected their dismay at the stresses, priorities, and incongruities of modern life. Philosopher George Grant came to recognize the impossibility of ignoring the social conditions that favoured the development of a mass society – the "forces that make our mass culture far too profound simply to be thought away." He also despaired of overnight solutions, claiming: "the belief that the forms of society can be easily changed by our choices is a relic of the faith in liberalism, and as limited as most of that liberal faith."[60] Few others shared this distrust of a proactive cultural strategy, and even Grant had to work up to it over a period of several years. More pervasive was the conviction that the general public needed to be made aware of its predicament, to be shown what it was missing at a time when technical expertise and a kind of blissful homogeneity appeared to have the upper hand. The promise of self-determination implicit in the democratic faith and so apparent during the Second World War seemed at odds with the realities of 1950s life, where convenience triumphed. Canadian cultural critics began to conflate the respective plights of the individual within the mass society and of the nation within the North American continent.

The concept of democracy is important here, but my purpose is not to analyse the political uses of the democratic ideal, nor to advance our knowledge of Canadian politics. Given the variety of political affiliations (when we can discern them) among critics of modern life and mass culture, to ask whether Conservatives regarded the humanities with a greater degree of admiration than did members of the Co-operative Commonwealth Federation (CCF) or the New Democratic Party (NDP) would be to subject a complex base of evidence to categories and judgments unsuited to it. Describing critics as the heirs of a particular political tradition is difficult. Many can be classified as conservative in that they opposed the ephemeral character of mass culture and the alienation from tradition that distinguished modern life. In some respects, they resembled what one historian called "cultural conservatives," who "find that society really is not much interested in their ideas and that they are in a real sense superfluous to the basic concerns of their own culture."[61] Conversely, the perspective they were trying to defend also had much in common with nineteenth-century liberalism. We can identify the impulse to edify or improve society with a liberalism divorced from the perpetuation of traditional social structures – one that "looked forward to the gradual extension of democracy to all social classes and eventually to all nations."[62] Any search for a definitive way of attaching a political label to cultural criticism is not helped by the likes of historian W.L. Morton, who saw his political party, the Conservatives, as the heirs of this liberal tradition.[63] George Grant was another such figure, in that the left has appropriated his anti-imperialism but ignored his attachment to religion. The right has adopted his religious thought but largely ignored his critique of corporate greed.[64] Much further to the left, contributors to the Labour-Progressive Party's *New Frontiers* saw their aspirations for a progressive culture "choked by a flood of the cynical degenerate products of U.S. commercialism" and vowed to "build a consciousness of our own Canadian cultural achievements and seek to develop and enrich them."[65] Liberals brought the Massey Commission – for some, the beginning of culture's institutionalization in Canada – into being, but the conservative weekly *Saturday Night* and the left's *Canadian Forum* had long provided space for critics of mass culture and of the complexities of modern life.

Both left and right saw their visions of the desirable society and its culture as victims of what had become, by the 1940s, the modern status quo. Cultural critics' political leanings, or their divergent ideas about the role of the state, may have prevented them from openly lauding each other's efforts, but they belonged to a critical community of thought whose borders were more permeable than those erected between the memberships of political parties. Much more important organizations than political parties in this regard were voluntary arts and educational associations, whose priorities were the protection and transmission of sometimes quite specific values and ideals. Characterized by one scholar as "umbrella organizations for mandarins,"[66] these organizations, especially the Canadian Association for Adult Education (CAAE), are more accurately viewed as drawing their members from populist rural social movements and urban elites.[67]

THIS STUDY

Setting the Scene

The frustrations addressed here did not arise with the beginning of the Second World War, and they were not by any means exclusively Canadian. It would be useful, then, to set the scene for my treatment of the years 1939–67. Historians of early-twentieth-century European culture cite a degree of popular discomfort with the mechanization of life, the proliferation of cheap, salacious literature, and the standardization of leisure.[68] Although this refrain of cultural and moral decay abetted by the march of science and industry had already been raised for generations by the early 1930s, that period emerges as a time in which some Europeans given to reflecting on the state of culture urgently expressed their dismay at the prospect of the masses "coming to power." Among these alarmed voices, Spanish critic José Ortega y Gasset's probably became the best known, but the years after 1930 were most notable for English speakers in that several earlier works, stretching back to Matthew Arnold's *Culture and Anarchy* (1869), through Gustav Le Bon's *The Crowd* (1895), Oswald Spengler's *Decline of the West* (1918), and Sigmund Freud's *Civilization and Its Discontents* (1930), appeared in English, as the Ortega and Freud works did, or came out in new editions.[69]

During the first part of the twentieth century, although Canadians had unprecedented contact with a range of European practitioners and works in the arts and literature, the American cultural presence in Canada came to dwarf that of Britain and other nations. Still, the conviction remained that U.S. culture "could be accepted because it posed no threat to Canada's British orientation and character: Canadians might be socially American ... but they continued to function within a British and imperial framework, a fact which would prevent them from being absorbed by their southern neighbour."[70] Late in the 1930s, even those observers aware of the many avenues along which American customs and enthusiasms had influenced Canadian daily life, and keen to see this reality acknowledged in Canadian literature, could not deny that the imperial tie remained strong. Authors Morley Callaghan and William Deacon noted with some disappointment that educators perpetuated the British attachment with the most vigour: "Every kind of pressure is brought to bear to keep up the Canadian tradition of having one foot in the European world, one foot in North America and the head up in the clouds."[71]

Callaghan and Deacon found what they considered the pretence of Britishness frustrating, but the "Canadian tradition" that they described – a tendency of looking to both Britain and the United States –

greatly influenced English-Canadian ideas about mass culture and modern life before 1939. This duality would continue in wartime and beyond. Although Britain's penny press and other distractions could be as lurid as their American counterparts, English Canadians given to expressing their opinions on matters of culture continued to recollect and represent Old Country life as more genteel, possibly because British commentators such as F.R. Leavis protested against mass culture so vehemently.[72] Despairing in 1934 of Canada's cultural poverty, Arthur Lower extolled the richness of the European (especially the British) tradition and set forth a number of conditions remaining to be met before Canada acquired the rudiments of a worthwhile national culture. Since New York was already entrenched as the North American metropolis, it would be practically impossible for Toronto to take up the same role in a nation already operating under a continental pattern – another variation on the colonial theme – that catered to a mass, U.S.-defined taste. Sensing the literal and figurative oceans between the seats of high and "popular" culture in the English-speaking world, Lower reckoned Canada as being adrift somewhere in between, concluding, "Our popular culture is not our own, no more than our culture in the more technical sense."[73]

American observers vexed by low- and even middlebrow culture – and there were several of them[74] – could not perceive as threateningly alien much of the mass entertainment that became popular in the 1920s and 1930s in quite the same way as their counterparts in Canada. It had, at least, sprung from their own nation. U.S. social scientists began relatively early in the interwar period to recognize mass entertainments as an integral part of the American urban fabric, effectively dividing a waning conservative critique of mass culture from a rising left-liberal one.[75] Despite thriving pockets of "high" culture in the United States, from which touring theatre companies frequently ventured north of the border, observers in Canada tended to identify newer forms of entertainment, leadership in technology, and material pursuits with the republic and to see what Lower called "culture in the more technical sense" as having originated and continuing to flourish in Europe.[76] By the 1930s, some sixty years after the introduction of universal education in Britain, a number of thinkers there believed that basic literacy, movies, and radio had opened up a marketplace for culture that served the instincts and interests of the masses without requiring them to dwell on life's more meaningful questions and that those forces were hastening the advent of a culture too base to be endured.[77] A colonial link, a common language, and a shared position as consumers of American works that dominated the popular field made the British critique more accessible in Canada.

The situation in Britain seemed dire enough, but British observers, thought that North American culture had gone even further down the road in its adulation of the popular. Perhaps the richest period examples of this may be found in C.E.M. Joad's monograph *The Babbitt Warren* (1926) – an extended treatment of American decadence and of Britons' alarming capacity for emulating it – and in Gamaliel Milner's attempt to link the fall of Rome with modern British tendencies.[78] Being North Americans who yet implicitly valued Old Country opinion, some Canadians concurred, though not without considerable helpings of self-deprecation. In an unpublished short story written in the late 1930s, University of New Brunswick economist Burton Keirstead invented a wit called Philip Gerrard who personified an upper-class British abhorrence for mundane pursuits, sensational literature, and the irredeemable sameness of the masses. As Gerrard leaves England accompanied by the story's principal character – John Forsey, a Canadian whom he met at Cambridge – he looks out over the throng of shipgoers at Southampton and wonders why he has been "so solemnly ambitious to waste my life trying to do something for people in the mass, because they always depress me so. I never feel so cynical as in a great crowd." During one of his subsequent trips to Canada, Forsey's wife, Nora, tells Gerrard: "There is nothing you can say in Canada which will make you smell worse to Canadians than to confuse them with Americans." With that, she sets Gerrard ranting: "They're all the same, so far as I can see. All suffer from the same hoof and mouth diseases, all offend with B.O. all lose their jobs because they don't shave with the proper razors, all wear the same clothes, drive the same cars, suffer the same clichés to pass in lieu of thoughts, read the same drivel and send their young to schools that 'pay dividends in character when your boy gets into business'. Now mind you I don't pretend to have been in this country for more than thirty-six hours, but I have studied the popular magazines."[79]

Outline of Study

This book's six chapters explore the dispositions and desires of some Canadians who professed to have studied the popular magazines and a good deal besides. The chapters emphasize particular themes but remain chronological in their sequence. The first two chapters (part I) both treat wartime. Chapter 1 explores how critics during the Second World War were able to link developments at home that they despised with various "enemy" characteristics, at the same time connecting their own tastes and standards with their own brand of cultural democracy. Chapter 2 introduces a wartime "culture of reconstruction," through which critics and their allies hoped to set the nation on a sound postwar cultural footing. The third and fourth chapters (part II) look at the postwar period up to 1957. Chapters 3 examines the postwar tension between science and religion through the eyes of critics and features a case study dealing with scientific programming on the radio. Chapter 4 looks behind the state's more overt involvement in cultural policy and at critics' deep pessimism about the efficient blandness of North American society. The fifth and six chapters (part III) examine the decade leading up to the centennial celebrations of 1970. Chapter 5 outlines a shift towards recognizing a broader definition of culture during the late 1950s and early 1960s, as concern over national cohesion mounted. Chapter 6 treats the anticipation of Canada's Centennial and Expo 67 as part of an already much-altered critique of mass culture.

In patrolling the borderlands between high and low, looking to uphold all that seemed tasteful, edifying, educational, or inspired and to dismiss the vulgar, vapid, anti-intellectual, or derivative, the English-Canadian cultural critic found ways to make distinguishing between these varieties of culture an expression of identity. By projecting the message that mass culture was producing Canadians who were somehow less themselves, critical observers who frequently had access to space in magazines and to the resources of the national broadcaster also made the vast middle ground between high and low effectively their own. Their critique helped ensure that when Canadians survey their cultural surroundings (domestic and foreign) they do so (sometimes ironically) on the basis of how these environs might nourish starving intellects or erode national mythologies.

This is not necessarily a bad thing. If English Canadians are today more familiar with the ways in which modern life and mass culture envelop and define them, if they live in a nation where private citizens and cultural institutions view the media as avenues of entertainment, as businesses, or as the means to construct identity, they should be aware of the role of wartime and postwar cultural critics. However elitist or unbidden their contributions might have been, critics struggled to balance the undeniable social benefits of democracy and modernization with their apparent cultural drawbacks. Studying critical disappointment at some outcomes of the subtle and symbiotic relationship between modern life and mass culture allows us – at least in the context of Canada's recent past – to understand a little more fully why academic and broadcaster Arthur Phelps could declare, shortly after the Second World War, that "some day the historians will tell our children's children how momentous were these hours. I think it's both a great game and a great duty for those of us alive now to try and comprehend what is happening and to take up our responsibilities as we see them in our own Canadian terms."[80]

Fretting over what people did with their leisure time may have seemed like a "great *game*" relative to the demands of war and external affairs during the 1940s through the 1960s. However, for those convinced that Canada needed to reconstruct itself culturally, cultural criticism was a solemn duty. In a society enamoured of the machine, and flooded with evidence that mass culture might become the *only* culture, duty called often.

PART ONE

War and the Culture of Reconstruction
1939–1945

I

Light from the Crucible of War

SUSPENDING CRITICAL SENSIBILITIES?

In English Canada during the Second World War, the discourse surrounding modern life and mass culture both drew on and contributed to the wartime environment. Respected as leaders within their communities, critics of contemporary developments often had to temper their concern for cultural matters with attention to their role as cheerleaders for the Allied "way of life." The experience of being at war none the less provided a platform from which critics tried to impart their understanding of how currents of cultural change affected Canada. They forged links between this understanding and the wartime circumstances familiar to Canadians. As they wrote books and articles or made broadcasts, cultural critics could act as if the war did not exist. They could criticize a film, for example, without commenting on its consequences for wartime morale. Pieces with a war "angle," however, stood a better chance of reaching a wider audience. Critics might associate certain cultural tendencies in modern Canada (or the Western world) with the documented or reputed traits and modes of living of enemies. Advertising, for example, might become a close relative of fascist propaganda. While critics might appreciate the material contributions of the scientific method, utilitarianism, and mass production to the war effort, some objected to the wholesale adoption of those principles, on occasion associating them with totalitarianism and cultural decay. While professing the requisite wartime reverence for democracy, critics hoped that its seeming tendency to empower mediocre forms of culture could be overcome by exposing the public to a greater variety of entertainments.

This chapter and the one that follows show how critics spent significant amounts of energy during wartime and in the early years of peace attempting to reinvigorate the democratic ideal by looking beyond its conventional political meanings and the often-romantic notions surrounding it.[1] Far from placing cultural matters on a shelf for its duration, the war brought into sharper focus some major aspects of the existing critique of modern life and mass culture. For some of English Canada's more articulate citizens, an overwhelming concern with defeating an enemy more threatening than impoverished taste offered an opportunity to conflate the two struggles.

Just over two years into the Second World War, Watson Thomson of the University of Manitoba's extension department declared: "The question of propaganda is really a much larger issue than the war itself or attitudes to the war." He referred to what seemed to him a troubling characteristic of propaganda – "its intimate connection with that profound crisis and transition in human affairs of which the war itself is an aspect and an episode." Crisis and transition were, for Thomson, part of the process of modernization, which tugged civilization between "individualist anarchy" and a type of conformity present elsewhere, he contended, in fascism and communism. Extremes of anarchy and totalitarian control, Thomson insisted, should be plainly "unacceptable to the liberal man of the west." Like a number of his contemporaries, he sensed a compromising way through this crisis. He also recognized how it might be difficult to convince the public to tread such a path, given that modernization had "collectivized life in a new and inescapable sense." In his estimation, new technologies of communication had fallen under the control of unscrupulous people, who, in the pursuit of profit, had victimized the ordinary citizen by treating him or her as part of the mass: "Men with dying roots and dwindling faith were subjected to the mass-producing processes of assembly-line labour, stereotyped 'culture,' mechanized 'pleasure.' Individualism and collectivism, in other words, have not had an even chance against each other. The scales have become weighted in favour of collectivism, and collectivism of a terrifyingly sub-personal, sub-rational quality."[2]

A war could work to suspend or to blunt aesthetic sensibilities in favour of pragmatic attention to public morale. As Jonathan Vance has shown in his study of the aftermath of the First World War, even though what he terms "vacuous requiems for the dead" would not satisfy many Canadians bent on erecting more enduring monuments, mythical – often melodramatic – representations of the war endured and were reprised after 1939.[3] The Second World War generated its own mythologies, which critics – even if they were so inclined – often failed to dismiss as appeals to sentiment. An example of this patriotic restraint comes from September 1943, when The *Canadian Author and Bookman* praised a maudlin collection of wartime poetry, *Watch the Sun Rise*, by Ontario high school teacher Dorothy Dumbrille, even though her work did not resemble the sort of critically acclaimed and clearly more modernist material then being turned out by established poets such as E.J. Pratt and A.J.M. Smith.[4] To their polite praise for the work itself, the editors added that the book's allegorical cover illustration of a woman facing purposefully eastward at dawn "happily epitomizes the position of Canada" but warned Canadians that the "new day" also "will be filled with vast responsibilities and obligations." They intended their praise for Dumbrille's verse to galvanize readers, presenting the war as a moment of reckoning, and they added: "It is part of a writer's task to carry such a message to the people. The writer who ignores this function, fails his great calling."[5]

As the editors' commentary indicated, a sense that writers had been handed an unprecedented opportunity to practise their craft in support of the war effort accompanied an acute awareness of every citizen's wartime duties and potential rewards. Those concerned with maintaining morale promoted works such as Dumbrille's because, no matter how unoriginal or saccharine, they served a noble and immediate purpose. Among Allied nations, that goal became the successful diffusion of an ironic message: strict compliance with wartime regulations and prolonged personal sacrifice would guarantee the maintenance of a democratic order.[6] Some commentators insisted that "the way to combat naziism is not by establishing it here 'for the duration', for if we surrender our freedom now it is doubtful we shall find it easy to regain once the war ends."[7] Yet expert guidance, even the level of regimentation necessary to ensure the efficient prosecution of the war effort, became more justifiable when invoked in the defence of individual freedom. Even though a number of critics considered the brand of democracy mythologized in wartime slogans only a half-measure, it remained difficult to criticize forms of culture that had become popular under a democratic system.

Writers were not the only ones called on to employ their talents in the cause of promoting wartime unity of purpose. Given the Nazi example of propaganda, and perceiving the need to counteract it with propaganda supporting the Allied democracies, broadcasters and filmmakers in Canada enjoyed enhanced status as a group that could decisively influence the prosecution of the war.[8] Columnist Raymond Davies considered every person involved in the diffusion of words and images as destined to make a difference, remarking: "to those of us still outside the armed services, those of us who are *opinion moulders*, history has given a central task, overshadowing all others."[9] In the midst of a war constructed as a choice between democracy and oblivion, *democracy* became more than a political term for cultural critics. Despite the journal's acknowledged mandate and its usual attention to party politics in Canada, the *Canadian Forum* instead of engaging wholeheartedly in homefront political combat, declared in an editorial that "we are all liberal democrats now."[10] Its editors, however, were not celebrating the achievement of a truce among political parties but honouring the ideals that characterized liberal democracy – ideals often cribbed as "The Four Freedoms" after a speech by U.S. President Franklin Roosevelt in January 1941 – which had become the *sine qua non* of wartime discourse.[11] This devotion both encouraged the denunciation of totalitarian nations' "brutal regimentation and overriding of the individual"[12] and allowed critics to scold a domestic population "capable of enjoying the benefits of democracy without having either the invincible ignorance or the deep wisdom necessary to fortify it against the perils which democracy brings."[13]

Wartime did not provide the first convenient occasion for suggesting that the artist, writer or performer could also be an activist, but exhortations of this sort were probably, before the war, more easily characterized as items on a political agenda. As one commentator on the left vowed in 1936, "there can be no full, free creative life for the individual except in harmonious association with his fellows ... so long as the good life is barred to the great masses of people by our social institutions and conditions this prerequisite is unattainable." Linking decadence and social inequality, he cited evidence of prior failures and suggested that catering exclusively to elite tastes – or more likely, maintaining the social inequalities that made a richer cultural life available to only the social elites – had been the cause: "Past civilizations have crumbled because of such top-heaviness. The artist should be the first to recognize this, since any satisfying practise of his art demands responsiveness from as wide a body of his fellows as possible."[14]

The war harboured a range of meanings. Early in the conflict, I.D. Willis, a self-employed writer living in Gananoque, Ontario, noted that during the 1930s it had become apparent that only adventure could grant Canada the maturity it lacked. To Willis, war promised adventure because it represented nothing less than "the margin of a great wilderness of doubt and uncertainty, uncharted, unknown, into which the nation must go to find a new order."[15] Looking back from close range, hardly a year after victory in Europe and mere months after the defeat of Japan, historian Arthur Lower saw both of the century's world wars as parts of a longer developmental cycle for Canada. He maintained that the wars cumulatively had made "an impact on Canadian life almost as great as a revolution," pulling Canadians irrevocably away from lives lived in remnants of the "simple old community of the nineteenth century." While he acknowledged the contribution of "other forces" in transforming Canada into a modern nation, he viewed the wars as trials that had "enormously accelerated our speed of departure from the old ways."[16] Commenting some thirty years later, historian Donald Creighton considered wartime a "fresh beginning in the Canadian experience" after a decade of dismal conditions in the 1930s. He cited the "immense and prolonged effects" of the war and added that the "pace and direction" of the nation were greatly altered.[17]

Whether one considers the Second World War, for Canada, an adventure culminating in a new level of national "maturity," one episode in an extended process of modernization, an unqualified departure from all that had gone before, or something else entirely, contemporary reports generally perceived war as typically modern, a mode of existence in which a person's circumstances could change quickly via contact with previously unfamiliar cultures or via disturbance of set patterns of life. Almost overnight, the general anxiety wrought by unemployment and economic uncertainty during most of the 1930s seemed much less acute, as attention turned to international matters and to the question of whether the nation's established "way of life" would survive the conflict. For the majority of Canadians, critiques of mass culture and modern life did not arouse much sympathetic action during wartime, and such concerns remained subjugated to a war effort that relied heavily on mass communications to help inspire sacrifice and patience. Still, questions about what sort of culture Canadians would draw from the crucible of war occupied some observers, and their thoughts on this and related subjects – public information, the light that enemy practices cast on domestic practice, the place of science and techology, and the relations between democracy and mass culture – constitute a rich body of evidence linking the weighty business of war with the less momentous issue of leisure and its uses.

A NATION IN TRANSITION

The Second World War burst in on a nation already in transition. Canada was not yet free of the disappointments plaguing it during the 1930s, and the war took Canadians still further from Stephen Leacock's Mariposa towards a society in which everything seemed to move and change more quickly. Cultural critics found it difficult not to discuss the differences between rural and urban life. During the calmer months of 1939, in an attempt to take "a measure of Canadian thought," journalist Peter Fraser spent some time perusing an Eaton's catalogue and a pair of large-circulation weekly magazines. Eaton's catalogue had long brought modern "city" goods to country customers. Comparing the Montreal-based *Family Herald* with the *Toronto Star Weekly*, he found the "earthy and rather pleasant smell of the one

[Herald] being balanced by the city-slicker aroma of the other" and gathered that there was "a superior mentality obtaining in Canadian rural areas." He cited the agrarian *Family Herald*'s ability to secure university professors as contributors, its sensible political commentary, and its relative lack of ads for patent medicines. In Fraser's estimation, the *Herald*'s song column, which reprinted old favourites such as the "Red River Shore," ranked well above the *Star Weekly*'s sentimental poetry and astrology features. He identified *Family Herald* subscribers, as a testament to the virtue of rural values, with the canny backwoods types portrayed in movies and dime novels, certain that it was "little wonder that rural characters in all popular fiction and in all Hollywood productions ultimately always triumph." He lamented the distance that modern Canada had travelled from the principles underlying a long-departed rural independence, which mass culture, ironically, had enshrined in the North American imagination. Appealing to a rural stereotype familiar to his predominantly urban audience, Fraser complained that fads and ephemeral concerns made it difficult for the modern city dweller to be much more than an easily distracted bystander. Unable to confirm that rural Canadians lived up to the image of the wise rustic that he had helped reinforce, he yet admonished town dwellers with that image, noting: "Canadians can thank heaven that their political bodies are still controlled by those on the back concessions."[18]

For more than a half-century leading up to the war, the nation underwent an extended phase of urbanization and industrialization, and the proportion of Canadians occupying the setting that Fraser had romanticized declined steadily. These powerful changes now serve as points of departure for much historical writing about late-nineteenth – and early twentieth-century Canada, especially in the sub-disciplines of social and labour history. However, the processes taking more people into towns and cities and making them wage employees had not run their course before 1914. Although the turn-of-the-century period boasted a more rapid rate of urbanization, it was only at some undetermined moment between the censuses of 1921 and 1931 that Canadians living in what the Dominion Bureau of Statistics defined as urban settings finally outnumbered those living in rural areas.[19] Yet the "old ways," or fond visions of them, seemed to remain part of the urban imagination even as rural areas obtained town amenities. One observer of rural life suggested that farm families had been isolated too long and were ready to become "up-to-date," to leave behind elbow grease in favour of electricity and join all the relevant co-operative marketing schemes they could. He remained certain that city dwellers would not alter their perception of life carried on away from the crowds and factories, declaring: "It is left to the urban orator to extol the blessings of rustic freedom. The agrarian knows the restrictions of his boasted liberty."[20]

Not only did North Americans migrate from rural to urban environments during the first part of the twentieth century, but the solitude supposedly conducive to freedom of thought and action was rapidly disappearing. More efficient methods of transportation and communication carried goods, people, and information to previously isolated areas, wearing down local customs and linking the inhabitants of such areas with provincial or national frameworks.[21] More people became familiar with the bustle and the fleeting transactions – both social and economic – of urban life. *Saturday Night* editor B.K. Sandwell observed that during the 1930s "in urban areas, and to some extent even in the country, the home has lost much of its importance as a social centre; motoring, the 'movies', public dancing places and restaurants provide the occasions for people to meet their friends."[22] In 1939, American philosopher and educational theorist John Dewey saw independence and strength in the isolation of rural life: "Before we engage in too much pity for the inhabitants of our rural regions before the days of invention of modern devices for circulation and information, we should recall that they knew more about the things that affected their own lives than the city dweller of today is likely to know about the causes of his affairs."[23] A few months before the war, Trans-Canada Airlines' new passenger service seemed like a potential boost for breadth of experience and national unity, but columnist Leslie Barnard doubted air transport's ability to improve society in any profound way. He longed instead for an elevation of the national disposition. "Our trust cannot be in streamlined fabrics, ingenious gearing, efficient engines, and unlimited miles per hour," he wrote, urging readers to temper their enthusiasm for the hyper-modern, space-conquering airplanes. Personal enrichment remained far more important: "our bodies might reach the stratosphere and our spirits still be no higher than the dull levels of prejudice and mediocrity along which it is sometimes easier to stumble than take flight from the ground."[24]

PUBLIC INFORMATION

Within six months, all able spirits would be thrust into partnership with the national war machine. Yet, as historian Chester Martin remarked at the time, Canadians went into the conflict with few illusions: "It requires almost an effort to recall the contrasts of twenty-five years ago – the ingenuous response of 1914, the bands playing, the haste to reach the scene in time to share in the adventure."[25] As it did elsewhere in the West, the coming of war in Canada further accelerated the country's transformation into a modern nation. In their work on interwar Britain, Peter Miles and Malcolm Smith emphasize 1940 as a cultural, as well as a military and political, watershed. Following the tense months of waiting at the beginning of that year – the "phoney war," bombs began to fall in Britain after Germany took the low Countries and much of France. The task of preserving morale during the early days of the conflict fell largely to those working in branches of government geared towards controlling what the public heard on radio, saw in cinemas and on posters, or read in newspapers and pamphlets. An appreciable portion of Britain's writers, George Orwell recalled, had been "sucked into the various Ministries or the BBC" regardless of their politics, because the government understood only too acutely the power of public information.[26]

The same pattern of state involvement in presenting the war to the public obtained in Canada, but to a lesser extent. A similar class or, more properly, a similarly literate and articulate group of Canadians commented on the nation at war. Most often, however, these observers volunteered their opinions, writing or broadcasting on a more freelance basis than their British counterparts. Canada's Bureau of Public Information (BPI) and its successor, the Wartime Information Board (WIB), lagged behind Britain's Ministry of Information (MOI) and the United States' shorter-lived Office of War Information (OWI) in relative size and sophistication. Despite their small size and opportunities for writers and broadcasters outside the public service, the BPI and WIB were where "many members of the elite had gained experience in managing public opinion." Some would later recycle the techniques honed during wartime in aid of the "humanist cause of the Massey Commission."[27] Somewhat upset by wartime leanings towards the CCF, at least one representative of the business community saw even the moderate members of Canada's information corps as "shrewd propagandists who have wormed themselves into key organizations where they can more readily control and direct the thinking of thousands of people."[28] However, browbeating Canadians about a perceived decline in cultural standards was not an officially sanctioned activity of any government agency during wartime.

Although the Canadian government had intended the BPI and WIB to oversee war news and commentary, to boost morale, and to present Canada's war effort in a flattering light wherever possible, their mandates, and the Liberal government's reluctance to be seen engaging in propaganda, limited their ability to address domestic affairs not plainly connected with the war. While the two boards did not directly employ an army of writers, broadcasters, and filmmakers in the way that Nazi Germany's propaganda bureau did, they used similar methods and no doubt contributed in at least a modest way to national solidarity in wartime.[29] With the establishment of the National Film Board (NFB) in 1939 under the direction of John Grierson, Canada acquired another potential avenue of influence over public opinion. Grierson was a pioneer in the genre of the documentary film, and his wartime NFB work – which he did not hesitate to call "propaganda" – brought carefully edited images of the war to countless Canadians.[30] Regardless of the profile or impact of government propaganda agencies, much of the measured reflection on homefront life and on the state of culture in Canada still came from academics or journalists who worked under wartime secrecy guidelines but were neither members of the government information corps nor bound to follow its lead. As a result, much of the wartime commentary on cultural trends survives in articles, broadcasts, and pamphlets that were certainly patriotic and probably served to boost wartime morale but originated with voluntary associations or individuals concerned as much with the direction of Canada's cultural development as with winning the war.

The state of being at war threw into sharper relief some aspects of the connection between modern life and mass culture. Advertisers, as might be expected, did not miss the opportunity to be topical in wartime. Augmenting the themes of pre-war campaigns pushing futuristic goods with new ads emphasizing the nation's military obligations, they strove to place would-be consumers in the vanguard of modernity and in the honourable company of Canada's armed forces. Advertisers associated their wares – often billed as products "of tomorrow" – with the same qualities that they had customarily trumpeted, such as reliability and efficiency.[31] These qualities took on a deeper significance in wartime because they had become essential for victory. Articles in Canadian magazines or topics featured on radio programs paid consistent attention to the war, whether they devoted considerable space to war news, reported on some aspect of troop or homefront life, or merely wished Allied forces well. Countless articles or programs failed to mention the war explicitly, but readers and listeners could feel its presence. Business reports noted increased industrial demand for commodities such as metals and rubber, sports leagues went on without many of their best players, and "women's pages" featured recipes adapted for rationing.

The overarching reason for these developments on the homefront did not need to be set out repeatedly for a public whose daily lives brimmed with reminders of their nation's commitment. Yet such an extensive awareness of the war did not transform Canada into a nation motivated solely by war. Even so, war reached deeply into the lives of even those who might be expected to contemplate more sublime states. Art critic Robert Ayre reviewed a late-1940 exhibition of contemporary Canadian works, declaring that "the war is still too new, still not urgent enough, in Canada to be a valid influence in our art." But he quickly qualified that remark to account for the conflict's impact on the everyday lives of artists and non-artists alike – people "seriously disturbed by the war." He noted also that, among artists, "some have gone into active service, some are giving all their spare time and energy to military training, and others are too uneasy to work whole heartedly, as if painting doesn't matter in times like these. I think it does; it matters very much; and that is why a show like 'Art of Our Day in Canada' is heartening."[32] Clearly, culture of a certain sort had not been forgotten. However, given Canadian society's complete involvement in the war effort, particularly during its early stages, when Britain seemed in gravest danger, proposing some sort of order for peacetime culture without reference to the wartime task at hand would have been foolhardy.

ENEMY CHARACTERISTICS AND CULTURAL CRITIQUES

War served as a great agent of change, altering the life of nearly every citizen, and, according to B.K. Sandwell, it stood as the one thing that "makes us willing to face risks and make experiments that we would not venture upon under any other circumstances."[33] About one millon "ordinary" Canadians joined the armed forces, and most of the rest of employable age filled jobs or managed households, where wartime needs at the very least circumscribed daily routines. For members of the intellectual or cultural elites who had not already enlisted their bodies or – perhaps more appropriately – their minds and talents in the struggle, to appear unmoved by the war emergency invited public contempt. Literary critic J.R. MacGillivray complained in 1941 that Canadian authors had not sufficiently engaged the war as a theme in their work and displayed "no apparent awareness of ideas and events, but a perfect isolation from place and time." He wondered what might remedy their insularity: "Did not somebody tell them last year to their gratification that in this war the front line ran right through their desks? Would that it did!" Despite a few exceptions, he noted that in 1940 "eighty per cent of our fiction has been devoted as usual to books for children, animal stories, and lurid tales of adventure on the frontier." Some short stories included reflections on wartime and were therefore somewhat more successful in their "imaginative interpretation of the common experience of people in this country." But that genre could not command nearly the readership that MacGillivray saw rushing to buy cheap novels that romanticized life on the western frontier.[34] In a nation mobilized to fight its enemies abroad, figures such as MacGillivray who thought about domestic cultural matters for a living, or those such as Sandwell who noted the impact of various kinds of change on Canadian life, considered it prudent to express their opinions on such homefront subjects by linking them, directly or obliquely, to issues arising from the war.

For most Canadians, the war was an uncomplicated struggle to join. It was sometimes billed as a "War of Ideals," in which opposing ideals presented themselves unambiguously, and A.W. Trueman saw it in rather stark terms, as "a war between people who have no religion, on the one side, and people who have, on the other; between people who have officially thrown aside decency and morality, and people who still cherish these principles and give expression to them in their lives, however imperfectly."[35] The assumption, by default, of proprietorship over decency and morality granted Canada and its Allies plenty of latitude to portray the enemy as inhuman. Waging war certainly seemed justified, and one magazine writer contended that it would be extremely useful in wartime to cultivate a "constructive hatred towards the enemy, a hatred akin to the spirit of the Crusaders."[36] Even peace-loving sorts, well-travelled and accustomed to seeking compromise in their daily lives and careers, found it easy to endorse the war as a moral struggle. Editor and clergyman Claris Silcox was aware of the resistance that some German church leaders offered their government and hence did not consider all Germans fully complicitous. Yet he viewed the war as worth fighting because it was "not only a just war but a holy crusade against the rulers of darkness of this world, against spiritual wickedness in high places."[37] For those convinced that Canadian society was itself prey to some of the same forces that had so perverted Nazi Germany and its Axis partners, the presence of features common to both enemy culture and modern Canadian life allowed them to practise their own brand of cultural stewardship while furthering the war effort.

Critics helped perpetuate a view of the wartime world in which the Nazis spouted propaganda or indoctrinated their youths, while the Canadians, the British, and later the Americans managed information or engaged in "education for democracy."[38] These distinctions were subtle, but important. German émigré sociologist Paul Lazarsfeld noted the North American compulsion to resist too close a devotion to public opinion while also avoiding authoritarianism. "We look at radio and its effects upon public opinion as a possible means of steering safely between these two dangers," he remarked. "Has it made, or can it make, us more amenable to social change without making us thoughtless and intolerant victims of propaganda stereotypes?"[39] The additional irony of assigning sinister impulses to Germany or heroic motives to the Allies for what were broadly similar propaganda efforts seemed lost on commentators who sought to maintain what little "decency and morality" they thought Canada could yet claim. To those concerned with the scourge of mass entertainments or the abandonment of cherished customs, Canadian society sat in grave danger of succumbing to the same influences. As historian Frank Underhill noted: "The phenomenon of the masses as we see it in Nazi Germany is so sinister because Germany only reveals the ultimate stage of certain tendencies in our contemporary world which can be detected in all countries."[40] By linking domestic cultural trends with enemy techniques, and vice versa, critics dissatisfied with particular aspects of the emerging modern order could express their frustration with those trends *and* remain faithful to the war effort.

Portrayals of enemy culture served as potent object lessons for Canadians even before the Axis powers had officially become Canada's enemies on 10 September 1939. A month before war broke out, one columnist, still flushed with sentiment stirred up during the King and Queen's visit in May and June 1939, expressed his belief that Canada's British and French heritage, as well as its friendship with the United States, outshone all its material riches and placed it in a distinguished company of nations. Conspicuously excluded from this group – "the peoples of whom we truly form part" – was Nazi Germany, which had earned a reputation since 1933 not only for its treatment of minorities, but for its extensive propaganda machinery and its thinly disguised use of crowd psychology as a political tool. The author of the piece, W.J. Healy, read German threats of war as examples of the same sort of mass manipulation exercised on a larger scale and directed outside Germany's borders. Although he was certain that Canadians possessed ample "spirit" to meet the challenge of war, Healy recommended that Canadians stand guard against Europe's propagandists, whose reliance on mass persuasion placed them foremost among "the darkeners of the sky of civilization, the war-mongers, who are most potentially dangerous in their planning to induce fear and nervous inaction."[41]

Mere weeks before Canada entered the war, Watson Kirkconnell suggested that a state of enmity already existed when he contrasted fascist and communist practices with the ethic of freedom – an ethic that he identified with Christianity and the democratic powers. Tying together the usually disparate realms of economics and religion, he blamed the modern economic system for the discord of the late 1930s, when nations that could not produce all that they needed threatened to take it by force from their weaker neighbours. Because they had abandoned their spiritual roots in favour of the rapid achievement of worldly objectives, Canada's soon-to-be enemies, Kirkconnell suggested, had sacrificed too eagerly at the altar of modernity. "The fascist and Nazi systems of Germany and Italy seem to be efficient and moving forward," he wrote, "but this is at the price of Christian liberty."[42]

With such a buildup in the months before hostilities began, it should not be surprising that critics shifted easily to more pointed critiques of enemy culture in wartime. Once war was declared, with few exceptions, earlier concern about the regrettable assaults on popular liberty in distant places such as Germany and Italy[43] gave way to full-scale denunciations of reputed enemy characteristics that might threaten – or perhaps were already endangering – civilization in Canada from within. Much of the anti-enemy rhetoric in wartime pamphlets, magazines, and radio broadcasts was designed primarily to raise spirits and swell recruitment. However, these sources contain more than the elementary hatred that writers such as Raymond Davies wished to incite. Among the patriotic calls for Victory Loan contributions and total commitment to the task at hand, several critics used the example of enemy culture to demonize tendencies perceived to be at the root of either ongoing or potential cultural decay at home.

Identifying the least flattering features of progaganda with the enemy most commonly involved indicating their role in the rise and perpetuation of the Nazi regime. Relative to Nazi Germany, Fascist Italy and Imperial Japan received less frequent attention from Canadian propagandists, although Prime Minister William Lyon MacKenzie King vilified those nations often in his wartime speeches.[44] As for Germany, commentators found it difficult to hide dismay that this northern European nation, with which the Anglo-American world had enjoyed cordial cultural and intellectual relations as recently as the mid-1930s, had strayed so far from the fold. By 1942, Frank Underhill could echo, as if stating a mathematical axiom, British writer and broadcaster J.B. Priestley's declaration that "Hitler, the vindictive doss-house dreamer, thinks and acts always in terms of the masses, and never for a moment in terms of the people."[45] Thanks to newsreel footage and frequent press coverage of party rallies during the 1930s, the Nazis had gained a reputation in North America as masters of spectacle and manipulation. Underhill alluded to a distinction between masses and people that differentiated a uniformly corrupted or deceived enemy mind from the sort of self-control that critics hoped Canadians still possessed: an independent will that enabled each citizen to determine when to co-operate in an enterprise such as a "just" war.

Identifying enemy propaganda with domestic advertising campaigns was an effective way of repudiating both forms of communication.

When Northrop Frye wrote that "it is not Churchill or Roosevelt but Mussolini who must pose for cameras and kiss the shuddering babies and generally advertise himself like a toothpaste to retain public favor,"[46] he referred chiefly to the contrasts between democratic and totalitarian polities but swung a double-edged sword. Frye knew that the image of Il Duce advertising himself "like a toothpaste" would resonate for readers familiar with the sort of heavy-handed, unsubtle approach often used to sell such goods to the masses. Correct or not, his implication that Allied leaders had secured popular support by simply doing their jobs also broadened the imagined distances between enemy and self and between the world of advertising and virtuous resistance to it. Identifying forms of culture with an easily maligned "other" was hardly an original strategy, but it was particularly striking in wartime because the time for dialogue between opposing nations had passed. Pre-war memories and stereotypes replaced direct interaction. As a tool for encouraging critical readings of even the most mundane aspects of one's own social and cultural surroundings, the enemy dictator proved useful.

The ideal of an independent will resistant to demagogues and hucksters and supported by a tradition of self-determination appealed to critics as a beacon to lead Canadians through the dark years of war. Canada, according to Arthur Lower, featured an "easy-going, not unkindly populace resting on the laurels of religious teachings and the mores of its pioneers," but its people needed informed direction, because they were in danger of a grave fall. He saw the "disappearance of fixed beliefs, the wearing out of the old traditions, the absence of a dynamic" as dangerous developments that could lead only to decline. Alluding to the Gospel of Luke, Lower saw Canada as "a house swept and garnished into which seven devils may be moving, devils of intolerance, of harshness, of gregarious unanimity, of panic fear, the conventional characteristics of the crowd."[47]

Despite such candid admissions of dread, critics often displayed a cautious fascination with the mass mind doomed to serve a succession of undeserving masters. In the spring of 1940, the Canadian Association for Adult Education devoted an issue of its *Food for Thought* to a discussion of propaganda and its intended effects. Its editor, British-born educator and broadcaster R.S. Lambert, noted that propaganda was best defined as a "*method* of influencing people," which, depending on the motives of those employing it, could be used for good or ill. Far from rejecting propaganda out of hand, he even hoped that the Allies might "leave behind them their early amateurism" and become more expert in the field. This was especially important since the military outcome of the war remained uncertain, and the Allies would need to maintain goodwill among themselves, neutral nations, and the conquered enemy.

However, given the immediate example of the Second World War, it seemed plain to Lambert that enemy societies had succumbed to propaganda in a way that Britain and other English-speaking nations could (or should) not. In aid of establishing a historical basis for this distinction, he suggested a crude national hierarchy of resistance to mass persuasion: "Individuals are more rational than crowds; and therefore the art of propaganda is particularly effective in swaying the beliefs and actions of people in the mass. Highly individualistic peoples are least susceptible to propaganda, and so are those with well-established traditions or customs, which resist irrational, as well as rational, innovations of thought."[48] Here "rational" and "irrational" referred not to the logical rigour of arguments put forward by propagandists, but to their format. Individualistic peoples tended to be difficult to persuade, through either protracted ("rational") argument or emotional ("irrational") appeal. To distance those in Britain and the Dominions yet further from what he called the "black art" of modern propaganda, Lambert added that, even though Britain's Lord Northcliffe pioneered in its study (but more so in its commercial exploitation) before and during the First World War, the British had all but abandoned such techniques between the wars. Hitler was thus free during the 1930s, Lambert suggested, to invest the term with the malevolent connotations that it held throughout the English-speaking world.[49]

In wartime Canada, therefore, identifying with the British tradition meant affecting a degree of detachment from enemy-style propaganda and from mass methods of maintaining popular solidarity or at least advocating controls on their use. One observer wondered how Canada would "steer its way between the sterile purism which dreads the contamination of 'propaganda' and the indiscriminate zeal of the flag-waggers."[50] To tread such a path, an organization such as the Wartime Information Board would need to represent its work as documentary of Canada's war effort, as a force for national unity, or as a corrective to the influence of enemy propaganda, which it essentially did.[51] In this sense, keeping the public informed of Canadian achievements on the battlefields of Europe or on the homefront suggested more of a concerted program of education than propaganda. In the field of education itself, fear of a Nazified generation was apparent. Citing the example of German youths, for whom they believed "conscience, civilized man's ethical guide, has been abolished," Ontario school officials added fuel to a century-old debate by proposing the inclusion of a religious component in the provincial curriculum, ostensibly as a preventive measure.⁵² N.A.M. MacKenzie, later an instrumental member of the Massey Commission, told conscientious Canadians that they could make themselves safe from would-be dictators by making certain that their educational system did not focus too much on training youths for particular professions without grounding them in the humanities. Because it produced community leaders familiar with the wisdom of the ancients and the moderns, a liberal university education, he argued, gave a population access to the cultural background that it needed to discriminate between right and wrong, forthrightly "meeting and defeating enemy propaganda."⁵³

With conscience and a tradition of free inquiry upholding the Allied cause, it scarcely bothered those in charge of promoting the sale of Victory Bonds that their spring 1942 campaign contained some powerful propaganda. The reader, addressed as "you" – an individual – saw a rank of blank-countenanced Germans saluting Hitler. These were the "faceless men, men without identity, who march with linked arms against machine guns if they are not ordered to stop, who beat old men in the streets, and send their own mothers to concentration camps because the Fuhrer says it should be so." The new Germany contained a new kind of powerless German, represented in the Victory Bond ads as "not just vicious, bloodthirsty men" but as "automatons, without wills or desires."⁵⁴ The campaign implicitly acknowledged, and was probably to a degree inspired by, the reported inability of cartoonists during the Second World War to "produce anything recognizable as the typical German soldier," whereas the First World War's "fat-necked barbarian, wearing a spiked helmet and decorated with the Iron Cross," had been ubiquitous.⁵⁵

The image of ordinary Germans driven towards war with little control over their fates did not go unexploited by those in Canada wary of mass culture and of the level of indoctrination presented in *Education for Death*, Gregor Ziemer's account of his life as a teacher in Germany.⁵⁶ However, these writers could further their own cultural critiques and serve Canadian wartime morale simultaneously by attributing Nazi success at deluding the masses to a fundamental weakness among the German people. In that vein, R.S. Lambert noted what he considered some telling German traits, which included an "admixture of sentimentality and brutality, which is alien to Anglo-Saxon hardheadedness." The Nazis had supposedly mastered the "cultivation of artificial in place of innate patriotism, distrust of individualism, and cultivation of the herd instinct, leading, through the German power of organization and attention to detail, to regimentation."⁵⁷ Lambert's early wartime vivisection of the enemy psyche led him to suggest that the "cultivation" of these tendencies could be blamed squarely on the Nazis, under whom such traits were "brought to the top," but that the tendencies themselves resided in the group and were easily coaxed out. He claimed that Canada, along with its allies, remained a nation of individuals drawn together in a common cause and that its people would do well to defend British traditions in peacetime as well. Lambert added disapprovingly that Germany had tried to imitate some of Britain's characteristic institutions in the late nineteenth and early twentieth centuries, but had came up instead with "traditions created by artificial culture."[58] Hitler had merely augmented an already derivative pattern with a convenient assortment of theories of race and destiny. "There," intoned the Narrator in one of Mac Shoub's radio dramas, "is the cursed culture that slits the throat of life with a brutal edge."[59]

Working under such assumptions, critics in Canada could quite easily portray enemy culture as inauthentic and use it as a model of what to avoid at home. While examining the decline of religious affiliation at one of Canada's oldest universities, B.K. Sandwell contended, as might be expected, that "the true business of higher education is to keep alive, and to make continually stronger, the traditional culture of the community in which it functions." However, he drew on a counter-example that the enemy had provided in order to chastise Canadian society and advocate the ideal of a responsible populace. Sandwell accused Canadians of breaking faith with the "true meaning" of culture. He made sure to note that culture was "certainly not identical with the meaning ascribed by Germans between 1910 and 1941 to their own word '*kultur*' but it contains more of the idea of discipline, and disciplined responsibility than we were willing to put into it during those same years."[60] The enemy could exercise discipline over a mass public but could hardly expect responsible behaviour from it. However well-deserved, Germans' Nazi-era reputation for thinking and acting en masse granted considerable licence to Canadians keen to promote responsible individualism at home. The war effort curtailed some domestic political freedoms, and, even though the regulations circumscribing life seemed to most Canadians part of a regrettable state of regimentation, several commentators reminded them that this plight was only temporary. The public had not been wrenched, at least not for the sake of conformity, from attachments or pastimes that they were free to choose. By drawing attention to the enemy's dependence on cultivating conformity, critics strove to condemn blind adherence to cultural forms that seemed popular but had flourished at the expense of existing values and practices. They hoped that Canadians would learn allegorically that their society could mature only by recognizing and building on the traditions that had shaped it thus far.

In pointing out the errors to which entire societies were susceptible, observers were fortunate to have a convenient enemy to make the metaphorical divide between punishment and redemption more recognizable.

In an address broadcast during the intermission of a radio presentation of Gounod's *Faust*, McGill Principal F.C. (Cyril) James spoke of Germany's Faustian bargain and its inevitable ruin. James considered Hitler "a modern embodiment of Faust" who showed complete disregard for "the code of laws and morals that has been carefully formulated and preserved by the untiring efforts of successive generations of mankind."[61] To James, the preservation of this code of laws and morals was synonymous with the Allied cause. Although enemy culture (or the conception of it that James and others shared) and the mass culture produced and consumed in North America were hardly identical, critics could draw parallels between the restricted nature of life in an Axis nation and the danger lurking behind the inanity and sameness of much of the fare that they saw at home. The Canadian people could be trusted to elect reasonably harmless governments or to fill the jobs opening up in an increasingly mechanized world, but their fitness to choose wisely between the timeless and the ephemeral remained suspect without some form of supervision, guidance, or access to the wisdom of cultural authorities.

One final illustration of the identification of mass society with enemy culture comes from a 1943 radio play in which the protagonist was a young German pilot flying over France. The playwright, with a flourish of unsubtle symbolism, separates the pilot from his squadron. Liberated from the "herd," the flyer begins to think about his indoctrination, which is presented as the antithesis of a Christian upbringing. Before long, he hears his superior officer's voice: "Remember ... you are no longer an individual. You are a cornice on the great edifice of the state. You must become a machine ... with eyes and ears and a voice. You must come and go like the hands of a clock, as though bidden by an unseen mainspring."[62] Tormented by guilt over the innocent people whom he has killed and maimed, he thinks of the Lord's Prayer and dies horribly when his plane crashes. The playwright left the listener to imagine that the pilot had been redeemed, either in the conventional religious sense or by rediscovering his individuality, but made it plain that the vast enemy crowd – of which he had been too long a member – could never be so fortunate.

THE PLACE OF SCIENCE AND TECHNOLOGY

What of the pilot's airplane and the breathtakingly efficient system that had created it? It would be misleading to argue that many Canadians regarded science, the technologies springing from it, or the application of scientific principles to social problems with great suspicion during wartime. Regardless of how the enemy chose to apply knowledge, science itself would retain an exalted position as the engine of human advancement.⁶³ Such was the level of interest in the frontiers of scientific and technological knowledge that Canada's national magazines ran regular features offering declassified tales of war science. For its stirring lay reader–oriented science pieces, *Maclean's* employed a number of freelance writers whose scientific credentials, if they possessed any, went unacknowledged. Most often relegated to the middle and back pages, these articles supplemented "real" war news in that they were literally reports from another front.⁶⁴ An aptly named feature, "The Science Front," ran in Sandwell's *Saturday Night* from late 1939 into 1943. The *National Home Monthly* geared its "Tuning Up for Tomorrow" series, inaugurated in 1945, towards a postwar bounty of supervitamins and household robots.⁶⁵ Looking beyond the immediate conflict with confidence that scientific progress would be maintained was a component of wartime culture. Advertisers, media, and government sources reminded the public that scientists and technicians would do their utmost to improve life on the homefront and to give Canada's military the equipment that it needed. Recruits might have grumbled in their mess halls, but at least one branch of the armed forces revised its menu early in the war to reflect new findings in nutritional science. Up-to-date military machinery demanded a well-nourished soldier operating at peak efficiency.⁶⁶

With few exceptions, wartime observers rendered military technologies and the science behind them as neutral objects. Science retained its pre-war prestige as one of modern life's most identifiable features, but as Sir Richard Gregory, editor of the British scientific journal *Nature*, argued in a pamphlet distributed widely in Canada, the enemy had "chained" its scientific workers to party ideology, effectively polluting science itself.⁶⁷ At worst, science emerged as an accomplice rather than the author of human misery – a "tremendously enthusiastic butcher, sitting on God the Fuhrer's right hand."⁶⁸ Yet such views – their rhetorical power turning on the personification of science – were relatively rare in Canada. More numerous were discussions of new ways of waging war that either emphasized the malignant will behind enemy science or presented the Allied use and development of wartime technologies as an attempt to keep pace with the enemy. Typical of this perspective was a phoney war–era article describing the "eager" adoption of anti-blackout drugs by German pilots. The *Maclean's* correspondent in London, Beverley Baxter, MP, emphasized national and ideological differences by asserting that it was "the instinct of a healthy young Briton to scorn the adventitious aids of science and to rely on his strong heart and clear brain." He conceded that Allied pilots would soon have to adopt similar techniques if they hoped to repel the Luftwaffe, but he intimated that these would be obligatory detours from their natural inclinations.⁶⁹

Presenting each new enemy weapon as an aggressive use of otherwise-benign scientific principles, journalists made Canadian and other Allied attempts to counteract those weapons sound like entirely defensive measures. Yet when these attempts proved successful, newfound Allied superiority in defensive measures could be used as propaganda. One cartoon portrayed the success of the Royal Air Force (RAF) in keeping enemy planes at bay by showing Germans reduced to firing handguns from biplanes.[70] Even the stories surrounding these defensive measures could be prescriptive of appropriate wartime social conduct. When German U-boats began using acoustic torpedoes to home in on the sound of Allied ships' propellers, reporter Blair Fraser assured readers that the (Canadian) National Research Council's response was technically competent. In presenting what he could of Canadian scientists' still-classified solution to the problem, he related the story of how war had brought tinkerers of differing backgrounds together: "The Navy wired Research Council, 'Can you do anything about [the torpedo]?' Research Council could. In the lab beside their little wharf a staff of college-trained physicists and shop-trained mechanics worked side by side for two days and two nights without rest."[71] The scientific expert and the craftsman were as much combatants as the paratrooper or the bomber pilot. More important, they had employed their expertise nobly against an enemy that compelled its technicians and scientists, contrary to the scientific spirit, to make ever-more-terrible engines of destruction.

During the war, observers often strove to impart the lesson that advances in science did not on their own pose a threat to humankind but that society should be vigilant about the motives behind their application. British author James Hilton (*Good-Bye, Mr. Chips*) argued that "it is not for a technician to hold back his skill because someone may misuse it." Physicist E.L. Harrington spoke of science as a servant of humanity, used best to save labour and provide "new pleasures," but he noted that science, for all its marvels could not save humanity from its own regrettable inclinations or, more specifically, from those of the broadcaster. "They cannot build a radio which will give to us the best in music but will not receive jazz, or that will bring us messages of cheer and pleasurable programs, but neither the rantings of a Hitler nor soap advertisements." His contrasting of "best music" and "jazz," "cheer" and "Hitler," reflected a conviction that even decisions about how to employ what otherwise seemed a dispassionate or even potentially beneficial piece of technology could have ramifications within the realm of culture.[72]

One could oppose, for example, technological changes that made workers redundant, but such opposition little affected the momentum of research and development, because the fruits of science and the scientific worldview had long since become identified with modern life and progress. As long as scientists and engineers continued to offer consumers ever-more-comfortable lives, their prestige grew and careers associated in some way with science became more desirable among young people casting about for secure employment. In an article written in the form of a letter to a generic "bright young man," William Hardy Alexander told his fictitious correspondent that, if he is interested in academe, he should seek a post in natural or applied science, because such positions were distinguished, offered reasonably good incomes, and rarely involved serious political or moral choices. Alexander went on to qualify his initial statements by offering advice about potentially troublesome disciplines within the sciences, but he maintained that these fields continue to flourish because society has not hesitated to invest its hope in them.[73] Investors had been pouring money into scientific research for decades, and defenders of the free-enterprise system portrayed it and science as inseparable partners ensuring material and social progress.[74] Even though journalist W.J. Healy believed that the war's first Christmas called for spiritual strength, he resigned himself to admitting that "mankind will go on living and developing and providing itself with improved appliances and better institutions."[75]

In such a climate, a 1940 editorial in *Canadian Forum* seemed merely to confirm what had long been obvious by declaring that the world's more advanced societies depended almost completely on scientists and engineers to conduct their daily business. Although both of the war's belligerent blocs were dependent in this manner, the writer went on to raise an important point. Throwing Allied and enemy conceptions of the scientific method into sharp contrast, he saw – supporting the Allied order – a spirit of rationality that was "incompatible with the organization of mass emotion," and he added that "societies based upon rational inquiry will survive their rivals in the long run, if civilization survives at all."[76] This suggestion – that an advantage rested with nations that did not rely on mass persuasion – also implied that the liberal democracies, like forthright practitioners of science, sought truth alone. They did not need to practise indoctrination founded on dubious science.

Given the associations developed in North America during the 1930s between Nazi theories of race, national destiny, aggression, and methods of propaganda, interested commentators could easily suggest during wartime that enemy applications of science also lacked civilized restraint. In 1939, W.C. Keirstead reflected on the need for dissension in a democracy, identifying totalitarian culture with the absence of a genteel, but rigorous, scientific spirit. "Dictators may make use of scientists to provide means for their predetermined ends," he noted, "but they use propaganda to secure mass responses." Keirstead had obviously seen newsreel footage of Nazi rallies, for he included virtually the whole range of cultural forms in his catalogue of social events turned to sinister purposes: "Music, ritual, ceremonial, regimentation, the cinema, the radio, the press, and emotional oratory are all used to arouse feeling, to produce uniformity of attitude, and to prevent critical thinking."[77] Keirstead suggested that critical thinking stood at the core of responsible scientific inquiry, and the troubling relationship between science and culture in enemy societies should become a touchstone for those hoping to criticize more recent developments in Canadian life. Wartime critiques thereby served a dual purpose, condemning the misuse of science for political ends while issuing warnings – such as Keirstead's – about the power of mass persuasion to affect Canada, as it had Germany and its allies.

Wartime changes to educational curricula, especially the emphasis on the engineering and technical fields, which suggested a decline in the pre-eminence of liberal arts and a shift towards vocational training,[78] caused some consternation. Such alarm arose in the context of a perceived need to educate citizens who could serve as mediators between humanity's material and spiritual requirements. As we saw above, N.A.M. MacKenzie recognized the crucial role that science was playing during the war but lamented, as others did, the tendency of universities to emphasize the technically-oriented professions. He claimed that "only incidentally do they serve the high sounding purposes" they might. He declared that such a narrow program made "no provision for problems of [an ethical] kind and assumes little if any responsibility for their cause and cure. Our engineers, our doctors, our dentists and all the rest leave our universities with university degrees, presumably the hallmark of the educated man and woman." Though needed desperately during the war, scientists, doctors, and engineers would be expected during peacetime, he argued, to take on responsibilities within their communities for which a university career spent sneering at arts electives had not prepared them.[79]

How a society decided to deploy its knowledge, and how it valued disciplines or pursuits other than the completely utilitarian mattered greatly to wartime cultural critics. Reviewing a compendium of John Dewey's work a few months before war broke out, classicist Eric Havelock suggested that the deeds of European fascists were already prompting some North Americans to question their own readiness to employ science and rationality as sovereign methods. He claimed that the flavour of pragmatism associated with Dewey's philosophy appeared to be relatively harmless during the American economic expansion of the late nineteenth and early twentieth centuries, when "the interaction of ends and means, of ideas and functions, seemed automatic." He added, however, that "as man progressively extends scientific technique to the purpose of dominating his fellow men, the activities of totalitarian communities are going to force the thoughtful to turn with renewed attention to that old-fashioned question, What after all is the chief end of man?"[80]

Much had changed between the wars, and the question of ends did seem old-fashioned in a world brimming with means and strategies. Commenting on military recruitment in Canada, journalist Albert Wakeman observed that it paled in comparison to 1914, suggesting that arousing enthusiasm for the present war was difficult because the whole enterprise had been "figured out in cold-blooded efficiency." Emotion had gone out of fashion, and "in place of the recruiting depots and the bands, and the reviews which coloured the last war, we have requests for enlistment of skilled mechanics, and training schools and secret sailings." Wakeman also suggested that an efficient war deprived those on the homefront of spectacle: "It is a long time since British people were called upon to pay for anything without being given some kind of show for their money."[81] To those seeking a balance between the pragmatic goals of winning the war and maintaining "civilization," the human price that a society paid for its preoccupation with technology and efficiency remained the prime concern. Early in the conflict, as he pondered the rush to safeguard Europe's artistic treasures, Morley Callaghan noted that the First World War had taken a great toll among artists and writers. He cited an interwar drought in British literature as compelling evidence of too great a fascination with science and advocated going further than keeping brilliant physicists out of uniform. He asked if it had "occurred to our governments that the true key men of our civilization are the men who make beautiful things."[82]

Making beautiful things took on a greater significance for critics during a time when much of the nation's labour, if not devoted to using the materiel of war, was producing it. Early in 1940, architect and teacher Humphrey Carver reminded Canadians of what had become an abiding feature of modern existence – the decline of craftsmanship in the face of mass production. Invoking John Ruskin and William Morris, Carver set aside their socialist politics to argue that Canada could lose what little authentic craft culture it had left if steps were not taken to imbue the relatively new field of industrial design with the essence of craft production – "the sensitivity of the hand." Carver recognized that the tide of industrialization would not abate. But he hoped, as others did, that handicraft could survive in Canada through some sort of integration with industry, avoiding the fate of the British arts-and-crafts movement – a "reactionary and sentimental spinsterhood." That handicrafts had become symbols of an artistic spirit indicated their currency as symbols of a world outside science, outside utilitarianism, and outside the efficient production of conformity. Manufacturing and distributing goods or services without much regard for what the public might buy by the truckload seemed somehow anti-democratic, but it had allowed consumers access to products and experiences formerly reserved for those with more money or patience. Recognizing this as one of the keenest contradictions defining the modern age, Carver repeated Morris's observation that "as a condition of life, production by machinery is altogether an evil; as an instrument for forcing on us better conditions of life it has been indispensable."[83]

Cultural critics in wartime Canada also had to grapple with a troubling paradox – major changes to the way Canadians earned their livings gave them more leisuretime while their jobs seemed to leave them fit for little else than a culture that someone else had made for them. Echoing philosopher Paul Schrecker, painter Lawren Harris and a band of like-minded critics warned: "if no systematic effort is made against the trend towards uniformity ... big business and mass production will efface all regional differences and smother the living creative effort of every individual."[84] Creativity in the home was also at risk. Asking her readers the rhetorical question: "Did you ever feel mass-produced?" Adeline Haddow agreed that mass production had come to stay but intimated that it need not destroy creativity or individuality. She prescribed a method for bestowing a sense of taste on the consumer and on the consumption of mass-produced goods: "Let her withdraw her watchful eye for a moment from the price ceilings and turn it upon the bad designs in cheap factory-made articles. Let her express her dissatisfaction and demand something better. Let her do her share in adapting the machine to a higher civilization."[85]

In wartime, mass production, science, and the rational deployment of resources aided the fight against enemies that used the same tools, albeit in a manner consistently and unironically identified with aggression, the pursuit of "irrational" goals, and uniformity. In the absence of significant differences in technique, distinctions between the opposing powers depended on the perception and communication of cultural differences. That task fell to articulate Canadians in the journalistic, academic, and artistic fields, who, like their counterparts in Britain and the United States, looked to simplify these distinctions further by pinning them on one central principle, present among the Allied nations, but absent from the enemy camp. The dilemma for this group of "perceivers and communicators" was that *democracy* – the principle that wartime necessity placed at the core of Western civilization – also played an elemental part in the proliferation of mass culture.

DEMOCRACY AND MASS CULTURE

Despite his inclusive, forgiving tone, when Northrop Frye declared that "Democracy is in essence a cultural *laissez faire*, an encouragement of private enterprise in art, scholarship and science,"[86] he did not mean to indicate unqualified support for the books, radio programs, or films that had become most popular in an expanding cultural marketplace. Rather, he wished to remind his readers that a liberal democracy, even though it emphasized the voice of the majority, made room for a considerable variety of expression, which in turn made possible challenging, enduring works. "There is more in life than democracy," one editor at *Canadian Forum* wrote, "though democracy may be the essential which sweetens the rest."[87] Thanks to the democratization of the educational and political systems, more people could now read, attend high school and university, and vote, but democracy's track record in the first part of the twentieth century offered little promise of cultural regeneration in the second part. Before the Second World War, cultural critics had come to identify democracy in North America with an impatient mass audience unlikely to think critically or to appreciate any but the most elementary historical, literary, or biblical allusions. John Dewey, whose brand of educational democracy Hilda Neatby vilified in the 1950s, noted that "one effect of literacy under existing conditions has been to create in a large number of persons an appetite for the momentary 'thrills' caused by impacts that stimulate nerve endings but whose connections with cerebral functions are broken."[88] Tabloid newspapers continued to run simplified, sensationalized stories ahead of, or in place of, war bulletins, articles on public affairs, or domestic items that seemed grey and lifeless by comparison. One incensed critic used verse to compare the hedonistic apathy of the tabloid reader to the alcoholic's preferred state: "As men who seek oblivion in drink / They dose their senses, dulling them with ink, / Afraid to think, afraid to try to think."[89] However, because Frye and others considered the liberal democratic ideal "something rooted in the broader and deeper concepts of culture and civilization,"[90] it warranted veneration not only as a worthwhile basis for differentiating the Allies from the Axis, but as a way to spur English-Canadian society to honour the "great tradition" of Anglo-American thought and to redefine the practice of democracy itself so that it implied more than the satisfaction of an unreflective mass.

Even if a full-fledged "cult" of democracy did not exist during the war, a professed affiliation with the defence, evangelism, or improvement of democratic life seemed mandatory for commentators seeking a sympathetic audience. Cultural critics added another dimension to patriotic calls for democracy's preservation. Author I.D. Willis was not alone in clinging to writer-diplomat John Buchan's idea that democracy existed as "an attitude of mind, of spiritual testament, and not an economic structure or a political machine."[91] More than sixty wartime pamphlets, books, articles, or broadcasts of Canadian origin featured as a principal theme the ideal of democracy or its application to some aspect of war or of civilian existence. Not all these declarations of democratic faith were pointed critiques of modern life or mass culture, but many expressed concern about the ways in which passive roles for the citizen/consumer had replaced the lively give and take that progressive thinkers associated with democracy in its ideal state. They could manage only, as E.M. Forster had put it in 1939, "two cheers for democracy."[92] For example, the *Citizens All* series of broadcasts, begun in late 1940 and published almost concurrently as the "Democracy and Citizenship" series of pamphlets, aimed in a general sense to help listeners feel part of a democratic system that reached outside politics into their daily lives.[93] Most significantly, wartime commentaries harboured a critique of the "hollow" democracy that critics saw passing for a much richer set of values. Considering the volume of British and American output on the importance of maintaining a democratic society, English Canadians had access to an arsenal of material in which democracy figured prominently.[94] Such publications were hardly bestsellers, but organizations such as the Canadian Association for Adult Education (CAAE), the Canadian Youth Commission, and local libraries distributed them in quantity to their members and to people who were inquisitive or motivated to explore public affairs.

For cultural critics during the war, this inquisitive segment of the population comprised the target audience – conscientious citizens towards whom they could direct expressions of support for democracy or concern for its welfare. The job of offering this audience "mass education"[95] in democratic living provided critics with a suitable vehicle for addressing troubling social and cultural developments. Just as in interwar Britain, where Daniel LeMahieu has shown that "what culture was appropriate for a democracy became a question pitting the forces of the market-place against the influence of an articulate minority,"[96] those constituting this sort of articulate minority in Canada took care to situate their calls for cultural reform within the framework of a quest for liberal democracy. They also took care to speak to those who owed improved employment or social status to the democratization of educational opportunities. Critics could cite their concern that mass culture was unsuitable for a democratic people because it distracted citizens from their vital wartime responsibilities, but they could also be confident that their audience "knew better" or aspired to a more refined leisure than movies or pulp novels. The prosperity of wartime relative to the previous decade seemed only to make this unsuitability more evident, leading one pamphleteer to note: "Most of us have plenty of money for the poor sort of stuff that many of our amusements dish up for us, for motor cars and gas, poor reading material, for all sorts of things that are not essential to comfortable and cultural living."[97] Even among organizations committed to principles of direct democracy, such as the credit-union movement, the perception that certain popular pursuits lacked some unspecified quality that made others "cultural" indicated their fear of the direction that an ostensibly democratic mass culture could take.

Any wartime observer could discern the ideological gulf between fascism and the Allied attachment to a democratic political and social order. Such difference was essential to the construction of the war as the "defence of democracy." The widespread belief that the "ideal of democracy is at stake; this force which vitalizes all our institutions is in danger," lent further urgency to the need to halt the enemy's military progress[98] and encouraged the individual to take a part in maintaining democratic institutions at home. To meet the variety of threats facing it, commentators had democracy appear in a variety of guises, from militant to nurturing. In their pamphlet *Dynamic Democracy*, Philip Child and John Holmes called for "an aggressive democracy on the march," ready to convince those not already suitably devoted to democracy that their hopes lay with its survival.[99] Even late in the war, the sense of struggle – of a torch passed from the English Civil War through the American, French, and even the Russian revolutions, and certainly on through the First World War – remained a vital way of expressing the idea that "The Fight Isn't New."[100] At the other end of the scale, R.S. Lambert adopted a flexible, less martial strategy. "As long as the enemy is inspired by the dynamic conception of a mission to change the world (even in a wrong direction)," he lectured, the enemy "must be countered by a similar dynamic conception of re-invigorated and improved democracy."[101]

Many Canadians were no doubt entirely satisfied with the rather practical argument that democracy must be preserved simply because the alternative was hateful totalitarianism. Staged spectacles such as the "If" day held in Winnipeg in 1942 drove this point home by depicting what Canadians might expect if they lost the war. "German" troops arrested bus passengers, a priest, and the city's mayor. They interrogated others at random and put them in concentration camps. Worship was forbidden and, as a final humiliation, teaching democracy in the schools was banned.[102] This simple model, which presented the public with a choice – confront democracy's enemies or face disaster – found its way into some of the wartime literature and commentary, among – treatments of democracy as a system in need of continuous renewal, if not redefinition.[103] I.D. Willis's first wartime pamphlet opened rather tamely with the exhortation to "accept our personal responsibility for conditions in Canada, and to study those factors which have brought them about," but it devolved towards slogans encouraging Canadians to put their "shoulders to the wheel" so that the enemy could be more speedily conquered.[104] More often, however, those who addressed democracy and its place in the war presented the image of a democratic culture that could, on the strength of its adaptable nature, rally citizens to its defence. Citing rigid enemy systems of thought and governance that tolerated no political or artistic opposition, Canadian commentators contrasted mass manipulation with the creative potential of a liberal-democratic approach or set democracy's practicality against the enemy's need to inhabit a "mystical nation-state."[105] Even in the midst of campaigning for more comprehensive social programs, Stuart Jaffary identified the democratic ideal's greatest cultural advantage. He contended that in offering "the largest measure of opportunity for the common man, both materially and spiritually," democracy allowed for "the fullest development of the human personality."[106]

While contrasting coercive totalitarian methods of instituting sweeping social reorganization with the gentler ways operating in North America, Father M.M. Coady, a pioneer in building Maritime co-operatives, also noted the difficulty – in democratic societies – of giving people what was considered good for them. "We want to attain our objectives," he wrote, "but we want also to do it in the free way. In our democratic way, the dynamics for social reconstruction must come from within."[107] Coady referred to the difficulty of coercing Canadians into accepting social innovations imposed from above, but his caution indicated that he thought it unwise for those committed to elevating tastes to insist that they alone were equipped to serve as cultural arbiters. In a democratic society, freedom had to be the prize of total war, and, despite an abundance of wartime ideas about what should be changed, critical observers could not object to much in contemporary culture without sounding as if they wished to censor popular entertainments. For the liberal democrat hoping to counter the power of mass culture by enlisting government protection for less "popular" pursuits, any cultural renaissance had to come through a broadening of the average person's experience, not through an abridgement of the consumer's freedom to choose. In its contribution to the "Democratic Way" series of pamphlets, the Canadian Teachers' Federation declared that "the enlightened state will, as far as is compatible with public order, avoid conflict with the awakened consciences of its citizens."[108]

While they condemned some domestic conditions by associating them with the enemy, critics also considered the freedom to produce or appreciate cultural works invaluable. "Cultural liberty," one observer remarked, would comfort and make more creative the artists, scientists, and writers "who in a mysterious way lead the great mass of mankind."[109] Northrop Frye approached the topic from a different angle, commenting that "the art which emerges under the cultural anarchy of democracy may be subtle, obscure, highbrow and experimental, and if a good deal of art at any time is not so the cultural achievement of the country is on a Woolworth level. But art under a dictatorship seldom dares to be anything but mediocre and obvious."[110] Relative to what was generally represented as the certainty of spiritual subjugation under a fascist regime, democracy held great promise for Allied nations – promise that few critical observers believed had been realized. Liberal democracy granted cultural producers the latitude to be subtle and highbrow, but it also allowed them freedom to be mediocre and obvious, and critics perceived the tendency of newer media to serve mass tastes as a dictatorship of sorts. While they chose repeatedly to point out the unpleasant implications of such a dictatorship, critics remained mindful that preserving the right to criticize and to promote "suitable" alternatives was more probable and desirable than overturning the complex and long-running historical process of modernization and the concomitant rise of mass culture. Instead of advocating measures that would mark them as cultural authoritarians, they proposed that the extensive democratization of culture – which had so far seemed to result mainly in troubling productions such as radio soap operas – could also aid the cultivation of more discriminating minds. Few engaged the question of how many people were capable of becoming "cultured," even though democracy gave more and more people the opportunity. B.K. Sandwell asserted rather bluntly that the majority would remain "uncultured" but could certainly escape ignorance and misery.[111]

In an atmosphere emphasizing the dramatic opposition between democracy and totalitarianism, inspirational works accenting the high stakes of the war and the moral rectitude of the Allied cause formed part of the propaganda effort. Such works also reflected a disdain for passivity. The idea that the Allied nations shared a liberal-democratic tradition came to the fore, and critics eagerly bound wartime resolve with the nineteenth-century British liberal tradition of Mechanics' Institutes and voluntary societies, the erudite egalitarianism of American democratic heroes, or the faith of religious stalwarts. "The great tradition of political freedom which is Canada's heritage has been shaped in the brave struggles of men motivated by religion and conscience," read one pamphlet, "in the old world and on Canadian soil."[112] In Canada, mass communications, higher rates of literacy, and advertising had operated to transform the public sphere, and, as Sandwell remarked, the previous century's notion that "all ideas will be judged according to reason and only sound ideas will ultimately prevail, has been shown to be far too optimistic."[113] Acknowledging the foundations of democratic thought while soberly accounting for the reach and persuasive power of the contemporary mass media seemed a more proactive strategy. Beginning in February 1941, the CBC presented its *Theatre of Freedom* series – twelve radio plays featuring such renowned writers and actors as Norman Corwin, Merrill Denison, Douglas Fairbanks, Jr., Elsa Lanchester and Charles Laughton, Raymond Massey, and Orson Welles. Selected because "they have all of them some message to give to Democracy," the plays further admonished listeners by emphasizing particular democratic virtues: "*St. Joan* is a study of tolerance, *An Enemy of the People* preaches the sanctity of conscience. *Strife* warns against extremism and pleads for moderation. *Valley Forge*, *Abraham Lincoln*, and *Victoria the Great* describe the qualities of democratic leadership." Here the producers hoped to represent the democratic tradition as an outgrowth of British, American, and Canadian experience – an Anglo–American recipe for orderly progress. Although many of the productions featured historical themes, the CBC had Norman Corwin's *Seems Radio Is Here to Stay* open the series in order to "bring home to us the vital power of radio to inform and unite our community in support of its ideals."[114]

Commentators and pamphleteers offering their advice to concerned Canadians maintained that the community had to be united because its attachment to a concept of democracy based on personal responsibility and effort appeared to be in danger of extinction. John Grierson swam against this tide, expressing a desire to leave behind what he admitted was the compelling rhetoric of individualism in favour of democratic consensus and a planned society.[115] Yet, critical contributions to the larger stream of motivational messages and cautionary tales more often emphasized the idea of liberal democracy as a neglected part of Canada's heritage – a heritage that must ultimately shape the culture surrounding even the most rudimentarily educated citizen. For example, Watson Kirkconnell's early wartime essays and speeches formed the basis for his short book *Twilight of Liberty*, which had the early working title "Canadian Credo." Kirkconnell chastised complacent longtime residents by celebrating immigrants' quick integration and their willingness to fight for their adopted country. Presenting the contributions of immigrant groups in this manner, he implied that Canadians already steeped in a tradition of democracy must strive to better exemplify certain presumably Canadian qualities. In September 1941, he suggested "Canadian Affirmations" as a possible title, he subsequently leaned towards "Holy War," because he thought that it "suggests something of the moral drive that we need in our thinking." The final title emphasized the enemy's threat to freedom and the urgency of democratic reconstruction from within.[116]

A dread of decay pervaded efforts to inform the population about the wartime threat to those basic rights that had been linked with democracy most memorably through Franklin Roosevelt's "Four Freedoms."[117] Such dread also sat, however, at the centre of wartime responses to mass culture. L.A. Mackay of the University of British Columbia noted the need to instil a sense of continuity in a democratic public: "If society were an organism, or if it were a machine, it would suffice that a small elite thought, learned and remembered; but in the world we live in, everyone, as far as possible, must remember the important things, or society falls in ruin."[118] Like others among his contemporaries also sensitive to decay, Mackay saw Britain as the origin and conservatory of an admirable democratic tradition. The stability of a slowly evolving culture and *noblesse oblige* – the responsibility of the privileged to be public-spirited and to set an example for those less fortunate – recommended the old country as a model for the Dominion.[119] Charles Phillips drew the line, however, at reinforcing British patterns of deference and an "aristocratic" sensibility in the teaching of history, civics, and literature.[120] One member of Parliament, Duncan McArthur, spoke highly of the democratic tradition but portrayed British democracy's trip across the Atlantic as a wasted effort. He contended that a vital sense of stewardship had failed to take root in a continental society whose social leaders had become wealthy and powerful too quickly. North American societies were hardly established before new inventions allowed them access to the continent's resources, which they "dissipated ... with prodigal wastefulness." Although the United States boasted a caste of millionaires, no invigorating sense of obligation could develop, McArthur suggested, where wealth and power were thought to be the products of individual skill rather than the natural outcome of a stable community and its roots.[121]

The appeal to a neglected democratic tradition, however, could carry the critique of contemporary society and its cultural preferences only so far. Canadians heard and read during wartime that they were protecting democracy, but democracy had become a rather nebulous concept. Wartime inspired a kind of "super democracy, when Jack is as good as his Master, and youth is as good as age"[122] – a situation that led some critics to suggest that the idea's force had been stripped away. One editorial lamented this loss and quoted T.S. Eliot's observation: "When a term has become so universally sanctified as 'democracy' now is, I begin to wonder whether it means anything, in meaning too many things."[123] Another commentator found continuous invocation of the democratic ideal to be like a "narcotic," but he added that "now it seems stale, flat, and unprofitable, because it creates an illusion, out of which you emerge with a headache of disappointment and despair."[124] Northrop Frye offered a qualification to the idea of an entirely noble democratic tradition, noting that democracy served as a sort of charm absolving Britain and the United States of their historical "capitalist imperialisms." The perception that "the word 'democracy' wanders through books, magazines, newspapers and speeches undefined and untranslated" bothered him even more acutely during the war's early stages.[125] Nearly two years later, Frank Underhill sensed no improvement, even among people whom he believed should have been more careful. In his view, the "most depressing feature" of the war was "not the battle news from across the Atlantic but the mass of stuff poured out by our editors, columnists, professors and best people generally on the subject of democracy and liberty." The apparent absence of an authentic commitment to democracy incensed Underhill and prompted him to complain that "when one is in the habit of reading fairly widely in current periodicals and books, and when one has submitted himself for some time to a tasteless diet of all this rehashed rhetoric of the nineteenth century, he gets the feeling that V stands for Vacuity."[126]

Democracy's *potential* for getting things right recommended it, but its reputation did not. B.K. Sandwell complained that the only appreciable changes in democratic culture in a long while had been "extending the franchise over an ever-widening area of the population." He argued that faith in a vast public's ability to assess and respond to the complex issues facing a modern nation was misplaced: "The accent has been too exclusively upon the quantity of the electorate and too little upon its quality."[127] Although wartime circumstances bound critics to express some form of support for democracy as an ideal, still they sought to distance themselves from a democracy that seemed to them no more likely to aid the achievement of that ideal than a recruiting poster. Even government-sponsored material on democracy offered some indication that, in the absence of continuous attention, democracy would reflect the qualities of a mass public that was easily satisfied and easily led. "Only the *best citizens* accept the duties as readily as they do the rights," declared one pamphlet distributed to armed-forces discussion groups.[128] Indeed, the uncomfortable sense that Allied nations had for some time been harbouring a rather ineffectual, delusional definition of democracy helped explain the drift of the 1930s. One playwright had a bold, progressive character declare: "Daddy went away to war in 1914 and saved the world for democracy. A depression wasn't big enough to undermine our self-confidence."[129] Ronald MacFarlane believed that majority rule was as prone to tyranny as a dictatorial system, but it was also much more likely to lead to a peaceful, ordered existence if guided by humanitarian principles and citizens who took responsibility for their own political and cultural fulfilment.[130] The unacceptable alternative to the ideal of the responsible citizen was a mass without a sense of history, unable to reflect on what sort of government – or what sort of culture – it was getting.

The messages that Canada could boast a rich democratic tradition and that the nation's enemies stood opposed to this tradition were simple enough to convey, and these received top billing from official and unofficial sources. Less evident, and less suited to a war effort demanding a united front, was the message that democracy must not be an instrument of its own downfall. "Man is not born a democrat," declared one educator, identifying democracy as more than a political designation. It took on the gravity, during the Second World War, of a cultural choice or a type of behaviour in need of "continuous creation and recreation."[131] Although critics echoed wartime strains of praise for the personal freedoms and mutual protection possible under a democracy, they worried that undue deference to it had contributed to a decadent mass culture. They also feared that such deference had favoured the chaotic, materialistic modern whirl, leading individuals, communities, and the nation away from the principles, tastes, and modes of living that comprised a budding national heritage. The wartime sanctification of a hollow democracy weakened the cultural elite's ability to insist that the supply of enervating, mass-produced cultural forms be somehow curtailed, but it also encouraged the creation and promotion of alternatives. I explore some of these in chapter 2.

Critical commentators, like their less outspoken neighbours, did not want to revisit a time when invincible ignorance had been the lot of many. "Fascism and ignorance go hand in hand,"[132] wrote Queen's University philosopher Martyn Estall, and the material benefits attending improvements in literacy, the development of new media, and increased leisure time seemed too obvious to allow contemplation of anything but further democratization. New media and more leisure time had certainly helped make possible mass culture, but they represented only one part of the path to cultural regeneration – the conditions necessary for the broadcast of a "deep wisdom" that would allow presentation of crucial elements of the Western tradition. A strategy for entrenching knowledge about how mass culture operated to standardize tastes underlay wartime commentary on democracy. By using the war's stark oppositions to expose the perils of democracy misapplied, critics could more forcefully argue that, if the public looked to them as its able representatives, cultural democracy would function best.

Critics portrayed the war as sobering evidence that, as modern life became more complex, mass culture seemed to render people less able to fend for themselves. Outside the well-worn critique of declining standards, there lay an awareness that war might also be a time of renewal, during which Canadians could recognize the intangibles that they wished to defend. As Cyril James noted: "This war is refining in the furnace some of the fundamental traditions and ideals of the human race, and those ideals are not utilitarian."[133] Neither did it seem that renewal would emerge from some example that the enemy had set or from an unsupervised democracy. On his program *Books and Shows*, John Coulter suggested that war, despite all its horrors, had some cultural uses. Younger poets had begun, he claimed, "to speak of the things of today in terms of today" – a development that contrasted sharply with the "inertia" of peacetime. He concluded that "if that inertia is proved to be an inherent characteristic of peace – then we should have to make the fearful admission, that the periodic recurrence of war is, after all, no evil, but a necessity, the essential instrument of regeneration which the Nazis and the Fascists claim that it is."[134]

While Coulter – or any other cultural critic – probably did not consider such regeneration worth the price that war exacted, he welcomed the sort of cathartic therapy that it induced, as long as traditional modes of conduct or culture would not be abandoned in the postwar era. He promoted the experimentation with and the reaffirmation of forms and ideals such as opera and democracy that had proven resilient and adaptable to new circumstances. His libretto for the CBC radio opera *Transit through Fire* (1942, music by Healey Willan) testified to the wartime notion that behind the worthy citizen stood a culture mindful of its origins but not constrained by them. To Coulter, new Canadian ventures such as those undertaken by John Grierson's National Film Board represented brave forays into hostile territory, "and Hollywood was the enemy." During the war, with the enemy metaphor at the peak of its persuasive power, this sort of rejection of popular film pointed a scornful finger at a commercialized mode of cultural production. Hollywood as enemy meant "flashy buffooneries, the deliberate triviality and trickery, the craven pandering, the cynical exploitation of what the mountebank commercarios of Hollywood believe to be the lowest common denominator of public sentimentality and lack of taste." Coulter believed that in documentaries and other more thoughtfully wrought productions the "canon of a true art of cinema is being laid down."[135]

To critics, canons could be updated or enlarged to reflect the emergence of latter-day talent or vision, and wartime did not preclude the recognition of new achievements. The artistic innovations and deliberate rebellions embodied in modernism did not make it an enemy. Modernist departures did not romanticize experience, commodify it or make it passive in the ways that mass culture appeared to do. Montreal's new train station met with approval in 1943 because travel remained an active venture, and the new terminal simply made travelling to or from the city more comfortable and aesthetically pleasing. That the station was completed in wartime made it more impressive.[136] Of course, the grand scale and modern finish of the building could be counted on to conjure bright visions of Canada's future, but the murals high on its walls lauded the doers and dreamers of the past as well as of the present, prompting one journalist to declare that it was "more than a station. It is a monument to the progress of transportation in Canada."[137]

Likewise, in the realm of the everyday, the war could deliver small rays of hope for Canadians exasperated with certain aspects of modern life. When federal industry minister C.D. Howe called an early wartime halt to cosmetic design changes in the automobile industry, he earned the admiration of an Ottawa columnist, who greeted the news with some relief: "this business of getting up in the morning only to see a new shiny car before your neighbour's door, and it looking all the world like a new kind of U-boat or destroyer, made life too complicated."[138] Though satisfying to some, such victories seemed isolated, temporary, and largely inconsequential, because dedicated critics of mass culture understood that war could bring substantial cultural improvement only if it assured the continuity of certain desirable traditions. Charles Comfort, head of Canada's band of official war artists, cited with alarm the case of wartime England, which stowed away paintings for safekeeping and where, reluctantly, evening concerts were "for a while abandoned." After making it plain that he considered the war effort Canada's top priority, Comfort warned that the single-minded pursuit of war aims without a parallel commitment to preserve art's place in the community would be disastrous – although "there are few of us unawakened to the gravity of the war," he had noticed "almost a pathetic eagerness to put first things first." This "tendency to treat the arts as non-essentials" would destroy the "very foundations of our civilization."[139] Another Canadian stationed in Britain sounded a more optimistic note, reporting that Kenneth Clark, director of London's National Gallery, had observed an increased propensity among ordinary citizens there to discard or at least to discount rigid class barriers in their appreciation of art. "In wartime when the static social grouping is broken down," Clark had said, "the tabu against art is broken down as well."[140] Although it is difficult to assess how willing average Britons or Canadians were to discuss matters pertaining to their nations' respective cultural scenes, war imparted an additional boost to the preservation of civilization through continuity of activity or continuity of interest.

"Civilization" included a religious tradition organized around the tenets of Judaeo-Christianity, and support for it among critics remained strong throughout the war. One treatise on the importance of religious freedom declared that its "extra-ordinary power of self-recovery and revitalization makes Christianity the best companion of democracy."[141] Claris Silcox explained that war, much like upheaval in any individual's life, "evokes both what is highest and what is lowest in human nature," and so individual soldiers most often displayed what was best in Christian society. War might well work to put soldiers back in touch with at least one aspect of their cultural heritage, but – like the technology that made it possible for war to be waged on an unprecedented scale – it could also erode confidence in traditional belief systems. Like Charles Comfort, Silcox worried about giving too much attention to the war and putting too much faith in fighting people and machines, so he instructed his readers to remember Rudyard Kipling's dictum that "men in barracks don't grow into plaster saints."[142]

CONCLUSION: FOCUSING THE CRITIQUE

Some critics found some uses for war – a harrowing experience through which, they believed, Canada would further consolidate its status as a mature nation. Expressing their dissatisfaction in terms of the bitter conflict itself, they sometimes used the potent example of enemy culture to warn Canadians against the depths to which the masses could be driven or acclimatized. They sought a balance between utilitarian and aesthetic perspectives. They recognized the value of democracy, while many of them worried that the cultural marketplace, as it had evolved, took into account only those kinds of entertainment that were immensely "popular" and hence profitable. Looking back on wartime in 1946, Richard Saunders claimed that many Canadians had been "shocked into the realization" that society's cultural foundations ran as deep as they did. He sought an unambiguous declaration of the "inner conviction of the rightness of our way of life"; during the war, he had noticed, the stresses of modern existence were best met with trusted weapons – the "inherited capital ... the ideas, the customs and habits, the institutions left to us as a heritage by our fathers and forefathers."[143]

Determined to reconcile the wisdom of the ancients with that of the moderns, most cultural critics steered clear of simply disparaging the current technological order or mass communications. To denounce these forces outright was especially counter-productive in wartime, for science and technology kept bombers aloft and even the most vacuous radio programs entertained munitions workers. Conditions convinced some "opinion moulders" that Canadians would emerge a stronger people only if they educated themselves and their children, not only about political matters, but about the humanism underlying liberal democracy.[144] As the conflict continued, critics found uses for the same media that advanced mass culture, having sensed that the much-discussed peace that would follow – whenever it arrived – would entail equally fundamental questions about the nation's social and cultural well-being. Most important for the nation's postwar culture, their experience of reflecting intensely on the wartime responsibilities and obligations of citizens would reinforce their vision of a reconstructed, democratic society that was more than the sum of its pastimes.

2

The Culture of Reconstruction

> If we are to get and keep this new world of which we hear,
> we must be mentally well-nourished and mentally tough.[1]
> B.K. Sandwell, 1941

Just as it would have been practically impossible to live in Canada during the years 1939–45 and not gather that a war was on, so too was it difficult to avoid talk of the postwar world to which Sandwell referred. By 1943, although millions were involved in the war effort overseas or on the homefront, one observer could note that the "favorite indoor sport for thousands of Canadians, including government officials and professional politicians, university professors, welfare workers and just plain everyday citizens, is post-war planning."[2] The term most often identified with the anticipation of peacetime, and with the variety of activities undertaken in preparation for it, was *reconstruction*. Politicians used it to evoke images of a prosperous nation grateful to those who served it in war, and businesses invoked it to market the same old products as somehow re-engineered for a new era.

The general excitement over reconstruction also presented an opportunity for critics of the cultural status quo to insist on rehabilitation. They agreed with the frequently repeated arguments that wartime had allowed Canada to modernize and to achieve an unprecedented maturity, especially in industry and international relations. However, seekers after a new cultural order hoped that Canada could be reinvented as a nation of citizens who heeded their responsibilities and obligations to the community and to the democratic ideal. Informed by some powerful assumptions about the kind of culture that an unguided populace would embrace – namely, a formulaic culture geared towards a passive audience – critics and their allies hoped to foster conditions in which "folk" and "high" culture could prove their worth by making postwar leisuretime not only entertaining, but edifying.

The concept of planning figured prominently during late wartime and the early years of peace, and, despite its potential for divisiveness in politics, hatching plans for peacetime appeared to be a promising way to avoid the disillusionment of the 1930s. The dream of a new common culture drawing on local or regional traditions and "civilized" activities seemed almost attainable in a wartime environment that cast the preservation and pursuit of such traditions and activities as indistinguishable from "active local citizenship of a positive constructive sort."[3] Yet within a few months of war's end, it seemed that the public had largely turned back to enjoying the material benefits of modern life. Among those convinced that Canadians could become a cultivated people if exposed to the right sort of influences, such a precipitous return to normality would not do. These cultural critics employed modern means of communication such as radio to absorb, refashion, and retransmit the rhetoric of reconstruction, advancing their critique of mass culture through an endorsement of alternatives to it. Without the seemingly boundless confidence that reconstruction encompassed, efforts to impart a basic appreciation of the Canadian and Western traditions would probably not have become quite the "search for identity"[4] that has fascinated and frustrated the few generations since.

During the latter half of the nineteenth century, the example of the dozen or so years following the American Civil War suggested that reconstruction was a task best undertaken once fighting had ceased. By the middle of the First World War, both Canada and Britain had recognized the value of preparing for the armistice, inaugurating reconstruction programs early but paying them little notice until relatively late in the conflict. As a consequence, planning for reconstruction did not become an integral part of the First World War experience. Its position among the committees and bureaucracies dedicated to administering the war reflected an early-twentieth-century zeal for social reform, but it suffered from underpromotion and the belief that agitation for peacetime utopias should rank behind more immediate concerns.[5] Given the historical connotations and career of reconstruction, even several months into the Second World War it still seemed presumptuous or incongruous to "discuss demobilization during a Recruiting Drive."[6] In general, historians of Canada have tended to treat reconstruction as an economic or governmental issue, and few accounts of Canadian culture and cultural policy at mid-century explore the concept as much more than an administrative moment.[7] Despite my contention that the critique of modern life and mass culture resonated with the culture of reconstruction, we must acknowledge the basic political and economic motivations behind reconstruction and the official bodies devoted to that goal. For most Canadians, the economic and social-welfare components of reconstruction justified the privations of wartime. Only as a kind of side-effect did the interest that they generated in the postwar period allow the prospect of reconstruction to become a vehicle for cultural and social criticism.

None the less, talk of the opportunities that Canada and its citizens would have in a world at peace arose early and surfaced consistently during the Second World War, with one frequent topic being the eventual demobilization of Canada's armed forces and their reintegration into civilian life. One magazine writer's explanation for a "resurgence of energy" among Canadians in the autumn of 1942 illustrated this symbiotic relationship between news of the war and bustle over reconstruction: "Isn't it because we realize that here, at last, is something bigger than ourselves, which not only must be done, but which is worth doing well and at whatever cost?" Although this journalist attributed the energy that he sensed to the engaging task of fighting a war, and conceived of reconstruction as a period distinct from wartime and succeeding it, he wanted Canadians to translate something of this spirit into the reconstruction period, and his further request for "a wide and healthy consideration of the spirit of reconstruction"[8] indicated that such a spirit had entered public discourse well before war's end. An appeal to what was both a formally and an informally acknowledged way of articulating material, social, and cultural ambitions for peacetime, this call to action joined literally hundreds of similar expressions of anticipation. Reconstruction was, in the words of one cultural critic, "a time when changes are expected by everyone and can reasonably be looked for."[9] Hope may have been deferred, but it did not go undeclared.

Elected authorities spoke of "Reconstruction" proper as beginning with the end of hostilities, and the mandates of Canada's two government-appointed committees on reconstruction – one advisory (the James Committee, founded in 1941) and one overseeing (the Turgeon Committee, set up in 1943) – reflected that definition.[10] The King government's well-publicized plans for postwar economic reconstruction helped make homefront austerity during the conflict seem bearable. Reliance on experts and adherence to social-scientific precepts, building since the early part of the century, lent those exercises in sanguine speculation still more authority.[11] Still, by so plainly preparing for the domestic and external problems of readjustment that would accompany peace, these officials contributed to an environment that privileged planning and encouraged the production of reassuring, if somewhat illusory, postwar visions. The prospect of cordial peacetime relations between business and labour – an odd team thrown in tandem by the war – was only one such vision.[12]

However improbable they seem in retrospect, dreams of co-ordinated goodwill or an enlightened democracy pervaded the discourse surrounding reconstruction. Here, the term *culture of reconstruction*[13] denotes that environment and the accompanying complex of attitudes, opinions, and aspirations directed (especially *during* wartime) towards the achievement of a more satisfying postwar society. Satisfaction, however, is relative to aims. Officially, "Reconstruction" was about easing the economic and occupational transition to peacetime, but the culture of reconstruction that leapt up around these more pragmatic intentions brought to light questions about the kind of society that Canadians could (or should) fashion once the war ended. Indeed, it gave the question of the state's role in planning for the period a distinctly cultural cast.

Although its initial power depended on there being a war from which to emerge, the culture of reconstruction, or the will to exploit it, did not evaporate suddenly with peace. Cyril James, chair of the Dominion Advisory Committee on Reconstruction, warned in 1943 that "we shall not, upon the morrow of victory, enter into a brave new world. If we are to attain the ideals for which we are fighting, every-one of us must continue during the postwar period to work with an energy and determination comparable to that which has been displayed during the last two years."[14] Such broad-based dedication would prove, like the culture of reconstruction itself, "illusory and short-lived."[15] Yet when the burden of war lifted and hosts of Canadians sauntered away from their noble intentions towards the material benefits of a more industrialized and urbanized Canada, cultural critics maintained the energy and determination to create a society serious about upholding lofty standards of citizenship and culture. For them, the culture of reconstruction was a singular atmosphere in which "civilization" and the conditions necessary for its perpetuation had at long last received some well-deserved attention. The most visible part of its legacy – taken up before the decade was out – was the Royal Commission on National Development in the Arts, Letters and Sciences (Massey Commission).

Following a treatment of the culture of reconstruction, including a discussion of planning as a powerful and malleable synonym for the exertion of authority, the remainder of this chapter examines some of the ways in which cultural critics attempted to graft their own vision of a reconstructed nation onto enthusiasm for more tangible things to come. The Canadian Association for Adult Education (CAAE) became a driving force. It helped create *Citizens' Forum*, an ambitious national radio series on public affairs structured around neighbourhood discussion groups. Its creators expected democratic encounters over plans to promote both awareness of the individual's role in the community and sensitivity to traditions that would guide behaviour, despite the rapid changes sure to characterize the transition from war to peace. *Citizens' Forum* is one of the richest sources available for exploring the culture of reconstruction and its place in the development of postwar cultural and social criticism, but it is not an isolated example.

Reconstruction's appeal as a theme brought at least three strategies for cultural rehabilitation to light. First, a movement to increase the number of community centres cited the pressures of modern life in arguing for the establishment of a network of these local havens for personal creativity and wholesome recreation. Second, in 1944, a collection of arts groups presented a united front to the House of Commons Special Committee on Reconstruction and re-establishment (Turgeon Commmittee), calling for aid in the struggle to augment public participation in cultural life. Third, an organization (the Canada Committee) initially dedicated to familiarizing foreign servicemen with Canada reinvented itself as the Canada Foundation, taking up the mission of promoting a vibrant national culture. These strategies existed concurrently and formed parts of the larger culture of reconstruction.

Critics insisted that a mass public equipped for little else but consuming household goods and the latest dances would harm chances for realizing a Canadian culture that was to be reconstructed on the foundation of the responsible individual. The critical response suggested that edifying and, if possible, homegrown material, presented locally or disseminated thoughtfully through the same media that commercial culture employed to reach its audience, would wean listeners, readers and movie-goers from the offerings to which they had become accustomed before the war. Although this longing for the cultivation of the discriminating – not necessarily "highbrow" – citizen through decidedly "middlebrow" channels proved too idealistic, those wishing to cast English Canada in a particular mould during the 1940s did much to lay the groundwork for a reinvigorated cultural nationalism that would develop in the generation to follow.

This chapter outlines the culture of reconstruction, including its emphasis on planning and on expanding its popular base, and their two major manifestations of it – the highly successful CBC program *Citizens' Forum* and several arts groups that sought to obtain or generate support for the arts. Their reconstruction-inspired response to the modern condition and to mass entertainment helped make mitigation of the effects of a commercial culture and an industrial society an integral part of Canadian cultural criticism.

THE CULTURE OF RECONSTRUCTION

Over twenty years had passed since the Great War, but a determination to avoid being caught unprepared for peace – as the Allies had seemed to be in 1919 – did not take long to surface once the second war began.

Even though the failure of diplomatic efforts to contain Axis aggression dampened spirits at the war's outset, it soon became plain that the overall tendency was to reckon in terms of victory – a tendency that one columnist attributed to a defiant reaction against the "sense of disillusion, in fact almost of defeatism, that was bequeathed to us by the last war and its aftermath."[16] Others, such as Ronald MacFarlane, saw grim determination as an advantage in itself. He reminded his readers that "to reconstruct the world in the 1920s men made assumptions which have since proven false. They were over-optimistic about the fundamental goodness and intelligence of men; as a result their dreams did not come true." Worse still, MacFarlane claimed, even small-scale improvements in humanity's standard of living and global security had not materialized. He took some consolation in 1942 in noting that the "statesmen of the world are not as optimistic about the coming state of perfection as they were in 1918. This is probably a healthy sign."[17]

Whatever Canada's government may have lacked in optimism, it made up for in sober preparations for the postwar period, although such measures hardly seemed to be high priorities at first. Early in the war, some observers condemned the "persistence with which our leaders avoid all genuine discussion of the 'way of life which we value above life' and sidestep most policies which would make the values of that way of life more actual to the masses of the people upon whom the burdens of the war are bound to fall most heavily."[18] Once it began meeting in 1943, the House of Commons Special Committee on Reconstruction and Re-establishment (Turgeon Committee) spent the bulk of its time determining how to employ and house returning soldiers and their families and how to manage the transition to a peacetime economy. Some of the committee's objectives affected policy immediately. Indeed, one motivation behind wartime controls on prices, supply, and other normally fluctuating economic factors was the need to cushion the economy, once peacetime capitalism was reinstated, against the same strains that followed the First World War. Reconstruction plans were not a rehearsal for a postwar overhaul of the economic system.[19]

Although the government authorized the creation of the Dominion Advisory Committee on Reconstruction under McGill University's Principal Cyril James only in early September 1941, James himself later traced official interest back to December 1939, when an order-in-council called for a committee of the cabinet to gather information on rehabilitation and reconstruction.[20] Foresight, some observers thought, would allow Canada to fulfil a new role in the world community and to help maintain peace. More pragmatically, Canada could sustain its own prosperity in ways that the makeshift solutions of the interwar period had not afforded. In 1940, Julia Grace Wales, a Canadian peace activist during the First World War and professor of English at the University of Wisconsin, commented that mere criticism of the social order would not transform passive citizens into active ones and advocated a positive program to combat a "profound distrust of all institutions."[21] The fact that academics such as Wales made up James's Advisory Committee was an admission that experts from many disciplines would be necessary for the adjustment to – as the University of New Brunswick's J.R. Petrie called them – the new "social, economic, and political folkways" to emerge from the war. Petrie believed that the universities, particularly the humanities, were to have a special place in maintaining a "civilized" perspective during such an abrupt transition: "Our sanity must be preserved. It is perhaps a pardonable prejudice to maintain that sanity will be provided by the universities, where at least an attempt is made to assess values and reach conclusions by methods that lie beyond the political hustings and market places of popular prejudices."[22]

Some of the programs associated with rehabilitation and reconstruction, such as technical and university education offered to veterans, have become familiar through historical writing, because the extension of such opportunities to individuals has influenced the nation's course since 1945.[23] Viewed in the context of the social programs inaugurated during and after the war, "official reconstruction" may not have generated the sort of tangible changes envisioned by Leonard Marsh's 1943 report on social security, but it helped reinforce a framework of expectation in which Marsh and others could propose their remedies.[24] The Canadian Council of Education for Citizenship (CCEC) saw reconstruction as enough of a public issue to constitute itself on a vow to "assist all Canadians in reaching an understanding of the problems which arise from time to time relating to postwar reconstruction."[25] The act of looking towards V-days became a part of wartime culture, and the official committees on reconstruction lent a name and some focus to the anxiety over what to do when peace came. Academic and broadcaster Arthur Phelps, like a number of his contemporaries, recognized that "our insistent problems are those associated with change and growth" and noted that such an environment had its cultural uses, for it was a kind of reckoning of the modern world to see where Canada fitted. He sensed the liminality of wartime, acknowledging strengths and weaknesses, including "the mind and power accumulating as a function of democracy in farm and labour groups, our sense of a total multiple dynamic experience with insufficient educational and cultural agencies for its interpretation and integration." The awkward task of taking on a more complex and demanding international role, despite a dearth of cultural resources at home, led Phelps to conclude, in a rather understated fashion: "We are in search of a society, we Canadians."[26]

Although we may be able to identify significant milestones in the government's reconstruction program, it would be difficult to discern when a culture of reconstruction first emerged in Canada. References to the postwar era as a node of public interest date from the earliest phases of the conflict. In January 1940, one observer remarked on the difference that a few months made: "Just as it was the custom, a year ago, to visualize the conditions of a new war, so it is now becoming popular to think about the time of peace."[27] Certainly by 1941, reconstruction had become a common enough subject of debate that some commentators comfortably noted differences in the way the Allied nations handled preparations for the postwar period. "More attention [is] given on this side of the Atlantic to what is going to happen after the war than there is in Great Britain," one writer declared, but he rightly recognized that "more seems to be happening in Great Britain which has a direct bearing on the kind of world we are going to live in when the war is over."[28]

Canada was at a safe distance from the war, and this physical separation from the various fronts allowed for more leisurely reflection on what sort of society would follow victory. Distance also meant more time to invest in bringing that result about through an enhanced public awareness of reconstruction efforts. By recalling the opportunities squandered after the First World War, "win the peace" – an international motto entrenched in Canadian pamphlet literature by 1941 – reminded the public that it was not enough to win the war; plans must be in place for peacetime.[29] Likewise, if volume of publications is a reliable indication, U.S. officials and opinion leaders were doing their best early in their war to make Americans reconstruction-minded.[30] Claris Silcox wrote to a friend about his travels to the United States during the first few months of 1942 as a participant in "a number of 'Win the War – Win the Peace' institutes on the Pacific Coast."[31]

Planning

Perhaps the most important element identified with "winning the peace" was *planning*. Within the culture of reconstruction, planning functioned as an implicit belief that existing flaws could be designed out of any system. The critique of modern life and mass culture held no prominent place in discussions of postwar planning, which focused on the material needs of Canadians. Yet noting concerns at that time about the desirability of allowing authorities to plan aspects of life and looking at doubts about the general public's ability to do much beyond electing those who could formulate plans can help us to understand the context that produced reconstruction-era strategies for cultural improvement. Espousing goals largely superfluous to the government's plans for economic and social reconstruction, and lacking a mandate to create authoritative agencies for cultural rehabilitation, cultural critics none the less developed their own strategies for an enlightened peacetime Canada.

"It has almost become an adage," one observer remarked in the CAAE's journal, "that after the war the 'old grey World won't be what it used to be.' A new world culture is being created; Science is developing it; the flux of peoples and nations is giving it periodic, temporary form."[32] Dynamic and unpredictable as this new world culture may have been, in Canada planning was deemed necessary to control the economic consequences of the transition to peace and as an individual strategy to ensure domestic security. Constructing an appropriate blueprint for the nation was a job for experts elected or authorized to act in the public interest, and planning for one's own family or business became a sign of conscientious citizenship.[33] Planning by science and industry would ensure the continuation of the material advances so central to convincing the public that conditions were improving.

Preparation for a "new order" based on the further modernization of Canadian society seemed to be a goal that everyone could embrace, but it remained laden with some pre-war baggage. Opinion regarding how comprehensive plans were to be depended primarily on people's political leanings, with conservatives favouring minimal controls and socialists eager to complete the installation of the welfare state. Some observers warned that any planning undertaken for the achievement of a new order would require a sensitivity to tradition and, above all, an active, well-informed citizenry to keep it from devolving into communism or fascism. In declaring that "we must chart a clear and resolute course for our national life," one of Canada's leading anti-communists, Watson Kirkconnell, advocated planning based on what he called the "seven pillars": religious faith, co-operation, education, justice, discipline, fraternity, and loyalty. "If we are faithful to these," Kirkconnell ventured, "we shall be able to preserve the best from the past and yet achieve such social and economic changes as may be necessary for human welfare."[34]

Planned well-being was obviously desirable, but some people insisted that it would come at a high price. Regimentation, so useful to the military and so necessary to the efficient distribution of scarce goods in wartime, world rankle afterwards. Conservative commentators and those representing business interests, quite predictably, placed considerable emphasis on this theme. Some vigorous denunciations of national planning – striving to identify such a state as unnatural and antidemocratic outside the exceptional context of war – carried on well into peacetime in the pages of *Saturday Night*.[35] It was not surprising to frequent *Saturday Night* contributor P.M. Richards that opponents of "free enterprise" had blamed it for the world's economic ills, but he expressed considerable alarm at "the readiness of the masses to accept this charge as just and disregard the obvious fact that whatever faults the free enterprise system possesses, it is nevertheless a system which was born of the people themselves and grew with them." This "organic" defence of free enterprise stood, for Richards, in clear contrast with schemes "imposed upon them from above, as a post-war 'New Order' would be imposed."[36] Other opponents of planning proposed that planners and legislators simply let the government pass the budget and adjourn[37] or suggested that Canadians wanted "security to make their own security"[38] more than a cradle-to-grave system. More imaginative commentators sought to equate rampant planning with the cruel machinery of war, the anonymity of troop life, or "a form of *escapism* which would entrust the whole organization of society to a number of worthy but fallible individuals who happen to constitute the state."[39] Illustrators producing editorial cartoons for *Saturday Night*'s business section, 'Gold & Dross,' imported or emulated the work of conservative British cartoonist David Low, ridiculing planning as the strategy of benighted socialists who would strip away the personality of the individual to impose an artificial uniformity of economic conditions.[40]

Despite conservative efforts to portray the situation otherwise, the economic reality, as C.A. Ashley contended, was that there had been "a large amount of governmental interference for many years; in fact it was largely the basis on which capitalism operated even before the depression, for what measure of interference, short of state ownership, could be greater than the institution of limited liability companies and of a protective tariff?"[41] Having only the spectre of regimentation and the fear of socialism to conjure with, supporters of what passed for free enterprise faced a public that, still smarting from the destitution of the 1930s, had largely warmed to plans for social security during the war. As might be expected, further left along the political spectrum, liberal and social-democratic commentators were ambivalent, or well-disposed, towards planning.[42] The Liberal government in Ottawa had erected the official apparatus of reconstruction and went ahead with its ambitious scheme of state-administered social-welfare measures.[43] Eminent CCF member F.R. Scott met charges that national planning was regimentation by contending that planning for defence and reconstruction would not mean so many restrictions on thought and discussion but might require some on property. Such necessary changes would meet with some resistance, he predicted sadly, because "most people will part with their freedom of thought before they will part with their investments." Scott called attention to what he saw as the equally regimenting mythology of self-made wealth by criticizing the contemporary reluctance to participate in collective, systematic solutions to long-standing inequities. Not one to back away from controversy, he went on to suggest that comprehensive planning was one positive lesson that Canada could learn from the Nazis – a lesson that England and France had already learned, to their detriment.[44]

Even though discussions of the scope and scale of planning as a strategy for national efficiency and recovery accentuated existing political divisions, the planning ethic benefited immensely from its association with the hopeful culture of reconstruction. Print advertising reflected this connection perhaps more than any other medium, as advertisers capitalized on planning's currency by conceiving campaigns that identified planning with security. Advertisers commodified security and made it the happy consequence of a decision to take charge of the future through planning. This decision, quite significantly, could rest with individual consumers or with some band of scientists or planners at the service of society, but consumers, by buying the advertised product, could assure themselves that they had helped to hasten the glorious postwar period. One ad campaign that recognized the power of planning on a societal scale came, ironically, from a company forbidden to advertise the type of product that it had become famous for producing. In 1944, Seagram's distilleries inaugurated a series of advertisements lauding the planners and researchers who had been invaluable to the war effort and would make the postwar years sublime: "No continent in the world is more fortunate in the tremendous improvements in everyday living which await it. That is because we are blessed with MEN WHO THINK OF TOMORROW!"[45] The ad implied that the "men who think of tomorrow" made the free-enterprise system as forward-looking as any other, with the added advantage that, as the incumbent system, it was committed – more than any other – to the maintenance of democracy.

Planning held appeal as an individual strategy, and advertisers invited consumers to manufacture their own security through foresight. A Royal Bank of Canada ad depicted a boy enjoying his "stamp" collection: "Young Bill is doing his own postwar planning. Every week he calls at the Royal bank, buys another War Savings Stamp and sticks it in his book. He has his own ideas of what he wants to do when the war is over – so he's saving for it now. Young Bill typifies the spirit of all Canadian youth ... a quality of self-reliance and personal initiative that has made our country great. No one is going to plan his future for him. He's taking a hand himself."[46] This copy made the rather common habit of keeping a savings account an intensely private act of "personal" planning. "Taking a hand" oneself precluded one's identifying with a mass public that always ran the risk of having its future planned for it. This theme remained a useful one for advertisers even beyond the immediate postwar period. A 1948 ad for Manufacturer's Life did not have to reach far back into the collective memory to tout insurance as personal planning, through which the insured party "places – and keeps – his own financial future and that of his dependents beyond the hazards of mere circumstance. He becomes a 'Young Man with a Plan' ... a more substantial citizen and a happier man because of it."[47]

Especially during the last two years of the war, the image of shedding military garb and "falling out" of rank appealed to those left at home as well as to people who had been or were still overseas. Again, advertisers picked up on this theme, hoping that the cheerful prospect of the soldier's return would prime families for some postwar spending. In this way they were as keen as their American counterparts to instill a sense of belonging to a new model army of consumers, whose reward would come with peacetime. In practical terms, however, it took some months after war's end before the majority of troops returned home, and some economic controls remained in place as part of Ottawa's reconstruction program. In the meantime, advertisers honoured the awkward transitional period, reminding consumers that they must practise moderation to keep inflation in check and that "the years of greater abundance, which are so surely ahead," would justify their patience.[48]

Wartime had done much to convince observers that the Canadian people could take on responsibilities beyond those of mere consumers, yet a number also contended that some aspects of life in peacetime would be complex and best left in the care of experts. Although it appeared somewhat anti-democratic to suggest that wartime decisions or major reconstruction plans should be made unilaterally by experts, even staunch opponents of state planning distrusted popular opinion. As Queen's University economist John L. McDougall complained, the great majority of citizens could not bring themselves to make the effort required in a democracy: "the people whose lives will be most deeply affected by it will not read the reports of the discussion in the newspaper, brief though they are. They will turn instead to 'Little Orphan Annie,' or will skip the paper altogether that night in order to see 'Tarzan' at the movies."[49]

More than two years after the war ended, Leonard Marsh could look back at the mid-1940s and note that "planning" was simultaneously a "fog" word and a "club" word – used to obfuscate and to silence opposition. "No issue," he contended, "is in greater need of clarity of thought. And none is likely to get it, if we toss the words 'democracy' and 'national planning' around as if they were magic wands, or sticks of dynamite, according to taste. And if we use other words along with them, like 'regimentation,' for example – which are excellent for begging questions, but don't do much to answer them."[50]

Precisely because of these varying connotations, the idea of planning held a prominent place in the culture of reconstruction. It could mean taking complete charge of one's affairs or abdicating responsibility for them to some central agency. Planners could be villains or visionaries, depending on one's conception of how instrumental governments were to be in bringing about what E.A. Corbett called that "far-off divine event towards which the whole creation moves."[51] Planning for peacetime, whether directed towards a return to rugged individualism or to the achievement of collective social and international security, formed a part of the cultural context and the culture of reconstruction because planning promised a level of control over an uncertain future. For cultural critics, the opportunity to shape postwar culture depended on their ability – during the conflict – to articulate their plans for it.

Spreading the Word

The wartime compulsion to think deeply about the sort of civilization that Canadians and their Allies wished to preserve did not always create unabashed planners for peacetime. As one such dissenter, B.K. Sandwell saw war as a kind of nexus of past, present, and future through which the nation would be reconstructed, but he found it impossible to ignore the war in favour of contemplating what still seemed to be a distant peace. Sensing more "intellectual activity" in the country since 1939 than in the preceding quarter-century, he noted a concurrent desire to gaze beyond the conflict: "Canadians of both languages are earnestly and passionately scanning their past and their present to discern their future which they now realize cannot be a mere continuation of the past and the present although it must nevertheless arise out of them."[52] Despite his own reserved attitude regarding reconstruction, Sandwell and his *Saturday Night* magazine capitulated in the summer of 1942, admitting that "discussion of the problems of the economic and social structure to be aimed at 'after the war' is becoming so voluminous and engrossing that we have decided to open a regular department for that purpose."[53] Even some writers on the left acknowledged that reconstruction would mean not revolutionary change, but rather a chance to put hard-won wisdom into practice: "the social lessons which progressively minded people have been teaching this long while seem to have been more thoroughly absorbed than they realize and the problems of the next years are more likely to be those of working out the implications of principles already accepted, rather than of framing new blueprints."⁵⁴ Often invoked as a generic reference to any sort of postwar plan, the metaphor of the "blueprint" recurred, and reconstruction items found a place in the *Canadian Forum*.⁵⁵

By mid-war, Canadians knew about the idea of reconstruction, often using it as a pretext for expressing their views on subjects only tangentially related to the postwar era, and occasionally exploiting it for gain. As we have seen in connection with the ideal of planning, advertisers and their clients seized on any theme that they read as current. In 1943 the Association of Canadian Advertisers, comprised of firms that advertised nationally, began to produce a monthly publication designed to keep members informed about the most salient reconstruction issues. As might be expected, individual firms, in the course of their quest to distinguish their message from competitors', found a natural fit between reconstruction's implicit message of service through preparation and the promotion of products such as insurance and home heating.⁵⁶ The Imperial Order Daughters of the Empire recognized discussion of the postwar world as an opportunity to nominate the Dominion for a greater role within the empire, be this shepherding old-country refugees or implementing members' suggestions for a healthier population.⁵⁷ Columnist Mary Lowrey Ross abandoned her usual conversational prose style, favouring verse for her satirical look at the widespread enthusiasm for reconstruction and the range of interested causes invoking it as the dawning of a new era. Although "A Reverent Ode to the Great Modern Goddess Panacea" poked fun at readiness to plunder ideas from platforms all along the political spectrum – "Take some from each, and all from some / And usher in the Millennium" – Ross noted an essential feature of the culture of reconstruction: even the most reluctant souls could not help but be engaged to some degree by the bustle surrounding preparations for peacetime. Her poem ended with an exhortation to participate or suffer the consequences:

> So turn from the ashes of yesterday.
> The fires of spring are on their way.
> Leap to the fire, adventurous man,
> Nor trembling cling to the frying pan.
> Don't be jittery, don't be dawdle-y.
> Better to leap than be shoved in bodily.
> Here's to the future and all who contrive it.
> And the Post-war world. Let's hope we survive it.⁵⁸

Whether or not it excited them to look towards peacetime with the rest of the nation, critics recognized that Canada had to win the war before "winning the peace". However, as two examples from 1942 well illustrate, merely acknowledging the war's paramount importance hardly guaranteed that one could ignore and thereby subvert enthusiasm for reconstruction. Although his magazine carried items on reconstruction, B.K. Sandwell remains the best example of opposition to dividing the nation's attention between the war effort and planning for peacetime. In March 1942, he railed at those "meddling liberals" who would too soon start planning postwar society: "the calm assumption that the issue of the war is settled and that the time has come to consider details of Reconstruction is another instance of the unbearable superbity of English-speaking people."[59] Such cautions against planning too far ahead only granted the culture of reconstruction further notoriety. They also emphasized the presumption that a society should be able to censure certain types of behaviour (in Sandwell's example, insufficient attention to the war) in order to achieve the desired result (victory). In contrast, three months later, war artist Charles Comfort repudiated a narrow focus on the immediate, affirming that, for those who truly cared about maintaining a civilized way of life, the war should be fought on two fronts: "There is almost a pathetic eagerness to put first things first. The danger is that in trying to do so, there is a tendency to treat the arts as non-essentials. We may, with the best will in the world, be destroying the very foundations of our civilization."[60]

Comfort and other sensitive souls faced the obstacle that government and public still seemed to conceive of reconstruction in terms that were too concrete. The widespread attention to topics such as jobs, housing, foreign policy, and social services reflected an entirely reasonable concern with those more material aspects of life but ignored, as some noted, "the moral, spiritual and intellectual resources which alone can sustain the best of plans for a better order."[61] Could a public so preoccupied be relied on to seek such a balanced perspective on its own? What methods might be employed to raise awareness of citizens' potential to shape not only their own material futures, but the culture that would emerge after the war?

It may have been "unbearably superb" to think about one task while completing another, but the aftermath of 1918 had taught "English-speaking people" and many more besides that correcting the social displacement resulting from war was not a simple matter. It required consulting recognized authorities well in advance of an armistice. Meeting in 1942, the Canadian Association for Adult Education (CAAE) attributed the "failures of 1919" to a "lack of realistic preparatory planning and to the failure to guide public opinion to a critical examination of the social processes by which these popular aspirations for a better world might be fulfilled." Yet the association's members feared "the alternative danger of producing disillusionment and despair by pursuing a policy of offering facile promises of unrealizable immediate goals."[62] Several commentators relished this aspect of reconstruction because it allowed them to position themselves as sober experts or authorities in the field of restoring a civilization lost to the ravages of modern life – of which war was a symptom – and its attendant mass culture.

One such authority was playwright John Coulter. On his radio program devoted to cultural criticism, he cheered the British Broadcasting Corporation's wartime ban on "songs of slushy sentiment, and all suggestive ones and those based on melodies lifted from the classics ... any form of debilitated vocal performances by male singers, and any insincere or over-sentimental style of performance by women singers"; expressed profound relief that, by banning such material "at last, democracy begins to silence its poltroons, and gird itself in sanity and dignity."[63] Outside his radio criticism, his own work spoke of a deep commitment to reconstruction and to the ideal of engagement with one's surroundings. Declaring that "social inertia is henceforth a crime," Coulter prefaced a pamphlet version of his and Willan's opera, *Transit through Fire*, with an implicit reminder of the banality of prewar mass culture and a dire prediction that if adults did not become involved in a thorough reconstruction effort, then "every means will be used to help the next generation forget the fearful lessons of the recent past and set their feet once more on the good old beaten paths. If they should do that they will, in John Ruskin's phrase, without doubt be everlastingly damned."[64] The libretto of the opera itself pointed to modern life as complex, disheartening, and disorienting, but rarely subtle. The protagonists – an idealistic young couple waylaid by the economic and spiritual stagnation of the 1930s – found purpose in wartime and hope in the reconstruction credo of avoiding old mistakes. The hero, armed with an MA, mocked an insular, materialist commercial world that refused to acknowledge the community's interests when he sang: "Only by spilling lagoons of blood / could again be stirred / the genius and generosity / of living democracy."[65] The costly purchase of a new order – a transaction presumably still in its early stages in 1942 – saddened Coulter. At the same time, it provided an opportunity for what he considered the more worthy elements of the human personality to take on leadership roles.

Transit through Fire was the first substantial "work" (i.e., not an article or critical talk) to present the problem of what could be done during the war to improve what would come afterwards. In venerating participation in a democratic, Christian community and disparaging the homogeneity of a continental or world order, it prefigured sculptor Elizabeth Wyn Wood's later call to "put our aesthetic resources forward"[66] as a means of national improvement. Putting aesthetic resources forward also involved moving out from under the shadows of both the old country and Canada's immediate neighbour to the south. Sandwell attributed a lingering, bifurcated provincialism to the perception that Canada was not "a mature and adequate society, and therefore cannot expect to gather many of the flowers of one." Britain and the United States deserved their own great literatures, and Canada was not far from achieving this same distinction. All that remained was the development of its own "cultured public."[67] John Coulter's vivid assessment of this need for a national cultural reconstruction by experts embodied the belief that the arts were "the sensitive antennae of the community" and recognized that this belief was not "shared by any but a pitifully small minority of the people of Canada, or of anywhere else." He contrasted the "big majority of people everywhere" with the noble but "unpractical and impossible minority" long denigrated as "at best the procurers of leisure relaxations, the cultural pastimes and graces which flower in times of peace."[68]

The problem of gaining a wider audience for the arts – in effect, expanding what Coulter called the "unpractical and impossible minority" – therefore stood for a few as an integral component of the culture of reconstruction. During the summer of 1942, the University of Toronto's A.S.P. Woodhouse noted: "To a far greater extent than was the case in the last war, this is a war of pamphlets." More important, he complained that the best and most plainspoken of the wartime pamphlets remained virtually unknown, except possibly to a small group of people who would have made it their business to read such material regardless of how widely it was distributed. Even though he insisted that "the man with little money to spend for expensive books is as much concerned to understand the causes and issues of the struggle as is the scholar,"[69] Woodhouse believed that the organizations producing and distributing these pamphlets had been unable to advertise their existence effectively. This inability constituted a major obstacle to the sort of education for citizenship that the war effort and beyond required.

Others sensed that more than pamphlet literature would be required if the reconstruction ideal was to affect a population accustomed more to entertaining spectacles than to the sort of individual contemplation that pamphlets demanded. Columnist John Baldwin declared: "the problem and its tentative solutions should be set out in churches, in farm and labour organizations, in Home and School groups, among undergraduates, and opened for discussion. By radio, by movies, by circulating exhibitions, a two-way stream of information, comment, and interest would be generated which would be invaluable."[70] Father M.M. Coady of St Francis Xavier University acknowledged economic needs and desires but emphasized the maintenance of cultural priorities through reconstruction. "We shall not lose our souls in doing these material things," he wrote, "if we have a right philosophy." This right philosophy demanded, however, that Canadians be "mobilized for continuous enlightenment."[71] As it turned out, one organization had, even before the war began, taken steps that would place it at the centre of such a mobilizing effort, and thereby at the centre of the culture of reconstruction.

This chapter now turns to the radio program *Critizens' Forum* – a joint venture between the Canadian Association for Adult Education and the CBC – that became the radio voice of reconstruction. The remainder of the chapter addresses three further manifestations of the culture of reconstruction – the push for local community centres, an alliance of arts groups that lobbied the Turgeon Committee in 1944, and the Canada Foundation, which viewed its role as the co-ordination of arts activities in Canada until the advent of the Canada Council.

CITIZENS' FORUM

The CAAE was only seven years old in 1942 but had already committed itself to emancipating the population from certain unpleasant symptoms of contemporary existence. Its first director, Ned Corbett, spoke in 1938 of a link between democracy and the basic goals of adult education: "The ambition of Democracy is to set men free. The ambition of Adult Education is the same, to set men free from government oppression, materialism, from bad taste in living, in music, drama, recreation, and most of all from the utter drabness of human life."[72] The CAAE also committed itself relatively early in its career to discussion groups as a vehicle for adult learning. To many adults, the format seemed less threatening than their memories of the school classroom or the college lecture theatre, and groups featured an added attraction: leaders could conduct each lesson in a "democratic" atmosphere.[73] The strategy was hardly original and had been common through the 1920s and 1930s, even among less conventional movements such as Social Credit and Technocracy, which relied on it as a means of recruitment.

By the later 1930s, Canadians hungry for edifying radio fare were also well aware of radio's potential as an educational tool. In Nova Scotia and Ontario, some educational organizations and extension departments had integrated listening groups with short broadcast series during the winter of 1938–39. These included the Workers' Educational Association (WEA) program *Labour Forum* in Ontario.[74] Director Corbett had been among those who founded the Canadian Radio

League in 1930, and he kept a close watch on educational broadcasting. He characterized the contributions of American panel and orchestral programs, and some of the talks on constitutional matters on the Canadian Broadcasting Corporation (CBC), as "definitely educational."[75] For some listeners, the better foreign examples of educational programming, such as the monumental 130-episode U.S. *Columbia School of the Air*, seemed to be all too fleeting and frequently replaced by poor substitutes. One Canadian devotee sighed, "Just about the time when we start to think about ordering the winter coal, Edgar Bergen comes back to the air, this time bringing with him not only his stooge Charlie McCarthy, but Bud Abbott and Lou Costello, Ray Noble's orchestra and Judy Garland."[76] By the end of 1939, the CAAE had made Manitoba and McGill graduate Neil Morrison its liaison with the CBC. Convinced that Canadian educators ignored radio at the peril of their objectives, it asked Morrison to organize forum programs, or, perhaps more accurately to *evangelize* them.[77]

The first nationwide venture into applying the discussion-group format via radio came with *National Farm Radio Forum*. The show's regional predecessors – *Inquiry into Co-operation*, *Community Clinic*, and *Canadian Farm Problems* – met with some success in organizing listening groups early in wartime. *Farm Forum* itself began in the winter of 1941, popular at least partly because it presented information that farmers could use to operate within their means.[78] Whether similar principles could be adapted from the needs of agriculture and applied to the broader sphere of pressing social and cultural problems remained to be seen. As one historian of educational broadcasting in Canada has noted, the war meant that the organizations co-operating to produce *Farm Forum* (the CBC, CAAE, and the Canadian Federation of Agriculture) found themselves using "rhetoric charged with connotations of social action; even traditional voluntary association leaders used terms such as 'postwar planning' and 'social reconstruction' to describe their general aims."[79]

By 1941, Neil Morrison had been hired as a member of the CBC's Talks Department. Although he outlined a scheme for a national-affairs forum program early in that year, it took some time to build commitment to such an undertaking, especially in the face of CBC General Manager Gladstone Murray's reluctance to stir up controversy for the corporation.[80] Not surprisingly, Morrison recommended in his 1941 proposal that any new talks programs be closely integrated with the adult education movement. However, he declared that programs using a forum model "should be planned to reach definite, large interest groups if they are to be most effective" and begged that "efforts and content should not be watered down by attempting to get universal appeal."[81] Murray resigned in mid-1942, and the corporation launched its "trial balloon" of that summer, *CBC Discussion Club*, independent of the CAAE. The program treated reconstruction and its role in the establishment of a "full, happy, democratic way of life."[82] The Talks Department, however, made no outstanding efforts to promote the show and made no plans to repeat it, at least not without help from outside.

Because of close ties between the CAAE and the CBC, embodied most convincingly in the person of Murray's successor and CAAE member J.S. Thomson, organizers and sympathetic CBC personnel soon floated ideas for a new program. By November 1942, those responsible for the successful *Farm Forum* displayed their eagerness to do more than preach to the converted about national affairs. Democracy remained the animating principle, but CAAE executive member Watson Thomson made no apologies for declaring that "the best thinking on post-war reconstruction problems should be presented to the minds of the masses of the people concerned, in the kind of way that would make for vital change to those who are in the majority." Elevating society through a culture of reconstruction, however, required a certain amount of duplicity. According to Thomson, community leaders such as the association's members had to face issues with "a certain moral earnestness" and to choose those capable of presenting the "best thinking." These capable people were to ask "questions as to the kind of society that the people of Canada really want or think they want. But we must have implied answers to these questions ourselves."[83]

By mid-December 1942, J.S. Thomson began trying to recruit a motivated co-ordinator for a national radio project, sensing somewhat apocalyptically that "out of the present world conflict there are dynamic forces likely to be released and unless they are encountered by some kind of intelligent understanding, might lead us to results that have a shattering effect upon the whole of our political and social life."[84] Members of the CAAE believed that the new venture should combine the appeal and reach of radio with the comfortable reinforcement of the local discussion group. In addition to the experience gained in putting *Farm Forum* and *CBC Discussion Club* on the air, the CAAE/CBC alliance could draw on the examples set in such publications as the YMCA's *We Discuss Canada*, in which the "tremendous task of winning the peace" featured prominently.[85] At the end of December 1942, members of the CAAE met and formally resolved to inaugurate the ambitious project, intending to draw on and amplify a culture of reconstruction by "stimulating and giving guidance to a process of public enlightenment and awakening regarding the issues of the war and objectives in the post-war world."[86] Those attending the meeting resolved that the present and the future could alternate as the focus of interest in the association's new strategy of education for reconstruction and acknowledged the power of planning, as well as the importance of public participation in making planning techniques "instruments of the achievement of a creative democratic society."[87]

In executing the project, the CAAE and CBC decided to concentrate on realistic means of achieving postwar goals while avoiding "a repetition of the sentimental and escapist idealism of much of the Peace and League of Nations activity after the last war."[88] Robert Boyer Inch became the first secretary of the project, having come to the CBC's Talks Department from a post with the League of Nations Society. While spending the early part of 1943 setting out the program's structure, Inch, in consultation with members of the CAAE's Inquiry Committee on the Postwar World, which included three future members of the Massey Commission,[89] started casting about for an auspicious name. An early working title had been "The Inquiry," and, perhaps inspired by H.G. Wells's 1933 novel *The Shape of Things to Come*, Inch scrawled "The Things to Come" and "Shape of the Future" on a carbon copy. After some deliberation, the planning group settled on "Of Things to Come: An Inquiry into the Post-war World."[90]

Keen to strike a balance between gravity and popular appeal, the program's organizers brought in writer Morley Callaghan to act as "Counsel for the People" during the first group of broadcasts in the spring of 1943. These were done without an apparatus of organized local listening groups, although such a structure was on the drawing board, to be implemented should the broadcasts evoke interest in forming a nationwide network of "inquirers." Claris Silcox, a well-meaning supporter of the program, reminded organizers that Europe might be invaded in 1943 and that forum broadcasts would then have to tread a fine line between enthusiasm and grave pragmatism. Silcox warned that "the minds of the people may be distracted by the casualty lists, etc. and many will be impatient at considerations of a problematical future Utopia." However, he still considered this a strong reason to view the program's "realistic consideration of the hopes for a new world after the war [as] a powerful contribution to national morale in dark days."[91]

The topics presented in what was known as the *Of Things to Come* spring series for 1943, show that from the outset organizers intended the series, through the discussion of issues germane to the anticipated postwar lives and material interests of Canadians, to introduce abstract themes. They chose topics such as "The Last Peace and the Next One," "Are Wartime Controls Here to Stay?," and "Social Security –

Housing"⁹² to draw in both the casual listener and the committed reconstructionist in search of postwar blueprints. The discussions were not so much about the inner workings of the League of Nations, price controls, or subsidized housing, but functioned as a means of bringing to public attention the principles that lay behind these.⁹³

The programs were scripted, and a brief look at the process of setting up the first one can show us how eagerly the producers presented reconstruction as a fresh start and how opinions were divided regarding how to "pitch" the shows. In preparation for "The Last Peace and the Next One," Morley Callaghan wrote to Watson Thomson explaining, in terms more reminiscent of a staged wrestling match than a public-affairs program, how three panellists – veteran newspaper editor John Dafoe, Robert McKenzie, a young adult educator; and an as-yet-undetermined champion of the "old order" – would square off in an entertaining, but thought-provoking half-hour. In a letter to McKenzie, Callaghan emphasized Dafoe's credentials as at best a lukewarm supporter of a thoroughgoing reconstruction. "I gather that he has no blue-print at all, in fact I doubt very much if Mr. Dafoe believes in a blue-print." The goal, Callaghan suggested, was to make plain the respective points of view of each man but to make sure that the progressive thinker – in this case, McKenzie – would be seen to have carried the day.⁹⁴ McKenzie expressed his reluctance to engage Dafoe as a "Well Meaning if Out-dated Old Sage" while himself playing the role of the "Impetuous, Eager Youth." He trusted the target audience to formulate conceptions of the panellists as "a by-product of our conflict of ideas not as a result of a conscious attempt to dramatize the conflict of Youth and Age."⁹⁵

After the spring series had aired a handful of episodes, audience response indicated that the program had been well-received.⁹⁶ Corbett worried, however, that the public might not be equipped to take the next step on its own. "The average man," he wrote to the National Film Board's John Grierson, "is full of a naive faith that officials are planning a new world and that as soon as hostilities cease these officials ... will pop up with blue-prints and all will be well."⁹⁷ The depth of Corbett's concern was not justified, as listeners wrote urging the CBC/CAAE alliance to make the program into a forum with organized listening groups, along the lines of *Farm Forum*. Comparing *Of Things to Come* to the fare customarily identified with commercial sponsorship, one correspondent considered "Mr. Callaghan's" program the most important on radio and complained: "We get too little of such programs and much too much soap [advertising]. I will admit there is a lot of good soap. I know it makes white clothes whiter, takes the dirt and grime out of overalls and works wonders with diapers, but soap will not remove that scale from the human brain."⁹⁸

The Radio Voice of Reconstruction

The spring series had situated the program in opposition to commercial fare and had all but convinced the CAAE that listening groups could succeed. In July 1943, National Selective Service called Robert Inch to active duty. He left the Talks Department and, with it, the forum program.[99] Before he departed, he reminded Corbett that the project had the potential to go beyond the territory already explored in public-affairs radio, envisioning it as an instrument for revitalizing democratic citizenship. Canada had "a possibility of creating something more or less permanent along the lines of the *Chicago Round Table* or *Town Hall of the Air* but better because it is operated by an organization owned by the people."[100] With Inch gone barely a month, the program's staff reaffirmed its desire to adopt techniques that would reach ordinary Canadians not normally given to seeking information on public affairs. Corbett found a basic level of popular awareness regarding war aims and believed that Canadians were willing to "accept sacrifices and submit to regimentation, for the purpose of winning the war," but considered their grasp of the larger implications of the return to peace "confused and lacking direction."[101]

Three weeks later, J.S. Thomson, having returned to his regular post as president of the University of Saskatchewan, but still involved with the forum project, argued eloquently in support of cultural "blueprints" for Canada's reconstruction. He compared reconstruction to the "intellectual and spiritual quickening" that characterized ancient Greek civilization, the Judaeo-Christian tradition, and the Renaissance. Plans to recivilize the postwar world, Thomson contended, echoed all these honourable precedents, because "the new spirit is first the possession of a few, almost a secret doctrine, but it spreads abroad and like leaven hidden in the meal, it works until the whole lump is charged with a new life."[102] Using radio to spur a "moral and intellectual revolution" among those making up "the whole lump" was a pragmatic decision. However, it acknowledged radio's persuasive power, and, more particularly, it reflected a desire to counteract the perceived effects of commercialized entertainments.

"To-day there is a culture that is very widely spread by modern technology, by the movies, by the radio, by cheap books, by music, dancing," Thomson explained. He challenged association members: "What good thing do you see coming out of Hollywood? And yet Hollywood is the cultural centre of North American life." The need to undo some of the damage that he saw, by competing successfully with Hollywood and the cultural shift that it symbolized, drove Thomson to claim that "the whole question of artistic standards in music, in dancing, in literature, in pictures, in radio programmes, and in the religious life of the Churches is related to this venture we have in mind."[103] Philosopher (and Royal Canadian Air Force Squadron Leader) Gregory Vlastos admonished *Citizens' Forum* organizers not to mimic Hollywood, but to be unambiguous. "Sad experience has taught us the need for the simplest, most vigorous and most interesting type of presentation. You notice that I avoid the word 'popular.' We do not wish to bid for interest at the expense of content."[104]

Thanks to the work of provincial organizers, and despite some controversy about which political parties might reap the benefits of planning a more liveable postwar nation via the airwaves,[105] *Citizens' Forum* debuted in the autumn of 1943 as a program with listening groups attached. George Grant replaced Robert Inch as secretary of the CAAE. In addition to helping prepare the reading material that went out to the groups, Grant attended to the central administration of the listening-group network.[106]

It was not long before the program had in effect because the voice of reconstruction.[107] Early in 1944, Mary Lowrey Ross began one verse of her satire on the vogue for reconstruction with a faux-Chaucerian flourish – "Sumer is icumen in / Lud sing rad-io"[108] – acknowledging the relationship between radio forums and longing gazes towards the postwar era. The Rev. F.W.L. Brailey saw *Citizens' Forum* as the "gymnasium and training ground for virile Christian citizenship," while the editors of *Canadian Business* claimed that the first few broadcasts "stressed class distinction, they sowed discord, and their chief appeal was to the discontented."[109] A chemistry professor at the University of New Brunswick wrote to the program's staff, congratulating it on extending the range of democratic participation.[110] Indeed, the forum concept had found its way into other educational endeavours, including the NFB's rural film circuit. The circuit adopted a forum-style discussion as part of its service, with projectionists often acting as itinerant group leaders. On the circuit, the critique of urban decadence met the myth of rural common sense, as one observer remarked on how the circuit films were "rather different from the typical bill of a city movie, not only because the purpose is different, but because the audiences themselves like more solid fare than make-believe romance or custard pies."[111]

Each group chose a name for itself, providing further evidence of this earnest atmosphere and an inclination towards "more solid fare." Names occasionally reflected support for a particular branch of the service (Corvette Group of Montreal), pointed to some distinguishing characteristic of members (Toronto's Parkdale Young Married Couples), denoted a meeting place (School House Forum in Barrie,

Ontario), or evoked a congenial atmosphere (Regina Friends Forum). A number used their name to celebrate the ideal of reconstruction: (transcending wartime surroundings and taking a role in shaping the postwar world, rather than waiting passively to be shaped by it): Phoenix Forum in Winnipeg, Toronto's Gropers, Scott's Brain Trust in Vancouver, and the Lachine Inquirers, the New Era Group, and the Higher Plane in Montreal.[112]

The notion of "activity" was cental to the culture of reconstruction, calling on individuals to maintain their end of the democratic bargain by taking time and expending effort to understand, and ultimately respond to, the challenge of modern citizenship. The challenge, as E.A. Corbett perceived it, lay in resisting the impulse to become part of the unresponsive mass. He wrote that community leaders could condemn apathy by showing Canadians that "they can't escape responsibility by refusing to take a hand in correcting the evils they deplore," and accordingly the job of those truly committed to a meaningful reconstruction was "to present as vigorously as possible the need for active citizenship."[113] An early *Citizens' Forum* pamphlet included the following prescription for the active citizen: "Democracy can be efficient - But first the people and their government must understand the difference between hopes and realities. If democracy means no more than getting out to vote once every four years then we've let our end down. Being an active citizen means more than reading the papers and listening to the news – it means finding out the facts, studying the problems and talking over proposed solutions with our neighbours, offering suggestions, making our views known and doing something about them in a constructive way."[114]

Columnist Violet Anderson wrote of the program: "How significant for our time – that Canadians should hunger so to become active citizens, participating in the solution of problems vital to their country! How democratic that it should be wide open to anyone wishing to participate, and to participate by the democratic method of discussion!"[115] However, at least one member of the program's staff thought discussions too contrived, too neatly packaged as a digest of moderate reform sentiment. Early in the first season, George Grant told a trusted friend within the CAAE that the program needed to embrace more than "middle of the way" or "mediocre" opinions, or else its group structure would accomplish little beyond its own survival.[116]

Grant's prescription would prove difficult to fill, and his warning would prove somewhat prophetic. *Citizens' Forum* reflected elements of the mass-culture critique in that it did not intend to pander to mass tastes or to prescribe courses of action to be followed slavishly. Yet it set out to incorporate techniques and strategies, such as a panel format similar to that of the American program *Invitation to Learning*, quizzes, and candid study materials that were visibly less "dry" and more "eye-catching" than wartime pamphlets.[117] It marked a compromise between the high-flying rhetoric of an engineered postwar order and the acknowledged persuasive power of mainstream radio. It clearly supported a liberal-democratic system that appreciated popular input, but it scorned the mob mentality that brought to mind Nazi "conditioning." By the end of the first season, CBC Programme Supervisor Ernest Bushnell praised the forum's at least partially fulfilled potential to engage a "wide, continuous" audience comprised of "the best and most responsive type of listener."[118]

Often made up of neighbours living on the same street, local listening groups came to symbolize a revitalized community ethic. Jean Hunter Morrison and George Grant wrote the reading material for these groups, and their work consistently praised communities in which people participated meaningfully. It also mourned the passing of a simpler time. In 1944, one week's material cited revolutions in transportation, communication, and production as causes of significant and disruptive changes to what had been the average Canadian's reassuring, if parochial, surroundings: "We no longer spend our days within the narrow bounds of a narrow community. In our sprawling cities and large towns we hardly know our neighbours personally, let alone the people who represent us in Parliament."[119] This modern malaise demanded a rededication to the community ideal and concerted local action. The 1944–45 season picked up where Grant and Morrison left off, devoting about half of its broadcasts to citizenship and responsibility, with the second exploring "participating citizenship" and *Citizens' Forum*'s contributions to that ideal.[120]

This rededication would, organizers hoped, help listeners and forum members to recognize their role within peacetime reconstruction. However, although it tried to provide a lively discussion that would entertain while it educated, the program's tone still seemed too lofty for some and may well have tempered enthusiasm for reconstruction among groups otherwise quite eager to educate themselves and advise postwar planners.[121] The officer-organizer of an armed forces listening group noted that the "broadcasts tended to lull the gunners into an advanced state of somnolescence, shared by myself. It was only *after* the broadcast was over and when the gunners were able to express themselves that the true spirit of discussion and free speech shone through."[122] To the program's organizers, however, this self-expression stood as an indispensable attribute of the active citizen. It was the purpose of the forums in urban communities, where spectating had come to replace the almost-lost art of social and cultural engagement. Within their own neighbourhoods, forum participants were to seek consensus actively rather than awaiting answers from on high, and organizers intended the panel segment of the program to serve as a model of civilized debate. One of the early movers behind *Farm Forum* and *Citizens' Forum*, W.H. Brittain, took a long-term view of active citizenship and of the role of the forum programs' in promoting it: "Progress is measured in centuries. The most we can do is give it direction. We can emphasize the importance of the twin-principles of responsibility and participation, for only with their full realization can any democracy thrive."[123]

Helping the public towards "full realization" of its role in shaping postwar society meant drawing a wide audience, and organizers seemed unable to achieve this goal. Despite the programme's appeals to democratic fundamentals, its tone sometimes created the impression that the majority was being ignored in the planning of *Citizens' Forum*. The lieutenant leading the aforementioned armed forces group asked, "is it necessary for the learned Joes, including Callaghan, to latch [sic] out with such phrases as 'economic bourbons', 'Pan-Germanic', and 'financial oligarchy?'"[124] In marked contrast to his initial reading of the program's reception, George Grant sensed a division in *Citizens' Forum* membership when he reported on the state of the project at the end of 1943–44, the first season: "We have in fact drawn a line. People above that line have become part of the *Citizens' Forum*, people below the line, the *Citizens' Forum* has not gone down to reach." Although he expressed dismay at an inability to attract a substantial membership for the listening groups, Grant consoled himself somewhat with the fact that it had at least caught on with a group thought to be unaccustomed to even a modest level of participation. "Among the middle class, the Forums have done a good job. Reading the reports and sitting in with the various Forums, one gets the sense that many people are studying citizenship for the first time."[125]

Just as it aimed at re-creating a community of communities, so *Citizens' Forum* encountered some of the forces that observers saw dividing the larger society. While the war was still on, organizers estimated that each *Citizens' Forum* episode reached about 500,000 listeners, and the study outlines accompanying both *Farm Forum* and *Citizens' Forum* reached over a million people a year.[126] Given the recommended forum size of ten to twelve participants, probably about twelve to fifteen thousand people were full-fledged members of the 1,200-plus local forums that Grant reported during the first full season. Even at its height, membership did not even begin to represent a significant fraction of the population, but it included community leaders – members of clergy, teachers, merchants, and professionals – eager to be seen at the forefront of cultural and social endeavours.[127] As long as the war and visions of its aftermath could sustain interest in the creation of a new democratic order, *Citizens' Forum* remained effective at defining participation in such projects as a requisite for active and meaningful citizenship.

As the war wound down and finally ended in 1945, the largely middle-class composition of the Forums' core membership – and the middlebrow tone adopted to build it – became more readily apparent. Radio had the same potential to affect listeners, but many of them no longer found themselves in circumstances where their support for reconstruction could be presented as having crucial postwar implications. N.A.M. MacKenzie had predicted as much in 1944, arguing that "the incentive will disappear with the end of the war" and that a backlash against attempts to influence public habits would develop, because "many of us value our personal freedom and we are inclined to think of freedom in terms of freedom from regulation and regimentation and restrictions and from taxes and government intervention of all kinds." The effort to plant seeds of active citizenship would decline; culture and history would collide, as "conditions and attitudes which have made it possible for us to do what we have done during the war will tend to change or disappear and will be replaced by other conditions and attitudes."[128] By 1946, E.A. Corbett could sense that the "old level of unity and urgency has disappeared since V-E and V-J days, and although there is evidence everywhere of interest in better education, and in social improvement, there has been a letdown and the average man is confused and frustrated in his desire to safeguard the principles for which the war was fought."[129]

In the absence of the atmosphere of urgency that characterized both wartime and preparations for the postwar period, *Citizens' Forum* became a public-affairs program much like any other, and its experts the target of comedy team Wayne and Shuster's good-natured ribbing.[130] The program had failed, as one historian of the adult-education movement noted, to develop the momentum necessary for continued local action.[131] The novelty of participating in reconstruction through radio was ultimately not enough to maintain enough active members to make it meaningful outside a collectively anticipated regeneration. Queen's University philosophy professor and Forum activist Martyn Estall remarked near the end of the war that "radio knows nothing of good and evil. It has no social purpose of its own."[132]

Panellists continued to simplify complex issues for listeners and refrained from preaching any form of revolution, and, as the candid lieutenant said of the first season's broadcasts, "most of the series exuded a phony aroma of 'culture.'"[133] Membership began to wane in

1945, and the first two years of peace saw the number of groups decline still further. Robert T. McKenzie, the young man cast as a foil for the old newspaperman Dafoe on the first broadcast, succeeded Grant as national secretary and recognized a potential audience. Mackenzie saw Canada as unique, claiming that "no other country makes similar use of radio in this two-way process of informing and developing enlightened public opinion." However, he admitted that any impact of the program would probably come through rather traditional community dynamics. "While the number of participants remains regrettably small, it should be emphasized that the program is playing an important role in developing well informed community leaders whose influence far exceeds their numbers."[134] After the war, such earnest determination to continue planning the better society through a rank of respectables seemed out of place. Even the program's organizers acknowledged that, on the whole, Canadians were most eager to resume "the unfinished business of personal living."[135] In a society learning how to consume again, emphasis on the democratic resolution of complex social problems overestimated the public's peacetime interest in such a project. One Nova Scotian educator complained to another in 1949 that *Citizens' Forum* now tackled issues "about which the average citizen knows little, and possibly cares less." As that Cape Bretoner saw it, *Farm Forum* had maintained its public appeal, but, for *Citizens' Forum*, only a reorientation towards "homey, down to earth problems" could bring back the membership numbers of wartime.[136] Despite a rather rapid demobilization of its own, becoming less earnest and more popular in tone was not part of the program's postwar agenda. Still, though deprived of the wartime hothouse in which it grew so quickly, *Citizens' Forum* ran until 1964 and served as a reliable indicator of the salient issues affecting the peacetime cultural and social climate.

BUILDING FOR CULTURE

Community Centres

Although *Citizens' Forum* was the product of a concerned and motivated group hoping to transform Canadian society by democratic means, other reconstruction-era critics of mass culture recognized the ability of governments on all levels to create a cultural infrastructure through which the seeds of "civilization" could be planted. Accordingly, their plans for the postwar cultural order assumed a rough equality among people, but not among those activities that people might choose to undertake. Three interconnected efforts to enhance the position of what could be considered "high" and "folk" cultures reflected these assumptions. The first – a movement to create a network of community centres – encouraged active participation in cultural and recreational pursuits as preferable to other forms of leisure. The second – an alliance of arts groups – made a case for the arts as the basis of civilization by presenting its plans for a national cultural infrastructure to the Parliamentary Committee on Reconstruction and Rehabilitation. The third – an agency called the Canada Foundation – emerged at war's end to encourage private philanthropy as a means of cultural patronage.

The idea of physical locales for cultural redemption in Canada developed before the Second World War. One forceful argument for establishing places where community members could gather to enjoy their neighbours' company and to participate in creative leisure-time pursuits came in 1925 from publisher Lorne Pierce. In *The Beloved Community*, his essay outlining the constitution and sustenance of a community-council program, Pierce predicted that the rural areas, especially when organized through rural schools, would provide the most fertile ground. Presumably more upstanding than the city dweller, the farmer would respond to such a scheme for reform simply because "his long contact with the soil has made him impatient with anything but the fundamentals. He detests sham; and the brightest candidate for odium, the individual marked for the speediest excursion to limbo and emptiness, is that citizen who would substitute swank and camouflage for the real thing."[137] Pierce would have to wait almost twenty years for disciples to take up his challenge. During the interwar period, a few community centres – such as Toronto's Woodgreen – had been established in Canadian cities, but early in wartime much of the responsibility for instilling democratic values and an appreciation for the arts still rested with the schools.[138] New, larger schools tended to be built in urban settings.

Although suburbs grew rapidly after 1945, it was impossible to know during wartime whether sprawl or the rebirth of existing neighbourhoods would result after the war. The average Canadian's postwar surroundings would need to be both a product of and a haven from modern pressures, which included more leisure. One pamphlet writer complained: "Children are not made to take root in unyielding pavement, bleak tenements or impersonal suburban dwellings. Space and neighborliness for individual expression and community development will become more than ever necessary as applied science brings increasing leisure hours from the field, factory, office and transport."[139] Urban planning's role in community development came to garner more attention, especially given an acute housing shortage – an issue to which *Citizens' Forum* devoted one of its first few shows in 1943. Hungarian-born architect Eugenio Faludi landed a job on Toronto's city planning board shortly after arriving in Canada in 1940 and achieved some celebrity during wartime as a prophet of prefabricated housing and new towns.[140] In essence, his advice was: plan, but don't plan ugly, utilitarian housing tracts for the masses, for such monotonous surroundings have contributed to the degeneration of youths.[141]

Most plans for the reconstruction of urban Canada left ample room for the discussion of postwar recreational and cultural facilities. This debate thrived on the tension between the initiative to "win the peace" through planning and the desire to preserve an unstructured existence. F.C. James, speaking to a gathering of Canadian architects, argued for the primacy of traditional and, above all, *personal* avenues of learning from one's community. "If community planning is to satisfy the souls of men, as well as the dreams of aesthetes," he cautioned, "it must take continuous account of these habits and traditions. It must recover for us the reality of home influences in moulding character, and of church and school in shaping the further development of human life." James emphasized the need for the accumulated wisdom of previous generations in meeting modern challenges: "If the things which Mr. [H.G.] Wells discards as 'stained glass' are not the fundamental verities of Western civilization, I do not know for what we are fighting."[142] Predicting that the postwar period would be a time of increased leisure, Stuart Jaffary commented in 1943 on the crucial role of guided recreation within the larger sphere of social services. "How eagerly this new arrival is to be welcomed and nurtured," he declared, "after our past decades of vacuous movies and the insidious passivity of 'spectating,' whether to the radio, sports, or politics!"[143]

By 1944, the community-centre ideal, the rejuvenation and evangelization of which became part of plans for the broader renewal of long-neglected urban areas, had more tasks than preventing juvenile delinquency. Community centres played a part in artists' lobbying efforts. Existing facilities, often ill-designed for the purposes that they served, had begun to show their age. Although he relished his work as a part-time art curator in London, Ontario, librarian Richard Crouch noted that when libraries had, in the early twentieth century, supplanted Mechanics' Institutes in organizing exhibits and debating societies, they still focused on "evolving and perfecting the means and methods for the democratic use and distribution of the book." Only gradually did they learn how to accommodate various other tasks, which could include, as they did at Crouch's library, hosting such new community events as *Citizens' Forum*.[144]

Given but few dedicated facilities, the desire to appreciate the arts in pleasant and purpose-built surroundings frequently underlay calls to design, build, and maintain a focal point for each community's postwar cultural life. The success of well-subscribed itinerant events such as the Dominion Drama Festival had convinced many, like one Maritime drama supporter, that "definite physical plans for artistic development are absolutely necessary to make us more closely knit and culturally lifted, if this present struggle for democratic privileges is to be worth fighting through."[145] Architects became involved early in suggesting model sites and plans,[146] and the most comprehensive statement of purpose appeared in the Royal Architecture Institute of Canada's *Journal*.

Most telling among these, and significant as a document of the reconstruction-inspired critique of modern life and mass culture, was musician Marcus Adeney's contribution. Expressing his reverence for Lorne Pierce as an unheeded visionary, Adeney recalled his own hometown of Paris, Ontario, during the 1910s, when "church organ and choir allowed for self-expression" and visiting lecturers were rare. "We reflected all that we had seen and known," he commented, adding that the arrival of the movies affected the town's cultural and recreational facilities, which were still well-used but inadequate. Adeney admitted that some integration with other organizations such as the YMCA, churches, and the CAAE would be necessary in many communities, so the organization of community centres would hardly be a grassroots effort. It would, however, be the site of a brokered anti-modernism, through which citizens could have access to a culture that critics considered more authentic than that produced in Hollywood. Foremost in his conception of the movement's tasks was its attention to and exploitation of "the deep impulse of every man toward a rounded life experience. Nothing is too rare and precious, no art too high-brow, no sport too simple or craft too humble, for the interests we must cater to."[147]

Adeney envisioned the centre as a "socially active" place, "with programs and resources always a little ahead of the average citizen's wishes and requirements." Citizens should be allowed access to a range of arts and activities – but only those that developed taste, appreciation, and skill. Amateur theatre, evening courses in art and handicrafts, folk dance, and sports programs in which community members themselves participated – rather than spectating – were already at the top of the agenda in towns that had organized their own centres.[148] A CBC-YMCA joint venture called *Sports College of the Air*, hosted by "Head Coach" Lloyd Percival and aimed at youth, generated a large, favourable response from its target audience.[149] Adeney and others, however, wanted these activities to become the staples of a larger, publicly funded network. He recommended against business's involvement in financing centres, not because its people would find a way to turn a profit but because "business cannot take a long term view. Its agents must follow and not lead public opinion."[150] The notion that a commercial presence could hurt community centres flowed from the assumption that profit-seeking firms would favour the most popular activities, leaving the more difficult, the more esoteric ones, to wither.

Inclined towards the public sector as its chief potential benefactor, the movement could play one particularly strong card. Though not of long standing, a well-established tradition of war memorialization[151] allowed boosters to tout their project as sacred to the memory of the fallen of the Second World War, whose numbers were still mounting in 1945. Unlike the period following the First World War, now it seemed that less acrimony existed over the question of ornamental versus utilitarian forms of commemoration, perhaps because rituals of remembrance had been developed by the later 1930s. Marcus Adeney cited a public-opinion poll showing that 90 per cent of Canadians favoured "useful" memorials, and he fused the motivations behind the community-centre idea with a sentiment that he knew would gather support: "But when we think of the arts and crafts, community planning, growth of mind and body for every citizen – all this nobly expressed in a building or group of buildings erected to the memory of the Fallen – we can draw no distinction between the useful and the monumental. Indeed, a Community Centre, designed by one equal to his task, would be the most splendid of cenotaphs."[152]

Boosters continued to present plans when peace arrived, and these embodied the same sense of mission that the movement's core supporters shared during wartime.[153] The belief persisted that Canadians needed instruction in matters of culture, so dissolute were their tendencies: "Many today do not know how to spend their leisure time constructively. They are attracted to the nearest or most advertised activity," Martyn Estall reported drily in 1946.[154] In proposing, as Estall had during the previous year, that the whole idea be funded extensively by local, provincial, and federal governments, CAAE director Corbett produced a fascinating catalogue of hopes, most of which had been expressed piecemeal in earlier declarations of purpose. In 1947, Corbett was justified in noting that "Community Centres in which our people can spend their leisure time pleasantly and profitably are widely accepted as an appropriate form of living war memorial."[155]

Supporters intended these centres to be places in which "comradeship, unity and devotion to a common purpose which characterized our life during the war can be maintained and developed in peace." Echoing his friend Estall's assessment of popular tendencies, Corbett called for the promotion of "worthwhile recreation" in the same way as commercial entertainments (which he called "special interests") were promoted.

He contrasted "better leisure-time experiences ... increased participation ... wholesome patterns of activity ... an active enjoyment of the arts" with "monotonous and repetitive" work, "an alarming number of persons rejected by our armed forces," and the creation of "juvenile delinquents."[156] Corbett wanted not to replace other forms of leisure, but to expose people to new ones, trusting, as Marcus Adeney had, that they would "develop taste, appreciation and skill, according to their experience and contacts."[157]

An Alliance of Arts Groups

A call for community centres constituted part of the presentation made by a united front of sixteen arts groups to the Parliamentary Committee on Reconstruction and Rehabilitation (Turgeon Commmittee) in late June 1944. This effort, dominated by representatives from the visual arts, has drawn some scholarly attention as a sigificant moment in the history of Canadian cultural policy.[158] The groups banding together declared that cultural matters deserved the same consideration that government had been giving to the social programs that, for many Canadians, defined reconstruction. This was an ultimatum to the state, asking that it identify implicitly with critics in the encouragement of non-commercial cultural forms.

Wartime, of course, did not bring about a sudden and overwhelming national epiphany, in which the public instantly recognized the arts as repositories of civilization, but it allowed cultural critics to relate the age-old theme of cultural decay to the neglect of both great works and new talent. Reflecting early in the war on artistic treasures and their value, Morley Callaghan noted that scientific and technical advances brought on by war were hailed as glad tidings, but that war's toll was considerable in human terms, "for the spirit needs beautiful and spiritual things to feed on, and not many of those things are around."[159] "Those things" did not always need to be highbrow, and they did not need to be stored away until the war had ended. A sculptor and chair of the umbrella group taking its reconstruction cultural plan to Ottawa, Elizabeth Wyn Wood drew on immediate wartime concerns to promote a more inclusive, but activist culture. She wrote that "artists and others of vision should act together to make our government understand that a nation's culture is an essential asset on its home front, before the world and before history." She carefully and clearly added that "by culture I do not mean literacy and gentility. I mean active, progressive, and creative achievement."[160]

An early draft of the "Artists Brief" to the Turgeon Committee listed a "capacity for intelligent and cultured living" as one of the goals of reconstruction.[161] Broadly similar in structure to many of the briefs to the Massey Commission, not only did the document prefigure such submissions, but its signatories believed that petitioning the committee might serve the nation's cultural development. This was a curious testament to the currency of the reconstruction ideal, in that the Turgeon Committee had no pretensions to the title of "state cultural agency," nor did it have the power to grant the artists' requests.

The sixteen arts groups collaborating believed that their audience would probably be interested more in the nation's economy than in postwar cultural prospects. Accordingly, they emphasized the economic and social benefits of investing in culture and the creative forces so instrumental in construction, manufacturing, and even radio.[162] Their brief called on the government to model Canada's cultural infrastructure on European examples. Notable among these was pre-war France – a place where "every original thinker, from dressmaker to building engineer, has found, not only opportunity, but promotion through public interest." Sweden and Denmark also received laurels for their integration of design and the manufacture of everyday objects. The final example, intended to be the most stirring, was Britain's generous support of music and the arts – some of the measures undertaken even during wartime – under the slogan: "The best for the most."[163]

The "best" elements of culture, however, were not widely accessible in Canada, and the allied groups proposed that the state undertake a "distribution of opportunity" to bring "all hands ... into the service of the state, for the welfare of the people, in peace as they are in war." This was hardly a vision of a nationalized culture. Still, the brief went on to recommend that the state initiate "a way of thought among the Canadian people [that] would create a vast enlivening movement." This would require a governmental body for the supervision of culture and all its branches, including crafts and the "everyday aesthetic values pertaining to the consumer." In the artists' plan, community centres would serve as concrete expressions of national purpose and as local gathering places for citizens seeking self-improvement.[164] One report on the brief made it plain that the sort of activities befitting centres would be those requiring mental effort and careful attention, predicting that "some day there will be a Community Centre at Mud Corners. It will be a spot where nearby folk will gather to hear good music and to see good pictures and shows. A spot where children and grown-ups will learn to make pottery, to act in plays, to blow saxophones and trumpets, to paint, to sing. It will be a spot for baseball games and picnics and concerts and discussions." Indeed, this same prophet predicted for the nation beyond Mud Corners a town-by-town, neighbourhood-by-neighbourhood renaissance, anticipating that "there will be many of these centres throughout Canada, and all of them will be focal points where Canadians may find outlets for artistic urges and food for cultural hunger."[165]

The Canada Foundation

The man who filed that report on the artists' presentation, Walter Herbert, was in a privileged position to assess it. As director of an agency called the Canadian Committee, he was responsible for a program supplying educational material on Canada to American and British officers stationed in Canada and had been weighing the pros and cons of a national cultural ministry since earlier in the war.[166] He was well-connected in Ottawa and advised staff preparing early *Of Things to Come* broadcasts.[167] Herbert lobbied for the sort of government involvement in cultural affairs that the artists' groups did in 1944, citing "colossal" indifference, which "must be undermined and dissipated; because our nation cannot achieve the spiritual maturity which will eventually make us great if our cultural life continues cramped and runted."[168] In the way of technique, he much admired Stephen Tallents's 1932 essay, "The Projection of England," which included the ultimatum: "If a nation would be truly known and understood in the world, it must set itself actively to master and employ the new, difficult and swiftly developing modes which science has provided for the projection of national personality."[169] Herbert did not, however, believe that the establishment of such an advanced state cultural apparatus would be simple. Writing to Liberal MP Paul Martin, he told the politician, as if speaking to a fellow member of some banned society: "Those of us who sincerely believe that artistic ferment has good-citizenship-building aspects will have to argue pretty vigorously against the cold-blooded realists."[170] When the war ended, so did the Canadian Committee's wartime mandate.

By October 1945, however, Herbert headed a new organization, the Canada Foundation, set up as a cultural clearing-house to publicize Canadian artists, writers, and musicians until a proper ministry of cultural affairs could be put in place. In the absence of the lump sum of $10 million that the artists' alliance had unsuccessfully requested as seed money for the community centres and their operating expenses, Herbert's organization set out to secure private funds for its work and to find champions for the culture crusade. Herbert even wrote to Mrs John Bracken, wife of the federal Conservative leader, again somewhat in the tone of a co-conspirator, about an upcoming CBC broadcast of another Willan–Coulter opera: "I suppose you have already planned to listen to 'Deirdre of the Sorrows' next Saturday afternoon. If you could induce Mr. Bracken to relax for three hours to listen with you, I think it would be good for his restless soul."[171] In the decade or so that followed, Herbert and his small staff served as advocates for the restless souls pursuing the fine arts and preserving distinctly Canadian variations on them. Typical of the organization's early-postwar work was an index of cultural publications – a project that continued into the mid-1960s.[172] Arising out of the reconstruction-era concern with the nation's cultural diet, the Canada Foundation existed as a kind of privately funded prototype of the Canada Council, which would not be endowed until 1957.

CONCLUSION: RECONSTRUCTION'S LEGACY

Thanks to the formal and informal attention that it received, the ideal of reconstruction was difficult to dismiss as a series of hopeful daydreams untimely dreamt during the dark night of conflict. The culture of reconstruction formed a part of wartime experience indistinguishable from the war effort itself – an atmosphere in which those not fighting overseas could be confident that life at home would be substantially better when bombers were finally transformed into lounge chairs.[173] Perhaps assisted by acute memories of hardships during the Great Depression, the idea of planning for peacetime gained credibility through more distant recollections of post-1918 disillusionment, as well as the more recent lessons of the New Deal, British efforts to construct a welfare state, and Canadian experience in that same field before and during the war.

The culture of reconstruction, though filled with a variety of plans for Canada's emergence from the war as a modern nation, also accommodated criticisms of contemporary life and mass culture. Some opponents of planning seemed to believe that, by resisting the extension of state planning into the era of peace, they were preserving, even buttressing, the foundations of the democratic ideal. *Citizens' Forum*, an invitation to planning for reconstruction that employed the modern means of radio and mass mailings but featured a town-meeting style, also billed itself as a bastion of democracy. At best, Canadians' cautious acceptance of some aspects of a planned society indicated an ambivalence towards large-scale efforts to structure significant portions of their lives. Only the most optimistic supporters of a new order could imagine that the public had been utterly remade by the promise of reconstruction. The University of Alberta's F.M. Salter recognized that "the common man" was probably most interested in peace, but he hoped that the average Canadian would also want "opportunities for self-improvement, control of his environment, and fruitful leisure." Salter also hoped that Canadians would reject consumerist impulses – that they would not want to live in "a world half slave and half free, no matter what delectable form the bondage may take."[174] That was early in 1946. As forecast, war's end brought widespread prosperity.[175] Once economic controls were lifted, the "delectable bondage" of new houses and better jobs drew many people. Convincing citizens of the pressing need to scrutinize their cultural surroundings would not be a simple task.

Still, cultural critics considered the stakes high enough to model what they considered desirable behaviour. With its localized group structure and emphasis on participation, *Citizen's Forum* was the most prominent example of a will to embrace new technologies – in this case, radio – and counter the influence of mass culture by making virtuous citizenship more accessible. Community-centre proposals relied on the perceived need to escape the passivity and uniformity of modern life. Although these efforts burned brightly for a short time, within two or three years it was clear that postwar patterns of living and consumption, including the consumption of culture, favoured the mass society.[176] For the ordinary Canadian, getting on with work, family, and personal security seemed a more attractive form of reconstruction than plans for community centres.

However, for the extraordinary Canadians who envisioned wholesale changes to the way in which their society would operate after the war, all was not lost. Their attempts to harness the culture of reconstruction institutionalized the critique of mass culture by privileging seeming antidotes to mass culture – radio forums, community centres, active citizenship. They proposed explorations via the considerable resources of the national broadcaster and the state to promote examples of authentic or worthwhile entertainments. Although they did not succeed in cultivating vigilance towards some of the same diversions that buoyed spirits on the homefront or towards the compelling promises of modern life, cultural critics drafted their own set of blueprints for a "proper" postwar Canadian culture against which English Canada would be measured well into the 1960s.

PART TWO

Postwar Realities, Shifting Perspectives
1945–1957

3

Science and Religion in a Mass Culture

In the months following the Second World War, victorious nations could begin devoting a greater measure of their energies to domestic issues less momentous than global military conflict. *Saturday Night* columnist Mary Lowrey Ross knew that her job was safe, however, because the planners, technocrats, and engineers whom she loved to satirize would not vanish anytime soon.[1] War had accelerated the already well-advanced institutionalization of scientific research and its application, and these same activities would become even more fundamental to postwar economies. After victory in Europe, as the transition to peacetime started to put plans for reconstruction to the test, the use of the atomic bomb complicated the task of preparing for life in a more technologically oriented world. Fears of nuclear war aside, solving what Charlotte Whitton called the "ghastly problem of our own genius" was intimately related to the citizen's cultural destiny. As she suggested of labour-saving inventions for work and home, "each advance threatens to make [mankind] more dependent, dependent not only for subsistence but dependent in his unused powers of growth, of leisure, of achievement."[2] Canadians also learned the strategic importance of keeping scientific secrets safe for the "free world" when certain of their allies became enemies in a new "cold" war.[3] Yet in a postwar environment where trust appeared to be given over to the rational, conspicuously modern natural and social sciences, many citizens found it difficult to let their religious attachments fall prey to scientism – the "apotheosis of science,"[4] the belief that "with the same techniques that have worked in the physical sciences we can eventually create an exact science of man."[5] The broader "cultural dichotomy" of "arts v. science" convinced defenders of the humanities that these would be endangered with the "approaching reign of a sort of 'scientism'; all too frequently, even now, are the Arts and Letters emasculated to serve the imperious demands of utility."[6] Some people saw religion as humankind's haven from the modern storm. Religion seemed vulnerable because politics, society, and culture no longer reflected "the essentially unchanging core of Christianity, but are based upon a new and radical reorientation of the spirit which is no longer Christian in essence but wedded to strange new gods."[7] This reorientation of the spirit, an increasing dependence on the scientific approach, did not necessarily mean an outright denial of the supernatural. Some of the nation's most articulate citizens argued for harmonious accommodation between these two forces that had otherwise been set at odds. Less than one week after the attack on Hiroshima, University of British Columbia president N.A.M. (Larry) MacKenzie could attribute the final victory "to the skill of our scientists who have produced our modern weapons including the atomic bomb, and to Almighty God who controls the destiny of all mankind."[8]

Science had been subject to criticism from some religious people for at least two centuries before the Second World War yet also acknowledged for generations as a symbol of modernity or progress. Rather than generating the sort of bitter, intricate theological debates prevalent during the late nineteenth century, the discourse surrounding the respective roles of religion and science in mid-twentieth-century English Canada dealt chiefly with what each mode of belief could offer society. The reflections of journalists, academics, church leaders, broadcasters, and others in English Canada during the late 1940s and early 1950s betray the way some perceived science or, more properly, faith in science as a troubling aspect of modern life. Historians have justifiably presented the immediate postwar years and the 1950s as a period during which the public put an increasing portion of its trust in experts,[9] but in 1951, when the Canadian Broadcasting Corporation (CBC) aired radio programs featuring experts in cosmology, philosophy, and psychology, listeners and critics did not hesitate to condemn the broadcasts as "Anti-Christian and Anti-Canadian."[10] While we are concerned more broadly here with responses to the seeming invincibility of science, the pivotal CBC series suggests that some observers viewed the union of a scientific perspective and the mass media as not only unorthodox, but heretical. Those cultural critics who saw religion as a cornerstone of a civilized heritage sought some control over the ongoing secularization of Canadian society. By holding religion up as a balanced and ultimately human activity centred on the individual, while ascribing to scientism the same disregard for the human personality that they saw in mass culture, they painted scientism as itself a variety of mass culture on the verge of displacing a more intimate religious tradition. In the eyes of those hoping to preserve a place for religion in Canadian cultural life, scientism seemed to require little of its audience – just like radio soap opera. Religion, however, had always demanded discipline and commitment, as well as harbouring a sense of reverence for complex music, representational art, and ancient wisdom.

Science established itself as an integral component of material progress long before 1939, and there existed no self-proclaimed pro-science lobby obliged to justify its growing authority. During the war, governments and industrial concerns underwrote the dramatic growth of research institutions and laboratories heralding the postwar arrival of what some historians have called "big science."[11] The federal "Minister of Everything," the former civil engineer C.D. Howe, was perhaps the most famous Canadian untroubled by such developments. He viewed the associated economic benefits as too good to pass up, likened science to a relatively unexplored hinterland, and welcomed the postwar convergence of scientific knowledge and economic power. He claimed a kind of divine right for this most modern arrangement – an "invasion by engineers of fields that are not strictly technical." This invasion was, for Howe, "another proof of the great importance of science and technology in the industrial and economic life of modern days" and would, he thought, only continue. He predicted social changes, telling the young engineers whom he addressed that they were in the vanguard: "In Canada, just as happened in Germany, the United States and England, training in some phase of engineering or science will become more and more essential to high executive positions in industrial and business organizations."[12]

Howe and others saw atomic energy as the newest hinterland ready for exploitation. However, even at a time when jobs exploiting such brave new technologies helped fuel prosperity in Canada, a desire for stability and security informed the relationship between science and religion. Although many religionists[13] conceded that science and technology provided the rapidly modernizing nation with its physical comforts, scientific hegemony had become identified with atomic terror, and did not inspire the confidence that it had before or during the war. Although a religious revival in post-1945 Canada may be attributed to a number of factors, not least a fear of nuclear war and annihilation, it indicated that faith in a higher power held considerable ground in a culture that had not yet fully accepted science as a part of its defining tradition. Cultural critics who supported a religious perspective did not attack the motivation for doing experiments or staffing laboratories, but rather warned against becoming infatuated with the fruits of technology or satisfied with the pat answers of the scientist in areas such as psychology where a religious interpretation still claimed some influence.

In reminding Canadians that science could do only so much for them, religionists contrasted a limited science with an all-embracing religion or constructed a picture of social decay in which science offered no comforting answers to the vexing questions of human existence and purpose. Commenting on the trend towards secularism in Canadian universities, B.K. Sandwell noted: "The Western World, save for a few aberrations like the Scopes Trial in Tennessee, is not in the least likely to set limits to scientific investigation in the name of any religion, for it has learned that the existence and nature of God are not a subject for scientific investigation, and that science can neither add to nor subtract from the content of faith."[14] Sandwell underestimated the capacity of his fellow citizens to employ religion as a refuge from a rather threatening postwar world. Some defenders of religion in Canada and elsewhere in the West had long sought to impose limits on the scope of scientific inquiry.[15] However, he was correct to suggest that in English Canada religion could no longer command the legal authority that it had a generation earlier during an extraordinary summer in Tennessee. In post-1945 Canada, this sort of limiting still took place subtly within a society that otherwise privileged science.

Although religionists were easily the most vocal doubters of science's value for humanity, some scientists were also keen to make peace between two cultures that they treasured. The wartime emergency had mobilized the physical and spiritual resources of the nation, and it would not be easy for Canadians to abandon the idea that they fought to maintain a way of life undergirded by the Western Christian tradition. As we see in the first section of this chapter, the decade or so following the war was a time of transition, in which some observers of science triumphant were still inclined to ask: towards what spiritual ends are we progressing? That such inquiries seemed to flare up during the early 1950s, though becoming less vehement within a few years, indicates that supporters of religion – at least with respect to any perceived assaults from science against its foundations – regained a measure of confidence in its ability to serve the spiritual needs of Canadians. The second, larger section of this chapter looks at the debates (and eight participants) in those years about the place of religion in a world dominated by science. Later in the decade, as the epilogue shows, critics of scientism remained, but their attention was more likely to focus on technology and the mass society as forces harming individuals, families, and communities.

SCIENCE TRIUMPHANT: BEFORE THE WAR AND AFTER

Scholars such as Carl Berger, Patricia Jasen, and Keith Walden have shown that the Second World War did not mark Canada's first exposure to modernity or to the sense of wonder and philosophical uncertainty generated by the advance of science.[16] However, a scientific outlook seemed to gain ground tremendously in the second quarter of the twentieth century. On the eve of war, Sir Francis Peabody, a fictional millionaire industrialist in one of economist Burton Keirstead's unpublished short stories, compared the interwar rise of science to a religious conversion several orders of magnitude beyond a nineteenth-century camp meeting: "It is the new religion, I tell you, and in America and I daresay in Europe today, whatever masquerades under the guise of science may be sure of commanding a degree of reverence and veneration which would move to envy a medieval saint."[17] Mocking the fascination with IQ testing and its ability to affect the social behaviour of parents concerned about their child's performance, Mary Lowrey Ross none the less sensed a profound generational shift: "Like most unscientific people they are profoundly impressed by Science and they accept its terms with the mixture of incomprehension and mystic faith that their parents reserved for articles of the Creed."[18]

Once hostilities began in 1939, and as the engines of battle became more complex and more terrible, scientists' role in the war's prosecution brought them an even greater share of public approval. An early-wartime CBC broadcast celebrated engineer and polio victim Elsie MacGill, who was heeding the noble calling of "hastening the peace to the world" by serving on the design team for the Hurricane fighter. It became a commonplace during the conflict to laud scientists and engineers for their tireless work. Scientists occasionally pointed out, as MacGill did, that their jobs were satisfying because "our goal extends beyond the war into the peace to follow."[19] Scientific effort was geared, rhetorically at least, to the promise of peacetime. The war made heroes of the scientists who attended university year-round to hasten their training, enabling them to assume active duty sooner and to improve the efficiency and safety of troops at the front.[20]

Science journalists rendered science less mysterious for the larger reading public. The subjects of wartime research became the stuff of everyday discussion, as weekly and monthly magazines began to run regular features offering declassified tales of war science, along with tantalizing speculation about postwar goods made better in the laboratory and tested on the battlefield. In *Saturday Night*, "The Science Front" ran under the direction of controversial science writer Dyson Carter and was the most engaging and critical of the magazines' science series. Winnipeg's Carter did not resemble the typical American science writer – "a professional journalist or public relations expert whose job it became to write about science, technology, and medicine for both the mass public and for general scientific audiences."[21] His work was not like that of his Canadian counterparts.

Many science features played on pent-up consumer demand for articles rationed during the war and helped create new demand for articles that were to come. Freelance science writers enthused over new or dramatically improved materials such as plastics and fibreglass emerging from wartime chemistry labs.[22] Leading the public to expect durable new materials and streamlined processes to accompany an overhauled world order constituted a vital part of the culture of reconstruction. When it began less than a month after V-E Day, *National Home Monthly*'s "Tuning Up for Tomorrow" series portrayed science as the tireless servant of humankind by inviting readers to acquaint themselves with at least basic scientific principles and, more important, to become accustomed to an accelerated pace of scientific innovation. The series slogan suggested that at least a nodding acquaintance with the latest news from the world of science would be socially beneficial as well: "Science is making tremendous advances on many fronts that are full of promise for tomorrow. Here are highlights to excite your imagination and illuminate your conversation."[23]

Despite the rosy picture that popular magazine writers painted, some scientists feared that the public still might associate science with the destruction rampant in war and sought to emphasize their benevolent aims and their commitment to peace. Some even tried to convince the Canadian public that it was fortunate to be receiving the blessings of science, given humankind's propensity for putting them to destructive uses. The themes of scarcity and war-weariness served University of Saskatchewan physicist E.L. Harrington well as he implored society to "catch up" to science. "That many of us must for the present do without the cars, radios, and numerous other conveniences we sorely miss is not due to any breakdown in physics," he explained, "but to a failure of our society to keep pace with scientific progress." He further chastised the human family: "It is not that we need less physics, as some have suggested, but rather that we do want [i.e., lack] a society worthy of the rich gifts physics has to offer." Harrington suggested how such a society might be created, mentioning the applicability of "certain social laws and principles that have become established and universally recognized," offering the examples of the Ten Commandments and Christ's teachings and advocating their scientific, or direct, application to modern problems.[24] Contrast that perspective with a wartime pamphlet written for troops still overseas, in which a CCF member of Parliament from Nova Scotia (and non-scientist) used the metaphor of "keeping pace" to urge the employment of science in the social realm: "Our task is to develop ourselves to catch up with the engines of science," wrote Clarie Gillis, "which have caught us all up and rushed past our understanding of how to use these powerful instruments for the good of humanity." For Gillis, religion remained in the larger picture, but as a feature "of the home and of the church," not possessing a "society-wide" applicability to the problems of modern Canadian life.[25]

Those differing opinions indicated that, regardless of one's desire to tackle social problems scientifically, during wartime science remained too valuable a tool to contrast it sharply with Christianity, the official faith of the Allies. Although he pointed less than five years later to the need to temper society's enthusiasm for science and materialism with a renewed religion, in his wartime book, *Seven Pillars of Freedom*, McMaster University's Watson Kirkconnell could not bring himself to name science as one cause of a weakening attachment to "religion as the motive force of civilization."[26] Others spoke out only slightly more boldly, blaming "unhumanized science" or enemy perversions of nature's laws for the horrors of war. Some, like chemist William Hatcher, recommended that, as a safety measure, educational curricula should be more effectively balanced between the sciences and humanities.[27] In *Saturday Night*, B.K. Sandwell condemned the practice of setting of one form of knowledge above others. "Now that the world is in the melting pot and everything is to be made over," he wrote, "it is interesting to conjecture whether a true higher education, directed to the maintenance, not of scientific industries, but of a true 'culture', must not necessarily have a good deal more to do with religion than that higher education of the last forty years in North America has had."[28]

Although few commentators expressed open hostility towards science during the war, some directly addressed the gulf between the spiritual and the physical, advocating an acknowledgment of faith by secular governments. Sandwell wrote in support of a national Day of Prayer held in early September 1942, admitting that few Canadians expected divine intercession in a war of planes and tanks, but reminding readers: "Prayer is not a force in that realm of the universe. But in the spiritual realm it is a force of tremendous importance. It need not change the mind of God, if it effectively changes the spirits of men through which God operates."[29] For one theologian, the "lag of moral, social and spiritual forces behind the mechanical force" became an even more potent theme after the brutal demonstration of applied science that ended the war in Japan.[30]

Such tame approaches to the fundamental differences between materialist and spiritual perspectives suggest that, even though general optimism existed about what science could contribute to postwar life, commentators did not often emphasize the corollary that religion could do little. Rather than speaking in terms of further human triumphs over ignorance and superstition, the prophets of postwar development assured Canadians that by 1950 they would see "Dame Nature still further ironed out."³¹ Canadian experience paralleled American in that the "spectacular achievements of wartime R&D [research and development] ... encouraged the belief that conscious application of 'Manhattan Project' [the cost-no-object scheme that produced the atomic bomb] methods to problems of poverty, health, housing, education, transportation, and communication might eliminate material want."³² In the light of such continent-wide optimism about the eventual alleviation of physical misery, at war's end even conservative religionists stressed rather quickly that the goal of religion was not to seek a return to an era before the age of science, but rather "to win man again for Christ, to win modern man as he exists here and now in his present social and political circumstances."³³

As the Canadian prophets predicted, scientists and engineers continued "ironing out" nature in the years following 1945, while resources and intellects that had been committed to military operations changed into more comfortable civilian garb. However, humanity still faced essentially the same problems that it had before 1939, as well as the new threat of atomic conflict. A return to peacetime priorities – the pursuit of security for one's family and a desire to put the cares of wartime to rest – only partially masked a new set of anxieties. Some of this anxiety must be attributed to the advent of atomic weapons and the ensuing doubt about humanity's future.³⁴ However, some of it arose in response to an increasingly complex society that a number of critics considered more oriented towards the acquisition of material goods and towards the social sciences, psychology in particular, as all-purpose balm for human problems.³⁵

Although historian Arthur Lower's prediction that "the magnitude of the issues we face will swing us back into our old mode of dealing with them, and that the second world war will see a renewal of our deep-seated Puritanism,"³⁶ did not come true in the months following the end of the war, the wartime reluctance among religionists to challenge the prestige of science began to break down. C.J. Eustace – a full-time executive in the Dent publishing house, a part-time intellectual, and a Roman Catholic – tried to restore a sense of mystery to the quest for a new order. He declared that "the period of transition through which we are now passing, described by various thinkers, both Christian and otherwise, as the 'twilight age,' is once again, under God, a time of trial and of faith, of obscurity and of prayer for those who believe and hope." He held significantly less regard for "those who have abandoned themselves to the formation of a brave new world in which nature alone and human efforts are to prevail." They were blind, for their errant lives had not equipped them to "see the work of the Holy Spirit, which is always prepared in secret within the souls of men." Eustace also spoke of the difference between spiritual and "naturalistic" views of the universe, accusing proponents of the latter view of employing the promise of a world transformed to persuade the masses that "they, too, are creatures of nature only, and if obedient to her whims can by their own efforts conquer the restlessness of the human heart and bend the cosmos to their soul's desire."[37]

As the magnitude of reconstruction sunk in after a war described by some observers as a millennial struggle between good and evil, religionists found that they could not mount an unqualified attack on science, because it had been so helpful in defeating fascism. Criticism of scientific method came to portray it as a powerful but incomplete form of knowledge or as a philosophy unable to deal with certain aspects of human life, emphasizing religion's potential to help the faithful cope with both the mind-boggling achievements and the ethical problems that science had exacerbated. Claris Silcox, a fixture in the United Church, addressed the topic of authority when he suggested that the scientists themselves had begun to ask questions that demanded a knowledge of the spirit. He mused that "in an age when the economists have become the idealists and the dreamers and are even unconscious of the laws of arithmetic, and when the scientists, in the wake of the atomic bomb, have suddenly become moralists, sociologists, exponents of political theory and even theologians, it behooves a mere theologian like myself to inject some realism into the discussion."[38]

Challenges such as Silcox's did not originate exclusively from the clergy or among self-proclaimed supporters of religion. Even when they took into account the triumphs of science in uncovering laws and processes only dimly understood just a few years earlier, journalists and commentators on science incorporated new standards into their assessments of its intrinsic worth. One marvelled at science's ability to gauge the infinitesimally small size of atoms, but betrayed a well-developed sense of spiritual symmetry when he estimated man's size at "about midway between a star and one of the three types of particles that form atoms" and concluded: "Science cannot tell you what your intelligence is made of, or your spirit, or your soul."[39] Although its application had ended the war, atomic fission had "added neither comfort nor convenience" to anyone's existence, claimed another writer: "Does anyone know any better now than 10 years ago why snow comes in crystals, no two alike?" Science had done much to reveal how the universe operated, the author admitted, but he asserted that it had done little – or could do little – to answer the question of *why* things behaved, reacted, or unfolded as they did.[40]

The question of purpose came more and more to characterize the discussion during the decade following Hiroshima and Nagasaki. Scientists offered theories on the mechanics of matter, but no compelling "story" to explain the universe. The scientifically derived narratives of evolution or explanations of psychosis, for example, only reminded people that their time on earth was short or trivialized their fears by attributing them to chemical imbalances in the brain. Reflecting on the place of religious belief and association in contemporary North America, Arthur Lower explained the significant appeal of religion over a scientific perspective: "So natural and strong is humanity's desire to transcend its own fate that this still remains the church's greatest asset. The assaults of science have not prevailed against it." He was providing a "job description" for modern religion in an increasingly secular Canadian society. From Lower's vantage point, the postwar world presented religion with an opportunity by creating an unprecedented need for comforting counsel and a need to acknowledge a realm beyond the physical. He declared that "today the instability of life induced by the great wars and by the very accomplishments of science produce not faith in the intellectual solution – "scientific humanism" – but distrust in it and a marked return to dependence on the emotional or religious solution."[41] Science could describe physical objects in nature and assemble systems of laws that explained how atoms collided, but it could not provide the means for identification with the infinite that had always been religion's stock-in-trade. Stella Keirstead found it odd that the question of immortality had become somehow "improper" and thought it "strange if in a world where science has demonstrated daily the indestructibility of matter, the unanalysable quality called life should be the only thing capable of being reduced to nothing."[42]

RELIGION IN A SCIENTIFIC WORLD: AIRING THE DEBATE

Getting Canadians to recognize this distinction between the material and the spiritual became a goal for religionists trying to counteract the moral chaos that some commentators attributed to a science-dominated world newly replenished with alluring consumer goods. Yet proponents of science – and the CBC featured three in 1951 – Fred Hoyle, Brock Chisholm, and Bertrand Russell – had distinctly different ideas. This section looks first at two scholars with objections to the extreme claims of science, then at the CBC talks, and finally at three responses to the CBC's triumvirate.

Objections to Science: Eustace and Kirkconnell

The output of two reasonably prolific "pillars" of the religious perspective – the Roman Catholic C.J. Eustace and the Baptist Watson Kirkconnell – exemplified some of the objections to science during the late 1940s and early 1950s. Their arguments, especially Eustace's, may seem alarmist or esoteric, but they addressed a common theme: a search for some means of controlling the results of scientific advance or of reminding the general population that life was not all about consumption and development. As one educator put it, "control of the bomb is not a scientific problem at all, – rather a social, ethical, and political one ... To deal with human energies you need people who have had the right training and experience, who are accustomed to dealing with people and irrational human values, who are able to see life as a whole, insofar as anyone may."[43] Some defenders of religion most vigorously promoted the idea that, even though science had considerable power as an explanatory tool, it was unable to address the needs of the whole person. They resented the growing complexity of science, as it resembled less and less applied common sense and became more the realm of the specialist.

Considering his vocation as a vice-president at one of Canada's largest publishing firms, C.J. Eustace was prolific in the latter half of the 1940s, arguing consistently for the supremacy of the spiritual dimension in modern life. He wrote several articles and completed at least one book in the decade following the war, but an article entitled "Science, Materialism, and the Human Spirit" best summarized his profound discontent with his surroundings. He began by exulting in the news from a conference at the Massachusetts Institute of Technology involving various "world thinkers."[44] Participants concurred that "scientists have contributed to the moral confusion of the age" and took this as evidence that scientific progress could never serve as the creed of a civilization. Eustace denounced the proponents of scientism, which he defined as the transference of scientific utopianism "from the field of knowledge to the society at large," for clouding the vision of the masses by suggesting that the human being was little more than "a natural animal." He comforted his mostly Catholic readership by suggesting that scientism had more thoroughly deceived and gravely affected Protestants, for many of whom, he believed, the "preoccupation with social welfare has altogether superseded the spiritual ideal of knowing, loving, and serving God."[45]

Eustace's writings typified the effort to impose rather absolute limits on the gaze of science: he thought the time ripe for a complete re-evaluation of the questions that science could be expected to address. The idea of separate spheres for science and religion was not new. But the argument that such limits should be imposed – not because science challenged religious dogma, but because it could not answer abstract questions about the purpose of existence – characterized the early postwar Canadian opposition to scientism. Eustace's article reacted acutely to relatively recent scientific developments. He assumed that Christianity existed, as did God, in the philosophical territory then being invaded by theoretical mathematics and emphasized the folly of scientists' move into this non-empirical "abstract" realm. Atomic science, riding a wave of postwar fame and fearful awe, had wandered where it could not claim to be true in the same way that religion could. He declared that "just as empirical science cannot deal with suprasensible reality, so scientific method cannot touch the apex of the human soul, or move man's will, or raise up his fallen nature." Without some sense of moral direction, he theorized, humanity's modern predilection for scientific analysis meant "progress divorced from the laws of God, as they must be applied in the moral order, and independent of the healing grace of the Sacraments, cannot hope to influence man's behaviour; just as scientific knowledge cannot hope to reveal the innermost secrets of God's Being to man." Eustace deemed these two different kinds of knowledge incompatible and suggested that science must be subject to religion because, although "it is not encroaching on Providence to work for an improvement of an order of things ... [and] the works of science and technology are good in themselves ... man is an infinitely nobler creature than the mere object of scientific research."[46]

As the president of a small Canadian university from 1948 through 1964, Watson Kirkconnell could hardly discourage research in the sciences, which had brought considerable prestige and financial benefit to institutions like his across the country. However, he brimmed with practical suggestions as to how modern youths could cope in a rapidly changing environment by maintaining a vigorous faith that kept pace with science. This perspective seemed to echo wartime opinion that stressed the need to build a society worthy of science, but the similarity ended there. Kirkconnell wished to see a society in which faith maintained its role as conscience and where religion did not represent the official creed of just another one of society's institutions. He considered knowledge of material and scientific factors important, but not totally adequate: "Only a profound religious awakening, transforming the very hearts and motives of men, can touch the core of the ulcer of our age. Intelligence is not enough."[47] In one of his commentaries on the state of education, he claimed that growth in knowledge had outstripped growth in character. "The chief defect of our Western civilization today is not want of scientific skill," he cautioned, "but want of a fundamental set of moral values, anchored to religious faith."[48] The medieval universities, Kirkconnell believed, had managed to synthesize an accommodation between science and faith, but he contended that this skill had been lost in modern times despite the stern lesson of the recent war, during which the spiritual ideals of the Allies inspired the attainment of their military objectives.

By advancing the possibility of an accommodation, Kirkconnell – perhaps unwittingly – attributed a syncretic quality to postwar Canadian culture, an environment in which science had established itself as a material benefactor, but where religion remained the force most able to render meaningful the lives of individuals most likely to distinguish themselves from the modern mass.[49] In reflecting on what a robust science meant to Canada, observers found it difficult to represent a measure of control over the ethical questions science raised by appealing to anything but a religious tradition. Expatriate academic Julia Grace Wales expressed her conception of the utility of religion in a utilitarian era: "True religious creeds are much more than bald scientific statements. Vital symbol enters into them. All the great statements of faith have pregnant phrases which we cannot afford to forget."[50]

The CBC: Hoyle, Chisholm, and Russell on the Air

One Canadian began to suspect, during the last few years of his life, that the *way* such vital symbols were delivered would play a significant role in getting them noticed. While his son Donald was away studying geography at the University of Chicago in early 1950, Harold Innis received a letter from the young man about a disturbing trend in American culture. *Newsweek* and *Harper's* had carried features on Immanuel Velikovsky, who posited scientific connections between biblical catastrophes, such as the parting of the Red Sea, and astronomical events.[51] Incensed at the uncritical way in which the public entertained Velikovsky's ideas, Donald wrote to his father about how the success of such "neo-fundamentalism" could only prompt "a sad commentary on the state of education in this country and the unscrupulousness of journalists. This Dr. Velikovsky is writing several large volumes on the subject and I have found that this fact is accepted by people as meaning that there must be something in it. Thus periodicals help the book trade and mass affects mind."[52] Perhaps the son was eager to demonstrate to his father that he understood some of the processes that the historian had been exploring for his soon-to-be-published works, *The Bias of Communication* and *Empire and Communications*. Clearly, Donald Innis believed that an insidious brand of religion was using the instruments of mass persuasion to challenge the scientific worldview and to obscure truths that science would eventually reveal. In Canada, however, the most striking incidence of a similar discontent with the manipulation of media arose a year later over the decision to broadcast three science series on Canadian radio. Opponents denounced a strong pro-science bias at the CBC, and the ensuing debate revealed that science was far from controlling Canadian society. The question of humanity's purpose remained the domain of religion.

To some Canadians, science not only stood as an alternative belief system, but had yielded radio, television, and movies and had thereby served to perpetuate a breakdown in Christian belief via these instruments of mass culture. This perspective conveniently ignored the fact that some members of the ministry, most prominently Alberta's William Aberhart, had been making broadcasts long before the CBC emerged in 1936 to oversee broadcasting.[53] After 1938, a CBC body called the National Religious Advisory Council existed solely to regulate religious broadcasting. Its role in influencing other aspects of broadcasting policy or practice remains unclear. From 1937 until the early 1950s, the CBC banned programs by individuals claiming supernatural powers or those that dispensed personal advice. Fortune-tellers, astrologers, handwriting analysts, dream interpreters, and the like found themselves off the airwaves entirely, as CBC officials attempted to prevent the dissemination of "pseudoscience."[54]

Although the CBC's Talks and Public Affairs Department took numerous controversial issues to the airwaves during wartime and afterwards, it had generally done so through the *Citizens' Forum* series, programs structured as debates, or one-off broadcasts exploring a specific topic. However, 1951, radio's last full year alone on the Canadian airwaves before the advent of television, featured a series of lectures by maverick Cambridge astronomer Fred Hoyle, a series including eminent Canadian psychiatrist Brock Chisholm, and another by the famous philosopher Bertrand Russell.[55] Although only a small fraction of the lectures explicitly disparaged religion, the airing of these series stirred up a discussion that reveals much about the relationship between science and religion in the national culture. Opponents considered such potentially controversial scientific material presented without a warning or an opportunity for rebuttal from the churches to be a betrayal of the corporation's commitment to defend the foundations of Canadian life. Respondents who wrote in support of 1951's lineup of scientific programming reflected on how rare and refreshing it was to hear scientists speak freely on the radio.[56]

Hoyle's series on astronomy (*The Nature of the Universe*) went to air first, in early May 1951. It consisted of eight talks and set forth the fundamentals of his findings in cosmology. He presented his "New Cosmology" in a fairly straightforward manner in the earlier broadcasts, and it was not until his eighth and final presentation that controversy emerged. Entitled "A Personal View," Hoyle's attempt to sum up, or to tie his previous lectures together, outlined his objections to criticism of an earlier collection of talks by him on the British Broadcasting Corporation's avant-garde Third Programme network. Hoyle spoke, he emphasized, "as a person, and not as a scientist" when he confessed that "the study of all these extraordinary facts has had an effect on me as a man." Perhaps listeners were expecting to hear how exploring the grandeur of the universe had reinvigorated Hoyle's faith. Instead, he asserted that working out *one's own* attitude towards such data was imperative, not a task to "leave to the theologians and philosophers." He went on to cite a brief history of Christianity's retreat before the incisive arguments of Darwin and his followers and to posit that the creation of the universe could now be understood entirely in scientific terms. Curiously, his most jarring assertion paralleled the distinction that C.J. Eustace made about the respective roles of science and religion. Hoyle said: "If the Christians are to find issues that lie beyond the purview of science, then they must look for them at a deeper level than the creation of the Universe."[57] Eustace, along with a number of other religionists, believed that there *were* no deeper issues than creation and that a science too bold to leave alone what they viewed as philosophical questions demanded a response.

Hoyle's personal view of how the branch of science known as cosmology had evolved, and of what it meant to his life, was of course both broader in scope and more detailed than the foregoing sketch. However, public condemnation of the broadcast fastened on the elements that cast Christian belief in a poor light and did little more than argue that airing such shows on the national radio network undermined the basis of an unspecified, but Christian, Canadian creed. One listener placed the Christian tradition at the core of national life, declaring in an unequivocal and rambling fashion: "For the C.B.C. to permit such an anti-Christian and atheistic man as Mr. Hoyle to enjoy time on the national radio and trample on and misrepresent our basic and traditional Christian ideals and way of Life as we in Canada have always respected and lived up to since the early beginnings, is definitely disgusting and even outrageous."[58] Despite such expressions of outrage and the "scores of wires and telegrams from Roman Catholic organizations and other religious groups criticizing the use of publicly owned facilities to attack religion,"⁵⁹ the CBC received more letters in support of the broadcasts than in condemnation, though less than seventy in all.⁶⁰ The most likely reason for the dearth of protest letters was that the CBC set aside airtime for two academics to respond to Hoyle's final broadcast the week after it aired.

The men chosen to counterbalance Hoyle's intemperate words were Ralph Williamson, an astronomer at the University of Toronto, and Father J.M. Kelly of the same university's St Michael's College. Williamson opened with an attempt at character assassination, dredging up Hoyle's spotty record as a wartime scientist, portraying him as an iconoclast with little respect for the wisdom of his more experienced colleagues or the urgency of the war effort. In trying to reduce Hoyle's influence on the minds of Canadians, Williamson pointed out a distinction between audiences: "It is one thing to try to sell a novel idea to a group of scientists, who are equipped with the experience and mathematical training necessary to determine whether the idea is worth considering further but it is very different when one talks to the non-scientific world." Presenting the public with a dollop of science via radio had been a grave mistake for the CBC, for listeners would uncritically lap up opinions to which they had been exposed. Hoyle had been negligent, his fellow scientist declared, in not differentiating for the public between scientific fact and his own ideas. In noting this tendency to conflate fact and speculation, Williamson placed Hoyle in the company of the notorious "catastrophist" who so enraged Donald Innis: "If we exclude Velikovsky's maunderings, Hoyle has committed the most glaring example of this kind of public flummoxing in modern times."⁶¹

Father Kelly, as might be expected, dealt with the religious implications of Hoyle's final broadcast, remarking that the cosmologist had "got into something beyond his depth" and that his "scientific straitjacket" would never allow him to answer questions with which philosophers and theologians were more comfortable. Kelly even indulged in a bit of science fantasy, predicting that if Hoyle "could be transported into the future for a few hundred millions of years he would still find men unhappy with the answers science gives them. It's no use saying this is due to the perversity of men. I think the more normal and valid conclusion is that science alone is not big enough or deep enough for man." Kelly lumped Hoyle's theory of continuous creation, or "little bangs," with the Big Bang model and dismissed both by declaring that "the real question of creation is this: Whence comes the thing that bangs?"⁶² The scholar/priest aimed to place an aspect of human existence beyond the reach of scientists such as Hoyle, who to him seemed bigoted and unable to understand why people might be most comfortable with an uplifting narrative of creation such as that in Genesis or an explanation of the afterlife that rewarded virtuous conduct. In allowing representatives of a religious perspective to respond to Hoyle, the national broadcaster practised a subtle form of censorship, placing a comforting buffer of traditional belief between the public and some of the more disturbing implications of scientific licence.

In September 1951, the Wednesday-night slot that the CBC's Talks Department had staked out in 1947, and which by the early 1950s was widely known to be "intellectual"[63] in tone, hosted another controversial series. Dr Brock Chisholm introduced *Man's Last Enemy – Himself!* on 5 September 1951. Structurally, this series differed from the Hoyle broadcasts in that the speakers were members of a group representing the psychiatric profession rather than a single presenter. The CBC made no plans to include a response from any religious organizations. Although the group contained Sigmund Freud's daughter Anna, distinguished American psychiatrist Carl Binger, and Ewen Cameron of Montreal's Allan Institute, Chisholm was clearly the main attraction. He was director general of the United Nations' World Health Organization, but in Canada he was still best known for his mid-1940s' pronouncements on the psychological treatment of children.[64] In 1946, while Chisholm was still deputy minister of national health, *Maclean's* published a digest of his public statements opposing traditional standards of behaviour as guides for raising well-adjusted children. He encouraged parents to be truthful to their children at all times, even advising them to divulge the truth about Santa Claus. On religion, Chisholm suggested that parents should tell their children what they believed to be true, but to avoid presenting their belief as fact.[65] In his 1951 message, Chisholm stressed tolerance, compassion, and understanding among individuals but remained firm in his insistence that the people who helped people with their psychological problems were "modern experts, not hereditary or traditional ones, who would advise on the basis of obsolete concepts, on long past certainties which they had learned in their childhoods from their ancestors' ideas."[66]

Within days of Chisholm's address, an ultra-Catholic paper, the *Ensign*, responded angrily.[67] In subsequent weeks, Ewen Cameron's lecture advocating the pursuit of scientific knowledge over "the old rule of thumb moralizing" again drew the wrath of the *Ensign* as well as of the Jesuit paper *Relations*, which reprimanded him, as the Anglican bishop of Montreal had, for "denying the grace of God."[68] Other commentators were more circumspect and seemed to appreciate, at least compared to Chisholm's earlier work, a more pastoral tone in the

1951 lectures. The *Prairie Messenger*, a weekly published at St Peter's Abbey in Muenster, Saskatchewan, commented on the series over the course of several issues. The editors found it "hard to imagine a man in Dr. Chisholm's high position opposing religion as such when the trend today is back to religion"[69] and considered the title and general implications of the series inspiringly reminiscent of Matthew 16:24 – "If anyone wishes to come after Me, let him deny himself."[70] It was difficult for any but extremists in Canada to make clear distinctions between the aims of psychology – as presented during the autumn of 1951 – and religion.[71] Unlike Hoyle's cosmology, the psychological talks could not be so conveniently dismissed as atheistic. One listener wrote that they were "full of recognition of the essential moralities by which we all strive to live our lives, and are in many ways a scientific examination, in terms suitable for an understanding of our world of today, of the eternal verities which were preached by Christ."[72]

On the heels of the psychiatrists came Bertrand Russell, in September and October 1951. The philosopher had turned his mind towards the problems and prospects of life at mid-century and had come up with a series entitled *Living in the Atomic Age*. As the series progressed, Russell made several concessions to modern life. His suggestion that a new system of virtues should replace the old, which had burdened humankind with "the load of sin," and his insistence that science had liberated society from the "great parts of traditional religion and morality [which] were inspired by man's bondage to nature,"[73] cast considerable doubt on the continued applicability of conventional religious belief. His final talk stressed people's quest to overcome conflicts with nature, with each other, and within themselves and again urged listeners to renounce the idea of sin in favour of embracing the techniques by which science attempted to resolve these conflicts.[74]

In Russell's case, as in Hoyle's, the CBC considered the material too controversial to broadcast alone. Following Russell's six-part series, the CBC aired a panel program featuring academics John A. Irving (Philosophy, Victoria College Toronto), D.R.G. Owen (Ethics, Trinity College, Toronto), and Edmund Carpenter (Anthropology, University of Toronto).[75] Although Russell alluded to a religious tradition as only one *part* of a philosophical/cultural burden to be set aside, Owen saw this as an endorsement of the scientific perspective. He accused Russell of knocking down a straw man that was not Christianity and argued that the disintegration and chaos threatening modern society was best countered by the sensitivity of religion. John Irving noted that even though Russell believed that applied science had "outrun man's capacity for moral sensitivity and political control," Russell did not seriously consider advances in the social sciences. Carpenter concurred but deemed more important Russell's idea that people must open their hearts to joy and cannot remain in fear, "which can only lead [them] to escape into the past and into mysticism, and we know there's no solution there."[76] The group could not come out and indict Russell as anti-religious, but that was never the point of the exercise. However incisive their criticism, another drama was playing itself out in a more public fashion.

What historian Marc Raboy called "an attack on the CBC from the extreme right" hijacked part of the agenda of the Parliamentary Committee on Broadcasting.[77] The pressure had been on since July 1951, when the more moderate B.K. Sandwell had judged Canadian radio an inappropriate place to question religion: "It may in the United States be the duty of radio to open its channels to any and every conceivable shade of opinion on religion and everything else. We have never felt that radio in Canada was under any such far-reaching obligation."[78] Despite the CBC's attempts to mollify or prevent protest by airing alternative viewpoints, the Russell series constituted its "third strike," and some sort of discipline for presenting unvarnished science seemed inevitable.

Although some degree of protest against or support for the Hoyle and Chisholm series had been evident from the time they were aired, Russell's presence, even rebroadcast, ensured a more public debate. Both Hoyle and Russell's series were transcriptions – pre-recorded talks from the BBC – so that CBC officials could "read ahead" and deliberate about allowing responses. The discussions within the CBC itself were illuminating. In the midst of the Russell series, Barry MacDonald, a CBC employee in Sydney, Nova Scotia, urged Supervisor of Talks and Public Affairs Neil Morrison to take further measures to counter the impression that "the CBC has jumped on a particular ideological bandwagon. The bandwagon seems to be driven by people who have discarded the traditional morality of Western society and put their faith in some fairly recent discoveries (and hypotheses) in the field of science, especially in the social sciences." MacDonald advocated a balanced perspective – he did not wish to see a general ban on scientific talks that disparaged or could be taken to disparage religion. He none the less maintained that in future the CBC should make certain that "scholars and students of high calibre who are basically Christian, or at least spiritual (as opposed to strictly materialistic) in their outlook," preface or respond to such controversial talks. Christian scholars, he continued, should be allotted time and prominence comparable to the scientists.[79]

Morrison decided that it would be prudent to investigate the issue of relative time allowed for religious broadcasts and to the three scientific series. The results of his assistant's inquiry were clear. The three series in question ran for a total of ten and half hours. Nationally broadcast programs "of a religious character" accounted by themselves for 214 hours of airtime per year, every year.[80] Although these statistics decidedly did not reveal the pro-science bias at which MacDonald hinted, another of his comments encapsulated the central paradox animating the relationship between science and religion in the early 1950s – the need to appear rational and objective while acknowledging that science had not done away with traditional beliefs regarding the nature of existence and moral conduct. MacDonald wrote: "the CBC can have no 'beliefs', except a general sympathy and accord with the basic ideas of our Canadian society. Certainly what we as individual members of CBC staff believes is irrelevant. So is the philosophic accuracy of either the 'traditional' or the 'new' school."[81]

By presenting talks on scientific subjects, the CBC reflected what it perceived as a burgeoning part of the intellectual world. During the war, science writers presented science in such a way as to make it seem less complex and more useful in daily life. Returning veterans swelled the ranks of technical college and university students and were expected to be more familiar not only with the theories of science but, in view of the atomic threat, with its importance in society and politics. Despite this democratization of science, several observers believed that one of the powerful "basic ideas" at the core of Canadian culture remained an attachment to the concept of a spiritual realm beyond the reach of physical forces. For the CBC it seemed *equally democratic* to respect such an attachment when trying to assess what the public wanted.[82] Its attempts to present both perspectives drew condemnation from one committed democrat, who saw the science series as an antidote to mass culture, noting that "these talks were far more important and significant to a democratic public than all the quiz programs, variety shows, soap operas, murder mysteries and disc jockey shows ever produced." He placed the issue in a Cold War context and reprised a credo of the reconstruction era: "We cannot maintain democracy nor can we defeat totalitarianism by imposing censorship. We must strengthen democracy by strengthening its basis, an alert and well informed, intelligent populace."[83] In her attempt to chronicle the acrimony over science programming in 1951, Miriam Chapin told her intended American audience that Canada was still "a deeply religious country, perhaps the most devout on earth. A Christian nation, it contains numerous minorities, Jews, Moslems, Buddhists, as well as deists and atheists. If nothing is to be heard on the air that offends any one of them, can any scientific truths be broadcast? Certainly Hoyle, Chisholm and the rest thought they were discussing science. Is Christianity so vulnerable an institution that none may presume to doubt its tenets?"[84]

Journalists were divided about allowing controversial science on the powerful medium of radio. In November, B.K. Sandwell added to his earlier commentary on Hoyle's program by arguing that "the questions whether there is a Creator and whether the life of the individual ceases at death are not scientific questions; these are not matters of knowledge, they are matters of faith; and the radio is not a suitable mechanism for disturbing the faith of anybody."[85] Wrapping up its coverage of the issue on New Year's Day 1952, *Maclean's* suggested that the "ancient struggle to root out heresy still goes on" and wondered how it was that some critics of the CBC could campaign to silence scientific programs in a society that valued freedom of speech. In advocating an end to behind-the-scenes attempts to censor ideas that appeared to ridicule or diminish the relevance of religion in modern Canadian society, *Maclean's* held up as exemplary the views of a theology student from Toronto's Wycliffe College. The student welcomed the opportunity that Russell's programs presented and rejected censorship, proclaiming: "Let not Christians hide behind artificial barriers but stand in the marketplace and declare Christ." Even in an era of prosperity and scientific marvels, the editor recognized the resilient nature of religious conviction: "To wilfully or capriciously shake another man's faith without offering him a better faith in return is one of the most vicious and wasteful acts a human being can commit. But to seek the final alliance of faith and reason is a high and noble purpose; and the man who seeks that alliance is not an enemy to faith.[86]" In his estimation, the result of declaring Christ in a materialistic world would not be the clear victory of one perspective over the other, but rather a commendable modern compromise based on a recognition of the limits of science and an appreciation of religion as a meaningful way of transcending them.

Responses: Owen, Coady, and Wallace

Although it had played a useful part in transforming the economic lives of thousands of Canadians sice 1945, science remained in an uneasy coexistence with religion because it still could not offer a "better" faith in return. Some religionists, however, read this sort of stand-off during a period of religious revival in North America as a portent of difficult times ahead or of creeping moral decay. During the year following the excitement over scientific programming, one of Russell's critics, D.R.G. Owen, published a slim volume entitled *Scientism, Man and Religion*, which he abridged and broadcast over the CBC as part of a series entitled *Christianity in an Age of Science*. In his essay "Science, Scientism and Religion," Owen opened by asking why the present age was considered scientific and by attempting to explain two important and, to him, intimately linked developments – "the decline of religious belief and the rise of the mass-society." He assigned blame carefully: "I ascribe these two related phenomena not to science, which is a certain method of investigation and control, but rather to scientism, a blind adulation of science which disregards or denies the limitations of the method."

Like C.J. Eustace, Owen used the term *scientism* to suggest an insidious ideology or a process of mass delusion. Like Eustace, he saw great value in the technical achievements of science but emphasized that science could not examine or resolve all the problems that humanity might encounter. Nor did the empirical principles on which science operated address "other methods of knowledge or the validity of other classes of belief." To Owen, science seemed much less versatile than religion, because "the fact that spirit and values, for instance, are intangible and immeasurable means not that they are unreal but merely that they fall outside the scope of scientific investigation."[87] Most important, Owen insisted that historically both religion and science had served as pillars of Western society, but both had been ill-treated at the hands of scientism – a "prevailing tradition," or "set of presuppositions," that involved "the rejection of all apparently irreconcilable beliefs. The tradition of our age can be given the name 'scientific' in the sense that the assumptions of which it consists are distorted generalizations of the valid limiting principles of science."[88]

Owen considered scientism and communism to be analogous. He saw an unfortunate paradox in the way in which the West spent so much energy resisting enslavement to communist ideology but paid little heed to the "internal threat" of scientism, which he claimed was just as destructive of freedom. "If this way of thinking wins the day," he continued, "the result will be a Western version of the mass-society in which man will be abolished as successfully as in the contemporary communist state."[89] Despite such a bleak prophecy for human beings under scientism, Owen took it as a "sign of hope" that "behind and beneath our modern culture are the insights of Ancient Greece and Palestine and of medieval Europe." If it did not forsake these insights, Owen suggested, contemporary Western society should be able to accommodate both religion and science, because "true religion does not dispute the well-authenticated theories of science," while "science proper, recognizing its limitations, passes no judgment on the reality or unreality of spirit, freedom, values and God."[90]

Despite the limitations of science, its power as a force for the improvement of everyday life also had to be acknowledged. Father M.M. Coady, who did much to improve the economic welfare of rural Maritimers because he believed that poverty affected the soul as well as the body, admitted in a 1953 address that religion or a right philosophy could provide for only part of humanity's needs and that "the formula for the good society of the future is not going to be taken out, like a rabbit, from some metaphysical hat; rather, it is going to be the manipulation of commonplace things, the re-patterning of the forces that determine the life of man on this earth." Coady included the basic physical necessities as well as economic security and freedom among the commonplace things that science could help provide. He had, however, anticipated objections to such a seemingly atheistic stand on science: "I can hear some of you saying, 'That is vile materialism. I thought he would come to that!' But I say to you that it is high spirituality – seeing the spiritual aspect of created material things. We should not be fooled by externals. Real spirituality goes deeper, sees God in material things, and recognizes that the laws of nature are His handwriting in the world He created."[91]

The principal of Queen's University from 1939 to 1951, Robert Charles Wallace was trained as a geologist but came to occupy, perhaps more convincingly than anyone else in Canada, the middle ground between a scientific and a religious faith. Staking out this territory in a lecture at Acadia University in 1953, he granted that the scientist "has become an important person in the modern world, for our civilization has become geared to his discoveries, and awaits the new aids to living that he may give." However, he seized on the fluid nature of scientific inquiry as evidence of science's status as an evolving perspective, not as truth. Wallace asserted that scientists could not embrace all forms of knowledge because they were not open to the possibility that the supernatural, as another "field of interest," had certain laws of its own: "One would like to feel that this objectivity is carried over into other fields of interest not connected with his scientific pursuits, but unfortunately this does not always prove to be the case."[92] Science had drastically expanded the body of knowledge necessary for a dramatic taming of the forces of nature, but the empty prospect of material abundance without spiritual satisfaction differentiated a faith in science from religious faith enough to convince Wallace that both would be necessary components of the fullest possible life. He reasoned that atomic science, despite its potential for destruction and its being considered the most modern and the most dangerous branch, had been pushing humankind back in the direction of religious faith. After offering an inventory of the contributions of science to a more abundant material life, he added: "Our lives are easier, we have more leisure: there is more entertainment: we should be happier. And yet there remains the question mark. Are we really happier? Have we found that peace of mind which is the object of our striving?"[93]

Wallace also invoked quantum theory in proclaiming science's limited power to solve certain kinds of human problems. He appealed to extremely simplistic interpretations of Einstein's relativity and Heisenberg's uncertainty principle to suggest that scientists were only just beginning to realize that some questions were insoluble via scientific methods.[94] Although he granted that some time in the distant future science might find a way to apply its methods to the "imponderables in life" – the questions that had been so far left to religion or philosophy – he returned to a familiar refrain, admitting that "much has been done by experiment in psychology to reduce to some measure of order and intelligibility our impulses and emotional reactions; and much more may yet be done by scientific analysis. For in many of our actions we are machine like." He sought, however, to exclude vast reaches of human experience from such an impersonal, mechanized treatment, arguing that "in our credo, in the faith which inspires us to go forward, in the deeper strivings of the spirit – in a word, in the things that make life worthwhile, science has failed to penetrate. In these realms we seek other support."[95]

Such a search for other means of support was an essential part of the response to the pressures and pace of modern life, which Wallace believed had tended to "rush us off our feet physically, mentally, and spiritually." The way in which science had transformed work and leisure made it an integral part of daily life for Canadians, but it could not address the restlessness of spirit that accompanied modernization. Wallace believed that, in view of science's continual evolution from one hypothesis to the next, a "grip on the things that are eternal" must be part of the scientist's personality. The explicit goals of science and religion, he noted, had led observers to perceive a significant gulf between the two. He attributed this tension to dogmatism on both sides and to distinct ways of viewing the "great edifice of truth" – scientists striving for ever-newer representations of it, and the faithful "feasting their eyes on scenes that have become dear to them."[96] Contemporary society needed a way to acknowledge the undiminished spiritual curiosity that one commentator called the "receptivity to the infinite which will not allow them to rest."[97]

Wallace thought that an effort "to examine, in this very modern age, the faith by which we may live" was long overdue and would lead to a greater understanding between scientists and the faithful – two parties that had erroneously conceived of their respective goals as antagonistic.[98] Wallace saw a divine purpose in the progress of humanity from age to age and suggested that science and religion were equipped differently so that they might complement each other. The contentious issue of authority, he claimed, fell away when religion was willing to admit, faced with hard scientific evidence about the physical world, that it spoke metaphorically on matters that were more properly the concern of science. Conversely, he warned scientists not to assume that they "had the complete vision." Wallace left his audience at Acadia with the message that the conditions were right for a truce: "The world of science and the world of religion are one world. We are nearer to achieving that greatly desired unity than at any time in the days that have gone."[99]

Wallace's plea for unity came near the end of a period marked by intense speculation on how religion could maintain its authority in the face of science. Commentators perceived the promise of unity in unlikely places. Watson Kirkconnell saw it in the medieval university, and D.R.G. Owen saw it in the ancient Greek civilization, in the Holy Land, and in the Middle Ages. Lister Sinclair found it in early-1950s' Canada. In a radio piece on Arctic survival, he reflected on the effortless way in which an Inuit hunter remained open to material and spiritual stimuli: "Arvik is a mixture of technician and mystic – like most men. What observation can teach – he knows. What doing can prove – he accepts ... Without books – he preserves the past. He seems to understand all the principles of science. And yet, he believes in spirits."[100]

The question of religion's place in an unquestionably scientific world would pale next to a more general discontent with mass culture and the technological society in the years that followed. Religion and science could be said to address different concerns, but "scientism," later reconceived by the likes of George Grant as an over-reliance on technology, would remain anathema to critics of contemporary society and its culture.

EPILOGUE: FOCUS ON TECHNOLOGY

The prestige of science during the war years owed much to its characterization as the right arm of democracy and to a growing trust in the scientific method as a rational way of addressing social problems. This transition certainly had implications for religion as a belief system and as a locus of social uplift. Religionists, like the scientific specialist, responded by claiming that their method was best suited to the task of helping people weather the pressures of modern life, some of which science had intensified. One of the most compelling episodes in this struggle involved questions about how relatively new methods of communication might be used, if at all, to present the quintessentially modern scientific worldview in a nation still conscious of the place of religion. By 1955, McGill zoologist N.J. Berrill wondered whether there was a "vital conflict" between science and religion. He answered in the negative, citing the common aims of the two perspectives and an essential "unity in all things," remarking that it "is more a matter of convenience for the benefit of our own understanding that we seize upon these intangible qualities of the spirit and set them apart from the physical world."[101] Although several commentators during the late 1940s and early 1950s spent a great deal of their energy setting spirit and body apart, that activity only served to acknowledge more acutely the power of science in contemporary Canada. The success of science and technology in exploiting the riches of the physical world could not be denied, and much of the era's discomfort with science was rooted in the search for a peace of mind less transitory than the physical comforts that boom-time brought to even the most remote corners of Canada.

Skirmishes along what B.K. Sandwell called the "science–faith borders" were less "vital" by the later 1950s. At mid-decade even the least religious of observers began to view the postwar religious revival as a rational coping strategy rather than as fanaticism.[102] Even the most strident critics of the modern condition identified not science itself, but the uses to which it was put, as the root of their concern. Berrill saw the complexity and pervasive nature of technology as a much more pressing problem, suggesting that "the differences between science and religion are fictitious if what we mean by science is that passionate search of the religious soul for the ultimate reality which he calls God." The danger arose, he thought, "only when science is converted to technology and becomes materialistic and when religion ceases to be the search for truth and says it knows all the answers." He concluded by chastising stiff-necked partisans on both sides, none of whom practised "true science" or "true religion." True science and true religion could be reunited because between them there existed "language barriers but no others. There is but one quest and science, religion and art are all on the same road."[103]

The concern with technology rather than with the work of pure science as a challenge to the role of religion began to reveal itself somewhat more vigorously by the late 1950s. The Toronto Conference of the United Church of Canada struck a committee to investigate automation, and, in his section of the committee's report, Harold Toye saw grave danger in the societal self-sufficiency that automation implied. Contemporary religion, he wrote, must "challenge the generally accepted authority of science, technology, industry, and military control which ignores God's Sovereignty and plays fast and loose with moral and spiritual values."[104] Despite the rather militant rhetoric, Toye directed his wrath at the societal tendency to think in selfish material terms rather than putting the community's welfare and Christian conduct first.

In 1959, John Irving testified to the lopsided nature of the contest between science and religion when a British schoolchild asked him, via the magic of a transatlantic radio link, which faith he would embrace if Christianity did not exist. He quickly suggested Hinduism, but he preferred Zen Buddhism "because no advance of science can bite into or destroy Zen-Buddhism."[105] Through the mid-1960s, philosopher George Grant complained of a widespread scientism, under which human needs were no longer central to technocratic governments. Journalist Pierre Berton sat in church and found an inflexible religion that could not or would not respond to modern conditions.[106] A year before Canada's Centennial, historian W.L. Morton spoke of a monolithic culture with little room for the spiritual or literary expressions that enriched life in bygone days. Science had come to determine the structure of daily and collective life to the extent that "only an Englishman such as Sir Charles Snow could speak of the existence of two cultures. To a North American there is only one, the scientific."[107] During that same year, Morton painted a bleak picture of contemporary life – of "perils unparalleled" – and added that "only a faith such as Teilhard de Chardin's, that such things cannot be in the Providence of God, will enable a man to be at ease in these times."[108] Amid buildings crammed with advertisements of participating nations' scientific genius, Expo 67's Christian pavilion showed its visitors "man in contention with himself" via the most modern methods of audio-visual presentation.[109]

As North American society came to be populated with what William Whyte in 1956 labelled "organization men," seemingly content to fit quietly into an order necessitated by technological advance and consolidated by bureaucracies, the postwar response to science as a trying facet of modern experience and an incomplete philosophy bore eloquent witness to religion's enduring place in Canadian culture. Despite swelling church memberships, the task of claiming a prominent and honourable duty for religion in a scientific age distressed some observers greatly. For the most part, however, their fears were misplaced. Religion managed to "maintain its visionary authority"[110] among people who were, their hopeful guardians believed, still inclined to seek explanations of life's purpose that were simple, familiar, and reassuring. Some movies and comic books proved perhaps more subtle enemies of religion. As an alluring alternative to traditional activities and community ties, mass culture brought Canada into ever more intimate contact with a modern world that offered much less spiritual guidance than psychiatrists on the radio. Yet when those who thought about the gulf between science and religion were moved to speak, they tended to emphasize the fluid and contingent nature of science rather than the powerful mass culture that often diverted people from questions regarding the universe or humanity's purpose in it.

Although the wartime infatuation with the promise of science is perhaps easier to understand more than a half-century later, the postwar efforts to make science responsible to tradition and popular beliefs, to adjust to the existential implications of nuclear weapons, and to retain religion as counsel and conscience were equally indicative of the times. Cyril James recalled the life of St Paul and described how difficult it was in 1955 to follow such an example amid threatening surroundings: "It was easier to walk with God, and work with Him, in simpler Eastern lands under Mediterranean skies than it is in a crowded bus on Sherbrooke Street in a world that is arguing about the atom bomb."[111] In the early 1950s, the combination of a religious revival with evidence that some scientists – such as Fred Hoyle and Brock Chisholm – had abandoned the sort of pious soul-searching common immediately after Hiroshima spawned jeremiads such as Owen's and hopeful calls for reconciliation such as Wallace's. Historians of science or of culture in Canada cannot ignore such attempts to safeguard religion's traditional place. Imploring their nation to leave room for the spiritual, supporters of religion in an age of science did not yet realize that the implicit need to live in both worlds – to transcend the borders between science and faith – was both an axiom and a commandment of Canadian life at mid-century.

4

Cultural Policy, Cultural Pessimism

Wartime and reconstruction revealed that although democracy became a powerful rallying cry, fear of easily distracted masses and of a perhaps-desolate utilitarianism – conditions that could be linked to modern life and to abuse of the opportunities that democracy afforded – threatened the hopeful vision of an enlightened postwar nation. The ambivalent reception that "religionists" gave the scientific worldview in the early 1950s showed that the longstanding contest between those two belief systems remained undecided. Their competition for time on the airwaves had only complicated matters. The 1950s hardly provided a respite for cultural critics, who claimed that the problems attending modern existence and the banality of mass culture had only intensified. Having struggled during the 1930s and savouring what leisure they had in wartime, many Canadians enjoyed peace and relative comfort once the troops returned home. Still, critical observers perceived an environment that, though more prosperous and ostensibly more carefree, accommodated an abandonment of the mental and spiritual engagement of wartime in favour of passive entertainment, material comfort, and social status based on consumption.[1] Critics reasoned that the ordinary citizen would be hard-pressed to extract himself or herself from these circumstances unless he or she chose "activities that will reveal his [or her] interests as a personality."[2] This prospect seemed unlikely without some form of intervention. As an exhilarating peace succumbed quickly to the uncertainty of the Cold War, the barometer of individual conduct was no longer the active citizen but the mass society.

Historians have not neglected the cultural dimensions of this environment but tended until recently to portray North America during the 1950s as a place where simple values re-emerged and (particularly in the United States) an uneasy consensus reigned. Because the *American* 1950s' experience represented the trajectory of the world's pre-eminent postwar commercial and cultural empire, it has become normative. In this version of events, although Cold War tensions dominated the international stage and affected domestic affairs all over the world, prosperity and a burgeoning youth-focused culture operated to make the 1950s a relatively quiescent time for the average North American – a reward for the collective heroism of the 1940s. General works on the United States in the 1950s cover political and diplomatic events assiduously and, with few exceptions, perpetuate the idea that the American public sought stability with an uncompromising passion.[3] Fortunately, studies such as W.T. Lhamon's *Deliberate Speed* portray 1950s' culture as anyting but placid. Lhamon noted: "Much of the speed, style, slapdash improvisation, and rushing instability in poems, songs, films and fiction offended keepers of maturing traditions." Such analysis enriches our view of a time that had been somewhat whitewashed by accounts conflating the banal frivolity of popular culture with the overall character of the decade.[4]

While the recent historiography of the 1950s in the United States has uncovered subtler hues, historical writing on Canada in the same years is still notable mainly for its fascination with the struggle between Liberals and Progressive Conservatives for political power and influence. When surveys of this period address Canadian "culture," they list some of the more prominent artists, writers, and musicians active at the time or describe how governments proposed to support a small, underappreciated and chronically underemployed arts community.[5] Any account should acknowledge broader political themes, but these may be exploited in more helpful ways. For example, a handful of historians have explored the difficult Cold War years. Although Canada did not have its own Senator Joseph McCarthy, foreign policy and national security were minefields, and much was done to Canadians, ostensibly for their own protection.[6] Only recently have students of the period come to appreciate that the history of social and cultural policy in postwar Canada is not the history of society and culture.[7] While Doug Owram's welcome work on the "baby boom" generation devotes long-overdue attention to Canadian society and its culture in the 1950s, he reinforces an interpretation of the decade as a comfortable nursery for those who would ultimately carry out more strident acts of dissent.[8] His rebellious young men and women of the later 1960s and early 1970s seemed to draw little of their anger from a sedate 1950s, absorbing only a sense of entitlement, which enabled them to seek justice and self-knowledge more obtrusively as they reached adulthood.

As contemporary observers well appreciated, however, the 1950s featured anxiety over juvenile crime, boredom, and the potential for atomic war, driving much of the public towards suburbs, censorship, and conformity to ready-made ways of life. Despite clear evidence that Canadians overall tended to manage their anxieties by consuming cars and double features at the movies, cultural critics' commentary on such trends provides a perspective lacking in empirical or anecdotal accounts. Suffused with despair and clearly biased towards autonomous thought, liberal education, and the accumulated wisdom of the West, critical dismissals of mass culture and prescriptions for "re-humanizing" modern life were genuine. In the light of the often-urgent tone of this critique, we cannot justify merely gazing at a veneer of contentment with the abundant life or assuming that "Culture" either flourished or did not. Attention to the variety of ways in which modern life altered social patterns and values, and focus on a manifest will to help "high" and "folk" culture compete for public attention with mass entertainments, both suggest that cultural critics saw the vast public as unwittingly subjugated but ultimately redeemable. Their success at selling this interpretation of how cultural supply influenced demand translated into unprecedented state support for the arts. The immediate goal was not a highbrow renaissance but undoing what Hollywood and the other capitals of mass culture had wrought. By advocating a wider range of cultural options for Canadians, critical observers hoped to establish self-improvement and a degree of eclecticism as attractive social norms and thus halt the common culture's perceived decline.

The end of the Second World War signalled only a qualified return to the abundant life for many Canadians, as many goods remained scarce and it would be some time before the armed forces pulled out of the fomer theatres of war. In this way the years 1947–49, during which full-scale consumption resumed, along with a peacetime agenda – subject of the first section of this chapter – cohere more readily with the 1950s than with wartime. This transitional period also coheres with the 1950s because some broad themes emerged – themes that continued to invite concern during the 1950s and beyond: pressure to conform to new norms in work and home life; consumerism and the commercialization of culture; and the perceived abandonment of cultural effort in favour of "empty" leisuretime pursuits. Most of the incidents or issues treated in this chapter – for example, historian Hilda Neatby's crusade against progressive education – arise before the later 1950s.

Scholars have long considered the Royal Commission on National Development in the Arts, Letters and Sciences (the Massey-Lévesque Commission – or simply the Massey Commission – treated in the second section of this chapter) to be the genesis of fascination with Canada's cultural well-being. It has become the central event in a "creationist myth" for cultural nationalists, despite the efforts of the 1920s, Second World War plans for cultural reconstruction, and the sort of earnest pulse-taking embodied in the Canadian Youth Commission's relatively brief career in the mid-1940s.[9] Those seeking to understand the Canadian cultural "elite" portray the Massey Commission as a watershed or at least as the first genuine acknowledgment of a desire to develop the nation's cultural infrastructure.[10] Often cited as a kind of highbrow census or nationwide cultural inventory, the commission had a short lifespan, (1949–51). Its report was not, however, the defining statement of an abiding 1950s critique of mass culture. Cultural criticism during this period ran wider, encompassing disappointment not only with cultural forms that had become popular but with change affecting such areas as education, business, and the family. Well over 400 concerned community, provincial, and national groups submitted briefs to the commission, and these are certainly valuable to the history of cultural policy. They also constituted readings of the cultural landscape in particular locales or by representatives of groups interested in a variety of activities as pastimes or livelihoods.

Part of the critical commentary on modern life and mass culture emerged during a relatively brief, but intense, nationalist re-evaluation of the Canadian arts milieu, broadcasting, and higher education. Unfortunately, this concurrence prompts us to see what Paul Litt called "the Donnish Inquisition"[11] as coterminous with interest in rooting out cultural heresies. In the absence of such a purpose-built institution, during the remainder of the decade it is more difficult to follow the later grumblings of cultural critics. Yet, in the years following the Massey Commission – as the third and fourth sections of this chapter reveal – commentators recognized that neither the war nor the commission had ushered in an era of enlightenment in Canada. Visions of a postwar democracy filled with attentive, independent, active citizens likewise did not materialize, and post-Massey denunciations attacked the forces that made Canada appear to be a "soft nation."[12]

The Massey Commission, however, exhibited two valuable characteristics. First, as a government-sanctioned examination of Canada's cultural life, it invited more frequent commentary on a wide variety of cultural topics. By the time its *Report* came out in 1951, cultural critics had floated a raft of suggestions for coping with a modern environment whose "ephemeral" entertainments they believed did little to promote self-improvement or recreation, despite the increased leisure time available to the average person. Second, a host of policy recommendations emerged in the wake of the commission's hearings. Yet many of the recommendations in that wide-ranging program took several years to implement, if they were implemented at all.[13] The vow to investigate broadcasting resulted in the mid-1950s, in a royal commission (Fowler Commission) on that very issue, around which still more critical readings of Canadian cultural life huddled for heat and light. This second state-sponsored look at the dynamics of cultural change in North America I explore more fully in the next chapter.

AN EMERGING CRITIQUE: THE LATE 1940S

Most Canadians found it simple to move into peacetime. With the conflict won, concern over the prospect of atomic war and the well-being of their own families came to occupy greater portions of their time and energy. Another, much smaller group saw cultural and social patterns established before the war as still troubling, intensified by further industrialization and urbanization during the war. Within two years of victory, much of the urgency and grim goodwill that characterized the relatively collectivist culture of reconstruction had ceased to matter to individuals occupied once again with their own affairs.[14] Curiosity and trepidation remained, but the war had equipped many Canadians with a sense of the world beyond their hometowns, and critics generally saw this as a positive sign.

In 1947, Arthur Phelps delivered what seemed to be a characteristic declaration of 1950s-style hope and despair. He wanted his audience – a university group in New Brunswick – to ponder some of the irrevocable changes that war had brought. "Ideationally, we are at the very vortex of our contemporary human tension," Phelps suggested. He also acknowledged that Canada and Canadians were a transformed people: "We performed what we called our war effort. We have become a big business concern. Our young people have gone to the far places of the world and come home again. Lifted from their localities, they have also criss-crossed their own country and made discoveries. They have slipped back now to their home places and laid their uniforms aside and they wonder about themselves and the Canada they find."[15] Phelps recognized that the war experience had been an education for many and hoped that citizens could now fix on the task of coping with profound change. Change, he noted, could frequently be attributed to the diffusion of dangerous goods or influences among populations unsure of how to assess their often-concealed qualities. Disastrous change for North America's Native population, Phelps remarked, came in the form of "whiskey and guns and syphilis." Change was a recognized condition of modern life. Yet modern life and its commercialized culture now seemed all the more dangerous to critics because the changes that these brought often made making a living and entertaining oneself seem such a harmless relief after years of wartime concentration. The consequences of common leisuretime choices seemed removed from the choices themselves. "Work out techniques for the universal distribution of the funnies," Phelps added wryly, "and you have psychiatrists and mothers huddling in drawing-rooms at troubled little private meetings and even fathers and Brock Chisholm wondering what in the world is happening to us."[16] Critics believed that Canadians would seek help for the symptoms out of concern for their own well-being, but would they recognize the disease?

While they worried privately about what the future held in store for their families, many Canadians also came out of the war aware that their nation had become more important on the world stage and that it needed to remain so. Even literary types could cautiously admit that a vigorous internationalism might be affecting Canadian literature. Poet A.J.M. Smith suggested that "Canadian literature which formerly aimed to be 'national' is now, here and there at least, taking on a cosmopolitan maturity."[17] The advent of the United Nations Educational, Scientific and Cultural Organization (UNESCO) late in 1945 raised spirits among those in Canada who saw the new internationalism as a civilizing force committed to "the intellectual and moral solidarity of mankind," even though the King government was either reluctant or ill-prepared to participate in it.[18]

Even as they sought a worldly sophistication, advocates of a civilized postwar Canada had to acknowledge the need for economic development. That development, however, also re-emphasized troubling modern tendencies. B.K. Sandwell, a long-time supporter of free enterprise, noted that the drive to compete with one's neighbours had certainly survived, and he remarked: "the world is so much with us that nobody can fail to realize that fact, except perhaps those that are dazzled by the false light of the goddess they worship ... The diseases of the age are worry diseases; the twentieth century is the century of the duodenal ulcer."[19] A return to the genteel ratrace after six years of war was hardly a reward for Canada's youths, and to Sandwell the quest for success, unlike the drive for achievement, seemed highly unnatural:

The 'shades of the prison house' which 'begin to close about the growing boy' are in the main the shadows, not of a struggle for existence, for we do not have to struggle much for existence today – not of a struggle for achievement, which is in accordance with our nature and a source of joy – but of a struggle for success, a struggle to keep up with the Joneses and ahead of the Smiths and not too far behind the Robinsons. I particularly want to stress that this struggle for success has nothing to do with the struggle for achievement. ... [The artist's] desire is to make the kind of music, the kind of picture, the kind of architecture, the kind of engine or machine even, which is the best he is capable of and the fullest expression of himself. That is the struggle for achievement, a great and noble and natural struggle; and in our time it gets sidetracked, before the youth is twenty-one, in favour of the struggle for success, and the result is a divided personality, a schism in the soul, which is fatal to happiness long before the inevitable tragedies of life arrive to darken it.[20]

While he did not advocate the bland security of the socialist state, Sandwell also considered the cult of success a perversion of the individualist ethic and therein as dangerous as socialism. He held up the artist's highly subjective and personal sense of achievement as a model that offered access to a noble set of values, while consumerism gave only temporary satisfaction and fleeting status. This was hardly a call for a new aesthetic elitism, but a warning that fitting into the mass society represented a denial of selfhood. If youths would only recognize – along with the rest of the population – that their daily work and leisure could be expressions of more than getting and spending, the nation as a whole could claim to have forged its own culture.

The promotion of Canadian industrial design combined a desire for aesthetic maturity and cosmopolitanism with the ever-present needs for employment and for practical items such as furniture. Even during wartime, a dull mass-production aesthetic and scant evidence of a design sensibility among Canada's manufacturers prompted some commentators to extol the virtues of a seemingly forgotten craftsmanship. Creativity and the opportunity to exhibit taste in daily living were not only, they argued, for an artistically inclined elite. Later in wartime, critics would argue for the adoption of new materials and production techniques by industrial concerns, so that "there might be some hope for beauty in daily life."[21]

By 1948, the "Design in Industry" exhibition had toured the country, and art and design critic Donald Buchanan, who had spent the previous few years advocating beauty in daily life, praised the National Gallery for initiating a "design index". This was a compendium of international examples from which Canadian designers and manufacturers could draw ideas for new products. Buchanan's stances against unnecessary ornamentation, pointless streamlining, and the defining of design trends by the larger American manufacturers joined other clear calls for Canadians to reclaim this territory for themselves by establishing such facilities as an industrial-design museum.[22] Good design was a counterweight to the necessity of mass production, and the adoption of a design index signalled a move to emulate the seemingly less market-driven standards of Europe. A quiz administered to fair-goers at Toronto's Canadian National Exhibition in 1948 showed them three floor lamps and asked them which they preferred. The experts and most of the respondents chose a functional and graceful lamp that happened to be unavailable in Canada. One observer wondered: "Must we regard it as an axiom that all lamps in Canadian stores are ornate? But then why should this be so?"[23]

However, many critics still perceived Canada as a nation without the history or character – in essence, without the culture – of its older Allies. About a year after the war, social planner Leonard Marsh, virtually a household name after 1943 for his role in advising the Canadian government on social-security policy, took a position at the University of British Columbia. To him, the choice lay between material and spiritual sustenance. He wrote to a friend of the sacrifice that he believed he was making: "I have always wanted to live – for a while, anyway – in this part of the Dominion. It has certain virtues; but you cannot believe how both Betty and I miss the realities and social maturity of Britain and Europe – even if it *is* good to get some food and fuel for a while."[24] Canada represented, as Marsh suggested, food and fuel at a time when both were still rationed in Europe. The sense that the postwar nation could trumpet its material blessings as a middle-sized power hardly constituted a cultural awakening, but such blessings provided a compelling theme for advertisers in the later 1940s. Molson's kept its name in public view with a "Today we live in a Greater Canada" campaign, which highlighted new processes and industries – "New Additions to the Family!" – that had become part of Canada's industrial development since 1945.[25] Not to be outdone, O'Keefe Breweries ran a series of ads celebrating "Canada Unlimited" and produced a book by the same name, pointing to material abundance as well as the abundant possibilities for Canadians and immigrants. The book provided a sketch of Canadian history, paid close attention to how great Canadians had conquered time, space, and other obstacles, and proclaimed the vast – but now vastly more conquerable – wealth of its hinterlands.[26]

Cultural critics could not deny that life on successive and far-flung frontiers had shaped Canadian experience and saw few indications that such an established economic pattern would stop shaping it during the late 1940s. Still, geologist R.C. Wallace predicted a cultural shift away from the exploitation of natural resources as a defining national characteristic. "Canada has been a pioneer," he declared, "and, like all pioneers, has turned her hand to carving out a home for herself from the resources that nature has provided." Wallace turned his attention to cultural matters and ventured that Canada "has as yet not been too greatly concerned with the beauty and refinement of that home, if only she could live in reasonable comfort. That stage should now be over, and the main attention should now be given to the things that endure."[27] More common than Wallace's wish that Canadians would seek beauty and refinement on their own were new variations on an ancient theme: *things* had come to matter more than standards of taste. Although this refrain echoed through the 1950s and beyond, critics began to comment on postwar society's materialistic tendencies even before all the goods had returned to the shelves.[28] Among those who denounced an overly grasping culture, C.J. Eustace unequivocally called the modern world "a chaotic and disordered place, in which men strive blindly for an abundance of life which they never seem to achieve."[29]

On the surface at least, life was better after 1945, but its purpose seemed less apparent to critics who could easily recall the resolve of the war. The fact that most Canadians enjoyed higher standards of living made the task of drawing attention to the allegedly dissolute nature of modern life more difficult. We revisit below the critique of consumerism, but critics found it indispensable to identify consumerism with fleeting rewards. They wrote and spoke of the urge to enjoy prosperity through spending as though they assumed that readers and audiences would be ashamed of acquisitive habits. What he saw as pointless consumption and hedonism alarmed Acadia University's new president, Watson Kirkconnell, who complained that the "masses of mankind in our age have been too preoccupied with the material wealth and industrial achievements of the day to have any philosophy of life at all." As the head of a Baptist institution, Kirkconnell could be expected to place spiritual integrity among the "things that endure" and to assure his audience that eventually, just as "Blomidon will be lost in the waters of Minas,"[30] humanity's earthly wealth would crumble.

In the later 1940s, cultural critics denigrated popular entertainments more directly than they had during the war, when the task of maintaining morale made necessary the presentation of positive plans for reconstruction or the identification of mass manipulation with the enemy. Dr J.M. Ewing, principal of Victoria College in Victoria, British Columbia, commented on some of the more prominent peacetime trends for his 1948 radio series *Our Changing Values*. Ewing professed nothing so forcefully as his belief that "we live today in a world whose social outlines are shadowy and insecure."[31] Dealing during the seven-week series with such topics as the demise of the "kinship group" family, divorce, youth, education, and leisure, Ewing urged his listeners to remember that the issues that he raised had *histories* – that they did not originate in contemporary Canada. He grounded his analysis and prescriptions for a better society, however, in more recent, localized observations. His remarks on leisure, made during the final program, are particularly valuable artifacts of critical concern. His approach also provides an example of the way in which critics began to broadcast their dismay, to make their analysis of the current cultural predicament more accessible to the public.

Admitting that he had "no hope of uncovering any profound truth" about leisure, Ewing none the less intended to "explore its possibilities," and in this spirit his talks ran for only fifteen minutes each. Beginning on an optimistic note, he claimed that the new leisure, no longer a privilege of the rich or even of the moderately well-off professional, had become "leisure for all" thanks to labour-saving devices, which increasing numbers could afford, especially since 1945. After enumerating and classifying some of the uses to which wealthy people had put their leisure in the past, Ewing noted that the wise or constructive use of leisure was hardly the private preserve of an upper class. Historically, he contended, this group had subordinated intellectual and aesthetic pursuits to creature comforts and pleasure, always seeking parity with the "current stereotype" of their own class.[32]

In Ewing's estimation, everyone should pay attention to the way in which the middle and working classes sought to imitate their wealthier neighbours, who themselves had forsaken taste for status. He suggested that middle-class leisure was especially derivative, replacing genuine experience and effort with sensation and consumption: "motor trips take the place of foreign travel; ... and the book-of-the-month is purchased instead of a rare first edition." In turn, working-class leisure seemed a "respectable and rather harmless" imitation of middle-class living standards, even though there had been "no lack of eloquence" on the prospect of the working class's redeeming itself by turning to its own traditions. Working-class leisure, Ewing noted, was doing nothing of the sort. Lowbrow movies and radio programs transcended social distinctions, dominating the common culture, while the "best" material remained hopelessly highbrow. He proposed a twofold solution that aimed at the growing middle classes, in effect admitting that the book of the month was preferable to none at all. It entailed rejuvenating reconstruction-era reform sentiment by reaffirming the school and adult-education commitments to lifelong learning and by bringing mass entertainments up to acceptable standards of taste: "So long as our motion pictures are shoddy and unconvincing, so long as there are radio stations that deluge their listeners with crudities and wise-cracks, so long as magazine illustrations lean more to eroticism than to art, just so long will our aesthetic level put us to shame." Peace and prosperity, Ewing admitted, made the avuncular tone of his commentary on leisure possible.[33] His simple arithmetic, in which bad culture drove out good and an enlightened middle stratum of society could serve as a new audience for "better" works, appealed to others eager to take action against cultural decline.

The attention that critics devoted to the scourge of the "comics" showed another reaction to an environment in which more time and money were available for entertainment. Conservative MP Davie Fulton targeted comics for censorship during 1948–49, and comic magazines, especially those that portrayed criminal activity or gruesome death, brought out a variety of responses from experts and parents. Some reviled the magazines as vulgar, some saw them as just another form of reading material. Federal Justice Minister J.L. Ilsley warned of the difficulty of framing a law that could discriminate between trashy and educational comics (of which a few series existed) and feared that banning such potentially enlightening ones as a "pictorial representation of the murder of Thomas à Becket."[34] Although it arrived too late to contribute meaningfully to the debate, the Canadian Association of Radio and Television Broadcasters found the comics a convenient issue on which to advance its argument that broadcast regulation should be taken out of the hands of the CBC. Rather than advocating censorship of crime comics, the association's member stations began airing *Teen Age Book Parade* in 1952. Hosted by novelist Charles Clay, the program claimed inspiration from such headlines as "Comic Books Help Saboteurs."[35] It also allowed the association to appear as an eager champion of post–Massey Commission cultural uplift by promoting "literature."

Whatever the motivations of its participants, the furor over comic magazines indicated a shift towards a more comprehensive critique of empty leisure and of the decline of cultural effort because critics denounced both the form and the content of contemporary comics. Addressing the form, with tongue only partially in cheek, Mary Lowrey Ross saw comics heralding an "Age of Illiteracy", in which works of fiction would go straight to the movie studios, to be released in "one big overall form for one big overall audience, and no questions asked."[36] Others condemned the content of comic books as hyper-real, claiming that the publications treated subjects that should have been repulsive to any normal person and glorified swift and decisive vengeance against enemies. The Canadian Federation of Home and School drew a direct connection between comics and youth crime and urged the federal government to begin "encouraging the growth of literature that will exalt rather than debase."[37] One worried writer/parent imagined a conversation she might have with her children about the ways comics desensitized them to violence and prevented them from reading "better" literature.[38] The observant comedy duo of Johnny Wayne and Frank Shuster, who consistently straddled the line between jester and conscience, broadcast a sketch in which one comics-addicted youngster spoke remorselessly of having killed his mother and, when later denied his daily dose of illustrated mayhem, suffered from "Disney spells."[39]

Everyday urban life was increasingly fast-paced, and an expanding mass culture had been offering compelling visual stimuli for decades. In the late 1940s, the postwar sense of wonder that Arthur Phelps spoke of in the spring of 1947 met the frustration of cultural critics who recognized that they did not have the power to control the production of those visual stimuli in the same ways that the commercial interests had done. The paradox of this period, however, was that the power to mount a resistance to potentially pernicious cultural trends – if this could be accomplished – lay with the state. Even people supporting attempts to bring a critical agenda to the attention of government reconstruction agencies knew that simply dictating or imposing cultural standards was not likely to create a discriminating public. *Citizens' Forum* broadcast a program on comics early in 1949, and, although participants agreed without reservation that comics were a low form of literature, a ban was out of the question. As one CAAE member noted early in 1949, "we will never become a mature people unless we learn to cope with our social problems as citizens and cease to depend at every turn on drastic government action."[40] It would, however, be only a matter of weeks before significant government attention would be lavished on the arts, letters, and sciences.

THE MASSEY COMMISSION: INVENTORY AND BLUEPRINT

By 1949, Canada had become a nation with one of the world's highest standards of living, and continued economic growth seemed assured. With such fortunate prospects came an ease that would allow for introspection. The sense that an important part of Canada's development had been too long neglected found support in political circles. In April 1949, thanks in large part to the efforts of a sympathetic and influential Liberal minister, Brooke Claxton, the federal government authorized a royal commission to chart a distinctively Canadian cultural course. In creating the Massey Commission, the government did not seem to share T.S. Eliot's opinion that "culture is the one thing that we cannot deliberately aim at."[41]

Just as critics of modern life and mass culture held a range of political views, they held differing estimations of the commission's approach. Some participated in its deliberations and even wrote learned reports for the commission on their particular areas of interest, while others kept their distance, complaining even before the *Report* had been issued that the body had gone too far, or not far enough.⁴² At the outset, however, the commission had a clear mandate to travel the nation hearing submissions from individuals, local, provincial, and national organizations; to report on the state of the arts, letters, and sciences; and, finally, to make recommendations to Parliament on virtually all aspects of culture except religion. This unprecedented attempt to plumb the depths of Canadian tradition and to shape the future brought the issue of cultural *authority* to the fore. Would it be consistent with liberal democracy for a commission to decide what sort of culture Canadians should have? Even if such a decision could be reached, how could this new national culture be made real?

Despite a profusion of "signs that we are passing out of pioneer and colonial conditions and becoming an independent, mature society," one group submitting a brief to the Massey Commission pointed out that the road towards complete independence and maturity would still be a long one. The fatigue and frustration created by the modern environment had forced many ordinary Canadians to "seek escape in mass entertainment which also does nothing to satisfy creative instincts, stimulate the imagination, or cultivate the mind – escapist movies, commercialized radio, primitive music, spectator sports, reading which is anodyne rather than stimulus, and so on. The result is mental and spiritual lethargy, an empty life".⁴³ These strong words exemplified a central theme of the early-1950s' critique of modern life and mass culture: the belief that most people had been drawn away from activities somehow representative of their genuine identities. One group of concerned citizens expressed their shame that Canadian film makers could not (or would not) interpret peacetime reconstruction: "We feel that there is abundant material in Canada to make first rate moving pictures. But when we saw a screen portrayal of the problem of the homecoming soldier was it a soldier in Canadian uniform? No, it was *The Best Years of Our Lives* with Frederick [sic] March and Dana Andrews returning to an American city to start life in the postwar period."⁴⁴ Frustration at the difficulty of convincing Canadians that their daily lives offered them few opportunities to be creative – that their inquisitive and imaginative talents had withered through no fault of their own – motivated a host of groups to suggest remedies via the Massey Commission. These solutions did not include banning mass-produced "popular" entertainments but rather stressed sustaining variety through the encouragement of artistic works and folk traditions outside the commercial mainstream.

Commission chair Vincent Massey and his colleagues received scores of submissions – over 460 in all. These constituted an inventory of the nation's tangible and intangible cultural resources and aimed at improving the access that residents of Canada's communities and regions had to "authentic" experiences such as live theatre, local arts and crafts, galleries, and university education. To characterize those individuals and organizations interested enough in cultural matters to submit a statement as constituting an entirely like-minded elite would be too simplistic. Taken together, the national, provincial, or local arts associations, ethnic groups, unions, trade concerns, and religious denominations offering their advice and experience represented much of the population. Amid the petitions for improvements to local or regional arts, educational, or broadcasting facilities, some briefs called for decreased regulation and declarations that nothing should be forced on a democratic people. Common to these widely varying opinions about the role of the state or the authority of cultural "experts," however, was the notion that certain varieties of culture remained above the sort then dominating the mass market. In a cultural environment that favoured the factory worker who wanted or needed to forget the real world instead of celebrating its beauties or addressing the tribulations of being human, the "liberal humanist"[45] fought an uphill battle.

In general, the organizations itemizing their perceptions of Canada's cultural past and their recommendations for its future addressed particular areas of interest. But behind these more specialized requests for support and changes to policy there lay a dread of artificiality, of appearing to impose an alien set of norms or expectations on a nation that had not long ago submitted gamely to wartime strictures. The Federation of Canadian Artists saw the arts as the "unfolding and evolving expression of the inner consciousness of the individual or society" and predicted grave consequences for any nation that would short-change the "natural development"[46] of its own culture. In answering its own question: "How can Manitoba people most effectively participate in a living and advancing Canadian culture?" one group's brief suggested that citizens' advisory councils be attached to the National Film Board and the CBC to recommend ways those agencies could better reflect the nation's history and diversity in future productions. Yet the idea of "natural development" was a fiction in that citizens who would step forward to serve on such councils tended to be people already involved in arts organizations and committed to at least a rough hierarchy of cultural standards. This assortment of "joiners" appeared before the commission because they refused to let the process of setting priorities for national development in the arts, letters, and sciences be anything less than the realization of a carefully debated consensus. The above-mentioned Manitoba group typified early-1950s' cultural activism by being "interested primarily in the development of the national culture as participants therein, and not in the development of a cultural enclave in Manitoba or in assuming the role of camp-followers or beneficiaries of a cultural development whose real centres and life are considered to be external to our own activities and interests."[47] During one hearing, a member of a university women's group in Regina suggested that any advisory board set up to monitor broadcasting should include supporters of soap operas, just as it should have people of different ages and religious backgrounds. This display of equanimity clearly caught Vincent Massey by surprise, and he remarked: "That is a very interesting suggestion – official defence of soap operas."[48]

Because an "occasion" such as the Massey Commission could draw greater-than-average community interest to the debate about cultural infrastructure it acquired an air of democracy, but the issues themselves remained on the surface rather peripheral to the average Canadian's concerns. Academics or artists made their presence felt through briefs and at public hearings because they could devote time and energy to fight for the preservation of what painter Charles Comfort called "those conditions which promote and support democratic 'spiritual' welfare." Comfort admitted that "the individual and institutional liberties implied in western democracy are understood by nearly all of us," but he cautioned his comrades in concern that the modern cultural system operated to restrict creative and "active" leisure, and he advised them: "Let us not forget that the welfare of the human spirit, and its freedom, is above all a supreme responsibility." With this task in mind, Comfort could see no real alternative to state involvement in cultural affairs – involvement that would allow for a diversified common culture unrestricted by what commercial radio or the local movie house offered. He hoped that an "instrument for assisting and developing the arts may be set up in Canada" along the path that Britain had followed, because he was certain that such an undertaking would play a "useful if not vital part in our spiritual regeneration."[49]

Commentators believed that this regeneration would not be a matter of allowing Canadians to sit back and soak up "culture." It would have to involve, as the Saskatchewan Arts Board's brief suggested, an acknowledgment of the many activities competing for even the rural resident's attention. "There are in many small communities, and many a side-road, talents, sensibilities and imaginings that are, or may become, the stuff of a vigorous cultural life," its brief noted wistfully. Yet current realities could not be discounted: "There are in this country people of many backgrounds and traditions, and there are none of us in Canada who have not felt the force of new and varied experiences. Out of this complex of tradition and new experience Canadians will have to create their cultural expression."⁵⁰ Under the rather ambitious heading of "means of improving the mind and increasing standards of social living," the Canadian Federation of Home and School included some of the demanding and clearly wide-ranging possibilities: "Lecture courses and classes in literature, languages, art, music, debating, dramatics, citizenship, the meaning and aims of democracy, growth of character, family and personal relationships, sex education, thrift, safety, handicrafts, etc."⁵¹ The unfulfilled promise of the community-centre curriculum lived on as well in proposals to solidify the position of the local library as a cultural hub.⁵² Without the germ of community that such venues offered, budding artists, writers, or musicians would be isolated, which could slow development of a national sense of cohesion. In the absence of a self-sustaining community of writers, for example, observers believed that reaching a certain level of literary achievement in Canada would prove difficult, and catching up with the reputation of Canadian notables in other fields would be less likely. The Canadian Authors Association remarked flatly that "the inarticulate nature of the average Canadian's patriotism results from the lack of a native literature commensurate with Canada's physical, industrial, scientific and academic stature, and with the proved character of its people."⁵³

In the majority of briefs and memoranda to the commission, the broadcast media and how to manage them rated at least some mention. For many of these respondents, the CBC emerged as another foundation of cultural improvement – an essential source of inspiration in communities too small or isolated to sustain much of an arts life. Pointing to the anticipated advent of frequency-modulation (FM) stations, one observer held up the prospect of "many more regional stations so that schools, universities, and even community centres may be granted operating rights."⁵⁴ In assessing broadcasting's potential for either providing or hindering access to a variety of perspectives and influences, critics tended to look to the CBC as a force that could mitigate the influence of commercial broadcasting. The corporation's policy of presenting programing of interest to the minority listener and to Canada's thinly-distributed population harmonized with their idea of cultural democracy. The American example of commercial radio, in contrast, indicated an attenuation of options for listeners and led one group to ask the rhetorical question: "Where is the 'Great Plays' series that used to be heard on N.B.C. on Sundays; where is the 'Columbia Workshop' on C.B.S. that produced [Norman] Corwin and other creative writers and artists?"⁵⁵ The big U.S. networks had abandoned such shows or moved them to times on the schedule for which they could not command the highest advertising rates. On private radio in Canada, too, the prime listening periods had (d)evolved to maximize revenue. Listeners took notice, ascribing more than offences against good taste to programs such as "Gangbusters – Superman – The Fat Man – Counterspy etc. These latter types of program teach of a world where physical force and brutality are the normal. They never admit desirable social forces, the fine arts, or normal human relations. This is destructive education. Thousands of dollars of school, social welfare and police effort must be used to neutralize the results."[56]

As well as representing the taxpayer, those who answered the commission's call for input also claimed to speak for a kind of silent army fed up with the lowbrow moneymakers crowding out less "popular" fare. Critics saw this restless segment of the public as relatively powerless in comparison to the mass-culture producer's image of the typical listener, reader, or moviegoer. The neglected group comprised the "many many reticent and unassuming citizens who are not often heard from, and would, I am certain, not want fine music and drama lost to soap operas, degenerate crime stories and the commercial hucksters."[57] By imputing a latent distrust of mass culture to the average citizen, critics committed to helping that same average citizen steadily improve his or her cultural surroundings also expressed their belief that all that people needed was variety. Some respondents to the commission, however, could claim to serve the public interest even as they served their own. Town Meeting Ltd produced a radio program called *Town Meeting*, which bore an uncanny resemblance to the American *Town Meeting of the Air* and preceded *Citizens' Forum* to air in Canada. In their brief, the program's producers made no apologies for presenting their itinerant forum over commercial radio. They had identified a show format that could draw a profitable audience and advertisers, but they also saw this venture as lending their brief and its primary message – freedom for the private broadcaster – an aura of propriety. Without portraying their audience as an elite, they pointed to a pool of people willing to become involved in community affairs without a lot of official prodding: "democracy depends on an informed minority. The kind of people who listen to *Town Meeting* are people who want to know the facts. They listen partly because of entertainment and partly because they want to make up their minds on what is true and wise."[58] In that he possessed the ability and interest to choose a stimulating program, *Town Meeting*'s model listener – like the "reticent and unassuming" citizens that arts groups invoked – was Everyman, but not just anyone.

Numerous emissaries to the Massey Commission believed that it should be the state's role to represent minority tastes and thus guarantee some variation from the broader North American cultural pattern.

Anthropologist Marius Barbeau sought preservation of Canada's folk heritage and saw Canadians' own stories as fundamental to the construction of a new identity. The continuous provision of opportunities to see and learn about fellow citizens, their daily lives, and their distinctive qualities, he believed, "would lead, in a very few years, to progress beyond reckoning. It would also bring to Canadians a cultural unity which it lacks when its attainments are only derivative and reminiscent of other lands and past ages."[59] Drama professor Emrys Jones issued a similar appeal for domestic, rather than foreign, dramatic art. In his estimation, any reinvention of cultural infrastructure should attempt to match the enthusiasm for amateur theatre, much of which he perceived to be at a novice level, with money to keep potential playwrights and actors in Canada. As matters stood in 1949, Jones saw companies performing the "older classics, foreign experimental plays, and modern 'hits' from Broadway, Hollywood or the West End of London, while Canadian manuscripts find grudging performances only through special awards for their production."[60] Such incentives to homegrown artists, however, became the legacy of the commission through the Canada Council after its formation in 1957.

Developments in the cultural and educational spheres troubled cultural critics deeply during the early 1950s. The Massey Commission appeared a step towards preserving what Raymond Williams has called the "great tradition," a tradition that "is itself always in danger of being vulgarized when it is confined to a minority culture."[61] Indeed, several commentators made this same distinction, asking that the outcome of the commission not be a rigorous set of rules about culture, because the great tradition was organic and able to subsume worthwhile works regardless of their origins. Others noted the positive role that immigrants could play in diversifying and enlivening Canada's cultural landscape if the principles of "cultural democracy" were followed.[62] Keeping the field open to a broad range of influences complemented those principles, but, given the way that the entertainment business worked, safeguarding variety and helping Canadian firms compete with their larger American counterparts would require some intervention.[63]

The sense that Canadians needed some form of guided regeneration did not vanish when the commission disbanded. Champions of a homegrown spiritual rebirth, whether they worked within the commission or alongside it, continued to see decay in every crooner and comic book and to despair more vocally of the social patterns – the conditions of modern life – that reinforced what they saw as the numbing existence of the average person. As patron of a formal bout of self-examination, the state assumed an unprecedented role in promoting the critics' understanding of what constituted worthwhile entertainment. It also furthered an interpretation of cultural democracy that emphasized the protection of minority tastes and aimed to inculcate a sense of popular guilt for not living up to them. Having taken on the question of Canada's cultural structure and prospects, the Massey Commission drew additional critical attention to the exigencies of contemporary society and to mass culture's seeming inability to engage difficult themes or address contemporary social concerns. The high profile, even notoriety, of the commission meant that the early 1950s provided more frequent occasion for critics to dismiss much of their environment as oblivious to the age-old questions that they believed must animate any culture worth having. In suggesting solutions to the problem of culture in a rapidly modernizing nation, critics acknowledged the accelerated rhythms of modern life as both context and cause for concern and named mass culture as an obstacle to individuals' fuller understanding of their responsibilities and opportunities in the social and cultural spheres.

CLASSIFYING CULTURE AT MID-CENTURY

The same month that the Massey Commission came into being, American critic Milton Klonsky published an article on mass culture in *Partisan Review*, the leftist journal especially vigorous during the 1940s in its attacks on commercial, or "low" culture.[64] In arguing that "comic strips, pulp fiction, movies, radio serials, commercial jazz and the rest are a direct result of modern technology and public education," Klonsky could not conceal his disgust at the way in which presumably beneficial causes had had such regrettable effects. He went on to shudder at the momentum and appeal of these entertainments. "Whether we choose to dignify these products by the name of Art is a semantic problem – what is central is that they usurp the functions of traditional art in setting the styles, the manners, the images, the standards and the goals of life for millions, almost as though they were the organs of an un-official state religion." He also noted the scope of mass or "popular" culture's appeal, declaring that "this sub-culture is wide enough to include the millionaire and the dime-store clerk, the President of the United States and the Negro sharecropper, the old and the young, in a truly classless and democratic consonance of spirit."[65]

Like Klonsky, Canadian cultural critics noted the power and the subtlety of mass culture and envied its apparent equability. They were aware too of how difficult it might be to achieve a "classless and democratic consonance of spirit" in Canada by merely asking an already motivated and interested segment of the population to report on the arts, letters, and sciences. The Massey Commission's inventory of educational, artistic, and scientific resources would be, the commissioners hoped, a spur to cultural nationalism, in that it would help identify, reward, and make examples of Canadians contributing to their particular fields of endeavour. But outside the confines of the commission and its quest to improve both infrastructure and attitude, cultural critics observed that most people did not know or did not care about how society and culture operated to marginalize alternatives to mass taste. Conformity, consumerism, and "empty" leisuretime activities became a part of the larger discourse on public affairs thanks in some measure to the creation of a government organization for perceiving and working to change the texture of Canadian cultural life.

In 1949, another American critic reintroduced a way of classifying cultural activity that had been prevalent during the 1920s – highbrow, lowbrow, and middlebrow.[66] Russell Lynes's revival of "brow" theory came not a moment too soon for Massey watchers, and a number of Canadian commentators adopted it. It was certainly possible to be conspicuously highbrow in post-1945 Canada, and around the time of the first commission hearings one art enthusiast warned against the dismissal of amateur attempts at creativity. "The art life of a country is weak when there is only passive consumption of works of art," Harold King wrote, adding that "the art life of a country is strongest when large numbers of people are active and producing, whether they give their whole time to it or not."[67] King's comments echoed the creed of the community-centre movement, which emphasized full participation in the planning, operation, and use of local facilities.

Of the reconstruction-era programs, community centres remained the most vital in the Massey years and indeed benefited from something of a revival of interest in their potential as local headquarters for whatever cultural development projects might arise from the commission.[68] Those who despaired that Canada had become too centralized – too much an urban country to go back to the land – considered improved rural access to cultural resources especially important. M.B. Mecredy sang the praises of the rural life but realized that it must take on some of the "better" attributes of town life if young people were to risk settling beyond suburbia. Even if local, provincial, or federal authorities could improve transportation facilities and take up his suggestions to improve cultural opportunities and education in rural areas, town youths were rarely game to leave urban comforts. This fact was for Mecredy all the more regrettable because "the hurly-burly of the fiercely competitive life of a business man, or the financial worries of a salaried man in the city has perhaps made him older physically than he would have become, living a country life." Recognizing that he had perhaps overestimated the harmful physical effects of city life on the average person, Mecredy none the less remained firm in his belief that the urban grind "has at any rate robbed him early of the mental and spiritual zest which were once his."[69]

To many observers, urban dwellers presented themselves as anxious and, harried to begin with, and tension over the new "cold" war only subjected them to an additional worry. From the end of the Second World War, but especially after the Soviet Union's successful test detonation of an atomic bomb in 1949, anxiety over the destructive potential of this terrifying class of weapon had been an element of North American life. In Canada, initial reactions to the atomic age were mixed. The *Montreal Standard* ran an "Atomic Age" essay contest, and many optimists dreamed of unlimited "clean" power and great leaps forward in technology.[70] Some more pessimistic sorts, both rural and urban, joined in worry over the consequences of misusing such power and hoped to press their own agendas home. C.J. Eustace intoned gravely that "the smell of the final cataclysm is now in the air."[71] The topic also prompted some nervous satire and some radio dramas with post-apocalyptic themes, although the mid-1950s would bring still more of this material.[72] The Atomic Age had brought with it a new kind of fear and a new wariness of what the University of Alberta's C.R. Tracy called humankind's "doubtful blessing."[73] The milestone of the world's reaching mid-century in one piece also meant that in mid-century retrospectives speakers and writers found a convenient occasion for reflection.[74] For cultural critics taking this opportunity, the first half of the twentieth century hardly seemed a story of unrelenting progress. For some, the contemporary scene represented an almost irremediable loss of control. Owing to its particular emphasis on the intertwined problems presented by modern life and mass culture, one source is worth examining at greater length.

Broadcast on New Year's Day 1950 and based on a series of articles published concurrently in *Maclean's* magazine by such observers as playwright and broadcaster Lister Sinclair and American media expert Gilbert Seldes, George Salverson's *In the Shadow of the Bomb* was a radio retrospective of the preceding fifty years. Resembling Sinclair's works of the 1940s, such as *A Play on Words* (1944), Salverson's piece was a gem of cultural criticism geared towards a middlebrow audience considered receptive to digests and dramatizations of history. It offered intelligent but, above all, intelligible commentary. Featuring a cameo appearance from University of Chicago Chancellor Robert Hutchins with his list of the ten most important people of the first half of the century, the program noted, as Sinclair's article had, the over-arching role of science in shaping history since 1900. Along with whimsical and prophetic looks at Canada in 1990 – where almost minute-to-minute inflation would drive up the prices of all the fantastic inventions that science had wrought – the piece featured sombre reflections on the carnage of two world wars. As promised in the program's title, the atomic threat did not go unacknowledged: "Now ... as science itself throws a shadow ... how well do we see? What are our moralities, our motives, our knowledge of ourselves and our time, as we are hurtled forward into the years of appalling climax and decision?"[75]

In attempting to increase "knowledge of ourselves and our time," one pivotal section of *In the Shadow of the Bomb* provided a biting critical account of the symbiotic rise of technology and mass culture. Admitting that the previous half-century had seen marvellous advances in such fields as transportation, medicine, and communications, the program's Narrator (played by Lorne Greene) declared: "In this world of 1950 there is almost nothing which is not the work of science, and the prestige of science is so great that almost nothing can succeed without it." The cultural impact of science, however, was best illustrated in what scientific progress had done to the rhythms of work life and leisure. Earning six dollars a week for fifty-seven hours of work, the labourer of 1900 could not approach the standard of living enjoyed by his 1950 counterpart, who took home $44 after a forty-hour week. By extension, Henry Ford and his disciples were responsible for the process by which the "mass-produced Model T, rattling over the roads of the world, led us to the glittering fantastic world of mass-produced entertainment!" In making possible the reproduction and transmission of identical performances, science "swept away the vaudeville acrobats, and jazzed out of hearing the dreadfully polite English comedy ... It's a wild, mechanized dance of the arts that begins with a nickleodeon, and ends with a flourish in a television set!"[76]

Having made this initial connection between science and the mechanization of cultural production, the Narrator met a character called the Showman, who professed and demonstrated an intimate knowledge of the modern entertainment industry's inner workings:

SHOWMAN: Mechanized labor produced leisure. Mechanized entertainment was created to occupy that leisure.
NARRATOR: That's neat.
SHOWMAN: Perhaps too pat.
NARRATOR: But it explains many things.
SHOWMAN: Yes it does. One thing it hasn't answered.
NARRATOR: Whether mass-produced entertainment means you must accept shoddy goods, along with the first rate?
SHOWMAN: Who can answer that? Who wants to? It gives us something pleasant to fight about, for a change.[77]

Salverson's formula of mechanization = mechanized entertainment came from the pen of the venerable American media analyst and critic Gilbert Seldes – who owed some of his insight to the inspiration of Theodor Adorno and Max Horkheimer.[78] However, Salverson, speaking through the Showman, had mixed feelings about mass culture and about efforts such as the newly embarked Massey Commission. The three final salvos of the above exchange were his and indicate that he found the question of mass entertainment's right to exist not only moot, but impossible to resolve and prone to elitist bias. Still, Salverson appreciated the opportunity to ask such questions and approved of the fact that Canadians could discuss the nation's cultural life in a more formal way via the commission's hearings.

In addition to fielding requests for performing-arts facilities and university improvements, the commission would find itself in a position not unlike that of the "great books" pedlar, though much less likely to recoup its investment. By 1950, the problem of sponsoring access to – or *distributing* via the mass media – what Salverson called "first rate" goods seemed to be no longer a debasement of the classics, but a symptom of the limited options open to those committed to minority rights within a cultural democracy. Not surprisingly, the commission's hearings dwelled on broadcasting, attempting to determine how to represent the cultural interests of Canadians who were not well served by fare in the commercial mainstream.

Mass distribution, the Showman concluded, was not entirely an evil thing. It had, after all, allowed such worthy productions as Laurence Olivier's *Hamlet* to be screened in places where stage productions of the play simply would not go, such as the fictitious Tank Town, Saskatchewan, where the prompter had been the star of previous local theatrical efforts. The Showman lauded the ability of the newer media to bring the best to communities either poorly situated or unable to afford more traditional means of experiencing great art: "Quality ... that's what mass-produced entertainment gave to Joe Public." Despite its multitude of entertaining options, the majority of the fare available owed its familiarity, and hence its popularity, to what the Showman called "the creation of an appetite." He confided that "to be successful, the manufacturers of the entertainment have to go even further. They've got to create the appetite. By creating a habit."[79]

The Showman also suggested that the consequences of creating leisuretime habits could be more grave than a parade of worthless movies. "Give the people what they want," he noted, "and make the people want whatever you give them" was the paradox on which the entertainment industry turned. Although the Narrator agreed that some of the industry's output was excellent, he knew that giving the people what they wanted "must mean more to our peculiar age than merely the happy distribution of art forms and casual diversion." The more profound effects of mass-produced entertainment, the Showman replied, would eventually be demonstrated in "the kind of people we have in this world ... who will have to solve some mighty tricky problems." Cultural products that did not exercise the audience's critical faculties would not equip that audience for the demands and mounting responsibilities of a "peculiar age." The studios would continue to produce films geared to adolescents, even though audiences would go to more sophisticated productions such as *Lost Weekend* and *Death of a Salesman* when such pieces were produced. As the Showman pointed out, "It isn't that people yearn for misery ... they want something true, and intelligent, said about their own lives." However keenly moviegoers might have longed to have entertainment provide answers to their personal crises, another observer complained that the movies none the less tended to standardize taste on a "vulgar level" and declared: "If Hollywood standards are low and false, so are those of the general public; and it is the latter, and not the former, which we should be concerned with changing."[80]

Although it would not arrive for another two years, journalists and potential critics certainly spotted television on the horizon.[81] The Showman hoped fondly that the new medium would affect the general public's tastes in a salutary way, by combining the artistic potential of film with the ability of radio to convey truth. He thought it more likely that each medium's less salutary qualities would emerge, mainly because precedents for the their trivialization and commercialization had already been set: "while movies have been busy running away from reality, radio has had to be a salesman to keep going."[82] The Narrator wondered what would happen if, like movies and radio, television's potential were restricted "to serving only the rudimentary appetites of the audience?" Salverson argued for a culture – and for cultural industries – that took a variety of tastes into account, including those of the minority. Catering to a notion of what the public wanted based on what it had been given in the past would not do. It seemed that the social and political stakes were a good deal higher in 1950, as the Narrator went on to inquire: "What will happen if they forget that, in a democratic society, there are not only many kinds of people, but that every human being has many interests and curiosities and desires ... and the function of a mass medium is to satisfy as many as possible?" He declared also that when entertainment represents or caters to a broader spectrum of interests and tastes it "cuts across the lines of highbrow and lowbrow, it helps people to grow up, to become citizens in a world of conflict, and complete individuals, not mindless robots in a dense mass waiting for the next dictator."[83]

Owing partly to Cold War anxiety and partly to memories of a conflict hardly five years over, the fear of an extended cultural adolescence for Canada moved critics to support the Massey Commission's overall motive – the development of "spiritual resources, which are less tangible but whose importance needs no emphasis."[84] In looking to an elevated common culture as essential to the achievement and maintenance of a national identity, critics had to determine which aspects of mass culture might affect that project. Approaches differed. Attempts such as Salverson's to distil wisdom about the ways in which mass entertainment affected and even attenuated the citizen's ability to exercise the democratic franchise sought a broad audience. Preaching directly to those whom he identified as intellectuals, Albert Shea, who would also eventually produce a layman's guide to the Massey Report, urged those "who would like more people to share their interest in certain ideas and principles" to put aside disdain for the canasta-playing masses and "go to them where they are." Shea insisted that there was a great need for "creative middlemen" who could translate or essentialize "the ideas we consider important," and he described the chief function of the effective intellectual: "He must be constantly dramatizing the battle for freedom, equality, creative living and international understanding. He must spell out his lesson in terms of personalities, human drama, action, of battles fought and won with the pen, the test-tube and the tractor."[85]

Finding ways to interest the average person in such lofty subjects often seemed like an exercise in marketing. As director of the Canada Foundation, identifying philanthropic individuals willing to finance the promotion of Canadian culture, Walter Herbert had indulged in a bit of marketing himself by the early 1950s. Despite his known connections to the incumbent federal Liberals, he was somewhat wary of the government's interest in cultural matters.[86] Part of his job, however, involved keeping abreast of any new publications, especially if they could be used to raise awareness among Canadians of their own folkways and the nation's newfound international stature.

By the time he crossed paths with Herbert in 1950, publisher Joseph Pollick had put out three issues of his *Canadian Life* – a project that Herbert assumed had folded, joining ill-starred and self-consciously literary periodicals of the postwar years such as *Reading* and *Here and Now*. Even though he wrote to Herbert, figurative cap in hand, to drum up some publicity for the magazine or possibly secure the Canada Foundation's endorsement, Pollick attributed what limited success his magazine had achieved to a middlebrow strategy of discussing "Arts without being 'arty' and to present the Humanities without being a soap-box or a pulpit." To him, the arts and humanities were indispensable elements of a democratic society, but he recognized a need to make them part of an entertaining package on the newsstand – i.e., part of leisuretime life. In an obviously ill-considered attempt to reassure Herbert that his publication's motives were pure, Pollick admitted: "to this end, when we do employ 'cheesecake', the fact that the woman is fully clothed only serves to enhance a man's thoughts; he might then conceivably read the Universal Declaration of Human Rights if it happens to be in the same issue."[87]

Like the wily publisher, critics knew what sold magazines. Harold Innis worked some of his communications theory into an essay that he called a "footnote" to the Massey Report, arguing that newspaper and magazine monopolies were involved in "a continuous, systematic, ruthless destruction of elements of permanence essential to cultural activity. The emphasis on change is the only permanent characteristic."[88] The media and cultural industries, Innis suggested, prevented the citizen from forming enduring links with his or her community and its culture by not challenging his or her intellect. Again, much like Gilbert Seldes, Innis believed that technology and mass production had cultural consequences, one of which was the debasement of literature: "Cheap supplies of paper produce pulp and paper schools of writing, and literature is provided in series, sold by subscription, and used as an article of furniture."[89] The number of printed works in circulation had increased dramatically, but much of this output appeared to neglect the world's, the nation's, and the individual's problems, both chronic and newly arrived.

CRITIQUES OF MODERN LIFE AND MASS CULTURE: THE 1950S

The three themes of conformity, consumerism, and emptiness permeated the critique of modern life and mass culture by the mid-1950. In the midst of what appeared to be a stable domestic environment, critics justified their alarm by pointing to the presence of all three factors in Canadian society and to the resulting absence of leadership and excellence. As much as they might have hoped that Canadians would act as individuals, critics began to speak more frequently and disapprovingly of a mass society whose members lacked the self-awareness and confidence necessary for a realistic assessment of their surroundings. Modern education, mass communications, materialism, and scientism, they argued, had subverted the reconstruction-era dream of developing responsible citizens, and the apparent hedonism of the 1950s compounded fears of a generation ever more incapable of appreciating its rich heritage. As this section seeks to show, for cultural critics the reconstruction-era ideal of reponsible citizenship (our first topic) had fallen prey to progressive education (according to Hilda Neatby), to an isolating affluence (*Crestwood Heights*), and to a bitter divide between the sciences and the humanities.

The Impossibility of Responsible Citizenship

By the time the Massey Commission disbanded, the state's strategy for the arts, broadcasting, research, and postsecondary education included unprecedented plans for funding academics, for exposing Canadians to "higher" cultural forms, and for preserving local and regional folkways wherever possible. One early success, though aided immeasurably by the expertise and prestige of noted British director Tyrone Guthrie, was the inauguration of a permanent Shakespearean stage at Stratford, Ontario.[90] For many cultural critics, triumphs such as the Stratford Festival were welcome developments, but hardly meant that they could – or that they wished to – abdicate their role as interpreters and consciences. Some believed that the state's more overt involvement in culture, via the Massey Commission, brought about what writer Hugh Garner called a "planted misconception" that the life of the mind in Canada had suddenly fallen under eminently capable stewardship.[91]

Far better, some said, to continue local efforts with "lecturers and teachers who are well trained, interesting and enthusiastic"[92] than to expect too much of an unwieldy national plan pitched too high, too soon. Defining its needs in terms of its largely female constituency, the Canadian Association of Consumers declared that "culture includes education for citizenship, and education in modern economics as it affects the home is very necessary now." Holding people's attention while helping them cope more effectively with a fast-paced world seemed more important here than helping them become film scholars: "Women want films depicting various aspects of consumer education, presented in informative, practical, interest-holding (entertaining if possible) ways, such as up-to-date information on good buying habits for textiles, clothing, meats, fruits and vegetables, household appliances, etc."[93]

Whatever their opinion of the federal government's visible hand, critics still behaved as though the vast public would not sense its own enslavement to modern rhythms and a commodified culture. Indeed, one well-researched aspect of Canadian thought in the 1950s has been economic historian Harold Innis's interest in communications technologies, particularly their subtly transformative social and cultural implications. Before his death in 1952, the final pieces of work that Innis produced were not revisions of his early ideas on the cod fisheries or the fur trade, but probing explanations of how culture was intertwined with the ways information and abstract ideas reached or did not reach the public. Although Marshall McLuhan's fame as an outspoken observer of such phenomena and popularizer of media studies would peak in the mid-1960s, Innis's probings profoundly influenced McLuhan's work during the 1950s.[94]

During the half-dozen years following the Massey Commission, critical attention to modern life – especially to more recent developments such as television and their capacity to aid or to impede self-improvement – became more pronounced. In drafting a document calling for broader access to the arts, artist Lawren Harris seized on the words of American author Alan Valentine, who perceived a great gap between the sort of culture that democracies had spawned and the type that they might achieve. Valentine wrote: "Until the common man personally confronts the magnitude of the duties he has assumed; until he insists upon quality in cultural as well as political leadership and therefore [in] himself, the practise of democracy will belie his promise." Littering his own declaration of faith, "Democracy and the Arts," with such exhortations to assume responsibility for elevating cultural standards, Harris expressed his belief that the masses could and should somehow be rescued, one at a time if necessary, from the grip of an "inexhaustible" supply of "pin-up girls, coca-cola virgins [and] boogie-woogie."[95] As Paul Rutherford has observed, with the introduction of television in 1952 Canadian commentators looked south to Americans' early experience with the new medium and tended to magnify the most alarming trends that they saw, even as they recognized TV's educational potential.[96]

Because such humanmade improvements to the material world and an advancing standard of living could have positive cultural effects, advocates of cultural improvement wanted to take advantage of the technological benefits of rapid change without becoming complacent about moral and aesthetic standards. Speaking to a group gathered for the purpose of gazing into "Canada's Tomorrow," McMaster University President G.P. Gilmour said that it was possible to accept new comforts while at the same time staying in touch with proven values. "Between the rosy optimism of those who foresee constant improvement of living standards and leisure and the pessimism of those who fear that man will become the slave of his own inventions," he reckoned, "there is certainly some middle path, which cannot be anticipated as inevitable but can be strenuously sought after as a duty and a possibility." The ideal citizens for "Canada's Tomorrow" would be, in Gilmour's estimation, "not leisured morons, living by push-button techniques while starving in mind and soul, but citizens of a free state, living by great ideals and exemplifying sturdy virtues".[97]

Those ideals certainly formed part of the original *Citizens' Forum* mandate late in wartime, but by 1953 that program's organizers had made some decisions about the sort of citizen that could reasonably be expected to follow the show. Responding to suggestions that their weekly offering was "too difficult and demands a degree of concentration and attention that the average listener is unwilling or unable to give," Isabel Wilson noted that there had been little demand for change from active participants and that "any attempt at 'mass' appeal would involve not only a different range of topics, but a drastic change in their presentation, both on the air and in the discussion material." She indicated that the whole apparatus was geared towards at least middle-brow abilities and interests when she acknowledged that there had been "no effort to plan for listeners with perhaps no more than an elementary school education."[98] Certainly no obstacles stood in front of anyone wishing to organize or join a local forum, but Wilson made no apologies for asking listeners to expect a certain level of competence and dedication from themselves and their fellow forum members. Weightier questions, such as "Has Canada a cultural future of her own?"; "What do we want from the CBC?"; "Is the city destroying our pioneer virtues?"; "What do we want from Canadian Television?"; and "The Church, Social Centre or Spiritual Community?" continued to dominate the program's schedule.[99]

Hilda Neatby on Modern Education

In view of the population bulge hitting the elementary schools about 1952–53, one of the earliest and most illustrative examples of cultural criticism arising in the wake of the Massey Commission had to do, quite appropriately, with how children were being educated and how their education could be expected to serve them as adults. Liberated from her duties with the commission, Professor Hilda Neatby took on the rather inexact sciences of pedagogy and child psychology, arguing as she had in previous years that "progressive" education as practised in Canada did not challenge children in the ways that they should.[100] Published in 1953, her indictment of Canada's educational system, *So Little for the Mind*, brought few new complaints to the table. Its chief villain seemed at first to be John Dewey, whose thought had been a profound influence on education and on its experts, especially during the generation preceding the 1950s.[101]

So Little for the Mind did not blame Dewey for the degraded state of education but rather cast stones at the vogue of his teachings and variations on them.[102] Neither Neatby nor the progressive educators whom she considered Dewey's disciples fully understood his educational philosophy, which James Kloppenberg argues had been "so distorted by generations of well-meaning but ill-equipped educational administrators that its original significance has been almost entirely lost." Indeed, in describing Dewey's assessment of the effects of modern life, Kloppenberg reveals a philosophy not far from that of cultural critics interested in allowing Canadians to exercise a latent curiosity: "Before the urban and industrial revolutions flattened children's experience at home, Dewey wrote, every day raised a multitude of questions about man's relation to nature and the individual's relation to those around him, questions that grew from children's experiences and could often be answered by their own independent investigations and encounters."[103]

Regardless of Dewey's original intentions, Neatby despaired that putting the student first – the progressive educators' accepted practice – had been a dangerous concession to modern psychological theories. Without some challenging standards and difficult tests at which children risked failure, she reasoned, "self-centred little automatons" would emerge from schools by the thousand. The desire to channel pupils only towards those subjects that they could master without much effort – and those that would translate directly into careers – infuriated Neatby. "Who is so bored and boring as a self-centred person?" she asked, and she supplied an answer: "Who is so happy and so free as the one whose pleasures and interests reach outward?"[104]

Neatby's complaints were hardly tentative responses to brand new problems, and she was hardly alone in her advocacy of liberal education as a way of equipping children for an adult world that, unlike the school experience, had seemed to become less forgiving. In 1941, Edward McCourt's satire of the educational system featured a utopian school-house that offered fantastic solutions to keenly felt problems such as the tendency to conform. This ideal school would pay dividends for the student "because he must now rely upon himself and not upon the herd for entertainment, he is able to develop a quality which our generation has almost completely lost – that of Self-sufficiency."[105] Worried that Canadian youths would never become culturally self-sufficient, Neatby "reached outward" to link arms with foreigners such as T.S. Eliot, Robert Hutchins, Sir Richard Livingstone and Sir Walter Moberly, all of whom, she believed, resented the untempered pragmatism of the Deweyites.[106] She also enlisted the views of like-minded Canadians, some of whom, such as McCourt, had been vocal on the subject even during wartime. These others had condemned educators for cheating students by allowing "the edge to be taken off their naturally keen minds with radio and movies"[107] or prefigured Neatby's tirade by complaining that progressive education ignored common sense and produced "shallow, unindustrious, pleasure-seeking, aggressive, and undisciplined people."[108] Arthur Lower's dismissal of the contemporary North American educational system as "highly utilitarian," and seemingly more so in Canada than in the United States, led him to conclude in 1948 that unless the gap between the truly "educated" – i.e., the beneficiaries of a liberal education – and the mass could be eliminated, Canadian schools would "always turn out a good many brilliant misfits and countless dull people who fit in all too well."[109] Business writer J.J. Brown warned that materialism had made the educational system an empty vocational exercise for many and had all but banished the idea of a "trained mind" attuned to such lofty ideals as " 'truth for its own sake', 'work for the fun of it', 'the instinct of craftsmanship', 'pride of accomplishment', and so on."[110] There existed pockets of tolerance, even support, for the newer methods. These recognized the stiff competition offered by radio, television, movies, and parental pressure on children to be socially successful. "That the latter pressure is translated by most children into an injunction to be popular with their peers rather than to make high grades," wrote one moderate, "is not surprising in a world where adult desires for status have often taken the place of pleasures and achievement, as goals to be aimed at."[111]

Although her own opinions did not define a critical consensus or chart a new course for Canadian educators, the significance of Neatby's work lies chiefly in her conviction that she was exposing a misguided group of experts who had managed, despite their democratic rhetoric, only make the various provincial educational systems training grounds for a dull acquiescence with the social status quo. Her critique of progressivist education was at bottom a critique of modern life, especially of such factors as its "theoretical exclusion of dogmatic morality; of the neglect and scorn of the intellect which results from pseudo-democratic equalitarianism; of the success-happiness fallacy; of the blind faith in scientific techniques and mass operations." Her proposed remedy included, along with a renewal of faith, nothing less than the "re-definition of democracy in terms of freedom and a return to the habitual and deliberate contemplation of greatness." Neatby believed that the modern educational establishment had jettisoned greatness and achievement in favour of social adjustment and success. The final aspect of her plan for reconstructing civilization seemed tailor-made for the flush 1950s; it was not the "futile" restoration of some bygone age but "a just appreciation at once of the uses and abuses of material comfort and well-being, a constant awareness that although scarcity may ruin health and happiness, abundance is no guarantee of either."[112]

Of course, the depth of Neatby's conviction could not guarantee that her contemporaries would agree with her assessments of education or of the larger society. In fact, one observer who advocated a middle way portrayed the historian and her antagonists as uncompromising partisans in what had become an intense debate during the winter of 1953–54.[113] Though somewhat alarmed at her conservatism, Neatby's former teacher Frank Underhill defended her on the grounds that "there must be something in the complaints which one hears on all sides, from parents, from employers, from university teachers, about the intellectual quality of the products of our high schools – their inability to read or to express themselves in writing, their boredom, their vulgarity, their purposelessness, their lack of curiosity or understanding about any kind of life except what is comprised in the experience of their own group, their failure to reach the position where they are on the way to become inner-directed rather than other-directed." He none the less betrayed his own pragmatic view of education's purpose, which was "not to make children happy in solving children's problems but to prepare them to solve the problems of the men and women they are to become."[114] By "inner-directed," Underhill meant self-directed – a quality that contrasted glaringly with the mass society, particularly with its reputation as a homogenizing force. Adding his support to Neatby's post-Massey project, Robertson Davies laid the blame for mediocrity at the feet of materialism. For decades, he argued, there seemed little need for liberal education in a nation of frontiers. "Material success could be made to serve as a cloak for a great deal of provinciality and downright stupidity. We still think of ourselves in pioneer terms, though we are now a wealthy nation of townspeople. ... Why should we bother with education beyond the standard which appears to serve us well?"[115] Ultimately downcast at the unlikelihood of reversing such a trend, during the winter following the publication of her book Neatby held faint hope that educators would uphold the long and honourable Western tradition, complaining that "they continue blandly to socialize for a society which threatens every moment to cease to exist."[116]

A volume of Neatby's of essays published once spring returned in 1954 gained less notoriety than *So Little for the Mind* but revealed just as clearly one of the directions of 1950s' cultural criticism. Entitled *A Temperate Dispute*, the collection extended her critique of educational expertise and included two essays with broader applications.[117] "The Debt of Our Reason" accused educational progressivists of hiding behind two vaguely defined, and therefore almost infinitely useful concepts: a democratic philosophy and the scientific method.[118] Even more relevant was Neatby's stab at the mass society, "The Group and the Herd," in which she worried that individuality had been lost and that a "herd instinct" prevailed. The ability to live in solitude and to enjoy leisure as an opportunity for achievement or understanding represented, for Neatby, an educated person and a goal for any society's educational system. A society would flourish only by hallowing the idea that "all we have learned, all we have achieved, derives from the individual who is in the group but who remains an individual; who cooperates and even submits, but who can, if he must, stand off from his fellows and tell them they are wrong." Her example of the herd instinct, somewhat predictably, was the Nazi youth camps, in which individuality and the spirit of healthy dissent had been repressed in the interest of uniformity.[119]

Loneliness in the Crowd: Crestwood Heights

If the mass society was so ephemeral and so detrimental to the individual, how did critics characterize people who seemed to thrive on the culture that it housed? In his satirical *roman à clef*, *The Chartered Libertine*, author and journalist Ralph Allen made these people the unwitting victims of commercial culture, fed mostly "movies about cowboys, plays about private detectives, programmes of recorded love songs, funny sayings by comedians, and serials about unhappy ladies." Critics such as Neatby appeared in the book as principled but powerless crusaders who longed to make room for "a piece of music that isn't a love song, some of it very old music that hasn't any words and takes nearly a hundred instruments to play; talks and lectures about science and books and about our own history; plays in which, sometimes, nobody gets murdered or even falls in love."[120] All over North America, living standards rose after the war, yet, except for the introduction of the new medium of television, the range of cultural and social options – the variety of pastimes and ways of life – did not seem to be expanding at the same pace. Identifying the sort of personality that could both define and perpetuate such an environment became something of a cottage industry. Acknowledging a debt to the more ambitious of the community studies completed between the wars,[121] some of the most influential work in North American social science after 1945 gathered data and anecdotal evidence to construct portraits of society, paying particular attention to the psychological effects of living in a mass society. American congressional hearings on the problem of juvenile delinquency reached the conclusion that the mass media "stood between parent and child."[122] In Canada, these reports of conformity and anonymity within the mass society and the corporate world found an attentive audience among cultural critics.

Sociologist David Riesman headed what was probably the most influential such project – a nearly decade-long survey undertaken during the "great Toqueville revival of the late 1940s to the mid-1960s" – which moved concerns about democracy's homogenizing tendencies into the foreground of critical discourse.[123] The result of his team's work was *The Lonely Crowd*, which introduced the concepts of "inner-directed" and "other-directed" that Frank Underhill used to distinguish between mature and immature members of society.[124] Riesman's concern was not so much with maturity as with explaining, through identification of causes and symptoms, the replacement of the inner-directed type of "social character" by the other-directed.[125] Canadian observers also considered the question of how this replacement had come about – how experience inside and outside the social and cultural fields shaped social character. Sociologist Murray Ross, an advocate of community centres after the war, echoed Riesman's findings, reporting that in mid-1950s' Canada the "average man in the urban centre finds his life has little meaning, his human relationships little depth or significance, his voice little importance in the affairs of his work or his community." This sense of feeling disconnected from local society drove the average person irretrievably into the arms of the advertiser and the cunning businessperson, as Ross explained: "In reaction, he turns to all kinds of escape devices which 'hucksters' and other manipulators of mass advertising have convinced him are the fruits of the good life to which he is entitled. Thus, he becomes a heavy consumer of tobacco, liquor, slick magazines, television, movies, and two-tone automobiles which cover up, in part at least, his loneliness and feeling of insignificance."[126]

In 1956, the same year Ross pointed squarely at what amounted to consumers' complicity in their own exploitation, a team of social scientists presumably much influenced by *The Lonely Crowd* published the results of its five-year dissection of a modern Canadian suburb. John Seeley, Alex Sim, and Elizabeth Loosley collaborated on *Crestwood Heights*, a thinly veiled study of Toronto's prosperous Forest Hill area. Sim had been closely involved with the *Citizens' Forum* project from its earliest stages, and Loosley had participated to a lesser extent. The team saw its Forest Hill study as an exercise in community psychotherapy, though admittedly as a diagnostic or descriptive – rather than a curative – phase of treatment. They noted that the community had "come to us for help" and assumed that what residents said and did could reveal deep-seated anxieties, but not assuming that "the patient knew what his problem was."[127] Residents spoke of problems related largely to adjustment to conditions that were not peculiar to the postwar era, but were characteristically modern in nature. For example, the corporate or professional career paths that many of the men in the neighbourhood followed led through a range of occupations, but shared the characteristics of hard work, "prudent boldness," and "ever-widening circles of decreasing intimacy." Conversely, many young women would "drift into school and into marriage taking things as a matter of course."[128]

Owing to Crestwood Heights/Forest Hill's wealth and reputation as a "desirable" area, that particular community hardly typified others in Canada or the United States, and the study's authors did not present it as typical. They did, however, structure their work using such categories as shelter, time, and career to show how even in a privileged neighbourhood with higher-than-average levels of education and income, modern life had functioned to establish values through stages of socialization over which community institutions presided. The suburb in question served as a factory for fitting people to norms that had little to do with personal achievement or self-improvement except where those served as pathways to wealth and status. The authors documented, in abundant detail, what B.K. Sandwell had described eight years earlier as the "terrible over-concentration on the struggle for self-advancement, the pursuit of the bitch-goddess Success."[129]

The anxieties surrounding this struggle for success were, for the authors of *Crestwood Heights*, the most prominent features of suburban life. Although the study was supposed to present these features objectively, its rendering of the neighbourhood as a hive of neuroses places the book among works critical of modern conditions, particularly those affecting families and gender roles. Despite its origins as an academic project, initially under the direction of the National Committee for Mental Hygiene,[130] *Crestwood Heights*, as David Riesman noted with some disappointment, "was not dense and allusive; everything is painstakingly spelled out," and therefore it could be read by the "educated non-professional reader."[131] Yet this accessibility remained an important addition to the critical arsenal during the 1950s. Even an extensive research project such as *Crestwood Heights* would not suffer for being directed at a motivated general audience. Communities might display a range of attitudes towards the dream of material success, but all of them needed to be advised of the ways in which such a relatively homogeneous dream had been propagated. As Alex Sim told an audience in 1957: "while one locality may vary with another in the intensity with which the dream is sought, believed, or realized, its universality extends as far as the message of the mass media is effectively extended." The dream could be identified by residents of the neighbourhood, but it had originated outside. "There is much more than dreams in Crestwood Heights that belongs to all North America," Sim continued; "there is the material culture, the literature, jokes, beliefs, styles, psychological theories, and fads, medical practices, political ideas, house furnishings, fables, fears, and hopes, all these are universal to North America yet caught and mingled in a given point in space and time in a special way."[132]

Neighbourhood culture was certainly susceptible to a multitude of forces and constituted a rich field of inquiry for social scientists, but by the mid-1950s some cultural critics had also devoted nearly a decade's worth of close attention to the ivory tower. Indeed, hopeful commentary on achieving a kind of equilibrium – between the natural and social sciences on one side and the humanities on the other – had been a feature of criticism well before the war.[133] In the mid-1930s, J.L. Synge remarked wistfully on the ability of the great scientists of the early modern period, such as Newton, to combine their scientific curiosity with an acute literary sensibility. "In the eighteenth century," he explained, "Science was a playful girl who whispered of conic sections, putrefaction, and refraction in the ears of bishops and marchionesses. Now she is a stern matron who stands beside the chair in every council of war or industry."[134] Especially after the Second World War, under the threat of the atom bomb, critics remarked often that the speed with which the sciences seemed to be displacing the humanities in higher education reflected deeper and rather distressing currents in society.[135]

Two Cultures? Sciences versus Humanities

However, scientific research maintained significant authority in the years just after 1945. Its credentials as the prime mover behind victory in war and as a source of increasing leisure could not be denied, but cultural critics exercised themselves over more than science's implications for religious belief. Especially while the Massey Commission met to consider how to help Canada's universities "keep up" with the sciences while preserving the tradition of the West, a number of observers anticipated British author C.P. Snow's late-1950s' work *The Two Cultures* by calling for improved communications between the dominant scientific and the beleaguered humanistic communities.[136] Among these peacemakers, Malcolm Wallace argued in a submission to the commission that such an entente could be reached, but not without some cultural breakthrough in which a "pendulum swing of popular interest once more restores to us an active faith in the Humanities." With guarded confidence in that sea change, Wallace identified an eventual return to the humanities with the modern Canadian economic and diplomatic goals of "enabling us to take our place in the world community of the future." He warned, however, that genuine respect for the "civilizing power" of the humanities would be an absolute precondition to the sort of maturity that the nation sought: "Our own people cannot grow to mature stature until they turn their interest to the moral, aesthetic and philosophic aspects of life; they will need the humanities to teach them to understand the history, the tastes and the thinking of other peoples."[137]

The Massey Commission ultimately recommended that government spend considerable public money on improving universities, and even on establishing new ones, to equip youths for life in the modern world. To critics, such an endeavour seemed to privilege the task of fitting graduates for specific kinds of employment rather than moulding their characters. The university had become, in the course of a generation, a training ground for technical pursuits, venerating the "narrow concepts of usefulness" that Arthur Lower suggested "proceed from the drive for the efficient society, the society 'on its toes', girding itself against its enemies within and without. If our energies are to be consumed in the fight against the enemy, what remains over for making ourselves better human beings, for building what we call 'civilization'?"[138]

Delivering an address dense with implicit disdain for the technocratic takeover of higher education, Lower's fellow historian Donald Creighton thought it impossible to overstate the case for the humanities "in an age characterized by the enormous prestige of the physical and social sciences and by the adulation accorded to technical training and what is reverently described as 'know-how.'" Arguing at first for the applicability of the humanities to the function of government, Creighton quickly shifted gears to praise the world that "vanished irrevocably in 1939, ... [and whose] intellectual foundations seem, in comparison with those of modern times, so solid and shapely." Creighton spoke as though the appeasement of mass opinion had utterly vanquished the humanities: "Nazi-ism may be said to have reposed on bogus anthropology; communism reposes on bogus economics;" he declared, "and there are times when the contemporary English-speaking world seems to place its total trust upon a bogus political science which has converted democracy into a vaporous pervasive incense, floating in a supposedly edifying fashion over nearly everything, and yet, oddly enough, arousing its devoted worshippers to truculence abroad and illiberality at home." This was not a denunciation of democracy, but an expression of disappointment at a slanted playing field. Clearly dissatisfied with the dominance of the sciences and social sciences, he wondered "whether the humanities would have lent themselves to such monstrous perversions."[139]

In the mid-1950s, the modern university also had its defenders. E.W.R. Steacie, head of the National Research Council, thought it unrealistic to adopt the humanistic biases of a cultural elite as a practical model of civilization. He also condemned science popularizers of the "ain't science wonderful" school, who seemed to focus only on new "gadgets" for mass consumption instead of stressing science's role as the method that helped create still more leisure time for humanistic pursuits. The cries of anguish over science and technology's eminence in the university or the world outside it, Steacie claimed, did not reflect the opinion of the average Canadian, because technology enveloped "what everyone, or almost everyone, does for a living." Indeed, he insisted that technology was simply the way a society determined what uses would be made of hard-won scientific truths, and there was no advance in the arts that could not also be harnessed for objectionable purposes. "If writing had never developed, there would be no yellow journalism and no comic books," the chemist surmised, "but I doubt if my humanist friends would agree that the development of writing was unfortunate."[140]

Unfortunately for the humanists, and for Canadians committed to "reconstructing" a nation populated by inner-directed individuals, the technocratic society remained the engine of prosperity in North America. Its culture of newer, bigger houses and cars, of television and comic books, seemed to offer the things that people wanted – products of democratic ingenuity. A.R.C. Duncan, chair of philosophy at Queen's University, expressed some frustration that society viewed the humanities as "a kind of top-dressing of ornamental culture on the solid foundations of science and technology." In doing so, he pointed to a problem that critics did not know how to get around: cultural improvement required a kind of dedication or effort that seemed to many like a replication of the work environment. Standing in opposition to pleasure and the plainly recreational effects of more passive pursuits, seeking "culture" outside of what was readily available seemed like asking for an extra helping of wartime austerity, like donning sackcloth and ashes for no good reason. Attention to cultural matters during the 1950s carried this connotation to the extent that Duncan confessed: "for many people the word 'culture' conjures up dreary images of long haired youths listening to Bach and Vivaldi instead of red-bloodedly jiving and skiffling, attending revivals of obscure Elizabethan plays instead of rioting with Elvis Presley, and wandering tight-lipped and white-faced around galleries of paintings instead of enjoying throbbing emotional dramas in glorious technicolour like Peyton Place."[141]

CONCLUSION: A WASTELAND?

Cultural critics upset with the prodigality of 1950s' culture and its subjugation to a manufactured mass taste frequently targeted the social implications of modernity. Educating, rather than merely lecturing, individuals about their vulnerability to a vapid commercial culture and the ease of suburban sameness came to be something of a mission. Critics paid close attention to the work of social scientists such as David Riesman, whose dispatches from an alienated United States provided a powerful framework for understanding Canada's trip down a similar path. To some, signs such as the pre-eminence of the sciences in higher education indicated capitulation to a technocratic modern order. In essence, the ideal of active citizenship most forcefully articulated during the reconstruction period remained important to cultural critics, who saw local or individual engagement with approved folk and high culture traditions as central to a vigorous nationhood, to social harmony, and to gradual emancipation from the too-easy yoke of mass entertainments.

The term *"reconstruction"* could no longer be applied so readily, but several of the same assumptions and goals remained in place. The state's interest in the cultural sphere only added a political dimension to the critics' existing struggle to make edifying activities and resistance to materialistic, homogenizing impulses indispensable components of a desirable common culture. In this sense, the 1950s held considerable anxiety – not comfort – for observers who made it their business to point out troubling symptoms of the mass society and its culture and yet attempted to treat their Canadian patients in ways that did not seem patronizing or anti-democratic.

The Royal Commission on Broadcasting began in 1956 under R.M. Fowler, but unlike the Massey Commission it spent its energy more on assessing the business and the politics of broadcasting than on analysing programming content or its social impact. Few Canadians seemed worried, as Arthur Lower was, that "television will repeat the story of the movie, but on a far more intimate scale, for it is carrying ideas, from pie-throwing upward, into every hearth and home." Lower's outrage at the prospects for domestic cultural development combined nationalist invective and conspiracy theory. The United States produced much of the objectionable fare inundating the Canadian market, but in his estimation Americans themselves were not part of the plot. U.S. popular culture was not "popular" at all but had been forced on the audience: "No doubt any society can be persuaded without too much difficulty to accept large helpings of sex in its daily diet, but that is different from asserting that these are 'what the public wants.' Still, Lower argued, the Canadian public distinguished itself from the American by being inherently more conservative, a further and more distressing indication that "much of what is served up to them in the way of 'popular culture' is, for them, an acquired taste."[142]

If cultural critics are to be believed, few Canadians cared about where or how they acquired their tastes and social habits. As they fitted into lives that seemed straight out of William H. Whyte's *The Organization Man* – a seminal mid-1950s' study of the mass society – it did not occur to many of them that their cultural choices were less frequently their own. In describing how the public had come to want what it had been given, George Salverson's "Showman" claimed to encapsulate cultural producers' low estimation of the mass audience. During the 1950s, the ease of being able to turn to an ever-increasing number of diversions, however simple or derivative, seemed to drive the act of "getting culture" even further upmarket, further from legitimacy as a democratic process. The mass society itself had come to represent the fruits of an injudiciously practised democracy. To J.B. Priestley, whose Toquevillian moment came as he toured the United States in 1957, this new society based on higher rates of productivity, inflation, and higher standards of living also featured "high pressure advertising and salesmanship," mass communications, and a majority-oriented "cultural democracy" that contributed to the prevailing sense that "you think everything is opening out when in fact it is narrowing and closing in on you ... You have to be half-witted or half-drunk all the time to endure it."[143]

When "getting culture" was linked with the search for a Canadian identity, as it often was during the 1950s and into the early 1960s, insisting on an identity that included an appreciation of the Western humanist tradition could seem unnatural and contrived. Sensing the difficulty of enforcing a hierarchy of tastes, critics began to favour a middlebrow ethic of self-improvement, through which citizens could acquire a rudimentary understanding of the basis for their nation's being and have access to cultural forms that explored the human condition. About 1950, observers considered radio and travelling exhibits valuable for providing stimulation to audiences that had no lively arts communities close by. Complete reliance on such methods of cultural uplift remained suspect. One group's contribution to the Massey Commission read: "The blight of passivity is the curse of our modern civilization, and we shall make a most disastrous mistake if we imagine that turning a radio button or watching a touring drama group is any substitute for singing in a glee club or putting on a play."[144] Reviewing Carl Jung's *The Undiscovered Self*, Robertson Davies concluded sadly that most of his fellow citizens preferred the anonymity of the crowd and a numbing presentism:"Our North American feeling that mass good-doing, corporate worship, and concurrence in a body of accepted opinion is 'modern' and 'efficient' conceals a dread of that loneliness which a soul must encounter when it turns inward toward itself."[145] To the cultural critic, the fleeting satisfactions of mass culture and the false conviviality of the mass society signified nothing more clearly than the convenience of empty lives.

PART THREE

*Full Circle:
A Broadening Definition of Culture
1957–1967*

5

Mass Media, Broadcasting, and Automation

By the mid-1950s, the question of what English Canadians might find if they turned inward to examine their individual or collective personalities had begun to worry critics of modern life and mass culture. While the broader educational aims of the mass culture critique continued to enjoy state sympathy, critics became less categorical about the space between high and low cultures. In the light of the assimilation of Canadian ways of life to a more generic North American model during the 1950s, social and cultural self-determination seemed more important than the maintenance of hierarchies. After the Second World War, but especially as more formal agencies for cultural development emerged in Canada during the 1950s, outspoken monitors of contemporary society feared acquiring reputations as dogmatic arbiters of taste. As Morley Callaghan reported rather matter-of-factly in 1957, it was "no longer respectable to be highbrow." He wrote, however, of the abiding need for a homegrown group that could set inspiring examples of engagement with art and with everyday life – "some kind of an aristocratic class formed of colorful men with minds of their own. I know that aristocracy is a dirty word in our time, but I call Thomas Jefferson a democratic aristocrat." Callaghan wondered if such a group could come into being and assert its will in time to save Canadians from an unpleasant fate. "Where is this new class of men respecting leisure and reflective idleness to come from?" he asked. He could not offer a definitive answer but wrote that he had "enough faith in the human spirit to know it must come if Canada is not to become a big railroad station with a soap opera on a giant television screen to divert those who are waiting to catch a train."[1]

Cultural critics responded in varying ways to their waning power to influence tastes or define (descriptively or prescriptively) a Canadian character impervious to "other-direction." During the later 1950s and early 1960s, critics did not tire of pointing out how they saw modern life and mass culture favouring structures that effaced desirable individual and collective qualities. They contended that those who cared little about the autonomous person, family ties, or national distinctions had increasingly mediated and systematized work and leisure. Three interrelated topics – critical objections to the state of the cultural "market," the embrace of a middlebrow cultural nationalism, and responses to the social implications of an automated workplace – reveal that critics' own remedies were no less meddlesome. Advocating a self-awareness that encompassed personal and national identities, many in English Canada's academic, arts, and journalistic communities became mediators too, as they attempted to cultivate an audience perpetually sensitive to the consequences of allowing foreign or unfamiliar forces to determine the sort of society that Canada would become.

The years around 1960 saw an escalation of the Cold War, and this contest of ideologies certainly formed a pervasive part of life. In Canada, the domestic scene remained slightly more sedate. The political shift towards John Diefenbaker's Progressive Conservatives during 1957–58 seemed to have few direct or immediate implications for those interested in cultural matters. The 1957 creation of the Canada Council as a central agency to fund the arts and academic research and the advent of an independent Board of Broadcast Governors in 1958 were each in the works before the political changeover.[2] Their existence symbolized the state's interest in culture. The practical tasks of governing media and shepherding culture guaranteed some public philosophizing about the relationship between them. Indeed, the Royal Commission on Broadcasting occasioned such debate and reflected critics' acquiescence to the television age.

Sensitive to the immediacy and rapid proliferation of mass communications, critics recognized the need to treat the electronic media, especially television, as fundamental to a new, wider public sphere, which held the promise of an enlightened democracy but seemed to deliver less. Several supposed that, as was the case in the business world, large firms would take over production in the cultural field, and their output would display the "adolescent" tendencies of which George Salverson's "Showman" character spoke with such familiarity in 1950.[3] The continental market for culture seemed to glorify image and sensation over substance and decorous behaviour. If these tendencies were ever to be corrected, the mass audience needed exposure to material intended for more mature minds and to material that would excite further interest in uncovering a latent Canadian identity.

Thanks to the post-1945 entanglement of Canada's economic and foreign policies with those of the United States and the basic similarities between the two nations, the search for a national identity apart from the American juggernaut has become a fixture in Canadian historical writing, as well as in the larger field of Canadian studies. Portrayals of that quest as either a worthwhile goal or a futile errand have been emerging for over forty years.[4] Historians have not examined the extent to which this search may also have been informed during the late 1950s and early 1960s by what some of the nation's more articulate citizens saw as a crisis of selfhood stemming from contemporary social and cultural trends. Cultural nationalism displayed an anti-modern side[5] in that it opposed accelerated continental integration as North America became a mass society, but this was not a nationalism biased against the electronic media. It signalled a qualified retreat from an "unconscious moulding by book culture."[6] Some critics suggested that exposing the public to Canadiana through works more "refined" than those that had been spilling across the border for at least two generations would help Canadians assemble their own national mythology. However elusive that goal may have proven since, the imperative of defining a vigorous national identity affected the ways opponents of mass culture pursued their aims. In little more than ten years, the desire for a thorough reconstruction, in which active citizens set the tone, had largely given way to a middlebrow approach that sought not to disturb or harangue people, but to facilitate any sort of activity outside an American-dominated commercial culture.

Although observers inside and outside Canada had been pointing for years to the humanities' decline in influence as compared to the growing authority of a scientific worldview, it was 1959 by the time Britain's C.P. Snow showed that these camps within the academy constituted separate worlds of their own outside it as well.[7] The era featured a revival of critical interest in the differences between science and the humanities. This revival most often included discussion of the cold, homogenizing qualities of the technological society that Snow had set in opposition to the pursuits that critics believed gave life its warmth and variety. Running through and beyond the revival of interest in the science–humanities dichotomy, the discussion of automation and its ramifications outside the workplace helped resurrect and emphasize an older opposition between humanity and the rhythm of the machine.

This chapter first outlines the media explosion of the period and its ramifications for national identity. Second, it looks at broadcasting through the lens of the Fowler Commission and the ensuing fine-tuning of the CBC. Third, it shows Canadians and cultural critics alike wrestling with the new world of automation. The ferment of the era fused the critique of mass culture with a powerful new current of self-conscious nationalism.

MEDIA EXPLOSION AND NATIONAL IDENTITY

Though hardly native to Canada, the image of a fickle or crooked cultural marketplace stood as one of the most compelling in the critic's arsenal during those years. Not only did this image equate mass culture with the financial interests of its producers, it intimated that the cultural marketplace had inverted one of the basic laws of commerce, with demand adjusting itself to the low quality of what was being supplied. The oft-noted fact that a large and self-sustaining market full of consumers who were not so different from the average Canadian existed close by – along with hundreds of canny mass media enterprises – only complicated matters. The mass media brought more new sounds and images into more and more Canadian households. By the later 1950s, critics who owed their livings to exercising skill with language and literature had to grapple with the amalgamation of new media and ultimately with the death of the old truism that the home – a place where one could structure one's own life – represented a refuge from the public arena. Producer and critic Mavor Moore expressed the temper of the times, noting that "the audience, meanwhile, is trying to become accustomed to a break-down of old familiar categories: 'talking pictures', a radio program called 'Stage '57', a television program called 'Producers' Playhouse', recordings of 'literature', magazines enclosing records, teachers who clown and clowns who preach, orchestras who act, dancers who sing, 'live' television shows partly filmed, music to read by or (for hens) to lay eggs by." These new types of entertainment contributed to such a sense of displacement that sometimes the average listener or viewer perhaps found it difficult to escape. "The world now comes into his home," Moore reported, "and he 'gets away from it all' not by retreating to his hearth but by 'going out' into the world."

Moore recommended that anyone who wanted to understand the modern world learn more about the new "co-operative arts" and contended that the manipulative power of advertising and applied psychology had made the relative positions of artist and audience ambiguous. "The mass media become more and more massive," he wrote, and he complained that "private or coterie art becomes either a mass fad or a total loss, and the maverick artist cannot gain access to any of the few power stations that control this Niagara."[8] Although he did not contend that public tastes should always emulate those of a cultural elite, he believed that altering one's work to suit a "mass fad" afforded the artist little creative freedom and deprived audiences of much that they might appreciate. The developments that Marshall McLuhan spent much of his working life explaining – transformations of the ways in which people communicate – were hardly fads. By the later 1950s, critics recognized that if they intended to act on behalf of the maverick artist and the ordinary Canadian viewer, they could not avoid these newer avenues of influence but must use them to counteract the narrowing of tastes that resulted from the proliferation of mass culture.

Into the 1960s, critics' attitudes towards the mass entertainments on offer remained unforgiving. Rock and roll, castigated first in the United States as a corrupting influence, primarily on the white teenager, had become a worldwide phenomenon by the later 1950s. It met with the wrath of Watson Kirkconnell because he considered it bad music to begin with, and all the more harmful to responsible Christian citizenship when "rock 'n' roll exploiters" began to market sacred and semi-sacred music arranged in their own style. Even though its supporters might represent it as "the proletarian music of the new democracy," he could not appreciate such ventures as "a vocal rendering of the 23rd Psalm ... in which the Lord became a rip-ranting, banjo-whanging cowboy and reverence was lost in the tinny vulgarity of it all."[9]

Late-1950s' youth, however, appeared to be genuinely enthused by the music and could not see the contradiction in listening to it, even as an increasing proportion of them entered universities staffed by those who had acquired their tastes in times dominated to a lesser extent by canned culture. Frank Underhill left McMaster University after a visit, disappointed at the assortment of movie magazines that his wife found in a residence hall and dismissive of students who would buy sheet music for songs such as *Gonna Get Along without Ya Now, Harbour Lights, The Little Drummer Boy, Only the Lonely Know the Way I Feel, Starbright*, and *Welcome New Lovers*. Such songs, Underhill suggested, trivialized important human relationships or emotions and had tapped into a lucrative youth market that consumed these songs " 'as recorded by' individuals of whom I had never heard but who were, I presume, heroes of the disk jockeys; and the dreary sentimental slush of their words must have surpassed anything even in the screen magazines." Underhill was probably right about the lyrics' sentimentality but neglected to give the McMaster students credit for at least playing these songs on the piano rather than merely buying the readily available recorded versions. He held these students up as evidence that Canadian higher education seemed to be infested by clients and patrons whose inclinations were towards personal popularity and lax standards "at the very moment when what is most needed is an austere and difficult struggle towards excellence."[10]

The belief that this difficult struggle towards excellence could be orchestrated by a small cultural elite had become less tenable by the time the Canada Council was formed in 1957. The cultivation of excellence in a broad range of endeavours remained an admirable goal, but the idea that such results could be enforced clashed with the ideal of cultural democracy. However, so too did abandoning minority tastes or aspirations in favour of the most popular fare. The Canadian Arts Council declared in a submission to the Royal Commission on Broadcasting that "to impose the preferences of a supposed majority upon all groups in the community is surely undemocratic. In a national broadcasting system there should be programmes for all classes of citizens, and for all tastes and interests."[11] The Canada Council and other organizations would reward excellence where it was to be found and would also attempt to sow the seeds of non-commercial culture, sometimes in places where they might not take root. The most popular radio and television shows would continue to be available, whether on CBC-affiliated stations, through the American networks, or via private channels. Neither were comic books and movies in any danger. Where critics of mass culture had some input, they represented their position as non-coercive: any attempt to offer the public a more diverse selection of cultural opportunities sounded less threatening and more democratic than preaching to it about the supposed intrinsic evils of lowbrow entertainments.

Experienced observers and student journalists alike recognized that either the fact or the appearance of meddling with culture would cause an anti-intellectual backlash or would simply fail because any campaign to transform public tastes would be too ambitious.[12] They had listened for long enough to the likes of Don Jamieson, a television executive who had a direct interest in agitating for a free market in broadcasting and predicted that the curtailment of lowbrow programming would meet with little success. He claimed: "an audience raised on hill-billy music won't appreciate a Mozart octette overnight." In assuming that "hill-billy" music and Mozart existed on opposite ends of the cultural totem pole, Jamieson misjudged an important component of the mass-culture critique. To critics, what he called hill-billy music would probably have been acceptable if it truly was the music on which the audience had been raised or if it gave the audience a sense of an authentic milieu. Nevertheless, Jamieson saw highbrow material (or that which had been labelled "highbrow") as unimpeachable in its quality, but as being no guarantor of individual or national morality or propriety: "in much of Europe, as cultural levels advanced, moral values declined. History records that the Gestapo played classical music to stifle the sounds from the gas chambers!" He argued for a vision of Canadian culture derived not from some arbitrary conception of wisdom or beauty, but through a reading of "what ordinary Canadians want": "I do not suggest that we must remain in ignorance of finer things in order to save our souls. Obviously, however, cultural development alone is not enough. The moral fibre of the nation must be strengthened at the same time." Accepted modes of behaviour must not be denigrated in the name of cosmopolitanism or refinement, Jamieson insisted. He called for programming to reflect the common person's conscience and complained of the CBC's "cultural" offerings that "some of the dramas, on the national service, do no such thing. The Canadian culture we seek must stem from all the people of Canada. It must not be the synthetic product of a handful of so-called free thinkers, as much as these people are entitled to a place in the overall scheme of things."[13]

It was difficult, in a Cold War environment that frequently equated the development of North American popular culture with political democracy and a kind of "people's morality," to speak of the imposition of cultural standards from on high as a practical policy. Even the critics themselves recognized how difficult overcoming entrenched popular tastes would be. In 1957, historian W.L. Morton broadcast a review of colleague Donald Creighton's *Dominion of the North*. Creighton wrote to Morton to apologize, claiming that he had missed the broadcast "because I had no idea that you would be the speaker and because, quite frankly, I am a little tired of the very familiar voices of that extremely small and almost unchanging group of literary and political critics who have been performing on C.B.C.'s *Critically Speaking* for the past ten or fifteen years."[14]

As much as the abandonment of cultural standards might leave the door open to an irresponsible "lowest common denominator," critics generally wished to avoid appearing "snobbish" or doctrinaire about culture. A period of intense speculation about the desirability of controls, directed largely at broadcasting, yielded a number of revealing articles in a new monthly called the *Canadian Commentator*. Opinion among the journal's contributors ranged somewhat, but none would suggest quotas or embargoes on particular forms of culture as sound cultural policy. Some made an effort to embrace works that were popular, but carefully done. For instance, Mavor Moore, particularly sensitive to this issue, wrote in favour of Agatha Christie's novels.[15] The prominence accorded cultural topics in a publication that otherwise featured articles on domestic (occasionally American) party politics and foreign policy made plain the political dimension of the culture debate in late-1950s' Canada.[16]

In his aforementioned condemnation of rock and roll, Watson Kirkconnell spoke of the "exploiters" eager to get into the "religious music racket" as simply the latest in a long line of Tin Pan Alley confidence men.[17] The United States had a fully developed and lucrative system of cultural industries that employed mass-distribution techniques similar to those in place in other commercial fields. In commenting on the nature of this market, legal scholar Ernest van den Haag grieved that there was no telling how many talented people had been lured into writing or performing for the bulk of the population. He suggested that long ago Dante was able to accomplish what he had because "there were no alternatives to being as good a writer as his talent permitted."[18] Academics, too, perceived the Canadian university orbit as relatively serene or, as Claude Bissell at the University of Toronto did, less business-like than the American one: "We have, for instance, neither the energy nor the resources to establish the specialized periodicals that flourish so abundantly in the United States, and that make the writing and publication of a learned article an exercise in marketing."[19]

Perceptions of such a shift towards the cultural marketplace made more tenable the case for the intentional protection of Canadian arts, letters, and folkways on nationalist grounds. Broadcasting became a central part of this vision, and extending such protection meant extending the broadcast network.[20] Donald Creighton proposed a new national policy in which closely regulated electronic media would play the leading role, promoting an elevated common culture by controlling and augmenting the supply of programming. "A national broadcasting system can do for us, in the realm of the mind and the spirit, precisely what these old and tested national policies have done in the political and economic sphere," he declared. His scheme for aiding home manufacture and consumption was based not on the exclusion or replacement of foreign material with Canadian, but on the belief that "a steady flow of live programmes along the east–west life line will express Canadian ideas and ideals, employ Canadian talent, and help unite our people from sea to sea and from the river unto the ends of the earth."[21]

Not all observers of culture could be counted on to favour such relatively direct methods, but, as with the democratic ideal, they rarely questioned the need to battle the forces of continentalism. Alan Thomas of the University of British Columbia's extension department recognized television's power as "the great stabilizer" and saw the act of carving out a Canadian space on the airwaves as an uphill struggle given the tremendous competition from programs that existed purely to entertain. However, he was concerned more with the method than with the goal, remarking that "the whole issue surrounding the 'Canadian content' of broadcasting hinges on the fact that the audience must be 'canadianized' or constantly reminded of the quality of its nationality. The question is whether this is the way to do it."[22] Again, the idea of making prohibitive laws or regulations to attain a rather abstract cultural end was a difficult proposition in a democratic society, but the end itself – a heightening of Canadian self-awareness – enjoyed the approval of most commentators. They cited the needs to avoid becoming "nobodies, shabbily dressed in bits of borrowed material," to correct an ever-deepening dependence on the United States, and to seek more than the "derivative and commonplace."[23]

Critics knew that "Culture" still intimidated much of the population, regardless of how much joy and pride its advancement might generate among an elite. After the Canada Council was set up, the educational and cultural sectors got in line to receive their various windfalls. Philosopher John A. Irving saw, however, little public will to justify the outlay on culture, largely because of its intangible qualities. He noted that education was "accepted as a means of improving our skills and techniques in order to increase our comfort and material prosperity. Culture is suspect because it aims at improving among other things, our tastes in art, literature, drama, architecture and entertainment." Irving carried the contrast further, pointing out how aspirations to culture seemed pretentious, perhaps even a denial of pleasure. "Education is valued because with it we are enabled to enjoy more of the pleasures which we share with the uneducated. Culture provokes resistance because in changing our tastes it seems to aim essentially at changing our natures."[24]

For a few other critics, trying to change tastes, assembling a heritage through such projects as McClelland and Stewart's Centenary Series in Canadian history, or constructing of a stately national capital seemed artificial. Writer Hugh Garner dismissed this bandwagon atmosphere as inauthentic, as "patriotism by persuasion, an attempt by misguided zealots to transfer love of country from one person to another by means of the written and spoken word."[25] Perplexed by what appeared to him a sudden upturn in attention to the health and welfare of a national culture, John McDade presented a typology of cultural hypochondriacs that included the "Logical Lamenter," "Anti-American Snarler," "Perfervid Anti-puritan," and "Short-haired Breast-beater" – a devotee of *Reader's Digest Condensed Books* who, convinced that "we tend to overdo all this culture stuff,"[26] represented an angry element in the middlebrow audience, distinguishable from the masses only in having a voice of its own. At bottom, however, the idea that Canadians needed and wanted an identity aroused less controversy than the possibility or the method of achieving one.[27] Whether the characteristics that would grant Canada an individuality among nations emerged through a laissez-faire approach or a concerted campaign, the process of discovering these had become an almost legendary activity. One satirist couldn't wait for the process to exhaust itself: "We've survived the Oxford group, Social Credit, hula-hoops, several wars and any number of isms – I imagine sanity will return, we'll forget the whole thing, and just be ourselves again."[28]

The desire to make new national distinctions was strong. Mass culture in the later 1950s and early 1960s was nothing if not conveniently consumable, and critics still contrasted this convenience with the determination required to gain access to and appreciate "highbrow" works. The extremely popular output of American studios, publishers, and networks had been especially convenient to the bulk of Canada's population for most of the century, so by the mid-1950s critics identified mass entertainments almost automatically with the United States. By later in the decade, U.S. cultural critics such as Dwight Macdonald had already spent much of their careers approaching mass culture as a kind of pollutant and wondering what they could do to expose and eliminate its sources within their own affluent society. To Canadian critics these sources were external, so doubly worrisome. By the early 1960s, their critique rested on the image of a cultural-commodities exchange dominated by Americans since well before 1939. Although improved communications technology had assisted in English Canada's asorption into an ostensibly lowbrow American fold, it also allowed the assertion of cultural nationalism.[29]

The tradition of identifying mass culture with an American influence helped reinforce the corollary notion that works of Canadian (and other non-American) origin possessed some greater merit. Despite decades of innovative and thoughtful American contributions to the arts and scholarship, many critics in Canada still looked to Europe for their literary and artistic models.[30] We may attribute this bias at least partially to the extremely visible mass-culture "machine" in the United States. Still, nationalism played a major role in creating a narrative of Canada's misfortune – a view in which high, folk, and now Canadian works were to be valued all the more because they had to contend with a neighbouring culture whose capacity for producing garish trivialities had seemed only to increase during the television age.

After completing his survey of contemporary French culture in 1954, University of Buffalo historian Julian Park embarked on a new project. He assembled a number of knowledgeable contributors to take snapshots of Canadian cultural life. Somewhat predictably, the group addressed Canada's progress in disciplines such as literature, music, art, the social sciences, philosophy, science, and education. These fields were all supposed to indicate the presence of a distinctive national culture, which Park defined simply as the Canadian's "recorded reflection of his way of life and his attitude toward it." An inventory of such activity might have sufficed as a "reflection" of the tastes of educated or especially creative Canadians. Park admitted that "obviously radio and television reach more people than perhaps all the arts combined" and also noted that the CBC "is performing both its cultural and national duty. It has three objectives – adequate coverage of the entire population, opportunities for Canadian self-expression, and resistance to absorption of Canada into the general cultural pattern of radio in the United States, supposed, rightly or wrongly, to be geared to a lower intellectual level." The CBC, however, could not alter the entire cultural playing field in Canada merely by pursuing these three objectives. Park described the trials of being Canadian in a continental entertainment market: "The Canadian who captures the attention of his fellow citizens in the realm of the lively arts has to be different from, and frequently better than, his competitor in America. He must stand more criticism, and this he gets in large measure from his fellows."[31]

Even an outsider such as Park could sense the ambivalence that his team of Canadian correspondents harboured towards the new "lively arts" of radio and television. Given the potential of these media to reach across distances, it seemed a matter of course that by the later 1950s communications had assumed a central position in the Canadian discourse about how cultures develop, change, and relate to others. Harold Innis, embracing the topic early in the decade, linked the survival of Canadian culture with a distinctly Canadian presence in print media and broadcasting. For him, "taking persistent action at strategic points against American imperialism in all its attractive guises" and "attempting constructive efforts to explore the cultural possibilities of various media of communication and to develop them along lines free from commercialism"[32] were essential to preventing the further erosion of cultural choices. An order of magnitude more compelling than print, the electronic media presented both a terrible challenge and a significant opportunity to those convinced that the mass society need not define the Canadian character. Providing credible opposition to mass culture, which Frank Underhill called a "dynamic form of American diplomacy,"[33] required direct competition for listeners and viewers' attention, not merely the disapproval that critics had employed in the past to denigrate salacious literature. Like Innis, critics had to develop a strategy for culture that accounted for new ways of communicating.

Through the later 1950s and early 1960s Marshall McLuhan stood as the most prominent figure concerned with understanding – and conveying an understanding of – mass communications. The scope of his work and its applicability to more than Canada marked it as an extension of Innis's later writings. McLuhan, however, placed greater emphasis on the psychological mechanisms behind media influence and – over time – exhibited less dread of the potential death of a Canadian culture.[34] McLuhan is chiefly notable here because his views were *exceptional*, tending to run counter to a more prevalent alarm about how newer methods of communications transformed or rendered irrelevant the values of the past or distracted the public from the task of synthesizing a vigorous modern Canadian culture. Critical of the under-use of new media (particularly television) in education, McLuhan clearly did not believe that these media created a passive public. Rather, he drew attention to the "great enlargement of reading interests which has resulted from movie, radio and television"[35] and saw newer methods of communications as a way to make the student an active learner. "Is it not this very shift in our society which makes the young so resentful of an educational establishment in which they are consumers only? They live with a technology which insists that they be co-producers in the very act of learning."

Yet McLuhan believed that society had done very little to acknowledge new opportunities and that students languished in a system where they "experience only a negative motivation with regard to a curriculum which ignores the undeveloped countries of our minds and which looks on the new media as the source not of culture but of trash."[36] By not assuming that mass communications automatically begot the mass mind, he placed himself outside the mass-culture critique, especially after his 1951 work *The Mechanical Bride*.[37] He rejected the frantic search for identity, suggesting that Canadians should be better satisfied with "simply becoming very much more aware of those tendencies and situations which have so long postponed the development of this dubious egotism."[38] He did not look so suspiciously at the connections between modern media, culture, and national identity as critics whose thought, action, and influence dwelled on guiding Canadians through a time of upheaval on the cultural front. Those connections themselves would affect the way in which the critique of modern life and mass culture proceeded and would be debated as Canadians tried to decide how to govern the contentious field of broadcasting.

THE FOWLER COMMISSION AND THE CRITIQUE OF PRIVATE BROADCASTING

Late in 1955, the Canadian government acted on one of the recommendations of the Massey Commission and appointed businessman Robert MacLaren Fowler[39] to chair a Royal Commission on Broadcasting. As some of those who appeared before it had hoped, the Fowler Commission eventually resulted in the alteration of Canada's broadcasting policy. Towards this end, much of its time involved discussing and hearing presentations on the rather technical matters of allocating frequencies, station licensing, broadcast financing, and regulation. It employed Dallas Smythe, a Canadian-born researcher who was then a member of the communications department at the University of Illinois, to study and classify a week of television programming by content. The commission stirred up the most revealing commentary on mass culture, however, by inviting individuals and organizations to appear before it. Some respondents portrayed themselves as objective observers, and others made no secret of their frustration with either the highly competitive television marketplace or with the officious bureaucrats who aimed to tame it. The standard-bearers for regulation and for the chaotic marketplace were, respectively, the CBC and the Canadian Association of Radio and Television Broadcasters (CARTB). These two groups opened the discussion with voluminous submissions and lengthy oral presentations. Although some of the more patently cultural (as opposed to technical/financial) issues came to the fore only after their presentations, a short summary of their positions can help us understand how supporters of both models could purport to serve the public interest.

The commission's first "guest," CBC Chairman Davidson Dunton, wasted little time before absolving his own network of greed. As an implicit condemnation of latter-day broadcasters whose stations were more investment than public service, he looked back to praise sainted pioneers in the field: "to them the country owes a big debt, to those people who did something to get it going in the twenties when the returns were not sure or enormous." He assured the commissioners that the CBC was not a business nor did it intend to let broadcasting in Canada come under the sway of advertisers and ratings, even though its programming had private sponsorship and its executives studied the ratings. It would not fill its schedule with material imported from the United States, even though such material was considerably cheaper to run than producing original programming. The CBC had shown, Dunton claimed, that "it is possible for a system to run counter to the usual pressures of economy and to deliberately produce Canadian programmes, deliberately distribute service right across the country." This defiant act, costly but deemed necessary for the sake of providing an alternative to American stations, had historically defined the public broadcaster's mission. The use of public funding to produce and schedule programming for a broader range of listeners and viewers put this mission under close scrutiny. "It is easier to operate a straight business," Dunton noted, for, because it ran on licence fees and then came to rely more on tax revenue, the CBC found itself constantly "weighing this elusive norm of public interest." As for varieties of culture, he emphasized that it was "not necessarily our job to see that just the highbrow things are circulated, or just popular things, or just the things the larger groups may want. I would suggest it is our job to see, on the whole, there is a comprehensive service containing in reasonable proportion a number of elements that broadcasting can communicate so well."[40]

T.J. Allard, executive vice-president of the CARTB, hoped that the Fowler Commission would help his organization get out from under the thumb of the CBC, which still regulated the industry. The association's brief called for a separation of powers in broadcasting much like the separation of the executive, judicial, and legislative branches in a modern government.[41] Despite CARTB's insistence that little if any difference existed between freedom to broadcast and freedom of the press,[42] and despite the litany of legal opinion that it cited to support this claim, its preoccupation with the business end of broadcasting shone through. The private station owners conflated the public interest and the freedom to broadcast as they liked. Asked about programming that was violent or served no discernible educational purpose, Allard replied that "good taste is something which can almost invariably be provided for by law" and cited the fact that comics were not banned but rules of content had been set out and publishers who wanted to stay in business would obey these rules. Allard's fellow board members struck a less puritanical note in offering examples of how they had policed their own programming. New Brunswick's representative on the board mentioned that his station carried the *Mount Allison Forum*, "a discussion sometimes of professors which can be quite dull." He humbly suggested that as a resident of his community he was well-equipped to judge how much "dull" was too much. "I am trying to run my station so that my community will be a little bit better because my station is operating there, and I do not think there is a regulation under the sun that can do it any better than that."[43]

Beyond the heated contest over the expansion of television licensing and the question of an independent regulatory body for broadcasting in Canada, a number of submissions addressed the cultural tone of programming and the issue of whether broadcasting was a business or a higher calling. At times the Fowler Commission became a forum for debating the commerce–culture nexus. Organizations normally occupied more with the state of higher education or planning the next concert season demonstrated a knowledge of how business imperatives had shaped the public's experience with the mass media business imperatives. For example, the Canadian Association of University Teachers (CAUT) noted that sponsors in imperfectly competitive markets (where name-brand recognition was as important as product quality or price) tended to spend the most on radio and television sponsorship. "It is a strange cross-section of the nation's business which assumes final control of our entertainment," the association's brief reported – "producers of soap, gasoline, cosmetics, stomach powders, automobiles, branded foods and household equipment."[44] The ads were memorable, but the sponsorship game certainly affected the sorts of programming that the public could expect. The Humanities Association of Canada, Fredericton Branch, agitated for a stronger CBC signal in central New Brunswick because the branch's members believed that audiences were not "getting what they want" from a local private station that none the less had high ratings: "It may be that CFNB, as it claims, is, on the whole supplying the majority of its listeners with what they want, but we must suspect surveys conducted among listeners most of whom can listen to only one station. And do surveys take into account that many people seldom listen at all because the programmes are so bad?"[45]

Representing the other side of the debate, civic politicians attended the commission's Winnipeg hearings in order to beat the local development drum, and this pattern prevailed in most other cities. By 1956, most Canadian "regional metropolises" had CBC television stations, if not some production facilities as well. Local boosters came to the Fowler Commission to aid groups of investors looking for second and third stations in their cities, reasoning that if the city were granted another station or stations, business *and* culture could be served. Winnipeg lawyer C.I. Keith, QC, represented the local symphony orchestra yet worried about the sort of message that increased regulation of the airwaves would send: "I would hate to see some kind of a... board made up of professors and musicians to devise programmes that the public will be forced to look at, heaven preserve us from that sort of thing."[46]

The business potential of private television appeared to boosters still relatively unexploited, and they claimed that local talent would thrive on local stations. Chairman Fowler subsequently dismissed this claim by pointing out that much of the material broadcast locally was "canned," – i.e., pre-recorded, probably in the United States.[47] In Winnipeg, Alderman Douglas Chisholm estimated that the previous evening's CBC broadcast of Franz Kafka's *The Trial* "may suit ten or twenty percent of the public, but the other eighty percent may not like it at all." He advocated an alternative source for local television, so that "the CBC could possibly find by surveys what the people actually want instead of as at present, what is felt is good for them." Alderman Albert Bennett later added to his colleague's implied charge of snobbery by praising what he saw as one of the national network's rare concessions to popular taste: "The only people who told me they did like a programme on CBC were two men who said they wanted to get home and see the wrestling on Saturday night."[48]

In the same city, others regarded Saturday wrestling telecasts as reflecting an abdication of the CBC's responsibility. A delegation from United College, which included Principal W.C. Lockhart and historians Stewart Reid and Kenneth McNaught, presented themselves as "teachers," not as interested parties. They did not dissemble. A national broadcasting system must be national, they suggested, but also look beyond the nation's boundaries for inspiration, preferably to UNESCO and to other Commonwealth countries. They saved their sharpest words for the state of the broadcasting industry in Canada: "Radio broadcasting and television have acquired three fairly distinct functions: they are at one and the same time agencies to influence, agencies to entertain and agencies to sell goods. In the public interest first consideration should be given to the educative function of broadcasting and last consideration to its use as an advertising medium. Increasingly, it seems to us, the tendency has been to follow the reverse order." These academics had nothing against entertainment, endorsing music-hall and modern-music broadcasts as examples of light entertainment suitable for the public airwaves. More important, however, they saw the overall picture as troubling. McNaught summed up this concern by agreeing with J.B. Priestley's comment about Canada's having "slipped one cultural stage" and suggesting that television "should be parasitic upon a lively theatre, but that we had T.V. and no lively theatre."[49]

It was fitting that those educators were among the first groups to address the commissioners, for some of the more revealing reflections had to do with the electronic media's capacity to educate as well as to entertain. Critics of commercial broadcasting found it frustrating that the lightest of light entertainment seemed to dominate during the hours when most people would watch or listen to broadcasts. They did not advocate banning this sort of entertainment but believed that its producers and station managers had not given anything more edifying a try in the same time slots. In response to a commissioner's question about financing only educational and informative programs publicly, and having entertainment finance itself, the Canadian Federation of University Women's Marion Gilroy replied: "I do not know where you could draw the line. One person's entertainment is another person's education."[50] Determining how much to expect of an audience, or how it might react to a steady diet of educational programming, remained a difficult task.

The allure of television as an educational medium continued to stir passions, even though its supporters harboured some reservations. One group expressed caution about putting too much stock in television because even though it suited adult education, in which "motivation is assumed, not developed," it might not be as suited to all levels because "the very ease of approach encourages passivity of mind."[51] Reached through television, the passive mind would be susceptible to dangerous influences. A Catholic group looked forward to seeing and hearing more "men of intellect" on the air in Canada but added – almost certainly referring to the notorious scientific broadcasts of 1951 on CBC –

"we can do without those whose faculty is to shock or affront the conscience of the nation." This same group believed that the potential benefits of using television as an educational tool outweighed the risks, for the self-interested false populism of the private broadcasters appeared to them the least attractive option of all: "any encouraged or tolerated policy of anti-intellectualism will dwarf the growth of this great land of ours, sap its heritage, endanger its stability and democratic institutions and mock that spiritual faculty by which men most nearly reflect the image of God."[52]

Aside from addressing the moral implications of catering to the lowest common denominator, several of the groups filing briefs with the commission dismissed the private broadcasters' tactic of lumping the electronic media and the press together as democratic institutions. The press catered to readers of a certain political stripe or recreational interest, and readers looked to other publications if they were no longer satisfied. Some critics resented the electronic media for carrying on "as though the listener or the viewer directly controlled the nature and quality of programs." Program ratings resembled newspaper- or magazine-circulation figures, measuring how many people had tuned in, but critics perceived and spoke of a diffused and distant horde of specialists at maximizing ratings, none of them responsible for the final product in the same way as the editor of a local paper. In contrast to what seemed to them the relatively simple example of the local newspaper, the Canadian Association of University Teachers took a different view of television. "The connection between the audience and the show is extremely complex, its brief declared. "Often it involves the following: business firm, advertising agency, show business agency, network, program producer, performers and audience. The ultimate decision rests with the source of the money – the sponsor."[53] Although the CBC sold advertising time as well, its policy of producing or buying broadcast rights to shows that could not command high advertising rates recommended it to critics. Groups that appreciated the variety in programming that this arrangement offered threw their support behind granting the public broadcaster adequate funding to operate as a "public service free from undue pressures."[54]

Although the press had to compete for advertisers as well, the public supposedly found the press easier to ignore, regardless of whether it was selling or editorializing. The intrusive and persuasive world of radio and television advertising, however, required "constant supervision so that it does not constitute an invasion of human privacy."[55] Privacy in the home seemed especially rare as both radio and television became familiar household fixtures. At one time radio listening had been a family event for which battery power had to be conserved, but by the mid-1950s individuals could spend hours a day looking at television, drifting in and out of the room while the set remained on. Having entered the physical space where the family lived, its convenience helped it penetrate family routines. One group's submission observed: "Different from the theatre and the cinema, which limit their plays to those who attend of their own free choice, television is directed especially to family groups, made up of persons of every age, of both sexes, of differing education and moral training." The family sat at home, susceptible to slow dismemberment via the Trojan horse of television. "Into that circle it brings the newspaper, the chronicle of events, the drama. Like the radio it can enter at any time, any home and any place, bringing not only sounds and words but the detailed vividness and action of pictures; which makes it more capable of moving the emotions, especially of youth."[56]

Canada had some distance to go before every home had a television set, but Fowler and his colleagues fielded plenty of questions about this new domestic appliance and its effects on children. On one occasion, a story of "good kids" out of control found its way into what were supposed to be more solemn proceedings. A visitor to the commission reported that the mother of two young boys had recently been able to observe them with and without television in the house. Deprived of their favourite programs, the boys slept soundly and were well behaved, but with TV on "the bed was always a tangle at night." To this tale, Fowler replied: "I am afraid that [television] is a fact [of] modern life and children will have to adapt."[57] As much as this sounded like a vote of confidence in the resilience of the baby-boom generation, parents worried that their children were seeing too many "scenes of aggression and mental torment" to cope intelligently. In addition to the mental disturbance that some of the more highly rated shows could engender, young viewers came in contact with other shows that might not have been violent, but could still "convey false standards and ridicule authority."[58]

In that "lynch laws, war and spy stories" loomed large in respondents' recollections of what they saw, the "social responsibility"[59] associated with respect for authority seemed to be missing from just about everything broadcast on the commercial airwaves. Paul Rutherford supplies a corrective to this notion in his study of television in Canada during the 1950s and 1960s. Even American stations, supposedly the source of much material of dubious value, broadcast a decent amount of "culture on the small screen."[60] Still, the perception that for-profit broadcasting entailed a fairly unadventurous adherence to formula persisted. "Humour for children on private stations is 90% little animals mangling bigger ones, and the other 10% consists of stammering, puns, and custard-pie throwing," complained an agitated group of Regina housewives. While they certainly held strong opinions about the direction that most television programming had taken, the prospect of setting their children down in front of the television if certain standards were met seemed to occasion little fear. In contrast, their confidence in the CBC's lineup of children's fare, which included such material as *Jubilee Road*, *Kindergarten of the Air*, the school broadcasts, *Camp Wilderness*, CBC *Stamp Club*, and *Folk Song Time*, reflected their approval of an equally wholesome adult schedule, which consistently offered "something of a challenging nature. It gives us good music, fair and objective political and international comment, drama, help with consumer and household problems, and discussions by well-informed observers."[61]

The recognition that television could provide "something of a challenging nature," through which the ordinary person could connect to the wider world outside the home – and to other Canadians – represented one facet of an altered critical landscape. High culture remained high, but the obvious utility of introducing it to audiences via the broadcast media could no longer be dismissed in the hope that millions would pawn their televisions to buy symphony passes. Lobbying for a healthy CBC was one thing, but it was quite another to see respondents to the Fowler Commission looking to the cultivation of spare-time intellectuals as part of the solution to an identity crisis. This was not an overnight transformation, but, as critics came to terms with how television had already assured itself of a place in the home, the critique of modern life and mass culture adopted an increasingly middlebrow sensibility.

Using the new medium to bridge the "gap between the increasing complexity of our society and the understanding of the average citizen"[62] seemed to be a direct method of equipping Canadians for their roles in a democratic country. One presentation predicted that the future would be bright for adult education: "the tastes, interests and capacities of the public are greatly underrated, both in the United States and in our own country."[63] Signs that increased literacy appeared to be delivering some long-awaited results boded well for an expansion of that segment of the population that pursued its own answers to some of life's more difficult issues. Fredericton humanists looked hopefully towards the paperback-book trade, noting that "the people of a growing democracy must be kept informed of developments in the world at large. The increasing sales, all over the Western World, of paper-backed books on politics, economics, science, art, philosophy, etc., seem to indicate that there is a growing demand for information on these and other subjects."

In Cold War–era Canada, posterity also mattered. The same Fredericton group told the commission that, although the increase in sales of public-affairs books encouraged them, it would be "tragic if some

Gibbon of the future, reflecting on the decline of North American civilization, could say of our use of television: 'They used it only to watch wrestling and to sell soap.'"[64] Again, to those presenting briefs on broadcasting, the CBC appeared as the antithesis of this lowbrow sideshow. Programs on the public network such as *Exploring Minds*, which began its run in 1953 and was an introduction to the world of the university; *Anthology*; and the satirical but sophisticated *Rawhide* represented accessibility and the ideal of movement from one interesting subject to another. They also revealed a move away from entertainment calculated only to appeal to base curiosities and instincts, leaving the individual with little of value. As a radio network deliberately dedicated to culture outside the mainstream, the BBC's Third Programme inspired some reverence among critics of mass culture,[65] but in North America it had become difficult to ignore mainstream entertainers and experiences or to abdicate knowledge of them if one hoped to reach the public. Additionally, in Canada, where highbrows had come to owe more of their pleasures to state assistance, justifying the expense on a small segment of the population was nearly impossible.

To several observers and participants in the broadcast field, much in the ordinary person's daily experience seemed vigorous, personal, and evocative of Canadian archetypes – therefore preferable to the sort of entertainment that private stations customarily carried. The radio and television employees' union went further: "Our people are developing their own folk art, and are making themselves known to each other across the land. And we know of no better folk art anywhere than 'La Famille Plouffe' and 'Jake and the Kid.'"[66] These were TV series about ordinary people, but they explored regional contexts that helped them to become folk art in a way that satisfied the contemporary sense of the term.[67] Other aspects of Canadian life could stand as representations of folk experience, and critics recognized that "omitting the accomplishments of industry, the settlement of the north, or sports and recreation, would indeed mean that a projection of Canadian culture was a service to a minority by a minority." Alternatively, more visibly using radio and TV to inform people about such immediate concerns as the technological revolution and its implications[68] would demonstrate that the CBC was fulfilling its public-service mandate. Perhaps to show solidarity with the national broadcaster's declared policy of providing a "comprehensive service," suggestions for programming tended to include plenty of opportunities to encounter high culture, but also a rather mixed bag of other fare. A Labour–Progressive Party representative outlined the consensus opinion of his provincial wing: "We would like to see a local 'pick of the stars' programme, more use of the local ballet groups, the development of a local T.V. drama programme," and he added that party members would welcome a series introducing Manitobans to their own history.[69] The British Columbia Parent–Teacher Federation exemplified the bourgeois–middlebrow more convincingly, asking for more programs on such subjects as "hobbies, manual dexterity, instruction and development in sports, dramatization of children's stories, adventures and animal stories, science and natural phenomena and field trips."[70]

The incomplete nature of such middlebrow programming made it an ideal vehicle for the acts of public service and community-building that many cultural critics hoped to perform. That is, introductory approaches to any subject assumed no prior knowledge of it and could concentrate on conveying one or two rather simple ideas at a time. The Canadian Mental Health Association (CMHA) saw television as powerful and potentially troublesome if not approached correctly, but it told the Fowler Commission that both radio and television could do much to help combat misunderstandings about mental health or even "to help people understand themselves and their emotional make-up," just by passing on a couple of elementary ideas.[71] In its experience with programs in its field of interest, the CMHA noted that, of the "good" and "bad" programs on mental health, all the "good" ones were reverent introductory shows. A comedian appearing on the *Ed Sullivan Show* in the autumn of 1955 exemplified the "bad" by doing a song called "I'm a Schizy Phreny." The CMHA called it "a burlesque on the behaviour of psychotic patients which was in poor taste."[72] It also lacked the earnest quality, the compulsion to provide an authoritative but simple primer on a given subject, that defined middlebrow culture.

In his brief to the commission, historian Arthur Lower outlined a strong nationalist position by equating "American Programs and American Control" with cultural imperialism. "The Canadian people, as those who have spent their lives trying to understand them know, are conservative, they do not crave much excitement: in a dozen different ways their psychology is different from that of the great city populations to the south."[73] Although Americans pioneered middlebrow culture, the two nations were different on that score as well. In the United States, it served an entrepreneurial function – culture could be bought. In Canada, although opportunities such as book-of-the-month clubs existed, the middlebrow path also became an avenue for instilling a sense of national cohesion. Defining an ideal Canada against the example of commercial culture that they found operating within the Canadian broadcasting system, cultural critics saw television as a potentially effective way of passing on a set of simple ideas about how that same commercial culture operated to the detriment of a Canadian identity. A group of scholars at Queen's University wrote its own brief and wanted the electronic media to "please and inform us and move us as civilized human beings, not simply as potential customers whose sales-resistance can be undermined right in our living rooms." It advocated an eclectic list of experiences brought closer by broadcasting – but still mediated. Like Marshall McLuhan, who saw the new technologies as extensions of the human nervous system,[74] it saw radio and TV as ways of "heightening and extending our enjoyment" of all those vital affirmations of humanity; via television "we can attend the Coronation and the Olympic Games and the Stratford Festival; we can go to church or to school or to Parliament or to the ballet or to the ball-park as well as, but not necessarily on the way, to market."[75]

The critique of private broadcasting heard at the Fowler Commission hearings was not purposefully anti-American, although it resented control by this larger and distinct market – an "artificial" monopoly like the one that supporters of private broadcasting in Canada saw hindering their plans for expansion. Neither situation could be represented as democratic. As one observer prudently commented, the commission insisted that "Canada find itself," yet she acknowledged one of the primary obstacles to this process of discovery by quoting from its *Report*: "The problem of influence on Canada from the United States is not ... mainly that American programmes are too bad, but many of them are, in a special sense, too good."[76] This "special sense" – the knack that American producers seemed to have for turning out unsophisticated but popular programs, books, or films – worried critics and prompted them to conflate more easily the issues of nation and taste.

Fine-tuning the CBC

The problem of a public system competing with the commercial media concerned commentators again in 1958, when private broadcasters finally obtained a regulatory board independent of the CBC. For its first twenty-two years, the CBC had regulated the trade that it plied, and some who had lobbied for adoption of that system in the 1930s again "expressed their wariness about meddling with the existing structure."[77] However, the uncoupling of the roles of regulator and broadcaster gave some relief to those weary of hearing how the national broadcaster seemed remote or unresponsive to popular tastes. In terms of the board's influence over the CBC's own programming, the new regulatory structure meant little, because assumptions about the relative value of highbrow and lowbrow programs survived. Some critics worked up again the arguments raised two years earlier in front of the Fowler Commission. They advocated a system whereby the most vacuous popular material could not simply drive out the rest as indicative of a complex and diverse modern society and essential to democracy. "If we can provide audiences with the programmes they want while keeping available to them programmes they ought to want," one observer of the rather inexact science of "broadcast planning" noted, "we can preserve freedom and cultural opportunity."[78] According to Mary Lowrey Ross, however, the audience for the CBC public-affairs program *Fighting Words* consisted of a "small though volatile minority," to whom the show's panellists all seemed to be inveterate eggheads, and a larger group, "prepared to follow a program with interest and curiosity even when its subject matter is considerably over their heads."[79]

The determined middlebrow audience that Ross described gathered a disproportionate share of attention from the hopeful critics seeking cultural improvement through a broadened awareness of social issues and participation in public affairs. Self-improvement became less arduous when all that it took was turning on the television. In 1957, the CAAE represented its long-running *Citizens' Forum* program as "an idea as old as the Greeks ... as modern as television ... and more essential than ever."[80] Even though it billed itself as democratic, in tune with the latest technology, and a repository of sane perspective on the stresses of modern life, its membership – and consequently the number of groups participating formally – had begun to decline drastically within two years of the war, much diminishing its status as the voice of the cultural and social activist. Despite its drop in memberships, its tone still concerned organizers. Having inaugurated a television forum to complement the radio edition of the programs, *Citizens' Forum* tended through the 1950s to feature fewer international topics and more family issues, and by the early 1960s this inclination was well established.[81] Participants were still being asked to consider some weighty subjects, but, armed with pamphlets from headquarters, an alert parent could follow the average week's discussion as easily as the better-educated viewer. With fewer operating groups and faithful members on the mailing list, however, those watching or listening without the prepared text formed the majority. Long-time staffer Isabel Wilson could wonder, with much greater justification than she had even five years earlier, if *Citizens' Forum* was not "now sacrificing the interests of the continuing groups to those of the wider listening audience."[82]

The originators of the series had envisioned these programs not as discrete experiences to be sampled or quickly forgotten, but rather as part of a nationwide endeavour, whose members assembled each week to form hundreds of neighbourhood *salons* and, organizers hoped, to put what they learned into practise immediately. For some of those who kept the faith through the 1950s, the suggestion that they had to tailor their noble ambitions to a less committed audience clearly struck a nerve. But could they simply abandon the field to situation comedies? Organizers worked to make the programmes more entertaining for the casual listener or viewer and less reliant on group discussions by relating current social questions to the audience's own experiences. This was a response to the post 1945 challenge of a larger pool of competing programs, and seemed necessary, given a public that was relatively self-involved by comparison to wartime listeners. In the universities, noted one concerned educator, developing "more intelligent producers and consumers of radio and TV" depended on a "long and arduous" vigil, during which "we must be on the alert lest our products delude our past, present and future constituencies with their insidious brand of Kitsch."[83]

Suggesting that his corporation was undertaking a project to reflect Canadian culture rather than to dictate it, CBC President Alphonse Ouimet declared in 1959 that the public broadcaster must present programs on a variety of subjects. "Canadian culture," he said, "embraces everything from sled-dog races to symphony orchestras, from comedy to opera, from good talks to jazz." These activities seemed to cover a fairly wide range, but behind this inclusive picture lurked the old assumption that the CBC should champion interests or inclinations that had not been represented adequately by commercial broadcasters.[84] Ouimet, however, intended to present the CBC's mission as non-discriminatory. He told a Canadian Club audience in Toronto that "any narrower view of a national broadcasting service would destroy the purpose of the CBC as a unifying force in Canada. If CBC were to direct its programs only to arbitrarily selected social and economic groups, excluding others, we would no longer be a unifying force, but a divisive force – a force dividing the nation and doing irreparable harm to our aspirations as a people and as a nation."

A socio-economic definition of the ideal listener or viewer would hardly have suited the democratic tenor of the times, and the president did not need to point out that the CBC had always offered fare with which better-educated Canadians and those with the money to attend live performances were at least broadly familiar. "I do not believe Canadians want cultural segregation,"[85] Ouimet said, adding that the CBC had never considered itself anything but an agent of integration. The intention behind offering a wide array of programming was not to cater to a highbrow audience, but to expose the casual listener-viewer to something unavailable in the mass-culture marketplace – something requiring a bit of effort. The CBC conducted its operations over two mass media but did not present itself as a purveyor of mass culture. Indeed, although its policy of variety had customarily entailed carrying some shows that were popular on U.S. commercial networks, the bulk of its own productions were still oriented towards information, education, and cultivating a broader knowledge of Canada.

Perhaps consciously broadening Ouimet's already inclusive-sounding embrace of sled-dog racing and opera, the CBC echoed T.S. Eliot in a 1961 print advertisement, declaring: "The culture of a nation is the sum total of what everybody does." Through the intercession of a public network that interpreted its mission as "reflecting" the nation's increasing diversity, the CBC promised its audiences personal introductions to "a thousand and one Canadians whom we will never otherwise meet."[86] In his book *Canada: Tomorrow's Giant*, a 1957 sequel to the successful wartime volume *The Unknown Country*,[87] Bruce Hutchison advocated getting out and seeing the countryside for oneself. This was not practical for many Canadians locked in to industrial work schedules. The CBC offered encounters with interesting people and "better" minds and a tradition that critics believed producers of mass culture had acknowledged only through insensitive plunder.

This effort at persuasion had a target – the many people whom Robertson Davies described as those "who have no interest in literature as such, and who regard reading simply as one, and by no means the best, of the means by which they achieve the sensation which is the only form of entertainment they know." This audience, in Davies's estimation, demanded attention. Though not littered with specialists in literature, it appeared to him to "have taste and standards."[88] Yet some observers harboured reservations about middlebrow culture. Robert Fulford concurred with Davies's hopeful assessment of the audience but followed the American critical tradition by denouncing the practise of simplifying or abridging the classics in order to market them.[89] Indeed, counter to the prevailing model of the 1940s and 1950s in which small-scale cultural efforts won praise, Fulford reckoned that the adult-education movement had created an appetite for localized culture and a little learning. He weighed in on the side of the purists, contending that "to destroy or dilute Mark Twain is surely more harmful than letting a thousand sheriffs mow down a thousand bad guys." He considered it a graver problem, however, that television had become less interesting since the mid-1950s, when an "aversion to 'problem plays,' dislike of unglamourous acting, disgust for plays which modestly fitted themselves to the intimacy of TV" had inclined much American fare towards an unchallenging and mediocre "Hollywood" style.[90] Television had followed a recognizably lowbrow path, Fulford argued, as it abandoned life's more difficult themes in order to boost ratings.

The problem of evangelizing a critical sensibility – with its emphasis on self-improvement – had become one of marketing that sensibility, of convincing Canadians that adopting a sceptical attitude towards commercial popular culture would be beneficial to them collectively and individually. Although there were certainly pitfalls to trying to induce a widespread interest in decidedly "cultural" pursuits, the ethic of popular participation and accessibility often overshadowed that of reverent appreciation. Money and support existed for what were clearly middlebrow projects.[91] This had been building through the mid-1950s with the publication of such items as the proceedings of a Canadian Westinghouse–sponsored conference on Canada's future and the suggestion of large cash prizes for achievement in the arts, letters, and sciences to be awarded at a Grey Cup–style festival.[92] The adult educators' manual for Shakespeare workshops condoned adaptation of plays, sets, and costumes to local circumstances in order to draw wider audiences.[93] The publishing house that put out the *Canadian Commentator* also introduced its own encyclopaedia, as well as the *Baxter Dictionary of Dates and Events* and a book that it called the *Hexicon* – a six-language dictionary for businessmen, scholars, and travellers.[94]

By the later 1950s, critics had for the most part welcomed or at least developed a tolerance towards compromise alternatives to the romance novel or the western movie, whether these flew the banner of quick edification or conscious Canadianism. This general acceptance of middlebrow works – as compatible with the struggle against a mass culture that seemed to have little or no educational value and also with the cultural nationalist position favouring a Canadian idiom distinct from the larger North American one – did much to define cultural criticism in Canada during the later 1950s and early 1960s. John D. Robins's venture, the *Encyclopedia Canadiana*, debuted in 1957. It assembled, as one booster noted, "most of the essential information about our nation and our people."[95] It could be at the same time a product, a pathway to personal development, and an act of patriotic scholarship.

Whether a particular work or genre had "blazed its own trail" or simply resorted to a convenient and profitable formula helped to distinguish between art and kitsch.[96] In valuing works that purported to educate Canadians in an entertaining manner alongside those that were innovative or artistic in a more traditional sense, critics acknowledged this principle but also subverted it by seeking essentially nationalist ends. Supporting the popularization of folk and high cultures as an affirmation of selfhood and nationhood, they reflected a new conception of the cultural marketplace as corrupted, but redeemable. By the early 1960s, courting the middlebrow aesthetic had matured as a strategy for binding together idealized personal and national identities. This was especially the case at the CBC, where the goal had always been to provide more than entertainment and where critics retained a heaping measure of direct and indirect influence.[97] One young public-affairs host, Patrick Watson, summarized this spirit of compromise: "we should arouse interest rather than just feed interests that have already been aroused."[98] When discussing plans for a new nature series for televisions, the program's creative team searched for a way to present genuine scientific knowledge in an accessible manner. The group planning the series hoped to affect a higher tone by avoiding the formulaic treatment of animals, exemplified in "contrived story situations; anthropomorphism; meaningless music; fiction; characters; travelogue; human involvement for its own sake." Still, the medium of television demanded that the programs appeal to the viewer for whom they might be an initiation to the world of science, and that the treatment be a digest of the most important principles. One member of the group insisted that the "overriding flavor will be utterly scientific, with complete reliance on subject matter and film quality to maintain entertainment values at a high pitch. (Need I remark that one can be utterly scientific and still be attractively colloquial and easy in style!)"[99] In seeking to serve an audience whose own familiarity with a particular subject was limited, these producers incorporated altered conceptions of high and low, of education and entertainment, that resembled those of the cultural critic.

WRESTLING WITH AUTOMATION

Although ideological differences defined the Cold War, the existential anxiety building since 1945 owed part of its menace to the image of scientific knowledge used in a destructive fashion. In the late 1950s, the "space race" and fears that the communist bloc educated its scientists more efficiently than the Western nations further worried those already willing to side with U.S. President Eisenhower when he warned of a "military–industrial complex" – an alliance interested primarily in keeping an uneasy peace.[100] Thanks in part to the industries that grew so vigorously and provided jobs in peacetime, a devastating war loomed. Large corporations controlled a larger portion of the economy and exercised unprecedented control over how employees did their jobs or related to their co-workers. Many people seemed to while away more of their leisure time than ever.

American journalist and cultural critic Bernard Rosenberg knew how the rest of the world viewed his homeland's dominant forms of entertainment in 1957, when he warned his readers not to blame capitalism, the United States, or democracy for mass culture. "If one can hazard a single positive formulation," Rosenberg declared, "it would be that modern technology is the necessary and sufficient cause of mass culture." Claiming that "all that really matters is the most recent industrial revolution," he described the trickling down of technology from advanced to less-advanced countries and their collective cultural great leap backward. For Rosenberg, it was clearly a bad time for any nation to be as technically competent as virtually the whole world had become, and he mused: "Maybe at a higher stage of development, society will be 'ready' for industrialization, with consequences very different from those we see around us in the here and now. Meanwhile, change followed by barbarous accommodation proceeds at an accelerated tempo."[101]

Although Canadian critics kept a close watch over a cultural arena charged with nationalist sentiment and were reluctant to appear uncompromisingly highbrow, their attention – like Rosenberg's – sometimes turned to the larger economic and social forces that defined life. These were the forces shaping the societies in which mass culture thrived. Since the Industrial Revolution, concern over the effects of labour-saving or reducing technology had accompanied such innovations Canada. In during the Second World War, opinion on the intrinsic value of increasing mechanization varied. Supporters often saw it as contributing to temporary bouts of unemployment or displacement, while detractors might link it with an excess of leisure time or the enervation of an entire generation of women.[102] Near the end of the war, artist Lawren Harris foresaw a society where "big business and mass production will efface all regional differences and smother the living creative effort of every individual," and he worried that art and artists would suffer most.[103] Once peace returned, youths and factory labourers were also in peril, not because they stood to inherit an increasingly comfortable – if monotonous – workplace, but because the ease of everyday life made "honest" work less attractive and because keeping up with better and faster machines at work often proved debilitating.[104]

Just as the neighbourhood structure – even the wealthy Toronto district portrayed in *Crestwood Heights* – eased acculturation to current social patterns, so the workplace also came under fire as a hive of conformity. Before the war, Charlie Chaplin's film *Modern Times* satirized the tyrannical assembly line, pitting people against machines. By the 1950s, commentary on the social and cultural effects of a rationalized, mechanized workplace had become less symbolic or metaphorical, and more sociological. In 1956, the former editor of *Fortune* magazine, William Whyte, brought out his book on corporate culture, *The Organization Man*. For more than a decade, it remained an influential reading of the sort of work environment in which a growing number of Canadians too found themselves. Along with the organization of people, the prospect of substantive changes to the nature of industrial employment in Canada alarmed several observers during the later 1950s and early 1960s. The one word likely to bring out fears of a bleak working future, with attenuated avenues for creative input from the individual worker, was "automation."

Automation displayed an impeccable pedigree as the offspring of modern life in that it entailed an entirely new level of mechanical control over already highly mechanized production processes. In purely practical terms, it represented a leap in what had been a gradual or predictably incremental process of technological change. Where the assembly line had broken down manufacturing into a series of repetitive tasks still performed by human operatives, automation proposed to take over even those, leaving a much smaller workforce for supervision and occasional maintenance. Well before 1939, a few concerned parties predicted how increased mechanization would affect the number of jobs available in Canada's industrial sector. Forecasts varied, usually according to the opinion holder's relation to the means of production, and the issue of displaced labour continued to crop up well after the term *automation* came into more frequent use by the mid-1950s.[105] Despite the immense economic significance of this new way of producing both simple and complex goods, our chief interest lies in automation's power to incite commentary from those critics for whom it conjured vivid images of social and cultural decay.

A term unheard of before 1948, *automation* initially came under the scrutiny of satirists such as Mary Lowrey Ross and Eric Nicol, probably because it seemed to occupy far and fanciful horizons.[106] It was not until the mid-1950s that Canadian observers, along with their American and British counterparts, paid an appreciable amount of attention to automation or its implications. Within a decade, a number of monographs had been published on the subject, although Canadians had written none.[107] In 1956, poet and essayist Kildare Dobbs delivered one of the earliest blows against the automated society, identifying the difference between industry as it had developed and the coming age of automated industry in which the "only job left for men is watching the machines that watch the machines." Industrialists, according to Dobbs, had lately "convinced themselves that automation is going to set the mass of men free from drudgery and so free for higher things." Boredom, however, seemed more likely than a spontaneous rush to contemplate the nature of existence or to create sublime works of literature. He cited the inadequacy of "do-it-yourself" hobbies for filling the idle hours created by automation and portrayed the "problem of leisure" as one of the gravest threatening society. Finally, he charged his fellow artists with the task of leading the resistance: "Automation is the latest refinement in the relentless social machine and it is the artist's job to assert in his own person through his art that man is not just a blemish on his inventions." The artist, and presumably his public, had a role to play in relation to the blight of automation, and Dobbs conceived of it as "not just a spanner in the beautiful works, a nuisance, an inconvenient item of statistics, but ultimately and absolutely valuable, the master and not the slave of the automats."[108]

A few weeks earlier, the organization that brought intellectual heavyweights to the shores of Lake Couchiching, Ontario, every summer made automation the focus of its winter conference.[109] Participants discussed unemployment, education, and how automated Canada was or could become. Eugene Forsey responded to another participant's proposal that American and British corporations automate some of their Canadian branch plants by likening such an experiment to "trying it on the dog in Canada."[110] This sort of overt nationalism, however, was not as common in contemporary discourse on automation. Equipping workers for such fundamental change, especially in their time away from the job, became a cultural concern. One group of university women presenting a brief to the Royal Commission on Broadcasting noted: "Automation points up the increased leisure we shall all have as our lives become increasingly mechanized. That this leisure can be enriched is obvious if we have a national radio and television network which part time at least will provide an adult education program geared to our interests and needs."[111] As J.R. Kidd of the CAAE suggested, North Americans were remarkably uniform in being ill-prepared for this latest industrial revolution, and a number of commentators agreed that the most urgent need was not distributing blame, but anticipating automation's latent consequences for the individual and the community.[112]

One leader in this regard, and probably most representative of a "middle of the road" perspective, was John A. Irving. He participated in the United Church of Canada's first approach to the issue during 1956–57, lending another dimension to the Toronto Committee, which was concerned primarily with how automation might affect the church and its mission. In addition to affirming the church's potential as a stabilizing force, the committee's report included part of an article that Irving had contributed to *Saturday Night*.[113] In the unabridged version, "Can Machines Replace Minds?" Irving familiarized his readers with automation by providing examples of its application and carefully defining the differences between it and more familiar forms of mechanization. He emphasized, however, that the machines themselves were able to accomplish intricate tasks only because humans had designed them to do so. Improvements to manufacturing technology had not created a new, independent will to rival the human mind.[114]

Despite such reassurances, critics also viewed automation as a force that could undermine those aspects of the social order that owed their stability to limited leisure or to a previously more gradual pace of change.[115] Some thought that under a new regime, in which leisure time was more plentiful, peace of mind would be first to depart. "As automation carries him to opulence," Bruce Hutchison wrote half-satirically of the average modern, "he cannot suffer ease without a tranquilizer pill." He also reckoned that, despite the nation's long tradition of harrowing work on various frontiers, "only a small minority" of Canadians possessed the fortitude to cope with "true leisure" – an ideal state that might well include working at activities that gave one pleasure. Hutchison predicted that the worker displaced by automation, faced with utter boredom, would rise up, throw off the bonds of idleness, and discover his own mind – "a machine as surprising and novel to him, on first inspection, as a Russian rocket and much faster, with a wider orbit." What he called a revolt against leisure looked suspiciously like a rededication to cultural effort – a project that Hutchison and other commentators took rather more seriously than he let on here. "With our new machinery, the real question is not whether we can have more leisure – for we certainly can and will –" Hutchison proclaimed, and he echoed a much better-known emancipator, "but whether a civilization so conceived and so dedicated to leisure can long endure."[116]

Like Irving, in an elliptical fashion, Hutchison praised a moderate course of action vis-à-vis automation. He did so for a middlebrow audience, which he believed would appreciate the paradox of automation and remain wary of the consumerist impulses that would accompany declining prices for mass-produced goods. Although examples of good design could conceivably find their way into more and more homes if their production was given over to the automated factory,[117] one of Julian Park's correspondents, Roy Daniells, had earlier portrayed the appliances and gadgets symbolic of material success as equally symbolic of a different kind of servitude: "Our domestic machines may be labour saving, but they conduce, not to leisure, detachment and contemplation, but to involvement, manipulation, and pride of cumulative possession. They do not free their possessors."[118]

Commentary from those who supported automation, though evocative of a new era of leisure, did little to dispel the critical notion that days spent "watching the machines that watched the machines" would be a blow to humanity. From the management side, columnist William Westley applauded the trend towards pliable and team-oriented workers, ready for shifting around in automated enterprises. Far from ignoring critical perspectives, he chose to see as a boon the shift from "the 'compulsive man' of industrial expansion to the 'adjustive man' of over-production" – a shift that David Riesman described in *The Lonely Crowd*. Automation, Westley enthused, tended to promote the "development of character types who 'can get along with others', who can compromise and be good fellows even while being unpleasant." He noted William Whyte's concern over "compulsive attention to the demands of the group, to the demands of the corporate family and our conformity to them," but ultimately dismissed it by putting the onus on the modern executive to guide industry through what would be an inevitable series of changes. While he acknowledged the possibility of failure, confessing that "all this could contain the seeds of our own destruction," Westley remained a booster of the approaching changes, seeing them as an opportunity for people such as him to reinvigorate themselves. "I am inclined," he wrote, "to view the future optimistically. As the compelling effects of automation spread through industry, changing the jobs, changing the workers, altering the whole pattern of our society, today's executive will need new skills to deal with a new challenge."[119]

The challenge for workers would be to maintain individuality as they moved still further from the craft ideal. However, if technology took over some of the industrial worker's most distasteful tasks, more time and energy would be available for hobbies and family. Despite the potential for more time at home, several observers found it difficult to be optimistic about the effects on family life of work in an automated plant. Alastair MacLeod of Montreal's Mental Hygiene Institute blamed the application of "machine values to living man" for removing healthy forms of stress from the industrial environment. Traditionally, the organization of the human family had allowed men to function as "aggressive, competitive, purposeful" providers and women to fill correspondingly deferential feminine roles. MacLeod explained how he saw the up-to-date working world defacing this delicate domestic picture. "Father no longer has opportunities for pursuing aggressive competitive goals openly at work," he wrote, suggesting that as a result, "some of his basic masculine needs remain unmet. Mother no longer feels she has a real man for a husband and becomes openly aggressive and competitive herself, even moving out of the home into industry in her efforts to restore the biological balance."[120]

The work week had been getting shorter since the late nineteenth century, and it looked as though father's time at work would decrease further in years to come. Having become somewhat more expendable at work, he faced the same fate at home. Social worker R.S. Hosking, a prominent member of the United Church of Canada's Commission on Christian Marriage and Divorce, held out some hope, urging men to make the most of time at home by becoming reacquainted with their own families.[121] Although it did so diplomatically, the commission presented automation, along with the trend towards women seeking work outside the home, as generally reducing family unity. Ultimately, these were only two of a host of pressures that made marriage a much more difficult state to maintain. The commission's first report noted that "many things threaten marital fidelity and family integrity in our society. Desire for sexual gratification is over-stimulated by much of our mass advertising, popular entertainment and printed matter. Rapid urbanization, industrialization, and the increased mobility of population have transformed long established patterns of family relationships." All these changes had shifted the priorities of married couples, so that all too often "pre-occupation with material ambitions and personal enjoyment threaten more durable values in human relationships."[122]

This certainly became a familiar refrain for critics who saw the transformative, impersonal forces of economic "progress" as the villain in family dramas, in the alienation of the individual, and in the automated workplace. Indeed, from the mid-1950s on, an austere future symbolized most powerfully by automation and unbridled scientism gave rise to a number of dystopian visions broadcast on the CBC's more "serious" radio and television drama series.[123] William Paluk's "Let the Machines Do It" was a comedy based on the premise that humans would eventually take on some characteristics of the computers that some were starting to trust implicitly. Only a mechanical malfunction broke the "molecular chain of efficiency" embodied in the world's vast computer network, and the play's characters lapsed into what would seem, to early-1960s' listeners, to be familiar human patterns of interaction.[124]

As a departure from the familiar and sometimes pleasurable rhythms of work, automation stood out among modernizing processes. Keeping pace with a creeping tide of automation in offices and plants, concern for its impact reached new heights during the early 1960s.[125] Having demonstrated its interest through the Toronto Committee in 1957, the United Church of Canada entered a more developed discourse in 1964 when it resolved to create a full-scale Commission on Automation. The commission's mandate was to encourage the just distribution of automation's fruits and to promote the benevolent uses of leisure. With those ambitious goals in mind, it ran magazine ads declaring that "the Christian task in these days of increasing automation is to bear active witness to these Christian principles, and so help to make sure that the onrushing robots mean a better life for all."[126] By the mid-1960s, cautionary voices inside and outside this intrepid band admitted that rapid technological change would proceed with or without the approval of Canadian society's self-appointed guardians.[127] They could only hope, as historian W.L. Morton did, that young adults would recognize themselves among the "first generation of humanity who will be fully mechanized, automated and electronicized."

The direst cultural implication of this shift was that, except for the professional artist's work, the new generation's leisuretime pursuits might soon represent Canadian society's principal opportunity to define itself in full public view. Critics came to recognize that the working out of personal and collective identities would have to acknowledge the impact of automation on the working lives of many Canadians. They did not, however, concede the struggle to mechanized and standardized cultural experiences. They hoped that presenting alternatives would appeal to a basic sense of individuality, probably best identified as a middlebrow grasp of one's own place within a developing nation. Urging his audience to be mindful of the immense differences between humans and machines, Morton alluded to an essential task for all individuals: "machines are not persons, and persons are not machines. Man was not made for the machine, but the machine for man. Sensibility, thought, love, these only men may possess, and never the most intricate computer." He left room for both technology and human ingenuity – most important, reserving some time for humanists such as he, who would continue to have plenty to think about: "I do know the world has moved an enormous distance since I worked at Brandon College, and I also know that I still have a little work to do."[128]

Late in the summer of 1957, *Maclean's* printed a translated excerpt from Gabrielle Roy's most recent novel, *Rue Deschambault*. Roy based the story loosely on her own childhood, and in one scene she recalled her mother's ability to remain in good spirits, regardless of the family's circumstances: "A hundred times a day Maman got a lift of joy from the world around us, sometimes it was nothing more than the wind or the flight of a bird that delighted her."

Roy's cheering memory, though fictionalized and set plainly in a bygone period, thoroughly vexed one reader. He wrote to the magazine's editors, asking: "How can Miss Roy write that tosh in this sixth decade of the twentieth century? ... The world around us is not the wind or the flight of a bird. It is the fearful energy of an atomic universe, it is hydrogen bombs, rockets, guided missiles, it is international tension and the threat of war, it is the danger of financial collapse and bankruptcy, it is the mechanization of life, it is the degradation of all spiritual values through the commercialism and popular entertainments of our time. It is the kind of environment that produces the angry man and the existentialist, characters so lamentably absent from Canadian writing. ... How could any intelligent person get a 'lift of joy' from it?"[129] The letter writer's brooding sense of doom encompassed several facets of life that had changed drastically for Canadians since 1945. The correspondent's disappointment at the state of the modern world – and Canadian literature's apparent inability to acknowledge it – existed side by side with hopes that the nation would soon manifest its own distinctive character. Unveiling that character, however, required paying close attention to the changing face of modern life and use of the obviously persuasive media to engage the public by reconstructing Canada in an entertaining but always uplifting fashion.

Unsure themselves of what Canada had come to mean to its inhabitants, critics equated the fragmentation of experience at home and at work with an overall decline in cultural standards and social cohesion. One of the chief drawbacks of this fragmentation was that no new personal responsibilities seemed necessary for the maintenance of order. Nothing like a repressive bourgeois sensibility existed to check a hedonism made public through rites of consumption or to oppose an empty leisure that appeared to exact little personal effort or promote little spiritual growth. The inner-directed society had become other-directed, and critics believed that too much was going on for the average person to retain a measure of individuality without some benevolent guidance. Earlier in the 1950s, it had seemed that cultural improvement was on the agenda to stay and that intervention to arrest the decline in public tastes might succeed. Faced with learning what anthropologist Edmund Carpenter approvingly called the "new languages"[130] of the mass media, most critical observers became less sanguine as the 1950s continued.

Many sensed a twofold loss. First, they feared that, given the pressures that they frequently defined as external to Canada, or at least external to an idealized Canadian sensibility that had not been allowed to develop, it would be difficult to maintain the drive for cultural improvement. In the climate of the Cold War, establishing an elevated common culture by letting the public choose freely from among a number of competing alternatives was advisable as a sound public-relations tactic. It seemed unlikely because of strong competition from the American cultural industries. With a shared language, and a host of other similarities linking the two countries, lowbrow cultural products became popular for the same reason in English Canada as in the United States – they appealed well enough to average tastes. Most critics believed that the only people with the power to improve tastes by offering a broader range of entertainments were the producers, advertisers, and media corporations already complicitous in the decline.

Second, critics saw a pattern of increasing anxiety accompanying further Canadian integration into a technocratic continental orbit. This pattern worried those still hoping that the individual could take up new leisure opportunities rather than looking "to corporate sources for the advancement of his interests, the satisfaction of his needs and the definition of his beliefs."[131] The convenors of 1963's Couchiching Conference opened one session by asking: "Have we, the children of the twentieth century, become enmeshed in the seaweed and algae of an ocean of doubt and perplexity?"[132] The specialization already required of workers who were newly threatened by automation contributed to critics' conviction that Canadians were already "at sea." It had become more difficult for individuals to establish values and tastes that were their own. Although observers had identified the pace of life as a source of anxiety before the turn of the century, this long familiarity had done little to diminish modernity's seemingly pernicious influence on the average person's psychological well-being or on fundamental social structures such as the family. Maintaining their fascination with the broader context in which cultures existed and changed, several commentators (with the notable exception of Marshall McLuhan) contended during the later 1950s and into the 1960s that the complementary relationship between technology and mass distraction could lead only to weakened national and personal cultures that would consist largely of the often-numbing selections available in the cultural marketplace.

The reconstruction era had welcomed highly structured community-focused attempts to wean citizens away from passive leisure, and supporters of the Massey mission greeted localized aspirations towards a humanist high culture with approval. In contrast, many in the band of critics now recognized a kind of accessible exceptionalism as a reasonably reliable path – though admittedly more roundabout than blind patriotism – towards a Canadian identity. Those concerned about how Canadians coped with new pressures, social trends, and cultural developments had since well before 1939 been refining their own understandings of what it took to maintain a healthy self-concept. During the later 1950s, many of them began to recognize the usefulness of engaging in nationalist or middlebrow strategies, which seemed more democratic or inclusive than conformity to highbrow standards.

A melding of some assumptions surrounding nationalism and democracy characterized the period. These assumptions – first, that Canada was a nation whose exposure to American mass culture had kept it from some important date with self-discovery, and, second, that the remedy could come only through widespread acknowledgment of the undemocratic nature of that process – complemented each other. Within reasonably edifying cultural productions, critics found elements of the active individual type and linked these with an emerging identity-focused nationalism. In addition to maintaining their praise for high and folk cultural forms, a number of critics came to recognize that supporting self-consciously Canadian efforts at popular enlightenment would seem less authoritarian than "shoving Culture down people's throats." It might also draw the moderately well-educated, middle-income middle manager disenchanted with anonymity into the struggle for a nation impervious to low cultural influences.

CONCLUSION: LINKING NATIONALISM
AND THE CRITIQUE OF MASS CULTURE

As national secretary for *Citizens' Forum* near the end of the Second World War, a hopeful George Grant saw a chance to model meaningful participation in community affairs through radio listening groups – a promising marriage of old ends and new means. By the early 1960s, Grant could point to what he considered a disturbing relationship between technology and Canadian life: "as we move to greater technological mastery (a movement that can only be stopped by war) the most pressing social questions will call forth judgments as to which activities realize our full humanity and which inhibit it." To Grant, and to others eager for the nation to become an example of "full humanity," conformity, alienation, and the disintegration of community and family were dark clouds behind the more visible silver lining of postwar economic growth, and it was essential to separate activities that built the good society from those that threatened it. In addition to proclaiming his determination to humanize urban life, to restore a creative element to the world of work, and to balance individualism and order, Grant asked, "How can we stimulate education (in its broadest sense) so that the new leisure will be more than a new boredom of passive acquiescence in pleasures arranged by others? How can we see that in rightfully cultivating the fullest equality we do not produce a society of mediocrity and sameness rather than of quality and individuality?"[133]

In a period that featured the arrival and entrenchment in Canada of such significant agents of change as automation and television, the problems of authority and influence remained central for critics. Just as industrial automation formed part of a seemingly inexorable process of modernization challenging labour and social activists, cultural critics found their own options limited. Although they professed to be democrats, some clung to the assumption that the Canadian public, given more leisure and no guidance, would choose unwittingly from among the worst of the alternatives open to them. Despite the unprecedented state interest in culture beginning earlier in the decade, critics could not assert any right or privilege to monitor or police entertainments or ways of life without appearing reactionary and anti-progressive. The trap of bland, secure employment and a limited culture was well-constructed in Canada and strongly resembled the one reputed to house so many Americans. Indeed, one of the editors of a well-known U.S. collection of essays on mass culture suggested that mass culture, instead of a democrating cultural opportunity, had severely limited the range of human activity. "A genuine esthetic (or religious or love) experience becomes difficult, if not impossible, whenever *kitsch* pervades the atmosphere." He proclaimed, more artfully than any Canadian critic of those years, that "only the genuine experience, as Flaubert realized, can satisfy us. It presupposes effortful participation."[134] Though not reduced to such a convenient epigram, devotion to effort as a foundation of worthy experience remained strong among Canadian commentators. By the early 1960s, several of them had been longstanding supporters of cultural forms that required some effort of the audience and continued to identify these as antidotes to commercial culture.[135] Such thought-provoking works could also calm the whirl of life and help to determine – more fairly than box-office receipts – what sort of culture best characterized or suited Canadians.

The concluding section of chapter three above suggested rather briefly that, compared to the decade or so immediately following 1945, the later 1950s in Canada housed more profound concern about technology's social and cultural implications. Though coined only in the late 1940s, *automation* – a term most properly defined as "the automatic control of the manufacture of a product through its successive stages"[136] – had by the mid-1950s acquired a greater currency and a broader meaning. In addition to the speculation arising about its consequences for the labour market, its spectre prompted questions about its potential to alter roles within the family and about what further leisuretime might mean for those people already believed to be using their time off work unproductively. Automation, as interpreted by a group more favourably disposed towards the craft ideal, meant not only a loss of control over even the simplest elements in the production process, but a transformation of work and working culture that would leave only consumers and machine-minders in its wake.

Founded on an aversion to the notions of advertising or marketing culture in what was considered the American style, critics' own preferences for leisuretime listening, viewing, or reading – make it complex or educational, make it about ourselves as Canadians or about the human condition – outlined an aesthetic that most people would not share. These preferences were well-rooted by the late 1950s and early 1960s. The most notable aspect of critics' approaches to the threat of mass culture was that they did not dismiss ways of making the fruits of art, literature, and scholarship more convenient and entertaining. A willingness to link self-improvement with a decorous patriotism and, most important, to do so in magazines, on radio, and on television spoke to a softening of old prejudices. Journalist Blair Fraser wrote of

Maclean's editorial strategy: "We think of a *Maclean's* reader as an intelligent person in a relaxed mood, and a great deal of what we offer is intended only for his entertainment and not for his improvement. However, we have serious purposes. We want to report Canada and the world to Canadians through Canadian eyes."[137] Of course, endeavours such as the Stratford Festival remained laudable as institutions requiring the individual to pay close attention. Relative to the mass media, these drew small audiences. Given a public unable to afford tickets to events such as live theatre on a regular basis, making the critique of mass culture part of the discourses of nationalism and self-respect, and rendering it more accessible via convenient means of communication, marked a notable transition from what seemed the relative elitism of the Massey Commission era.

Cultural interchange between nations, for good or ill, had been present long before mass communication was practicable. Canada in the late 1950s, as a member of the United Nations, the North Atlantic Treaty Organization, and the Commonwealth, could not afford to cut itself off from a culturally rich and diverse but increasingly troubled world. As Malcolm Ross put it, "If no man is an island, no culture is an island in the day of Sputnik and the ICBM. But long before these dreadful signs of our littleness and our oneness had appeared in the heavens, the intermesh of the national cultures was far advanced. Communication does not always beget communion." Ross believed that this global awareness presented an opportunity: "at least now under the same dark sky, we can huddle together in a jiffy and, from Rome to New York, Toronto to Tokyo, trade our terrors and forge our hope."[138] Observers such as Ross saw value in looking outside Canada, for spiritual as well as artistic reasons, while making certain that Canada's cultural credentials were displayed to their best advantage.[139] Julian Park's observation about the CBC and its "duty" only hinted at the environment that Canadian entertainers inhabited – at least partially of the critics' creation. Holding Canadian acts in special esteem, they contended that these should be aimed at an audience with relatively mature tastes. If performers, writers, or artists sought a measure of critical approval at home, their work had to exhibit something of a cerebral quality, employing themes that were somewhat complex, illustrating some aspect of the Western tradition or presenting some episode of Canadian history.

Even Canadian television comedians, remarked Mary Lowrey Ross, did not "sit down on freshly painted benches, or involve themselves with wild loops of pizza dough."[140] Whether this was a folkway – as she argued – or the result of a need to provide entertainment clearly diverging from an American model, critics' identification of intrinsic cultural value with the rejection of slapstick and formulaic sentiment did not mean that only the "best" or most "authentic" books, films, or dances would do. It took until the early 1960s, however, for a pattern of compromise – today more familiar and institutionalized in CBC production values, Canadian content regulations, and numerous other aspects of cultural policy and practice – to emerge. While nationalist sentiment undoubtedly played a part in prompting some Canadian observers to portray American cowboy films and teen music idols as the uninvited Other, so too did disdain for the perceived vacuity of mass culture reinforce the will to produce or encourage more meaningful – and homegrown – alternatives. The question of whether critics were nationalists first or highbrows all along is moot when we consider that both these points of view influenced their reading of the late 1950s' cultural landscape and helped set a decidedly different tone for the arrival of another dynamic decade.

6

The Long Long Weekend: Centennial and Expo 67

Straining to discern the shape of celebrations still almost ten years away, journalist Peter C. Newman expected that the excitement surrounding Canada's Centennial would last "a whole year, not just the week-end we now devote to Dominion Day." His information at the end of 1957 came from Alvin Hamilton, a member of John Diefenbaker's Conservative government and one of the first to press for a commemorative effort that was not only reverently nationalist, but therapeutic. Hamilton complained to Newman that "the emphasis on Dominion Day in the past has been too much on baseball and not enough on national background" and went on to fuse two terms that observers of culture in Canada had been finding increasingly compatible: "we want *mass participation* in the Centennial." Echoing the powerful rhetoric of active citizenship contained in the culture of reconstruction, he could add hopefully that the Centennial year would bring "a rededication of the Canadian people – a resurgence of the national conscience."[1]

Hamilton's was an "official" look ahead – outlining one vision of what the state might accomplish in staging Centennial-year activities. During the late 1950s and the early 1960s, few observers speculated "unofficially" about the cultural opportunities of 1967.[2] This situation changed somewhat during mid-decade, when much of the planning for Centennial and for the 1967 World Exhibition in Montreal (known colloquially as "Expo" or "Expo 67") took place. These years are most often remembered as a time when civil disobedience challenged civil commentary as the dominant mode of addressing the contradictions of modern life. The mid-1960s also stood near the end of a transitional period during which critics gradually recognized that the maintenance of strict cultural hierarchies was largely incompatible with the promotion of an enlightened common culture. Two decades after the Second World War, it seemed that engaging the audience in an enterprise such as Centennial would mean organizing a year filled with events less earnest and more easily-consumed than the sombre and personal postwar reconsecrations a generation earlier.

Historians of 1960s' Canada have tended to characterize the mid-decade as a time in which the federal Progressive Conservative Party unravelled and "radical dissent and counter-cultural efflorescence"[3] began to take hold. Acknowledged most recently with a treatment by Pierre Berton, 1967 was clearly a milestone for Canada. For nationalists, the years leading up to the end of Confederation's first century housed a certain urgency, as if the nation would be called to account on reaching some mystical age of majority.[4] That need to display progress towards nationhood derailed neither anxiety over the pace and injustices of modern life nor the evolution of the mass-culture critique. Though not directed specifically towards preparations for Expo or Centennial, perceptions of how difficult individual and collective self-determination had become still led some in the early and mid-1960s to note – perhaps none so vehemently as George Grant in his 1965 *Lament for a Nation* – that little seemed worth celebrating.

The prefiguring of Centennial and Expo reveals much about the period's cultural context. Because the Centennial year's activities required intensive planning and critics did not stop addressing Canadian life, the period 1963–67 presented a distinctive juxtaposition of "official" and "unofficial" outlooks on what constituted worthwhile culture. As organizers told Canadians and each other how they thought the nation's Centennial should be celebrated and how they wanted the world to encounter itself at Expo, they drew on existing and evolving assumptions about modern life and the mass mind. Faced with the task of national self-definition, besieged by an apparently ahistorical mass culture and a relentless continentalism, they displayed an unprecedented, but not unheralded, flexibility. The preservation of local, regional, and "ethnic"[5] folkways characterized the planning of Centennial-year events, some of which were also constructed to engage the attention of twenty million people.

Given a year to get beyond the holiday-weekend mentality, would hordes of Canadians take time to seek some deeper knowledge of their collective identity? If the ambitious goal of meaningful mass participation was to be achieved, the nation's history and mythologies required distillation into more accessible forms than, for example, the CBC's public affairs programming of the early 1960s.[6] CBC drama producers and programming staff began planning for Centennial as early as 1962, discussing strategies for making history more accessible and even for satirizing the Centennial itself.[7] Like the chautauquas that travelled their rural circuits prior to the Second World War,[8] Centennial sought to improve its audiences, but was responsive enough to offer something for everyone. It was primarily a nationalist festival that revealed the limits of critics' influence and pressed organizers into determining how to transcend the habits of spectatorship that had grown up around Dominion Day. At Expo 67, the bulk of the national pavilions and exhibits celebrated human ingenuity under the theme of *Terre des Hommes* – Man and his World. Despite the jolly, futuristic impression left with many visitors, an underlying determination to break from the World's Fair precedent set in Seattle (1962) and New York (1964) lent Expo a faint museum-like air. A few pavilions envolved the dehumanizing power of raw progress and commercialism – the legacy of considerable sympathy for this alternative viewpoint during theme development in the mid-1960s.

The process of working out what to commemorate and to display as artifacts of Confederation's hundred-year career hardly seemed democratic. It involved much behind-the-scenes manoeuvring and was not immune to internecine political struggles.[9] Neither was the staging of a Universal Exhibition to be trusted to staff unfamiliar with international protocol or standards. These events were not, however, a one-way process, in which a booster elite simply told organizer-functionaries exactly how to commemorate Canada's heritage or how to confirm its status among technologically advanced nations. Most organizers within the Centennial Commission and Expo administration were well-disposed towards the liberal-democratic aims of the cultural critic. Well-educated and possessing a stake in the cultivation of a Canadian exceptionalism, they were none the less aware of the power of good public relations. John Fisher, the Centennial commissioner, had been a broadcaster with the CBC, well-known in the 1940s. Expo's Director of Operations Philippe de Gaspé Beaubien epitomized the literate executive. He had an MBA from Harvard and, like many of his collaborators on the project, considered Expo to be in an entirely different category from events such as the annual Canadian National Exhibition in Toronto. A cast of distinguished advisers from the sciences and humanities took charge of refining the exhibition's theme.[10] Still, by suggesting suitable ways that Canadians might *participate* in Centennial, organizers reflected both the influence of mass culture *and* its changing critique. Although Expo was a fascinating display of all things modern, featuring some of the most advanced means of audio-visual communication, a reluctance to give in and simply amuse the millions who came to visit must also be read as a reluctance to place entertainment above the more complex theme of humanity's conduct in a world that it had come to dominate.

By 1964, during the early part of what one historian has called the "High Sixties," an atmosphere of idealism, activism and experimentation enveloped Europe and the United States,[11] but seemed largely to aggravate Canadian cultural critics' disappointment at the general disengagement that they sensed in Canada. Hugh Maclennan remarked on a "new kind of unrest that afflicts every society in the West, our own included," but, too often for his liking, youths in 1964 seemed directionless.[12] Halifax broadcaster Norman Creighton surmised that even elementary-school textbooks had ceased to cultivate a sense of adventure and consequence in youths. In the old "Royal Reader," he recalled, "life was real, life was earnest. In the wings lurked the pinched faces of poverty and starvation, waiting to pluck down those who had not learned their lesson: that work is a virtue, and idleness the most deadly of sins."[13] The less conventional standards applied to artistic expression and behaviour in the early 1960s had not revoked critics' licence to insist that cultural choices carried moral or social consequences, but such a relaxed atmosphere made judgments such as Creighton's seem all the more puritanical.[14]

While Centennial and Expo drew on a critical tradition that valourized heritage, participation, and a humanistic perspective on technological development, they also accommodated a new relativism by acknowledging the need to convey their message in stimulating and dynamic ways. From his vantage point in 1965, artist and curator Moncrieff Williamson found the prospects for Centennial year and beyond pleasing and also pointed out some of the changes that had made these happier times possible. "Thanks to television, to radio, to survey courses at Universities, the plethora of art reproductions and superb art books, to what Malraux refers to as the 'museum without walls,'" he reported, "our flocks are larger than ever before, numbered in millions and considerably more intelligent and receptive in their acceptance of new, progressive thought.[15] This shifting scene (examined in the first section of this chapter) would add ferment to preparations for Centennial and Expo 67 (second section) and help to bring together the nationalist critics and a militant younger generation (third section).

A SHIFTING POPULAR CULTURE

Anticipating Centennial year allowed critics to continue airing their perennial complaints. In the early and mid-1960s, they found some fresh justifications for those grievances by doing what made them cultural critics: looking to their immediate surroundings and offering suggestions. Although the buildup to Centennial year provided some ready-made occasions for commentators to present their recipes for social and cultural improvement, there was no shortage of such commentary *outside* that context. Rapid technological change and a quickly shifting popular culture bestrode the Canadian scene. Critical observers might still have considered these to be externally imposed burdens inhibiting the realization of national identity or personal enlightenment, but they also admitted that Canada had become fully integrated into what sociologist Jacques Ellul had called the "technological society."[16] George Grant's aforementioned *Lament for a Nation* turned on this same unhappy admission but is probably best remembered for linking the demise of John Diefenbaker's brand of conservatism with the triumph of a technocratic system in North America. Observers treated the problem of carving out a Canadian space in the midst of those conditions as an urgent one, even when they did not explicitly address the upcoming anniversary of Confederation.

In Canada between about 1963 and 1967, life did not come to a halt in anticipation of a millennial experience. In Quebec, there were signs of instability, mainly because the province had experienced substantial economic and social changes since the beginning of the decade. This was a setting in which more radical separatist elements had begun to find their voices. The creation in 1963 of the federal Royal Commission on Bilingualism and Biculturalism put an unprecedented emphasis on dualism in government and indirectly on regional identities. The fact that issues such as separation were being discussed alarmed some people, but also spurred an already palpable desire to arrive at a more inclusive definition of Canada in time for the Centennial.[17] A new phase of constitutional wrangling began and brought in its train – eventually – such welcome developments as official support for multiculturalism and the acknowledgment of aboriginal entitlements. In national politics and foreign affairs, this was the Pearson (or post-Diefenbaker) era, and repairing relations with the United States as well as finding Canada a new flag loomed on the agenda. Of vital interest to citizens of all ages and backgrounds, "socialized" medicine began to gain a foothold in most provinces, having made some inroads during the previous few years.

1963–64 hardly denoted a radical departure from recent patterns, in which critical observers began to reconceive of the public as less passive. While the boundaries between high- and middlebrow had become somewhat more permeable, a cultural hierarchy still existed. Sometimes an authoritarian strain reappeared in the critique of mass culture, but these occasions only served to emphasize that culture, like the modern world, was a complex web in which consumers (formerly portrayed most often as victims) could express preferences and in doing so forge a popular culture. As a representative of the old hard line whose political sympathies had swung from democratic socialism towards the Liberal Party, Frank Underhill's mid-1960s' distrust of the "equalitarian democracy [that] tends to produce a regime of collective mediocrity" faithfully reprised his own wartime thoughts on even older trends. He remained convinced in particular that "the anti-intellectual strain in our society has been accented by the rise of the mass media in the fields of entertainment and information."[18] Convincing Canadians to spend their leisuretime at creative hobbies or activities in which they were participants rather than spectators could still involve warnings, like Underhill's, against the lowest forms of mass culture.

Several commentators harboured lofty ideals but had of late more readily accepted the challenge of promoting their vision for Canadian society through wider accessibility rather than through an appeal to divisive cultural hierarchies. For the most part, critics saw middlebrow programs and works presented from a didactic nationalist perspective in a positive light, but the sympathetic CBC was no longer the only Canadian network providing television service once the Canadian Television network (CTV) went on the air in 1961. The newcomer, like many of the private broadcasters that had joined it, had few resources for producing programs of its own. Consequently, it carried a significant proportion of American shows already highly rated in that market.[19] This effectively increased the supply of programming aimed at a mass audience and was but one factor assuring continuity in the criticism of vacuous entertainments. A heightened concern about the social effects of automation – a topic treated in the preceding chapter – also served as an indicator of continuity.[20]

For commentators eager to counteract tendencies towards conformity and mass production in the cultural and educational fields, the spectres of commercialization and needless devotion to organizational efficiency remained powerful rhetorical devices. In an article for *Canadian Forum*, Robert Fulford suggested that the CBC had sprouted a corporate ethic and had all but lost the sense of community that enabled it to produce innovative programming. To Fulford, this bureaucracy was "so paralyzing that its dead hand is extinguishing, one by one, the centres of quality and integrity which were painstakingly created in the 1950s and 1940s."[21] Beneath Fulford's distrust of bureaucracy lay the assumption that, when a creative or educational organization adopted the trappings of the market, the results of its efforts would soon become a commodity. Still, his reaction was hardly surprising, given the sharp distinction between market forces and the national interest that continued to characterize commentary on both the origins and the career of Canada's broadcasting system.[22] Arthur Lower saw the same sort of chasm dividing the rare and virtuous scholars from the useful but undistinguished administrators in Canadian universities – where "the powers of the world beyond our walls" (embodied in a culture of "bosses" and "promotions") appeared to have overwhelmed a system esteeming creative scholarship and the search for knowledge.[23]

Impressions converged of bloated university administrations and a bureaucratic CBC indicated critics' displeasure with the idea of cultural institutions' acquiescence to patterns prevalent in a science and technology–oriented business world. However, critical observers displayed an even stronger sense that the proliferation and abuse of modern means of communicating would render the intended functions of those institutions less and less relevant to more and more people.[24] If they did not pay more attention to the way people interacted with the media, education and culture would be entirely commodified and less likely to cultivate independent minds. James Gonsalves purveyed an image of a mass audience oblivious to even the most basic strategies of enrichment. "Drive around your city or around our country," he urged his readers, "and look up. Antennae rise like bayonets, in orderly suburban battalions, raggle-taggle armies from unpainted shacks and huge tracts of urban decay. Little blue screens illuminate places where no book has ever been or will probably ever go.[25] The idea that viewing television could replace or even preclude reading was hardly new. Indeed, the fact that Gonsalves did not elaborate on what he meant by "book" indicates that he expected his readers to understand how squalid social conditions and mass-produced culture could reinforce one another. For him, the presence of "books" (i.e., literature of a certain standard above the pulp novel) signalled personal autonomy. There was an element of national pride at work, too. At a time when President Lyndon Johnson's campaign for a "Great Society" targeted inadequate housing and educational opportunities in the United States, the suggestion that Canadians were likewise suffering in squalour (but had managed to keep their televisions) no doubt troubled those who regarded this country's situation as less dire and the personality of the average Canadian as slightly less pliable.

As they had since 1945, critics grappled during the mid-1960s with how to enlist popular interest in projects that – by trumpeting the virtues of a more diverse, participatory, and complex culture – would berate the public over its benighted condition. Hyperbolic or not, Gonsalves's portrayal of row on row of TV-addicted households set up an effective contrast between "intellectuals" and the masses and brought up the pressing issue of how activists keen to remedy both social and cultural problems could "enter the little blue worlds where the people live ... in terms that are meaningful to them."[26] Although the will to enhance the cultural life of every citizen persisted, critics found it difficult to maintain such clear distinctions between total absorption in mass culture and selective use of it. People disposed of their leisure-time as they pleased and – as Raymond Williams has suggested – often did so by patronizing seemingly unrelated or even "contradictory" entertainments such as theatre and football.[27] During the early 1960s, this transgression of boundaries already appeared to be commonplace in Canada. A film or a television program, even though it might be classified as popular, could simultaneously draw attention to the stresses of life and serve as an escape from them. Of one such programme, *Petticoat Junction*, television critic Dennis Braithwaite wrote: "Take anything in the show, the general store, the rotunda of the hotel, the high-backed wooden chairs in the dining room, and it can be seen that they function as artifacts of an age that our generation hates to leave and for which our youngsters would like to have the key."[28] Regardless of viewers' reasons for tuning in, Braithwaite's willingness to grant the program some significance indicated that critics had begun to look at popular entertainments less prejudiciously.

Finally, the problem of maintaining national unity also informed the mid-1960s' cultural context. The earliest years of the Quiet Revolution made Quebec's separation seem more than a remote possibility, and the diffuse nationalism – to which a number of commentators warmed about 1960 – crystallized around this troubling prospect. The Bilingualism and Biculturalism Commission met to examine old divisions and to enumerate the differences and the common ground between what appeared, more than ever, to be two solitudes. Increased attention to Quebec's grievances resonated with preparations for the Centennial, and, even outside official channels, thinking of ways to instil or revive a more general sense of nationhood became something of a pastime. From 1962 through 1967, *Maclean's* ran "Your Questions about Canadiana" – a regular feature dealing primarily with antiques. Plans for a television series consisting of 100 episodes from Canadian history were well in hand by 1964.[29] Under the auspices of McClelland and Stewart, the Canadian Centennial Publishing Company put out part of its Canadian Centennial Library series during 1965. Trading on the newfound yen for historical icons, by the end of 1965 the Lyons Tea Company had begun to include trading cards depicting historical scenes in every box of its product.[30] Journalist R.T. Bowman had been doing historical research and was working up *It Happened Today* – a series of radio programs on Canadian history intended to increase "Canada consciousness." He proposed airing his segments after the evening news in order to gain as large an audience as possible. More important, he wanted to reach people who might not consider themselves sophisticated or well-educated but possessed some capacity to appreciate the roles that Canadians – French- and English-speaking – had taken in the development of their own country. "In its present place, or after the proposed 'Readings from the Classics,'" Bowman wrote, "I feel we are reaching intellectuals, who probably know something about our history, or shut-ins and blind people. Of course I would like to make life more bearable for shut-ins and blind people, but we are going through a crisis as a nation, and I think it would help if the ordinary 'Joes' knew there were many exciting, fascinating things about Canada."[31]

MORE THAN A BIRTHDAY PARTY

By the middle of 1963, when the constitutional "crisis" of which Bowman spoke was only beginning to attract attention, the idea of Centennial had matured to the extent that the federal government's newly-formed Centennial Commission could present "national stocktaking and rededication for the future" as its goals for 1967.[32] These terms of collective enterprise and devotion eerily recalled the mid-1940s. In much the same way as anticipation of war's end had done, Centennial offered critics of passivity a forum in which to promote "healthier" ways of living and of interacting with neighbours. Citing some of the same old distractions and updating the list of troublesome influences, one malcontent thundered: "Do you realize our grandchildren will have half again as much leisure as we have today? What are they going to do with this time? Sit and watch television, resort to alcohol, sleeping pills or perhaps look for kicks misusing the new mind drugs such as L.S.D. or heroin?" Canada had not experienced violent rioting or widespread civil disobedience, but powerful images of the nascent drug-addled counterculture in some of the largest U.S. cities demanded a corrective in the form of simple, participatory recreation. Merely following the spectator sports that helped build American television networks and the CBC during the 1950s was not enough, and the speaker urged a "reawakening of our physical development, not only in the field of exercise, but in an intelligent choice of hobbies."[33]

Within the Centennial Commission itself, planning for the officially sanctioned parts of the year-long celebration looked beyond hobbies and towards 1967 as a transcendental experience, not only a recreational or diversionary one. In mid-decade, critics no longer viewed recreation and diversion as entirely antithetical to personal enlightenment, and in planning Centennial events organizers straddled the crumbling wall separating vigilant educator from circus promoter. "Exciting" and "fascinating" events were to be stepping stones to a widespread familiarity with elements of Canadian history and culture and would thereby suggest a distinct identity within North America. An interviewer asked Commissioner John Fisher if Canada would see any substantial changes following Centennial – if there would be "something more to it than just a big birthday party?" Fisher admitted that community infrastructures would benefit but hastened to add: "It's also a spiritual thing. It's taking stock. It is looking back to say 'thanks'. It is looking at today and saying kindly to each other 'let's build' and it's looking ahead. It's an emotional involvement."

Fisher knew that his organization could not hope to co-ordinate all the projects undertaken in small towns across Canada, but he insisted that Centennial "doesn't just mean firecrackers and bands... When you look back a hundred years from now we'll look pretty small if all we've built is a bunch of sidewalks."[34] None the less useful sidewalk and the ephemeral fireworks display found a place, but for idealists or practically minded local interests these did not suffice. Many Canadians may well have associated such amenities with Centennial for years afterwards (and why not?), but sidewalks and fireworks housed no local symphonies and hosted no amateur sports leagues. For those purposes, the federal government matched municipal and provincial funding to erect Centennial concert halls and arenas.[35]

The Centennial era's legacy in concrete also included such buildings as the National Library and Archives – a project in the works long before 1967 – and generally reflected an appreciation for architectural modernism among those who approved the plans. However, organizers intended Canadians to experience Centennial in a more *abstract* fashion, as a moving recognition of the happy historical accidents and political compromises that bound them together. True to John Fisher's reminder that posterity mattered, the design process for the Centennial symbol marked another instance in which the commission did not want its mega-project to look "small." An explicit call for a symbol suggestive of "simplicity, spirituality and beauty" indicated a desire to meet universal and timeless artistic standards, and its method showed contempt for amateurish or politically divisive designs. The resulting competition favoured graphic designers who could be relied on, as professionals, to evoke Canadian dynamism and unity without appealing to specific historical events or leaning unduly towards one founding tradition. The commission received unsolicited submissions from the public but did not consider them seriously.[36] The symbol was to be a "State Emblem" used by "governments, voluntary agencies, organizations (excluding commercial enterprises) and individuals ... separately and distinctly from any wares or services they are selling or distributing."[37] Despite isolated complaints that graphic designer Stuart Ash's stylized maple leaf too closely resembled the Star of David,[38] the symbol's clean lines replaced the cluttered look of arms, finding their way onto – and frequently dictating the shape of – countless local Centennial projects, including sidewalks.

The year's single most costly project provided evidence that those in charge, like the broader community of cultural critics, were prepared to adopt methods previously dismissed as little better than advertising strategies. Amalgamating the concrete and the abstract, and appropriate to the legend of the railway as a unifying force, Centennial organizers commissioned a "Confederation Train" with historical displays on board. The train testified to critical influence in that its displays featured a linear historical narrative, and, because it had been designed to accommodate a steady stream of visitors, it incorporated long-held assumptions about the general public's attention span and inclination towards the unsubtle. In its fifteen cars, the train would be an enthralling introduction to the "story of Canada." Its designers had taken pains to make sure that the travelling exhibit would "not be a museum train, but a vivid tableau of living history. The viewer will participate in a series of dramatic experiences as he passes from car to car."[39] In addition to researching American experience with the "Freedom Train" of 1947,[40] some organizers wondered whether the Confederation Train should be executed in a quaint locomotive-and-Pullman-style – "a huffing wonder" – or as a sleek, diesel-engined number that would probably require a spectacular paint job to attract "teenagers and young adults already blasé about atomic energy and space capsules." Regardless of which motif they chose, planners thought it imperative to construct the displays "to stimulate rapid movement wherever possible."[41] Ultimately, they favoured the modern chassis, and Canadians flocked to it as forecast. The train made over sixty stops on its cross-country tour, and, to serve communities not on the main rail lines, eight "Confederation Caravans" took to the highways in May 1967.[42] Like the train, the caravans themselves were the products of time-consuming craftsmanship, but they too presented only the briefest of glimpses into the lives of British or French forebears, pioneers or living luminaries. There were textual displays, but these hardly predominated. Instead, sights, sounds, and artifacts were meant to convey an instant impression of the era depicted. In most cases, these impressions suited the "heritage-building" purposes of the travelling exhibits but could not even hint at a place's or a period's complexities. "We move into a street and listen to the clatter of horses' hoofs and the jingle of bridles," read one piece of advance publicity for the caravans; "the street is our access to the English culture of 1730 to 1830."[43]

One last dimension of the Centennial experience made it noteworthy as a reflection of mid-1960s' fluidity. This was the rediscovery of a vigorous "popular" culture in local Centennial events, which, however briefly, stood in contrast to the norm of mass-produced leisure. Aside from the larger enterprise of Centennial as a nationwide year of celebration, towns, cities, provinces, and even corporations held literally hundreds of festivals, homecomings, and pageants, without as lengthy a planning period.[44] None came close to matching the portability, scale, or expense of the train and caravans, but neither could any be called completely spontaneous. Although locally organized events took on a variety of forms, the broad mandate of commemoration exercised a strange discipline over many of these activities. In making reference to the ordeals of settlement and development, or glossing over instances where settlers imposed their will on aboriginal populations, these local events tapped into what passed for local folklore or at least – like Nanaimo's Bathtub Race – arose through a light-hearted identification with their natural surroundings. Critics had long complained that mass culture was not authentic or worthwhile because it sought only to entertain people and rarely addressed more sublime or troubling states. Breaking the spell of distractions such as commercial television – entering "little blue worlds" to engage the occupants – required a sense of showmanship and compromise thoroughly incompatible with an older critical tradition of detachment from the entertainment "industry." However, Centennial was a distinctive kind of elite-sponsored venture in this regard because engagement subsumed entertainment – or at least the two coexisted for a time – and allowed ordinary people to mark the occasion in a way that appeared to be less mediated than everyday leisure.

Because it was an ever more abundant byproduct of modern life, organizers knew that the theme of leisuretime would be a major element of Centennial-year events. A set of Centennial posters urged Canadians to knit sweaters, support local projects, plant Centennial gardens, and hold family reunions,[45] – all activities intended to counter the mechanization and standardization of work and life outside work. Complaints about mechanization and standardization had been around for decades, but acknowledging the pervasive nature of technology and bemoaning continental pressures had become more common.[46] Expo both personified and responded to this environment, celebrating technical achievements while asking visitors to think about the resulting changes to society. As one art critic reviewing works commissioned for the then-new Toronto airport noted: "I know it's cliché to drag in the jet age, but it's true all the same that it has provided us with the one totally accessible image of our time, with all its implications both for the good life and as an instrument of massacre."[47] It may well have been entirely a cliché to raise the issue, but this familiarity indicated that the maladjustments of critics had become somewhat more mainstream concerns, fit for eventual reinforcement in the public culture of Centennial year. A script detailing the National Film Board's 1965 plans for its space at the Canadian National Exhibition in Toronto provided a foretaste of this reinforcement, vilifying passivity with gripping displays. It called for separate rooms, each portraying leisure as blessing and as curse. On the curse side, sepia-toned images would confront the viewer: "unemployed men standing at the U.I.C., men and women sitting disconsolately in tatty rooms, staring out of windows; men sleeping on park benches; a group of young hoodlums, leather-jacketed, standing on a corner or acting up in some way; an arrest taking place; rising through scenes of passive crowds at some spectacle, through mob scenes, scenes of the early Nazi years (the book burnings, perhaps), to scenes of war and mass destruction. The implication of the images should be immediately clear to an audience, even at the risk of their being clichés (this can be avoided by their being *good* images of their kind)." As a matter of course, the blessings of leisure received adequate space, but there planners preferred "restful images of nature" or "people dancing, playing instruments, picnicking, engaged in sports" over depictions of ready-made entertainments.[48]

Not a World's Fair

Before Expo 67, two World's Fairs took place in North America in rapid succession, and Canadians could be forgiven if they anticipated Montreal's event as their country's turn to share the same spotlight.[49] Seattle's 1962 fair took place under the banner of "Century 21 – Man and Science." The theme of Canada's pavilion there was a rather pedestrian "Canadian Science and Industry Serve Mankind," and an expected tourist overflow north into British Columbia seemed just as exciting to one reporter, who listed the highlights of the Canadian pavilion's exhibits: a town-sized dome for use in the Arctic, an A.V. Roe Company machine for harvesting and finishing timber on fifty-foot wheels, rocket models, satellites, and cargo capsules for moving commodities along oil pipelines.[50] A Canadian visitor to the fair noted an odd combination of technological utopianism and entertainment and concluded that the public had somehow been duped: "The theme is space age but the muse was P.T. Barnum."[51]

Two years later in New York, "Peace through Understanding" opened on the site of 1939's "World of Tomorrow" fair. It featured a mix of national and (U.S.) state pavilions, along with a strong corporate presence from such companies as Coca-Cola and DuPont, all clustered around the "Pool of Industry."[52] Like the Seattle fair, it sought to liberate patrons, at least temporarily, from their present concerns by emphasizing a marvellous future in which scientific knowledge would lead to comfort and social harmony. This, of course, had been the tone of the 1939 fair. Lister Sinclair believed that he had the measure of such events, suggesting that "people go to a World's Fair for entertainment, and excitement. They also want to get a glimpse of the Future; new developments, new inventions, new worlds opening out! They are not interested in the past, except perhaps in a very few items that are particularly unusual, and particularly interesting (e.g. Michelangelo's *Pietà* at the New York Fair)." He was certain, however, that "visitors to a World's Fair do not come to be educated, or indoctrinated, or to improve themselves, or to go to work."[53]

However, organizers did not intend Expo 67 to be a World's Fair or a "static commemoration"[54] of human achievement. Instead, it was a "Universal and International Exhibition" duly recognized by the world governing body. Organizers immediately differentiated it from the commercial heritage of fairs and affected a design sensibility that evoked the decorum of an art exhibition.[55] Drawn from a 1939 book by French author Antoine de Saint-Exupéry, the theme of *Terre des Hommes* itself received a great deal of preliminary consideration, and author Gabrielle Roy later recalled that it was intended to become no less familiar than "the 'melodic signal' that identifies the broadcasting station."[56] In May 1963, Roy went to Montebello, an estate between Montreal and Ottawa, to be part of a gathering of artists, architects, writers, academics, and scientists that resolved to make the theme provocative rather than perfunctory – to take pride in technological developments while recognizing the newer existential questions that those same developments had introduced. The theme remained sovereign, with advisory committees "ever mindful not to stray from the THEME elements outlined at the Montebello conference."[57] Pavilions with names such as Man the Producer, Man the Creator, and Man in the Community represented varied aspects of the overall theme and pointedly raised such questions. Lucien Piché, head of the Expo theme committee, reported to Expo's Board of directors that those in attendance at Montebello had decided "to display Man and Man's bearing on his environment rather than his subjection thereto."[58] Even the American pavilion, expected to offer an unvarnished advertisement for the wide-open way of life, seemed to respect the theme, "ostentatiously avoid[ing] the outmoded idea of progress."[59]

Technology's place at Expo indicated organizers' ambivalence towards it. One journalist spent time wandering through the theme pavilions and remarked: "Expo is dominated by technology, but it is a gay, often pop technology that you meet – technology that is confident enough to laugh at itself, even to question its own role. Thus the pavilion on Man the Producer flings out a string of questions: 'Do you think that Technology offers you material riches or faceless conformity?' or again 'Do you think Technology permits you to listen to the universe or prevents you from hearing yourself?'" On the whole, he saw "the good humour and non-commercialism" of Expo as creating a suitable environment for showing "technology as an occasionally wayward friend rather than a forbidding perfect taskmaster."[60] Those planning the federal government's pavilion certainly made an effort to display a dynamic Canada but also sought to evoke the idea that a more fulfilling progress came through preserving a community structure in which everyone could participate. H. Leslie Brown, head of the Canadian Government Committee for Expo, explained the process of naming the pavilion as an odyssey leading back to a folk image of Canada: "We [at first] coined terms from prefixes and suffixes of the Latin and the Greek – they had the sounds of pharmaceuticals and paint, of science fiction and of the carboniferous era." Such names as Trylon and Unisphere were the stock in trade of the 1939 and 1964 New York fairs and found their way onto the Expo site (Biosphere, Polytrope) largely via the foreign and commercial pavilions. However, these held little fascination for the federal organizers, who wanted to scrutinize the uses to which science had been put. The group finally settled on an Inuktitut word, *Katimavik*, which it translated as "gathering place." "In the right connotation, and with supporting words," Brown added, "it can say 'gathering place for those who wish to understand the world.'"[61]

For most visitors, spending a few days at Expo probably meant wandering from pavilion to pavilion without rushing to attend many cerebral events such as the Man and His World lecture series.[62] Trying to understand the world did not seem like a recipe for an enjoyable family vacation, nor would it have sounded like fun to the sort of carefree young people invented for the novel *Expo Summer*.[63] The world of business further adulterated the impossible vision of an earnest Expo, as DuPont, Kodak, Canadian National, and a host of others showed up and received their share of visitors. Still, innovative exhibitors such as the Czechs, distinctive exhibits such as Canada's own Labyrinth, and especially the "vigorous contemporary idiom"[64] of the Christian Pavilion made their own lasting impact because they dared to leaven the gospel of material progress with questions about its social implications. As Robert Fulford noted, "At Expo, the cinema, as a branch of mass culture, caught up technically with the high culture of the previous half century... What T.S. Eliot's *The Wasteland* [sic] was to poetry in the early 1920s, Expo cinema was to movies." The sense of involvement that critics had for years considered wholly absent from mass culture constituted a key ingredient in several pavilions and marked a kind of détente between the worlds of spectacle and edification. "After Expo," Fulford remarked, "it became possible to envision a world in which all the resources previously available to private industries and show business – film, lighting, models, carefully organized environments – would be used by professional educators to bring new exhilarating life to the school systems."[65] One legacy of Centennial year would be a blurring of the boundaries between popular culture and the more formal culture of commemoration. The other would be a new type of nervous energy, an anxiety that Canadians could do still more to discover those inherent tastes and values that they had just celebrated so convincingly.

FULL CIRCLE

In view of the number of commemorative and celebratory events available to the public during 1967, it is perhaps difficult to recognize that the mid-1960s was notable in Canada for essentially the same reason that it had been considered transformative elsewhere.[66] In fits and starts, chiefly in Europe and in North America, protests over nuclear weapons, racial discrimination, environmental abuses, U.S. involvement in Vietnam, and a number of other issues formed the basis of a counterculture[67] that permitted committed individuals, especially student activists and radicals, to live and pursue their interests outside traditional patterns. In Canada, this embrace of distinctly unconventional ways of life occurred on a smaller scale. It none the less indicated that a much more politicized element had emerged to denounce the same commercialism, technocracy, and seemingly systematic denials of "social justice" motivating those whose activities I outline in this book. Although they could not bring themselves to live communally and their political leanings may not have been as consistently left–liberal as the new corps of agitators, critics' discomfort with some of the dominant trends in Western society had been as profound for more than a generation. In that sense, they too constituted a counterculture – a more sedate, humanist one – that also encouraged self-improvement, opposed the standardization of experience, and sheltered a view of cultural democracy that often transcended their individual circumstances or affiliations.

As extraordinary as 1967 was for Canada, no single year or event marked the end of the road for the "veteran" critics who had been promoting resistance to fast-paced modern life and an unreflective, commercialized mass culture. Still, over the course of a few years in the mid-to late 1960s, the locus of discontent seemed to migrate outside this "intellectual elite" towards a group enamoured perhaps more of revolution than of reconstruction. The veterans held out hope that an awareness of alternatives to mechanized routines and to the unambitious, sentimental appeals to instinct that seemed to dominate the cultural landscape could still help the harried man and woman in the street become "active" citizens. Organizers constructed Centennial with this sort of active citizen in mind. Although planners accounted for the scale and haphazard nature of local celebrations, their conceptions of suitable cultural activities still reflected a bias towards uplift through experience. These new experiences, however, were to be appealing and aboveboard. A Regina man's rather inventive idea of forming a Company of Centennial Hitch-hikers met with John Fisher's refusal – it was illegal, and the Centennial Commission already had more intensive, elaborate, and spectacular schemes to bring Canadians together.[68]

Known for his conservatism, historian W.L. Morton could nevertheless step outside that role in 1967 to chastise a society in which progress had come to mean what was good for business and that let corporations "pollute the water we drink and bathe in, and poison the air we breathe, and into which our children are born. War criminals we had; now, doing these things, we have peace criminals." He could join a motley band of "historians and critics of human behaviour" in recognizing the "supreme irony of the fact that [pollution and similar human-made disasters] are the outcome of the historic periods of Enlightenment and Optimism, of Progress and of Science." More true to form, Morton went on to admit that he might be stating things rather starkly, but he still made it plain that those elements of modern life challenged a sense of order and purpose that had long been useful. "This is a new, uncertain, unexplored world indeed," he said – "the same relativity, the same sense of higher velocities, the same sense of unpredictability, the same sense that nothing is what it seems, but is boundless power working to no end and directed to no goal, pervading all other areas of human concern, thought, art and behaviour." He mourned what sounded like the recent passing of a beloved age, noting that "speculation has replaced reflection, reality beauty, and no one knows how to behave or dress, or cut his hair anymore. If he does, it is because he is a stuffy and obtuse traditionalist. Chaos, ladies and gentlemen, has come again."[69]

Less troubled by chaos and hoping to outline "the problems of being a dissenter in modern Canadian society," Stewart Goodings, associate director of the Company of Young Canadians (CYC), spoke of five assumptions that were in essence that organization's articles of faith. In order of presentation, youths must be involved as "fully-participating members of society"; universities should "make students maladjusted to society"; Canada, in that it is "liberal, progressive, technological," is part of the American empire; the Cold War is less important than the wealth differential between the "first" and "third" worlds; and a "generation gap" exists. He addressed the concerns of youths, but also – perhaps unintentionally – praised the sort of critical engagement with the world and with society that less youthful commentators had been promoting since at least the Second World War. The CYC's resolve to promote "constructive dissent" had much to do with a distaste for commercialized culture and the technological imperative. On the assumption that a proper university education should produce feelings of maladjustment, Goodings elaborated, "if students can read the great literature of the world and remain uncritical of television commercials and pulp magazines; if people can read Shakespeare and remain satisfied with the Beverly Hillbillies; if people can read about democratic experiments and remain satisfied with our Parliamentary institutions; if people can observe some of the lessons of history and remain unconcerned about the arms race in the world today, then these people have clearly missed the boat at university."[70]

Morton's alarm at chaos and the accelerated pace of life, and Goodings's clear dismissal of contemporaries who had gone to university but not obtained an education, hardly denoted a deliberate passing of any torch. Critics had long expressed dissent through their cautionary evaluations of tastes and choices, expecting perhaps to induce the restoration of an idealized public sphere. Although one can point to incongruities such as "anarchy clubs,"[71] youths of the mid-1960s cared less for order and less for gradualism than did the more decorous contrarians and reformers whom they succeeded. These two groups shared a disdain for conformity and for the stifling integration of commerce and taste that marginalized dissent by making it seem either highbrow or subversive in comparison to a mass, media-driven culture. The symbolic importance of commemorating a national anniversary with a large round number (100) attached and of hosting a prestigious international exhibition was bound to elicit commentary on the state of Canadian society. For those who had experienced Canada's cultural "cold war," the relatively short period leading up to and including 1967's most prominent attractions offered some of the last opportunities to exercise influence before members of a generation that had known only postwar conditions emerged as more radical and clearly identifiable critics of the established order. Conspicuous as the first year when Canadians tried too hard to relax and be themselves, 1967 did much to inaugurate patterns of commemoration and self-examination that have – especially *since* then – exemplified English Canada's approach to the questions of its own cultural vitality and validity.

Conclusion:
A Secret Understanding

When he looked back on a life spent encouraging continuous learning and determined self-improvement, adult educator Ned Corbett thought it fitting to close his memoir with a statement of what he called "my own belief."[1] Instead of a time-worn maxim reminiscent of his Nova Scotia birthplace or of the raw northern Alberta homestead country where he spent much of his early career, Corbett selected a short passage from one of E.M. Forster's essays published at the beginning of the Second World War. There Forster – and by association Corbett – described the sort of exclusive group with which he would gladly identify, even in an age known for its attachment to democratic rhetoric: "I believe in aristocracy – not an aristocracy of power, based upon rank and influence, but an aristocracy of the sensitive, the considerate and the plucky. Its members are found in all nations and classes and through all ages, and there is a secret understanding between them when they meet. They represent the true human tradition, the one permanent victory of our queer race over cruelty and chaos."[2]

As a title for the collection in which the same essay would appear twelve years later, Forster chose *Two Cheers for Democracy*. This choice reflected both enthusiasm for the potential bounty of modern life and dissatisfaction with its unpleasant outcomes – sentiments also present in the circumspect attitude of many English-Canadian cultural critics at mid-century. Although they desired social equality for all, these outspoken observers also bemoaned a culture based on amusing a mass public. They cited a shortage of eccentrics – a shortage that some thought might be overcome by cultivating audiences that would "respect leisure and reflective idleness."[3] This was not merely an admonition to leave Dad alone once he lit his pipe and settled down with the evening newspaper. It formed part of a more complex critique of postwar Canadian society, where most people seemed to demand little of themselves culturally, even though the technological changes characterizing their environment allowed them to engage in a variety of pastimes that their parents had found too expensive or distant a generation earlier. Canada in the wartime and postwar years became a modern nation, but some observers thought that placing complete trust in scientists and rejecting old ties seemed foolish. To be appropriately modern was to "look at things in their relations," just as women's columnist Adeline Haddow suggested her wartime readership do when choosing furniture. "Lovely to have heirlooms," she declared, "but terrible to have nothing but heirlooms!"[4]

Much as many early-twentieth-century social reformers feared the effects of industrial "trusts," by 1939 many English-Canadian cultural critics were well-placed to recognize the economies of scale present in broadcasting, film distribution, and publishing in North America. Considerations of national self-determination aside, they sensed how changes in communications technology had helped create an alternative reality against which artistic triumphs, pressing issues in a community (locality, region or nation), or even the routines of daily life seemed unable to compete. As one editor complained: "Sales clerks ignore one while practising quiz answers to themselves."[5] Especially after the war ended, life offered comforts and diversions – bread and circuses – that worked to pull the public away from an ethic of production that was set, both implicitly and explicitly, against a newer consumerist paradigm. Faced daily with the gulf between producer and consumer, between individual and mass, between culture and entertainment, critics' efforts likewise evolved into a twofold strategy.

First, in an era marked by the state's further incursion onto the field of social welfare, it was not terribly incongruous to find the state becoming a force in the realm of culture, and cultural critics played an instrumental role as advisers to what has customarily been portrayed as a nationalist project. It was a nationalist project, but not *entirely* so. The CBC, with its potential to counteract the market by offering deliberately educational or Canadian content became – and remains – a major vehicle for reminding Canadians of the world outside the entertainment "industry." This is all the more remarkable because the corporation itself has had to compete in the same field. Second, while the prospect of bringing high culture to every small town appeared to be expensive and rather artificial in the light of the mass audience's reputed attachment to being given "what it wanted," critics looked to an elevated common culture not as a consolation prize but as a corollary of unmasking the conformity and false democracy of the cultural marketplace. Reconciled to the fact that a nation's cultural landscape could not be remade by fiat, critics urged Canadians to become selective and intelligent consumers of culture. This middlebrow sensibility took a firmer hold late in the 1950s and blossomed in the 1967 Centennial celebrations – a spectacle orchestrated by the state but steeped in folksy leisuretime rituals such as canoeing and marked by the repackaging of the nation's history into caravans.

The optimism of late wartime led critics and social activists to envision conditions in which an idealized public sphere[6] could counteract the community-destroying forces of modern life. One enthusiastic observer made no secret of his hopes: "New channels of personal and social expression are desperately needed; trickles have already appeared for these channels. Dare we hope that the flood will follow, and that a mild renaissance of social and cultural expression is in the offing? Signs can be discerned; perchance the spiritual lethargy of years is being cast off."[7]

We have tended to think of figures such as Matthew Arnold as archetypes of a Canadian cultural elite – the sort of people for whom the Massey Commission represented great strides along the path of cultural progress.[8] However, even within such undertakings as the commission and the community-centre movement during wartime, emphasizing the effects of modern life and mass culture constituted a critique of progress itself. Critics sought a continual re-evaluation of the nation's cultural life and expressed their desires in terms of opposition to trends *and* to accommodation of new media. By the mid-1960s, "culture fatigue" had become a common ailment, perhaps because cultural critics and self-proclaimed experts were trying too earnestly to engineer a New Jerusalem. One newspaper writer preferred to let matters resolve themselves, conflating the venerable Couchiching Conference and beat poetry and by default embracing the television western: "Away, away with the lot of you, and take your berets and sandals with you. Better Paladin with his black hat than Stanley Knowles with no tie."[9]

Doug Owram has written: "No phrase had more power or meaning in the 1960s than 'participatory democracy.'"[10] The generation that he studied was one that dressed for dissent and later had its rebellion set to a soundtrack, but we should not conclude that the 1940s and 1950s were somehow without their agitators. Cultural critics were committed to democratic instincts and institutions, but they could hardly trust the system – as it had unfolded – to serve what they believed were everyone's best interests. Many of them recognized by the mid-1950s that their mission was to help construct a common culture to incorporate traditions and fads alike. Northrop Frye outlined the problem of cultural criticism as one of brokering an uneasy accommodation between taste and authority. "Democracy is a mixture of majority rule and minority right," he wrote in 1967, "and the minority which most clearly has a right is the minority of those who try to resist a passive response, and thereby risk the resentment of those who regard them as trying to be undemocratically superior." Here, Frye pointed allegorically to an important aspect of culture: that certain forms and categories of it seem to need protection, as do the civil rights of minorities surrounded by a powerful majority. A society needs to strike a balance between instincts ("the passive response," mass culture) and discipline (action/participation, high and folk culture). When he addressed the idea of cultural democracy, of majorities and minorities of taste, he sought accommodation and synthesis because he was speaking "not so much of two groups of people as of two mental attitudes, both of which may exist in the same mind."[11] To possess the impulse to be oneself and yet to strive for improvement is likewise a contradiction that can drive a person or an entire nation to "face risks and make experiments that we would not venture upon under any other circumstances."[12] Studying how cultural critics professed their understanding of the manner in which modern life and mass culture reinforced one another against the background of profound change is to take part in mapping the allusions and memories that defined Canada in the generation or so during and after the Second World War. Their increasing enthusiasm for imparting that perspective via radio and other mass means mirrored the Canadian public's increasing attention to those same media. Wary of the dangers of modern life and mass culture, and working consistently to show Canadians that there were "better" ways to spend their leisuretime, cultural critics emerged from relative obscurity to find themselves on radio and television – that is, in the marketplace. Duty had led them there.

Notes

INTRODUCTION

1 John R. Seeley, R. Alexander Sim, and E.W. Loosley, *Crestwood Heights: A Study of the Culture of Suburban Life* (Toronto: University of Toronto Press, 1956), 14.
2 Willson Woodside, "'Insolence of Material Success': What It's Doing to Modern Man," *Saturday Night* (25 Dec. 1948): 10. A recent treatment of Weaver is Joseph Scotchie, *Barbarians in the Saddle: An Intellectual Biography of Richard M. Weaver* (New Brunswick, NJ: Transaction, 1997).
3 In his *Channels of Influence: CBC Audience Research and the Canadian Public* (Toronto: University of Toronto Press, 1994), Ross A. Eaman complains that the CBC has "seldom been associated" with cultural democracy, and he rather unproblematically presents cultural democracy as the practice of "serving the lowest common denominator" – a strategy antithetical to the needs of minority audiences (ix–x). Cultural democracy must be defined much more broadly to include both mass and minority audiences, for disenfranchising minorities in favour of majorities is decidedly undemocratic. In a more historically-specific sense, both minority audiences and the CBC were central to cultural critics' ideal of representing more of the populace because they could hardly help but notice that private stations already served the larger public by carrying the most "popular" programs.
4 Allan Greer, "Canadian History: Ancient and Modern," *Canadian Historical Review* 77 (Dec. 1996): 575–90.
5 Stephen Azzi, *Walter Gordon and the Rise of Canadian Nationalism* (Montreal: McGill-Queen's University Press, 1999); Morris Zaslow, *The Northward Expansion of Canada, 1914–1967* (Toronto: McClelland and Stewart, 1988); John Richards and Larry Pratt, *Prairie Capitalism: Power and Influence in the New West* (Toronto: McClelland and Stewart, 1979). Surveys include: Alvin Finkel, *Our Lives: Canada after 1945* (Toronto:

J. Lorimer, 1997); Robert Bothwell, Ian Drummond, and John English, *Canada since 1945: Power, Politics and Provincialism*, rev. ed. (Toronto: University of Toronto Press, 1989); J.L. Granatstein, *Canada 1957–1967: The Years of Uncertainty and Innovation* (Toronto: McClelland and Stewart, 1986); John English, *Years of Growth, 1948–1967* (Toronto: Grolier, 1986); Donald Grant Creighton, *The Forked Road: Canada, 1939–1957* (Toronto: McClelland and Stewart, 1976).

6 There are many regimental chronicles and soldiers' recollections, of which George Blackburn, *Where the Hell Are the Guns? A Soldier's View of the Anxious Years, 1939–44* (Toronto: McClelland and Stewart, 1997), is probably one of the better-written. More recent academic treatments include: Desmond Morton, *Victory 1945: Canadians from War to Peace* (Toronto: HarperCollins, 1995); W.A.B. Douglas, *Out of the Shadows: Canada in the Second World War* (Toronto: Dundurn Press, 1995); J.L. Granatstein and Peter Neary, eds., *The Good Fight: Canadians and World War II* (Mississauga, Ont.: Copp Clark, 1995); David Bercuson, *Maple Leaf against the Axis: Canada's Second World War* (Toronto: Stoddart, 1995); Granatstein, *Canada's War: The Politics of the Mackenzie King Government, 1939–1945* (Toronto: University of Toronto Press, 1990 [1975]) and *A Nation Forged in Fire: Canadians and the Second World War, 1939–1945* (Toronto: Lester & Orpen Dennys, 1989). Accounts that present less "official" sides of war are Michael D. Stevenson, *Canada's Greatest Wartime Muddle: National Selective Service and the Mobilization of Human Resources during World War II* (Montreal: McGill-Queen's University Press, 2001), Terry Copp, *Battle Exhaustion: Soldiers and Psychiatrists in the Canadian Army, 1939–1945* (Montreal: McGill-Queen's University Press, 1990); Ruth Roach Pierson, *'They're Still Women after All': The Second World War and Canadian Womanhood* (Toronto: McClelland and Stewart, 1986).

7 Eva Mackey, *The House of Difference: Cultural Politics and National Identity in Canada* (London: Routledge, 1999); Kenneth McRoberts, *Misconceiving Canada: The Struggle for National Unity* (Toronto: Oxford University Press, 1997) and *Beyond Quebec: Taking Stock of Canada* (Montreal: McGill-Queen's University Press, 1995); Stephen G. Tomblin, *Ottawa and the Outer Provinces: the Challenge of Regional Integration in Canada* (Toronto: Lorimer, 1995); William D. Gairdner, *Constitutional Crack-up: Canada and the Coming Showdown with Quebec* (Toronto: Stoddart, 1994); Robert Chodos, *The Unmaking of Canada: The Hidden Theme in Canadian History since 1945* (Toronto: Lorimer, 1991); Michael Oliver, *The Passionate Debate: The Social and Political Ideas of Quebec Nationalism, 1920–1945* (Montreal: Véhicule Press, 1991); Peter Brimelow, *The Patriot Game: Canada and the Canadian Question Revisited* (Stanford, Calif.: Hoover Institution Press, 1986); George Melnyk, *Radical Regionalism* (Edmonton: NeWest Press, 1981).

8 J.L. Granatstein is perhaps most representative of historians concerned primarily with the distribution of money and power via state cultural agencies. See his "Culture and Scholarship: The First Ten Years of the Canada Council," *Canadian Historical Review* 65, no. 4 (Sept. 1984): 441–74, and George Woodcock, *Strange Bedfellows: The State and the Arts in Canada* (Vancouver: Douglas & McIntyre, 1985); Bernard Ostry, *The Cultural Connection: An Essay on Culture and Government Policy in Canada* (Toronto: McClelland and Stewart, 1978).

9 Mary Vipond identifies this elite as a force binding literary and artistic nationalists together during the 1920s. Vipond, "The Nationalist Network: English Canada's Intellectuals and Artists in the 1920s," *Canadian Review of Studies in Nationalism* 5 (spring 1980): 32–52. See also her PhD dissertation from the University of Toronto: "National Consciousness in English-speaking Canada in the 1920's: Seven Studies" (1974). The only monograph on the multifaceted activity in this field is Maria Tippett, *Making Culture: English-Canadian Institutions and the Arts before the Massey Commission* (Toronto: University of Toronto Press, 1990).

10 Colin D. Howell, *Blood, Sweat and Cheers: Sport and the Making of Modern Canada* (Toronto: University of Toronto Press, 2001); Russell Johnston, *Selling Themselves: The Emergence of Advertising in Canada* (Toronto: University of Toronto Press, 2001); H.V. Nelles, *The Art of Nation-Building: Pageantry and Spectacle at Quebec's Tercentenary* (Toronto: University of Toronto Press, 2000); Jonathan Vance, *Death So Noble: Memory, Meaning, and the First World War* (Vancouver: University of British Columbia Press, 1997); Keith Walden, *Becoming Modern in Toronto: The Industrial Exhibition and the Shaping of a Late Victorian Culture* (Toronto: University of Toronto Press, 1997); Lynne Marks, *Revivals and Roller Rinks: Religion, Leisure, and Identity in Late-Nineteenth-Century Small Town Ontario* (Toronto: University of Toronto Press, 1996); David Monod, *Store Wars: Shopkeepers and the Culture of Mass Marketing, 1890–1939* (Toronto: University of Toronto Press, 1996)

11 Nancy Christie and Michael Gauvreau, *A Full-orbed Christianity: The Protestant Churches and Social Welfare in Canada, 1900–1940* (Montreal: McGill-Queen's University Press, 1996); Doug Owram, *The Government Generation: Canadian Intellectuals and the State, 1900–1945* (Toronto: University of Toronto Press, 1986); Ramsay Cook, *The Regenerators: Social Criticism in Late Victorian English Canada* (Toronto: University of Toronto Press, 1985); James Struthers, *No Fault of Their Own: Unemployment and the Canadian Welfare State, 1914–1941* (Toronto: University of Toronto Press, 1983).

12 Judith Stamps, *Unthinking Modernity: Innis, McLuhan, and the Frankfurt School* (Montreal: McGill-Queen's University Press, 1995); William Christian, *George Grant: A Biography* (Toronto: University of Toronto Press,

1993); Graeme Patterson, *History and Communications: Harold Innis, Marshall McLuhan, the Interpretation of History* (Toronto: University of Toronto Press, 1990); Philip Marchand, *Marshall McLuhan: The Medium and the Messenger* (New York: Ticknor and Fields, 1989); Arthur Kroker, *Technology and the Canadian Mind: Innis/McLuhan/Grant* (Montreal: New World Perspectives, 1984).

13 Valerie Korinek, *Roughing It in the Suburbs: Reading Chatelaine Magazine in the Fifties and Sixties* (Toronto: University of Toronto Press, 2000); Reg Whitaker and Gary Marcuse, *Cold War Canada: The Making of a National Insecurity State, 1945–1957* (Toronto: University of Toronto Press, 1994); Paul Rutherford, *When Television Was Young: Primetime Canada, 1952–1967* (Toronto: University of Toronto Press, 1990). Notable are two works by sociologists: Mary Louise Adams, *The Trouble with Normal: Postwar Youth and the Making of Heterosexuality* (Toronto: University of Toronto Press, 1997), and Peter Li, *The Making of Post-war Canada* (Toronto: Oxford University Press, 1996).

14 Philip Massolin, *Canadian Intellectuals, the Tory Tradition, and the Challenge of Modernity, 1939–1970* (Toronto: University of Toronto Press, 2001), 5, 18.

15 Maria Tippett, *Making Culture*, especially chapter 6. In her *Art at the Service of War: Canada, Art, and the Great War* (Toronto: University of Toronto Press, 1984), Tippett portrays the First World War as an earlier catalyst in Canadian cultural development.

16 Paul Litt, *The Muses, the Masses, and the Massey Commission* (Toronto: University of Toronto Press, 1992). On Massey's personal connection to the arts, see Karen A. Finlay, *The Force of Culture: Vincent Massey and Canadian Sovereignty* (Toronto: University of Toronto Press, forthcoming).

17 A.B. McKillop, "Culture, Intellect, and Context," *Journal of Canadian Studies* 24, no. 3 (autumn 1989): 12.

18 Gerald Friesen, *Citizens and Nation: An Essay on History, Communication, and Canada* (Toronto: University of Toronto Press, 2000). Ian McKay, *The Quest of the Folk: Antimodernism and Cultural Selection in Twentieth-Century Nova Scotia* (Montreal: McGill-Queen's University Press, 1994); on construction of the folk ideal, see 301–2.

19 D.L. LeMahieu, *A Culture for Democracy: Mass Communication and the Cultural Mind in Britain between the Wars* (Oxford: Clarendon Press, 1988); Michael Kammen, *American Culture, American Tastes: Social Change and the 20th Century* (New York: Knopf, 1999) and *The Lively Arts: Gilbert Seldes and the Transformation of Cultural Criticism in the United States* (New York: Oxford University Press, 1996); Joan Shelley Rubin, *The Making of Middlebrow Culture* (Chapel Hill: University of North Carolina Press, 1992).

20 Doug Owram, *Born at the Right Time: A History of the Baby Boom Generation* (Toronto: University of Toronto Press, 1996). See also John Kettle,

The Big Generation (Toronto: McClelland and Stewart, 1980); Robert Collins, *You Had to Be There: An Intimate Portrait of the Generation That Survived the Depression, Won the War, and Reinvented Canada* (Toronto: McClelland and Stewart, 1997).

21 John Coulter, "Books and Shows," talk number one, second series, 24 Nov. 1942. William Ready Division of Archives and Research Collections, McMaster University Library (McM), John Coulter Papers, Box 36, f. 2.

22 Vance, *Death So Noble*, 6.

23 Historians have been attentive to the documentary record. On Canada, see Mary Vipond's articles: "The Beginnings of Public Broadcasting in Canada: The CRBC, 1932–36," *Canadian Journal of Communication* 19, no. 2 (1994): 151–71; "Financing Canadian Public Broadcasting: Licence Fees and the 'Culture of Caution,'" *Historical Journal of Film, Radio, and Television* 15, no. 2 (June 1995): 285–300; and her previous volume *Listening In: The First Decade of Canadian Broadcasting, 1922–1932* (Montreal: McGill-Queen's University Press, 1992); David Skinner, "A System Divided: A Political Economy of Canadian Broadcasting," unpublished PhD dissertation, Simon Fraser University, 1997; and Raboy, *Missed Opportunities*. For a still more politically focused narrative, see Frank Peers, *The Politics of Canadian Broadcasting, 1920–1951* (Toronto: University of Toronto Press, 1969), or E. Austin Weir, *The Struggle for National Broadcasting in Canada* (Toronto: McClelland and Stewart, 1965). On Britain, see Paddy Scannell, *A Social History of British Broadcasting, 1922–1939: Serving the Nation* (Oxford: Blackwell, 1991), and Asa Briggs, *A History of Broadcasting the United Kingdom* (Oxford: Oxford University Press, 1979). On the American alternative to the state-influenced model, see Michele Hilmes, *Radio Voices: American Broadcasting, 1922–1952* (Minneapolis: University of Minnesota Press, 1997); Susan Smulyan, *Selling Radio: The Commercialization of American Broadcasting, 1920–1934* (Washington, DC: Smithsonian Institution Press, 1994).

24 Paddy Scannell, *Radio, Television and Modern Life: A Phenomenological Approach* (Oxford: Blackwell, 1996).

25 Frank Chamberlain, "Radio Is Our National Theatre," *Saturday Night* (27 Dec. 1941): 22.

26 E.M. Forster, "What I Believe" (1939), in *Two Cheers For Democracy* (London: Edward Arnold, 1951), 82–3.

27 A.B. McKillop, "Nationalism, Identity and Canadian Intellectual History," in McKillop, *Contours of Canadian Thought* (Toronto: University of Toronto Press, 1987), 6. This essay was originally published in 1974.

28 Nicholas Brown, *Governing Prosperity: Social Change and Social Analysis in Australia in the 1950s* (Cambridge: Cambridge University Press, 1995).

29 One wartime writer referred to a group outside the political power base – "not so much those upon whom rests the responsibility of conducting the

present war, but those individuals whose position entitles them to public hearing and public respect, and whose prominence enables them to be powerful factors in the shaping of public opinion. This tendency is showing itself not only among political figures, but among people eminent in education, in literature, in business and in religion." J.S.B. Macpherson, "Where Does Canada Stand in the World of Future?" *Saturday Night* (13 Feb. 1943): 6.

30 Northrop Frye, *The Modern Century: The Whidden Lectures 1967* (Toronto: University of Toronto Press, 1967), 29.

31 T.J. Jackson Lears, *No Place of Grace: Antimodernism and the Transformation of American Culture 1880–1920*, first pub. 1983 (Chicago: University of Chicago Press, 1994), xvii.

32 Andrew Ross, *No Respect: Intellectuals and Popular Culture* (New York: Routledge, 1989), 5.

33 LeMahieu, *A Culture for Democracy*, 103.

34 Forster, "What I Believe," 82.

35 Antonio Gramsci, *Selections from the Prison Notebooks of Antonio Gramsci*, ed. and trans. Quintin Hoare and Geoffrey Nowell Smith (London: Lawrence and Wishart, 1971), 12.

36 Quotation from: Anna Siomopoulous, "Entertaining Ethics: Technology, Mass Culture and American Intellectuals of the 1930s," *Film History* 11, no. 1 (1999): 48. Richard Pells, *Radical Visions and American Dreams: Culture and Social Thought in the Depression Years* (Middletown, Conn.: Wesleyan University Press, 1984).

37 Callaghan to Robert T. McKenzie, 12 Feb. 1943, NA, CBC, RG 41, vol. 187, file 11–18–5, part 5, CBC broadcasts on *Citizens' Forum*: *Of Things to Come*.

38 Vipond, "The Nationalist Network," 34.

39 John Coulter, "Books and Shows," talk number seven, second series, 5 Jan. 1943, McM, John Coulter Papers, box 36, f. 2.

40 Barry Ferguson, *Remaking Liberalism: The Intellectual Legacy of Adam Shortt, O.D. Skelton, W.C. Clark, and W.A. Mackintosh, 1890–1925* (Montreal: McGill-Queen's University Press, 1993), 233.

41 Paul R. Gorman, *Left Intellectuals and Popular Culture in Twentieth-century America* (Chapel Hill: University of North Carolina Press, 1996), 10.

42 Jackson Lears, *Fables of Abundance: A Cultural History of Advertising in America* (New York: Basic Books, 1994), 126.

43 Marshall Berman, *All That Is Solid Melts into Air: The Experience of Modernity* (New York: Simon and Schuster, 1982). Likewise, Charles Taylor notes how modernity can be seen with equal validity in two ways – as more intense since 1945 or as a process operating since the seventeenth century. Charles Taylor, *The Malaise of Modernity* (Toronto: CBC/Anansi, 1991), 1.

44 E.A. Corbett, "Adult Education," typescript (1938), 3. NA, Robert Alexander Sim Papers, MG 30, D 260, vol. 11, file 11, Canadian Association for

Adult Education (CAAE), correspondence, minutes, pamphlets. The late-nineteenth-century understanding of modern life seemed ambivalent and self-serving in prompting such uses of the term as: "in these remote districts the rush of modern life and thought had not as yet induced that feverish restlessness, which is the bane of our nineteenth century life." Maud Ogilvy, *The Keeper of the Bic Light House: A Canadian Story of To-day* (Montreal: E.M. Renouf, 1891), 64; "a mass of little luxuries – trifles too light and various to be describable, all the nameless inelegancies of modern life, with its superfluities, its pretence of intellect, its discriminating taste." G.M. Robins, *The Tree of Knowledge* (Montreal: John Lovell and Son, [1890]), 317; "how much less does the habitual drinker care for pictures, music, books, lectures, and a hundred similar features of the best modern life than the man who abstains from alcoholic poison?" Lilian M. Heath, comp., *Platform Pearls for Temperance Workers and Other Reformers* (Toronto, 1896), 125.

45 Richard D. Brown, *Modernization: The Transformation of American Life, 1600–1865* (New York: Hill and Wang, 1976), 12–14. Leo Charney and Vanessa R. Schwartz, "Introduction," in Charney and Schwartz, eds., *Cinema and the Invention of Modern Life* (Berkeley: University of California Press, 1995), 1–12.

46 Warren I. Susman, "Culture and Commitment," in Susman, *Culture As History: The Transformation of American Society in the Twentieth Century* (New York: Pantheon, 1984), 187. Matei Calinescu wrote of "bourgeois modernity": "The doctrine of progress, the confidence in the beneficial possibilities of science and technology, the concern with time (a measurable time, a time that can be bought and sold and therefore has, like any other commodity, a calculable equivalent in money), the cult of reason, and the ideal of freedom defined within the framework of abstract humanism, but also the orientation toward pragmatism and the cult of action and success." Matei Calinescu, *Faces of Modernity: Avant-garde, Decadence and Kitsch* (Bloomington: Indiana University Press, 1977), 41–2.

47 Charney and Schwartz, *Cinema and the Invention of Modern Life*, 5. Salvador Giner, *Mass Society* (London: Martin Robertson, 1976), 166ff.

48 A.L. Kroeber and Clyde Kluckhohn, *Culture: A Critical Review of Concepts and Definitions* (New York: Vantage, 1952), 291. See also Terry Eagleton, *The Idea of Culture* (Oxford: Blackwell, 2000). Raymond Williams calls culture "one of the two or three most complicated words in the English language." Williams, *Keywords: A Vocabulary of Culture and Society* (London: Fontana/Croom Helm, 1976), 76. Julian Park offered: "The culture of the English-speaking Canadian is simply the recorded reflection of his way of life and his attitude toward it." Julian Park, ed., *The Culture of Contemporary Canada* (Ithaca, NY: Cornell University Press, 1957), v. The Canada Council saw culture as "activities and interests that go beyond

supplying the basic requirements of existence and give to it beauty, pleasure and meaning, and so interwoven with everyday life as to be inseparable." Canada Council, *The Canada Council and the Arts* (Ottawa, 1959).

49 Rutherford applies this definition regardless of "whether the creator and/or distributor is a private company (Canada's Wonderland), a public corporation (the Canadian Broadcasting Corporation), or even a voluntary association (a parent–teacher association)". He also *implicitly* contrasts "high" culture with a mass culture "accessible to very large numbers of people, unlike opera, much scholarship, and even folk art." Paul Rutherford, "Made in America: The Problem of Mass Culture in Canada," in David H. Flaherty and Frank E. Manning, eds., *The Beaver Bites Back? American Popular Culture in Canada* (Montreal: McGill-Queen's University Press, 1993), 260–1. In his defence of popular culture, sociologist Herbert Gans bemoaned the power of the traditional definition of mass culture as the "symbolic products used by the 'uncultured' majority." Gans, *Popular Culture and High Culture* (New York: Basic Books, 1974), 10.

50 Chandra Mukerji and Michael Schudson, *Rethinking Popular Culture* (Berkeley: University of California Press, 1991), 3. Ray Browne defined popular culture rather broadly, as that which "embraces all levels of our society and culture other than the Elite – the 'popular,' 'mass' and 'folk.' It includes most of the bewildering aspects of life which hammer us daily." Ray B. Browne, "Popular Culture: Notes toward a Definition," in George H. Lewis, ed., *Side-Saddle on the Golden Calf: Social Structure and Popular Culture in America* (Pacific Palisades, Calif.: Goodyear, 1972), 10.

51 Some of the best-known critics and students of U.S. culture used the terms *mass culture*, *popular culture*, and *kitsch* to refer to "television, radio, Hollywood movies, mass-market paperback books, most advertising, and other mass-produced goods and art." Neil Jumonville, *Critical Crossings: The New York Intellectuals in Postwar America* (Berkeley: University of California Press, 1991), 151.

52 In 1960, Irving Kristol presented popular culture as a class-specific entity that had recently vanished and mass culture as a pervasive and often-invasive environment in which all of us live. Irving Kristol, "Democracy and Mass Culture: High, Low, and Modern," *Manchester Guardian* (8 June 1960). Raymond Williams wrote that one "cannot describe the bulk of this material produced by the new means of communication as 'working-class culture'. For neither is it by any means produced exclusively for this class, nor, in any important degree, is it produced by them." Williams, *Culture and Society 1780–1950* (London: Chatto and Windus, 1958), 319–20.

53 Among the better works addressing these themes are Leon Hunt, *British Low Culture: From Safari Suits to Sexploitation* (London: Routledge, 1998); Jackson Lears, *Fables of Abundance: A Cultural History of Advertising in America* (New York: Basic Books, 1994); Arthur Marwick, *Cul-*

ture in Britain since 1945 (Oxford: Blackwell, 1991); John Fiske, *Understanding Popular Culture* (London and New York: Routledge, 1991 [1989]); Michael Denning, *Mechanic Accents: Dime Novels and Working-Class Culture in America* (New York: Verso, 1987); Kathy Peiss, *Cheap Amusements: Working-Class Women and Leisure in Turn-of-the Century New York* (Philadelphia: Temple University Press, 1986); James Gilbert, *A Cycle of Outrage: America's Reaction to the Juvenile Delinquent in the 1950s* (New York: Oxford University Press, 1986); Janice Radway, *Reading the Romance: Women, Patriarchy, and Popular Literature* (Chapel Hill: University of North Carolina Press, 1984); Roy Rosenzweig, *Eight Hours For What We Will: Workers and Leisure in an Industrial City 1870–1920* (New York: Cambridge University Press, 1983); Dick Hebdige, *Subculture: The Meaning of Style* (London: Methuen, 1979). For articles, see Dominic Strinati and Stephen Wagg, eds., *Come on Down? The Politics of Popular Media Culture in Post-war Britain* (London: Routledge, 1992); 'Forum' on popular culture in *American Historical Review* 97, no. 5 (Dec. 1992); and Stuart Hall and Tony Jefferson, eds., *Resistance through Rituals: Youth Subcultures in Post-war Britain* (London: Hutchinson, 1976).

54 David Whisnant has described such efforts to remake culture among those considered culturally deprived as "systematic cultural intervention[s]." Whisnant, *All That Is Native and Fine: The Politics of Culture in an American Region* (Chapel Hill: University of North Carolina Press, 1983), 13.

55 David Paul Nord, "An Economic Perspective on Formula in Popular Culture," *Journal of American Culture* 3 (spring 1980): 25–7.

56 Lawrence W. Levine, "The Folklore of Industrial Society: Popular Culture and Its Audiences," *American Historical Review* 97, no. 5 (Dec. 1992): 1380–1. (One of the first uses of the phrase "folklore of industrial society" occurs in Marshall McLuhan's *The Mechanical Bride: Folklore of Industrial Man* [New York: Vanguard, 1951].) Levine's *Highbrow/Lowbrow: The Emergence of Cultural Hierarchy in America* (Cambridge, Mass.: Harvard University Press, 1988) presents the "sacralization" of culture and the imposition of hierarchies on it at about 1900. Michael Kammen's *American Culture, American Tastes*, addresses a more recent critical embrace of popular culture. Andrew Ross emphasizes the oppositional power of popular culture. This perspective, he argues, improves on the "more well-known, conspiratorial view of 'mass culture' as imposed upon a passive populace like so much standardized fodder, doled out to quell unrest and to fuel massive profits." Ross, *No Respect*, 4.

57 Levine, "Folklore of Industrial Society," 1381.

58 John Carey, *The Intellectuals and the Masses: Pride and Prejudice among the Literary Intelligentsia, 1880–1939* (London: Faber and Faber, 1992), 210. Daniel LeMahieu notes that cultivated elites in early twentieth-century Britain shared a "fundamental allegiance to the notion of cultural

hierarchy" and that "few intellectuals challenged the centrality of this concept." LeMahieu, *A Culture for Democracy*, 103.
59 Dr J.M. Ewing, "Our New Leisure," seventh in the series *Our Changing Values*, broadcast 22 Sept. 1948, CBC Trans-Canada Network, 5–6, Neil M. Morrison Papers, NA, MG 30, E 273, vol. 28, Public Affairs Scripts Broadcast 1943–51.
60 George Grant, *Philosophy in the Mass Age*, ed. William Christian (Toronto: University of Toronto Press, 1995 [1959]), 6.
61 "The early-twentieth-century conservatives said no to modern painting, or to stream-of-consciousness fiction, or to Coolidge prosperity, or to the New Deal so often that they seemed unable to say yes to anything ... In fact, the conservatives valued many things, ... religion, the classics, church architecture, useless knowledge, beauty, and the land, and they desperately wanted the world to stop wasting time, money, and energy on destructive diversions and to get on with the really important things in life." Crunden, "Introduction," in Crunden, ed., *The Superfluous Men: Conservative Critics of American Culture, 1900–1945* (Austin: University of Texas Press, 1977), xi–xx.
62 As Patrick Brantlinger notes: "Democratization was to be made effective through universal education and an extension of industrial prosperity to all classes and nations. But the change would occur through the elevation of the 'the lower orders' or 'masses' toward the standard of living of the upper classes rather than through the 'leveling' of those upper classes ... 'culture' became a key term in nineteenth century liberal theory, for it was by diffusion of culture partly through state-supported schools that 'the masses' could gradually be pacified and brought into the fold. To cite Matthew Arnold's title again, 'culture' was to supplant 'anarchy.'" Patrick Brantlinger, *Bread and Circuses: Theories of Mass Culture as Social Decay* (Ithaca, NY: Cornell University Press, 1983), 31. On liberalism in Canada during the early twentieth century, see Barry Ferguson, *Remaking Liberalism*, especially the final chapter on the "new liberalism."
63 W.L. Morton, "Canadian Conservatism Now," paper given 30 Jan. 1959, McM, W.L. Morton Papers, box 47, Articles, A–Ge, also annotated for *Conservative Concepts*.
64 Louis Greenspan, "The Unravelling of Liberalism," in Arthur Davis, ed., *George Grant and the Subversion of Modernity: Art, Philosophy, Politics, Religion and Education* (Toronto: University of Toronto Press, 1996): 201–2.
65 See Margaret Fairley, "Our Cultural Heritage," *New Frontiers* 1, no. 1 (winter 1952); 1–7 and inside front cover. On the American side, even Erik Barnouw, who had worked for the National Broadcasting Corporation and later wrote a massive history of radio in the United States, held a sharply cynical view of his nation's system, in which commercial sponsorship of quality material was an exception to the rule. See the foreword to Erik

Barnouw, ed., *Radio Drama in Action: Twenty-five Plays of a Changing World* (New York: Rinehart & Company, 1945), vii–ix.
66 William R. Young, "Making the Truth Graphic: The Canadian Government's Home Front Information Structure and Programmes," PhD dissertation, University of British Columbia, 1978, 91–2.
67 Raboy, *Missed Opportunities: The Story of Canada's Broadcasting Policy* (Montreal: McGill-Queen's University Press, 1990), 75. Ron Faris, *The Passionate Educators: Voluntary Associations and the Struggle for Control of Adult Educational Broadcasting in Canada 1919–1952* (Toronto: Peter Martin Associates, 1975).
68 Hans Ulrich Gumbrecht, *In 1926: Living at the Edge of Time* (Cambridge, Mass.: Harvard University Press, 1997); Leo Charney and Vanessa R. Schwartz, eds., *Cinema and the Invention of Modern Life* (Berkeley: University of California Press, 1995); Modris Eksteins, *The Rites of Spring: The Great War and the Birth of the Modern Age* (Toronto: Lester & Orpen Dennys, 1989); Carl E. Schorske, *Fin-de-siècle Vienna: Politics and Culture* (New York: Vintage Books, 1981). For primary material, see Anton Kaes, Martin Jay, and Edward Dimendberg, eds., *The Weimar Republic Sourcebook* (Berkeley: University of California Press, 1995).
69 Ortega y Gasset's *The Revolt of the Masses* appeared in 1930 and was available in English by 1932. Peter Goodall, *High Culture, Popular Culture: The Long Debate* (Sydney: Allen and Unwin, 1995), 23ff. Sigmund Freud's *Civilization and Its Discontents* (London: Hogarth Press and Institute of Psycho-Analysis, 1930) was translated almost immediately, and F.R. Leavis's *Mass Civilisation and Minority Culture* (Cambridge: Minority Press, 1930) provided a summary of thought critical of mass culture.
70 See chapter 5 – "Leaning 'On a Foreign Walking Stick'" – in Maria Tippett, *Making Culture*, 127, 142–5. See also Tippett, "The Making of English-Canadian Culture, 1900–1939: The External Influences," paper delivered 28 April 1987, York University (Toronto: ECW Press, 1988).
71 Morley Callaghan and William Deacon, "The National Forum: Can Canadian Literature Be Distinctively National?" radio address, CBC, 13 Nov. 1938, 7.
72 See especially Leavis's *Mass Civilisation and Minority Culture* (Cambridge: Minority Press, 1930).
73 A.R.M. Lower, "Colonialism and Culture," *Canadian Forum* 14, no. 163 (April 1934): 264–5.
74 Joan Rubin sees critics during the 1920s through the 1940s as more engaged or threatened by "middlebrow" forms, such as the Book-of-the-Month Club or literary programs on radio than by works without any pretence to edification. Further, this critique of the middlebrow did not seem to develop in earnest until the 1940s. Rubin, *The Making of Middlebrow Culture*, xii–xv. See also Crunden, ed., *The Superfluous Men*, introduction.

75 On this phenomenon of acceptance, see chapter 4, "Social Scientists and 'Deviant Entertainments,'" of Paul R. Gorman, *Left Intellectuals and Popular Culture in Twentieth-century America* (Chapel Hill: University of North Carolina Press, 1996). See also Michael Kammen, *The Lively Arts: Gilbert Seldes and the Transformation of Cultural Criticism in the United States* (New York: Oxford University Press, 1996), 327.

76 Chapter 5 of Tippett's *Making Culture* presents a sample of American arts groups travelling in Canada or available for appearances. On the way that Europeans came to identify dominance in certain cultural forms with American productions and production values, see Richard Pells, *Not Like Us: How Europeans Have Loved, Hated, and Transformed American Culture since World War II* (New York: Basic Books, 1997).

77 The British conception of the "problem" of mass culture is well covered in John Carey's *The Intellectuals and the Masses:* In *A Culture for Democracy*, Daniel LeMahieu more directly addresses the struggle to present "high" culture within a democratic, as opposed to an exclusive, context.

78 C.E.M. Joad, *The Babbitt Warren* (London: Kegan Paul, Trench and Trubner, 1926); Gamaliel Milner, *The Problem of Decadence* (London: Williams and Norgate, 1931).

79 B.S. Keirstead, "The Boundaries," unpublished, n.d. [1938], 19, 122. University of New Brunswick Archives, Burton Seely Keirstead Papers, UA RG 81, 3.1.1.

80 Arthur L. Phelps, "Community and Culture," Founder's Day Address at the University of New Brunswick, Fredericton, 18 Feb. 1947.

CHAPTER ONE

1 The sort of power that the term *democracy* could (and does) wield illustrates a phenomenon that critics certainly sensed, but which historians, especially in the field of culture, now view as a commonplace: "[We recognize that] experience is mediated by language, that our access to experience in the past as in the present is decisively shaped by its encoding in particular rhetorical conventions." Richard Wightman Fox and T.J. Jackson Lears, "Introduction," in Lears and Fox, eds., *The Power of Culture: Critical Essays in American History* (Chicago: University of Chicago Press, 1993), 5.

2 Watson Thomson, "Education and Propaganda," *Canadian Forum* 21, no. 253 (Feb. 1942): 328.

3 Jonathan F. Vance, *Death So Noble: Memory, Meaning, and the First World War* (Vancouver: University of British Columbia Press, 1997), see especially chapters 6 and 7, quotation from 219. The National Film Board's *On Guard for Thee*, released during 1940, traced the growth of Canada's self-confidence from the Great War to the end of 1939. Battle footage from the First World War moves into interwar industrialization, and the Depression

gets rather less attention than the prelude to it. The royal visit of 1939 is also a highlight. Another example was the radio presentation of a letter, supposedly from a Canadian airman named "Jimmy" who had written to his parents before he died. Jimmy had abundant faith in democracy and reminds the audience of its duty to bring about peace. [Posthumous Letter from 'Jimmy'], broadcast 27 Dec. 1942, NA, CAVA/AVCA: 1988–0167.

4 The modernist reaction to sentimental Victorianism was well under way by the 1920s. Ken Norris, "The Beginnings of Canadian Modernism," *Canadian Poetry* 11 (autumn–winter 1982), 56–66.

5 *Canadian Author and Bookman* 19, no. 3 (Sept. 1943): front cover.

6 The American government and advertisers managed to equate tasks that defined the national war effort – enlisting, saving, and producing – with the defence or potential improvement of the individual family's life. Robert B. Westbrook, "Fighting for the American Family: Private Interests and Political Obligation in World War II," in Fox and Lears, eds., *The Power of Culture*, 195–221.

7 Leslie Roberts, *We Must Be Free: Reflections of a Democrat* (Toronto: Macmillan, 1939), 248.

8 An associate told broadcaster Norman Creighton that Creighton would probably not be pulled away from his wartime serial *The Gillans* by Selective Service because he was working in radio. Allan Dill to Norman Creighton, 8 March 1943, DAL, Norman Creighton Papers, MS-2, 689, B4.

9 Raymond A. Davies, "Writers and Artists Must Work for Offensive," *Saturday Night* (19 Sept. 1942): 19.

10 "Winning the War," *Canadian Forum* 20, no. 237 (Oct. 1940): 198–9. The political contest surely went on during wartime, and its intricacies can be followed elsewhere. See J.L. Granatstein, *Canada's War: The Politics of the Mackenzie King Government* (Toronto: University of Toronto Press, 1990); Brian Nolan, *King's War: Mackenzie King and the Politics of War, 1939–1945* (Toronto: Random House, 1988); Robert Bothwell and William Kilbourn, *C.D. Howe: A Biography* (Toronto: McClelland and Stewart, 1979); Reginald Whitaker, *The Government Party: Organizing and Financing the Liberal Party of Canada, 1930–1958* (Toronto: University of Toronto Press, 1977); Walter Young, *Anatomy of a Party: The National CCF, 1932–1961* (Toronto: University of Toronto Press, 1969); Granatstein, *The Politics of Survival: The Conservative Party of Canada, 1939–1945* (Toronto: University of Toronto Press, 1967).

11 The four were freedom of speech, of worship, from want, and from fear. For a good example of how pervasive and resonant Roosevelt's speech was in Canada, see George W. Brown, *Canadian Democracy in Action* (Toronto: Ontario Department of Education, 1945).

12 Thomson, "Education and Propaganda," 328.

13 "Begin Now?" *Saturday Night* (27 Dec. 1941): 3.

14 John Fairfax, "Art for Man's Sake," *Canadian Forum* 16, no. 187 (Aug. 1936): 24.
15 I.D. Willis, memorandum to Justice J.T. Thorson, [1940]: 12. NA, Canadian Authors Association Papers, MG 28 I 2, vol. 1, Ontario.
16 A.R.M. Lower, "Canada, the Second Great War, and the Future," *International Journal* 1, no. 2 (April 1946): 99–100.
17 Donald Creighton, *The Forked Road: Canada 1939–1957* (Toronto: McClelland and Stewart, 1976), 37.
18 Peter Fraser, "What Our Thinking Canadians Really Think About," *Saturday Night* (18 March 1939): 2.
19 *Historical Statistics of Canada,* 2nd ed. (Ottawa: Statistics Canada, 1983), series A67–A69.
20 H.M. Cavers, "Progress and the Farmer," *Canadian Forum* 19, no. 224 (Sept. 1939): 189. Hector Charlesworth ascribed the popularity among urban dwellers of the "theory that the best Canadians were raised among 'the large vistas' where they could in summer time perform their ablutions in "the old swimmin' pool" to the rural origins of many men in Toronto's business and professional class. Hector Charlesworth, *I'm Telling You* (Toronto: Macmillan, 1937), 212–13.
21 Harold Innis was deeply concerned with the economic and cultural effects of communications and transportation technology, especially in his later works. For a more recent intellectual history along these lines, see Stephen Kern, *The Culture of Time and Space, 1880–1918* (Cambridge, Mass.: Harvard University Press, 1983). Jeremy Wilson presents one Canadian example of this standardization process in his study of changes to the scale and substance of political campaign issues in the BC interior in Wilson, "The Impact of Communications Developments on British Columbia Electoral Patterns, 1903–1975," *Canadian Journal of Political Science* 13, no. 3 (Sept. 1980): 530.
22 B.K. Sandwell, *The Canadian Peoples* (London: Oxford University Press, 1941), 116–17. Sandwell also named these factors as rivals of the church as a social hub.
23 John Dewey, *Freedom and Culture* (New York: Putnam, 1939), 44–5.
24 Leslie Gordon Barnard, "Postscript to a Letter," *Canadian Author* 16, no. 2 (April 1939): 7.
25 Chester Martin, "Trends in Canadian Nationhood," in Martin, ed., *Canada in Peace and War* (Toronto: Oxford University Press, 1941), 26.
26 Peter Miles and Malcolm Smith, *Cinema, Literature and Society: Elite and Mass Culture in Interwar Britain* (London: Croom Helm, 1987), 232–3, 239. See also Robert Hewison, *Under Siege: Literary Life in London, 1939–1945* (London: Weidenfeld and Nicolson, 1977), especially chapter 1, "Barbarians at the Gate."
27 The WIB was the successor to the Bureau of Public information, established in 1939 to co-ordinate information about King George VI's and Queen Eliza-

beth's royal visit. Though small, it included several members of other Canadian cultural and social-reform organizations. Young, "Making the Truth Graphic," especially 74–80 – a listing of staff. Paul Litt, *The Muses, the Masses, and the Massey Commission* (Toronto: University of Toronto Press, 1992), 40. The Ministry of Informations interests were broader than those of the WIB, and the ministry was also influenced in the direction of cultural study, during the early stages of the war at least, by the presence of some dynamic members of the unorthodox British social research group Mass-Observation. Gary Cross, "Introduction," in Cross, ed., *Worktowners at Blackpool: Mass-Observation and Popular Leisure in the 1930s* (London: Routledge, 1990), 2–3.

28 "The Job Ahead," *Canadian Business* 17, no. 1 (Jan. 1944): 18.
29 Young, "Making the Truth Graphic," ii, 1–6, 17.
30 H. Forsyth Hardy, "Democracy as a Fighting Faith," in *John Grierson and the NFB: Papers Presented at a Conference Held at McGill University 29–30 October 1981* (Toronto: ECW, 1984), 90. See also Gary Evans, *John Grierson and the National Film Board: The Politics of Wartime Propaganda* (Toronto: University of Toronto Press, 1985)
31 Particularly around the time of the New York World's Fair of 1939, a rash of ads emerged touting the futuristic qualities of certain products. Firestone Tires ran "As Modern As the World of Tomorrow"; General Electric reminded consumers of the benefits of research with "Test-tube Babies," a campaign emphasizing the economic spin-offs of a forward-looking society. Some examples of war-related print ad campaigns were: "Two shoulders to the same wheel" (1941); "Canadian Nickel: Serving Today ... Preparing for Tomorrow" (1943); and "Westinghouse Wartime Precision" (1943).
32 Robert Ayre, "Art of Our Day in Canada," *Saturday Night* (28 Dec. 1940): 25.
33 B.K. Sandwell, "War Gets Things Done," *Saturday Night* (22 March 1941): 14.
34 J.R. MacGillivray, "Fiction," *University of Toronto Quarterly* ("Letters in Canada" issue, 1940) 10, no. 3 (April 1941): 292–3, 299.
35 A.W. Trueman, "Our Present and Future Problems, with Suggestions for Their Solution," *Echoes* 160 (autumn 1940): 11.
36 Raymond A. Davies, "Canadian Workers Must Learn to Hate the Axis," *Saturday Night* (1 Aug. 1942): 10. See also Davies, "Management Too Must Learn to Hate Fascism," *Saturday Night* (15 Aug. 1942): 14.
37 Claris Edwin Silcox, *The War and Religion* (Toronto: Macmillan, 1941), 3. Les Callan drew a cartoon for the *Toronto Star* in April 1941 featuring a "free democracy" rifle pointed at a swastika and a "Hitler's axis" rifle pointed at a cross. "War Aims," Original at NA, accession number 1990-608-208.

38 A number of pamphlets and articles published during the war used this phrase or variations on it to emphasize the need to inculcate the fundamentals of the democratic tradition. See the later section of this chapter, which deals with democracy.
39 Paul Lazarsfeld, "The Effects of Radio on Public Opinion," in Douglas Waples, ed., *Print, Radio and Film in a Democracy: Ten Papers on the Administration of Mass Communications in the Public Interest* (Chicago: University of Chicago Press, 1942), 66.
40 Frank H. Underhill, "The People versus the Masses," *Canadian Forum* 21, no. 252 (Jan. 1942): 311.
41 W.J. Healy, "Canada," *National Home Monthly* 40, no. 8 (Aug. 1939): 1.
42 Watson Kirkconnell, "The Price of Christian Liberty" (1939), presidential address delivered in Winnipeg before the Baptist Union of Western Canada, reprinted in the *Canadian Baptist* (10 Aug. and 24 Aug. 1939): 5.
43 One observer suggested that significant confusion existed in England and Canada regarding the important distinction between democracy and liberalism and that Nazi and fascist regimes were at least nominally democratic in that they were "popular." H.N. Fieldhouse, "Dictatorship and Democracy," *Queen's Quarterly* 47, no. 2 (summer 1940): 161–4.
44 Young, "Making the Truth Graphic," 128–40.
45 Underhill, "The People versus the Masses," 312.
46 Northrop Frye, "War on the Cultural Front," *Canadian Forum* 20, no. 235 (Aug. 1940): 146. In this case, Mussolini merely met Frye's need to name an Axis leader.
47 A.R.M. Lower, "Look on This Picture and on This – A View of Canada in 1941," unpublished, dated 27 Oct. 1941, 1, Queen's University Archives (QUA), A.R.M. Lower Papers, box 19, B 430.48. See Luke 11: 24–25.
48 R.S. Lambert, "Mind under Fire," *Food for Thought* 1, no. 5 (May 1940): 3, 17. Lambert had also been especially keen to see his former employer, the British Broadcasting Corporation, become more adept at propaganda. See Lambert, *Ariel and All His Quality: An Impression of the BBC from Within* (London: Victor Gollancz, 1940), 303–6.
49 Ibid., 4–7. In a review of Canadian wartime efforts in propaganda, the author portrayed these endeavours as informational, with "hate" propaganda conspicuously absent; see especially 14–15. Looking back on the 1930s, NFB director John Grierson noted that resistance to activities resembling propaganda was high, in his estimation because "it was not generally allowed that information services were proper to democratic government." John Grierson, "The Changing Face of Propaganda," [1944], NA, Canada Foundation, MG 28 I179, vol. 37, file 6, Grierson, John, National Film Board. This piece was eventually published as "Democracy's Propaganda," in *Free World* 9, no. 1 (Jan. 1945): 37–40. On Northcliffe of Fleet Street, see LeMahieu, *A Culture for Democracy*, 111 and passim.

50 Watson Thomson, "Education and Propaganda," *Canadian Forum* 21, no. 253 (Feb. 1942): 328–31.
51 Young, "Making the Truth Graphic," iii.
52 F.D.L. Smith, "Religion, at Long Last, Gets into Education," *Saturday Night* (4 July 1942): 36.
53 N.A.M. MacKenzie, "The Universities in a World at War," speech at Sir George Williams College, [1944], 12, University of British Columbia Special Collections (UBCSC), N.A.M. MacKenzie Papers, box 96, folder 2.
54 "YOU against the Faceless Men!" (1942).
55 "Talk of the Town," *New Yorker* (7 Feb. 1942): 7.
56 Gregor Ziemer, *Education for Death: The Making of a Nazi* (London: Oxford University Press, 1941). W.H. Brittain saw "conditioning" as the reason behind some of the remarkable results that the Nazis achieved but was certain that Canadians could not be conditioned in the same way. "The Role of the Canadian Association for Adult Education" (1944), 2–3. NA, H.R.C. Avison Papers, MG 30 D 102, vol. 5, file 26, C.A.A.E. 1944. See also R.S. Lambert, "Youth, War and Idealism," *Food for Thought* 1, no. 8 (Oct. 1940): 3–13.
57 R.S. Lambert, "Why Germany Is Like That," *Food for Thought* 1, no. 3 (March 1940): 3. See also G.M.A. Grube, "Hitlerism Is the Enemy," *Canadian Forum* 19, no. 228 (Jan. 1940): 320–2. Sir Robert Falconer characterized the German nation under Nazi rule: "They are impelled by an arrogance of race, a hubris of ethnic complacency, a sense of the incarnation in them of a divine naturalistic force, which has degraded their youth into an immoral, indeed, I should say, a sub-moral state of mind." Robert A. Falconer, "Foreword," in Philip Child and John W. Holmes, *Dynamic Democracy: Problem of Strategy in the World War of Morale*, Behind the Headlines Series, vol. 1, no. 9, May 1941 (Toronto: CIIA/CAAE, 1941), 1.
58 Lambert, "Why Germany Is Like That," 9–10. Chronicling ways in which Germany had "parodied" Britain, Lambert listed Bismarck's attempts to instil devotion to the monarchy, the fostering of commercialism and industrial capitalism, and Wilhelm II's desire for a colonial empire.
59 Mac Shoub, "Thunder On, Democracy!" broadcast 8 July 1942, as the CBC *Play of the Week*, Concordia Centre for Broadcast Studies, CBC Radio Drama Archive, M007813.
60 B.K. Sandwell, "Religion and Education," *Saturday Night* (16 Aug. 1941): 7.
61 F. Cyril James, address during the radio intermission of Gounod's *Faust*, CBC Trans-Canada Network, 30 Jan. 1943, McG, F. Cyril James Papers, MG 1017, Addresses and Other Papers, 1943.
62 Anon., "Thine Is the Kingdom," broadcast 21 Jan. 1943, CBC Trans-Canada Network, 10, McM, CBC Scripts Collection, reel 19.
63 Donald Avery, *The Science of War: Canadian Scientists and Allied Military Technology during the Second World War* (Toronto: University of Toronto Press, 1998); George R. Lindsey, ed., *No Day Long Enough:*

Canadian Science in World War II (Toronto: Canadian Institute of Strategic Studies, 1997)

64 Typical of the *Maclean's* pieces were Creighton Peet, "Your House of Tomorrow" (15 Sept. 1943): 12–13, 43–5; Leonard L. Knott, "Chemistry Fights" (15 May 1942): 24–5, 46–7, 49–51; Wallace Rayburn, "Medicine Goes to War" (1 Sept. 1943): 18–19, 32, 34–5, 37.

65 Lawrence N. Galton compiled the "Tuning Up for Tomorrow" series, which began in the July 1945 issue of *National Home Monthly*. It fits best under John Burnham's category of "Gee Whiz!" science. John C. Burnham, *How Superstition Won and Science Lost: Popularizing Science and Health in the United States* (New Brunswick, NJ: Rutgers University Press, 1987), 5–6.

66 Kenneth Johnstone, "New Army's Food Is Streamlined," *Saturday Night* (18 Nov. 1939): 22.

67 Sir Richard Arman Gregory, *Science in Chains*, No. 12 in the Macmillan War Pamphlets series (London: Macmillan, 1941). In the same series, Julian Huxley contributed "Argument of Blood," which dealt primarily with Nazi race thought. Both sources were recommended in the CAAE's "Pamphlet List" for 1945.

68 In a stunning departure from his usual cheerleading role, science writer and communist Dyson Carter reminded critics of Soviet science what Hitler had been doing with the fruits of German scientific labour. "When Science Kneels to Pray," *Saturday Night* (25 Oct. 1941): 10.

69 Beverly Baxter, "London Letter – Science at War," *Maclean's* (1 Feb. 1940): 9, 35. Baxter developed this idea of misused science further in "The Mind of the German Soldier," *Maclean's* (15 Dec. 1941): 9, 44–5. See also Rolfe Williams, "Jap Using Drugs to Enslave Conquered Peoples," *Saturday Night* (2 May 1942): 6.

70 "The enemy are starting ... ," *Saturday Night* (4 Jan. 1941): 23.

71 Blair Fraser, "Hush-Hush Science War," *Maclean's* (15 Jan. 1945): 5–6, 41–3. C.D. Howe considered the scientist an unsung hero whose contribution would be acknowledged properly once the war had ended. "Address to Rotary Club of Montreal," 11 Feb. 1941, 3, NA, Clarence Decatur Howe Papers, MG 27 III B20, vol. 140, series 89, Articles, Speeches, Books.

72 James Hilton, "Mr. Chips Faces the Facts," Number 9 in the Series *Let's Face the Facts*, broadcast 15 Sept. 1940, CBC. E.L. Harrington, "Physics and Society," *Culture* 5 (1944): 285.

73 William Hardy Alexander, "Noli Episcopari (Letter to a young man contemplating an academic career)," *Canadian Forum* 19, no. 225 (Oct. 1939): 220–3.

74 P.M. Richards, "Democracy Worth Fighting For," *Saturday Night* (9 Aug. 1941): 26.

75 W.J. Healy, "Christmases in Years to Come," *National Home Monthly* 40, no. 12 (Dec. 1939): 1.

76 "End of an Era?" *Canadian Forum* 20, no. 234 (July 1940): 101.
77 W.C. Keirstead, "Discussion in Democracy," ibid. 18, no. 218 (March 1939): 378.
78 See Massolin, *Canadian Intellectuals, the Tory Tradition, and the Challenge of Modernity, 1939–70* (Toronto: University of Toronto Press, 2001), especially chapters 3 and 4. Paul Axelrod, *Making a Middle Class: Student Life in English Canada during the Thirties*. (Montreal: McGill-Queen's University Press, 1990)
79 N.A.M. MacKenzie, "The Universities in a World at War," speech at Sir George Williams College, [1944], 12, UBCSC, N.A.M. MacKenzie Papers, box 96, folder 2. Quoted passage from MacKenzie, "The Future of the Arts Course," speech to Universities Conference, [1942], 6–7, UBCSC, MacKenzie Papers, box 96, folder 2. W.C. Graham to Gordon Sisco, 7 July 1943, United Church of Canada Archives (UCA), Commission on Church, Nation and World Order, Box 1, f.8 – Correspondence. For a more consciously religious interpretation of the same issue, see R.D. Maclennan, "The Continuing Aims of Higher Education," *Culture* 4 (1943): 495–503.
80 E.A. Havelock, "The Philosophy of John Dewey," *Canadian Forum* 19, no. 22 (July 1939): 123.
81 Albert C. Wakeman, "New Year Thoughts on the War – and After," *Saturday Night* (6 Jan. 1940): 7.
82 Morley Callaghan, "If Civilization Must Be Saved," *Saturday Night* (16 Dec. 1939): 6.
83 Humphrey Carver, "Home-Made Thoughts on Handicrafts," *Canadian Forum* 19, no. 230 (March 1940): 386–7. The owner of a large Hamilton construction company took Carver's notion of integration one step further, arguing that handicrafts were neither "interests of the dilettante [nor] hobbies of the intelligentsia. In these days of increasing leisure time, and in view of the ever-widening demand for entertainment, amusement, and pleasure, these gifts have a definite and growing market." Joseph M. Pigott, "Youth and a Trade," *Maclean's* (15 May 1940): 18, 51. Even an advocate of modern architecture admitted that the Industrial Revolution had spawned "ugly factories and products which disturbed artistic people" before efficiency and economy were accepted as components of good design. George Laidler, "Modern Building," *Canadian Forum* 19, no. 223 (Aug. 1939): 154–6.
84 Lawren Harris et al., "Community Art Centres," *Canadian Art* 2, no. 2 (Dec. 1944–Jan. 1945): 62.
85 Adeline Haddow, "Individuality and the Machine," *Saturday Night* (20 June 1942): 21. Joy Parr presents the empowered postwar housewife in *Domestic Goods: The Material, the Moral and the Economic in the Postwar Years* (Toronto: University of Toronto Press, 1999), which explores the design and consumption of household fixtures and furnishings.
86 Frye, "War on the Cultural Front," 144.

87 "Education for What?" *Canadian Forum* 21, no. 250 (Nov. 1941): 229.
88 John Dewey, *Freedom and Culture* (New York: Putnam, 1939)
89 May Richstone, "Tabloid," *Saturday Night* (7 Dec. 1940): 15.
90 Frye, "War on the Cultural Front," 144.
91 Buchan was perhaps better known in Canada as the first Baron Tweedsmuir, governor-general from 1935 to 1940. Willis began one of his pamphlets, *Democracy: A Tripod* (Port Hope, Ont., 1940), with this quotation from Buchan's autobiographical *Memory Hold-the-Door* (London: Hodder and Stoughton, 1940), 220.
92 "So two cheers for Democracy: one because it admits variety and two because it permits criticism. Two cheers are quite enough: there is no occasion to give three. Only Love the Beloved Republic deserves that." E.M. Forster, "What I Believe," in *Forster, Two Cheers for Democracy* (London: Edward Arnold, 1951), 79.
93 One of the more comprehensive broadcasts in this series was: Terence William Leighton MacDermot, *Can We Make Good?* fourth broadcast in the *Citizens All* series on CBC, broadcast 15 Nov. 1940, published as no. 4 in the *Democracy and Citizenship* series (Toronto: CAAE/CIIA, 1940).
94 On the American side, Thomas Vernor Smith, Glenn Negley, and Robert Bush produced *Democracy vs. Dictatorship* (Washington, DC: National Education Association, 1942), a resource package for the teaching of democracy, which noted such publications as F.L. Bacon and E.A. Krug, *Our Life Today* (Boston: Little, Brown, 1939); Ryllis and Omar Goslin, *Democracy* (New York: Harcourt, Brace, 1940); L.J. O'Rourke, *Our Democracy and Its Problems* (Boston: Heath, 1942); and Lewis Mumford, *Faith for Living* (New York: Harcourt, Brace, 1940). Not listed as teaching material was Smith's own *The Democratic Tradition in America* (New York: Farrar and Rinehart, 1941). In Britain, support for and invocation of the concept was no less vigorous or wide-ranging. See Harold J. Laski et al., *Where Stands Democracy? A Collection of Essays by Members of the Fabian Society* (London: Macmillan, 1940); David Thomson, *The Democratic Ideal in France and England* (Cambridge: Cambridge University Press, 1940); Julian Huxley, *Democracy Marches* (New York: Harper and Brothers, 1941); J.B. Priestley, *Out of the People* (New York: Harper, 1941); Godfrey Elton, *St. George or the Dragon: Towards a Christian Democracy* (London: Collins, 1942); and Josiah C. Wedgwood, *Testament to Democracy* (London: Hutchinson, [1942]).
95 Martyn Estall, "Learning for Living," *Canadian Affairs* 2, no. 16 (Oct. 1945), 3.
96 D.L. LeMahieu, *A Culture for Democracy: Mass Communication and the Cultural Mind in Britain between the Wars* (Oxford: Clarendon Press, 1988), 3.
97 Nova Scotia Credit Union League, "Is Ignorance Bliss?" [1940], 2.

98 Prior to the dissolution of the German–Soviet entente, writers and broadcasters also noted the differences between communism and liberal democracy but seemed to find it easier to demonize the Nazi, Italian fascist, and Japanese regimes as enemies of democracy. See, for an example from the pamphlet literature, the quoted piece by the phlegmatic but committed I.D. Willis, *Democracy,* 1–2.

99 Philip Child and John W. Holmes, *Dynamic Democracy: Problem of Strategy in the World War of Morale, Behind the Headlines Series*, vol. 1, no. 9, May 1941 (Toronto: CIIA/CAAE, 1941), 5. On radio, "You Are Democracy" (broadcast 2 Dec. 1944) was a good example of such direct appeals; NA, CAVA/AVCA: 1976–0066.

100 *Government by the People*, Canadian Post-war Affairs: Discussion Manual No. 5 (Ottawa: King's Printer, 1945), 6.

101 R.S. Lambert, "Youth, War and Idealism," *Food for Thought* 1, no. 8 (Oct. 1940): 11.

102 Winnipeg "If" Day, Fox Movietone Newsreel, 1942, NA, CAVA/AVCA: 1978–0203.

103 H.N. Fieldhouse did not subscribe to the notion that democracy and dictatorship were mutually exclusive and cautioned his readers to avoid using "democracy" as a synonym for "liberalism." Fieldhouse, "Dictatorship and Democracy," 162–3. D.G. Davis, *Parents and Democracy* (Toronto: Ryerson, 1941); Julia Grace Wales, *Democracy Needs Education* (Toronto: Macmillan, 1942); Charles E. Phillips, *New Schools for Democracy, Behind the Headlines Series*, vol. 4, no. 6 (Toronto: CIIA/CAAE, 1944); George W. Brown, *Canadian Democracy in Action* (Toronto: Ontario Department of Education, 1945)

104 I.D. Willis, *What Do Canada and Democracy Really Mean to You?* (Port Hope, Ont., 1940), front cover.

105 B.K. Sandwell, "You Take Out What You Put In," third broadcast in the *Citizens All* series on CBC, 1 Nov. 1940, published as No. 3 in the *Democracy and Citizenship Series* (Toronto: CAAE/CIIA, 1940), 6; MacDermot, *Can We Make Good?* 6; Canadian Teachers' Federation, "I'm Free to Choose," No. 3 in the Democratic Way series (July 1943), 8–10.

106 S.K. Jaffary, "The Social Services," in C.A. Ashley, ed., *Reconstruction in Canada* (Toronto: University of Toronto Press, 1943), 119.

107 M.M. Coady, "Blueprinting Post-War Canada," *Culture* 4 (1943): 161. University of Wisconsin English professor J.G. Wales, a Canadian, wrote during the war that institutions in democratic nations deserved space to adapt to rapidly changing conditions because these institutions were "of long and organic growth." Julia Grace Wales, "Pro, Not Anti: A Principle of Integration," *New Age* 2, no. 31 (8 Aug. 1940): 9–10.

108 Canadian Teachers' Federation, "Freedom of Conscience," no. 4 in the Democratic Way series (Jan. 1944), 20.

109 MacDermot, *Can We Make Good?* 16–19.
110 Writing at a time when Germany and the Soviet Union were not yet at war with each other, Frye condemned both ends of the political spectrum, adding: "This something broader and deeper neither nazism or communism possesses." Frye "War on the Cultural Front," 144–6.
111 B.K. Sandwell, "Who Are Culture's Custodians?" *Saturday Night* (7 June 1941): 11.
112 "I'm Free to Choose" (July 1943), 6, quotation from "Freedom of Conscience" (Jan. 1944), 4.
113 Sandwell, "You Take Out What You Put In," 18.
114 The remaining plays, in order of presentation, were *This Precious Freedom, The Flying Yorkshireman, Hellas, A British Subject I Was Born,* and *The Fall of the City*. "Radio Hits the Mark!" *Food for Thought* 2, no. 2 (Feb. 1941): 15. At the conclusion of Norman Corwin's play, actor Phillips Holmes enumerated radio's contributions to "keeping democracy alive." *Seems Radio Is Here to Stay*, broadcast 2 Feb. 1941, NA, CAVA/AVCA: 1981–0100.
115 John Grierson, "Education and the New Order," address at the closing banquet of the CAAE annual convention, Winnipeg, 31 May 1941, 9, McG, John Grierson Collection, MG 2067, container 4, file 110.
116 Kirkconnell to William Clarke of Oxford University Press, Toronto, 5 Nov. 1940, 30 April, 29 June, 6 Sept. 1941 and Clarke to Kirkconnell, 22 May 1941, Acadia University Archives (AUA), Watson Kirkconnell Papers, Material on *Twilight of Liberty*, P1/11.2.
117 Young Men's Committee, National Council, YMCA, *Canada and the Four Freedoms* (Toronto: Ryerson, 1944); "Freedom and Scientific Dogmatism," *Food for Thought* 3, no. 3 (Nov. 1942): 5–6; J.E. Middleton, "Roosevelt" (poem), *Saturday Night* (21 April 1945): 3; "You and Me and Reconstruction," CBC Discussion Club, 28 Aug. 1942, NA, CAVA/AVCA: 1984–0164, reference copy at: 1982–0043/63.
118 L.A. Mackay, "About Tradition and Modern Education," *Saturday Night* (26 July 1941): 14–15.
119 B.K. Sandwell, "Liberty and Commitments," *Saturday Night* (20 Sept. 1941): 3.
120 Charles E. Phillips, *New Schools for Democracy* (Toronto: CIIA/CAAE, 1944), 15–16.
121 Hon. D. [Duncan] McArthur, "Education for Democracy," *Saturday Night* (7 Dec. 1940): 45. Creighton, *The Forked Road*, 20.
122 W.P. Percival, "Freedom of Educational Opportunity," *Canadian Geographical Journal* 26, no. 12 (June 1943): 289.
123 "Winning the War," *Canadian Forum* 20, no. 237 (Oct. 1940): 199.
124 MacDermot, *Can We Make Good?* 7.
125 Frye, "War on the Cultural Front," 144.

126 Underhill, "The People versus the Masses," 311.
127 Sandwell, "You Take Out What You Put In," 19. Sandwell had written along similar lines prior to the war. See "Totalitarian Democracy," *Saturday Night* (29 April 1939): 1.
128 "Canadian Hurdles," Canadian Post-war Affairs: Discussion Manual no. 4 (Ottawa: King's Printer, 1945), 82 (emphasis added).
129 John Chastey, "Bridge to To-morrow," broadcast 1 Jan. 1943, 18, McM, CBC Scripts Collection, reel 9.
130 Ronald Oliver MacFarlane, "Canada Tomorrow: Canada and the Post-war World, Part One," *Behind the Headlines Series*, vol. 2, no. 3, Jan. 1942 (Toronto: CIIA/CAAE, 1942)
131 D.G. Davis, *Parents and Democracy* (Toronto: Ryerson, 1941), 3.
132 Estall, "Learning for Living," 5.
133 F. Cyril James, "Stained Glass," address before the Royal Architectural Institute of Canada, 20 Feb. 1943, McG, F. Cyril James Papers, MG 1017, Addresses and Other Papers, 1943.
134 John Coulter, "Books and Shows," second series, talk number one, broadcast 24 Nov. 1942, 5, McM, John Coulter Papers, box 36, f. 2.
135 John Coulter, "Books and Shows," talk number three, First series, 30 June 1942, McM, John Coulter Papers, box 36, f. 1.
136 "Montreal Central Station Opening," script, 14 July 1943, NA, CBC, RG 41, vol. 252, file 11-39-8, Montreal Station Opening.
137 Gerald Clark, "First Stop to Tomorrow," *Maclean's* (1 Sept. 1943): 20, 45.
138 "Frozen Streamlines," *Ottawa Journal* (22 Nov. 1940).
139 Charles Fraser Comfort, "Art and the Community," Speech at the Opening Ceremonies of the John Gordon McIntosh and Wilhelmina Morris McIntosh Memorial Building, University of Western Ontario, 26 June 1942, NA, Charles Fraser Comfort Papers, MG30 D81, vol. 35, file 1.
140 Douglas Le Pan, "The Arts in Great Britain in Wartime," *Canadian Art* 1, no. 1 (Oct.–Nov. 1943): 13.
141 "Freedom of Conscience" (Jan. 1944), 6.
142 Claris Edwin Silcox, *The War and Religion* (Toronto: Macmillan, 1941), 6.
143 Richard M. Saunders, "Introduction," in Saunders, ed., *Education for Tomorrow* (Toronto: University of Toronto Press, 1946), ix–x.
144 John Macdonald, "The Corner Stone of Democracy: The Discussion Group," (Toronto: Ryerson, 1939); C. Cecil Lingard, "Why National Leadership in Education Is Vital," *Saturday Night* (21 Dec. 1940): 6; "Education for What?" *Canadian Forum* 21, no. 250 (Nov. 1941): 229–30; Canadian Teachers' Federation, "I'm Free to Choose," No. 3 in the Democratic Way series (July 1943), 5; L.A. MacKay, "Liberal Education Needed for Healthy Democracy," *Saturday Night* (27 May 1944):

11. "Government by the People," *Canadian Post-war Affairs: Discussion Manual No. 5* (Ottawa: King's Printer, 1945), 60.

CHAPTER TWO

1 "Begin Now?" *Saturday Night* (27 Dec. 1941): 3.
2 Leonard L. Knott, "Post-War Preview," *Montreal Standard* (magazine section), 30 Oct. 1943.
3 John Grierson, "Education and the New Order," address at the closing banquet of the CAAE annual convention, Winnipeg, 31 May 1941, 11. McG, John Grierson Collection, MG 2067, container 4, file 110.
4 This is Blair Fraser's term and the title of his popular history, *The Search for Identity: Canada Postwar to Present* (Toronto: Doubleday, 1967).
5 Desmond Morton and Glenn Wright, *Winning the Second Battle: Canadian Veterans and the Return to Civilian Life, 1915–1930* (Toronto: University of Toronto Press, 1987), 98–9, 106; Craig Brown and Ramsay Cook, *Canada 1896–1921: A Nation Transformed* (Toronto: McClelland and Stewart, 1974), especially chapter 15: "O Brave New World ..." Brown and Cook note wartime activity by social gospellers and a surge in nationalism but little excitement surrounding the postwar era as distinct from immediate reforms. Barry Ferguson chronicles some academic interest in reconstruction among Queen's University political economists, but this interest flickers to life only very near the end of the First World War, gathering strength in 1919. See especially chapter 9 of Ferguson, *Remaking Liberalism: The Intellectual Legacy of Adam Shortt, O.D. Skelton, W.C. Clark, and W.A. Mackintosh, 1890–1925* (Montreal: McGill-Queen's University Press, 1993). Maria Tippett's *Art at the Service of War: Canada, Art, and the Great War* (Toronto: University of Toronto Press, 1984) contains a chapter ("Lest we forget") on interwar efforts to memorialize the war via art exhibitions and the sense that war had – in an indirect way – contributed to a welling up of nationalist sentiment during the 1920s. On Britain, see Paul Johnson, *Land Fit for Heroes: The Planning of British Reconstruction, 1916–1919* (Chicago: University of Chicago Press, 1968) 1–9; and Kenneth O. Morgan, *Consensus and Disunity: The Lloyd George Coalition Government, 1918–1922* (Oxford: Clarendon, 1979), especially chapter 4, on social reform.
6 Albert Shea, "Blueprint for Demobilizing," *Saturday Night* (14 June 1941): 11.
7 One recent exception is Peter S. McInnis, *Harnessing Labour Confrontation: Shaping the Postwar Settlement in Canada, 1943–1950* (Toronto: University of Toronto Press, 2002). More typical approaches may be found in Peter Neary and J.L. Granatstein, eds., *The Veteran's Charter and Post–World War II Canada* (Montreal: McGill-Queen's University Press, 1998). Another

recently published collection – Greg Donaghy, ed., *Uncertain Horizons: Canadians and Their World in 1945* (Ottawa: Canadian Committee for the History of the Second World War, 1997) – contains a handful of articles on reconstruction. These include, Francine McKenzie, "Canada and the Reconstruction of Postwar Trade, 1943–1945"; Hector Mackenzie, "The White Paper on Reconstruction and Canada's Postwar Trade Policy"; David Slater, "Colour the Future Bright: The *White Paper*, the Green Book and the 1945–1946 Dominion–Provincial Conference on Reconstruction"; Peter S. McInnis, "Planning Prosperity: Canadians Debate Postwar Reconstruction"; and Dominique Marshall, "Reconstruction Politics, the Canadian Welfare State and the Ambiguity of Children's Rights, 1940–1950." Though informative on Canadian reconstruction policy, they show little interest (with the possible exception of McInnis and to a lesser extent Marshall) in reconstruction as a public experience or in its cultural dimensions. For more on the official side of reconstruction, see David Slater, *War, Finance and Reconstruction: The Role of Canada's Department of Finance 1939–1946* (Ottawa: Department of Finance, 1995). Paul Litt, *The Muses, the Masses, and the Massey Commission* (Toronto: University of Toronto Press, 1992); Maria Tippett, *Making Culture: English-Canadian Institutions and the Arts before the Massey Commission* (Toronto: University of Toronto Press, 1990).

8 John Baldwin, "Approach to Reconstruction," *Saturday Night* (24 Oct. 1942): 28.

9 Marcus Adeney, "Community Centres in Canada," *Journal of the Royal Architectural Institute of Canada*, no. 2 (Feb. 1945): 21–3, 39.

10 Charged respectively with advising and with overseeing plans for the transition from war to peace were the Dominion Advisory Committee on Reconstruction, under McGill University Principal F.C. James, and the House of Commons Special Committee on Reconstruction and Re-establishment, chaired by James Gray Turgeon, MP. The Advisory Committee advocated the creation of a Department of Reconstruction. When that department was formed in 1944 under C.D. Howe, the committee disbanded.

11 In *The Government Generation: Canadian Intellectuals and the State, 1900–1945* (Toronto: University of Toronto Press, 1986), Doug Owram viewed the reconstruction period as a logical place to end his account of the transformation of the Canadian civil service. Not only did those years teem with evidence that intellectuals had found a place within government, but also economic reconstruction was chiefly about engineering the speedy removal of wartime controls. See also Ferguson, *Remaking Liberalism*, 230.

12 James Allen's cartoon depiction of figures personifying Labour and Industry united behind a co-ordinated plan to tackle postwar problems, while the steam shovel of Wartime Unity moves into action, illustrated the "strike while the iron's hot" mentality of reconstruction. "Let's Break Ground Now," *Saturday Night* (8 March 1941): 33.

13 As of this writing, I am not aware of any other studies using this term.
14 F. Cyril James, address during the radio intermission of Gounod's *Faust*, CBC, 30 Jan. 1943, McG, F. Cyril James Papers, MG 1017, Addresses and Other Papers, 1943.
15 Ron Faris, *The Passionate Educators: Voluntary Associations and the Struggle for Control of Adult Educational Broadcasting in Canada, 1919-52* (Toronto: Peter Martin Associates, 1975), 153.
16 Albert C. Wakeman, "New Year Thoughts on the War – and After," *Saturday Night* (6 Jan. 1940): 7.
17 Ronald Oliver MacFarlane, "Canada Tomorrow: Canada and the Post-war World, Part One," *Behind the Headlines Series*, vol. 2, no. 3, Jan. 1942 (Toronto: CIIA/CAAE, 1942)
18 "Winning the War," *Canadian Forum* 20, no. 237 (Oct. 1940): 199. Ardent democrat I.D. Willis warned business interests that returning veterans would demand "real improvements in all phases of our national life which must go deeper than mere social insurance." I.D. Willis, memorandum to J.T. Thorson, [1940], 13, NA, Canadian Authors Association Papers, MG 28 I 2, vol. 1, Ontario.
19 Maxwell Cohen, *Governmental Machinery of Wartime Controls and Its Relation to Postwar Problems*, Report to the Advisory Committee on Reconstruction (Ottawa: King's Printer, 1942), 28.
20 Advisory Committee on Reconstruction, *Report* (issued 24 Sept. 1943) (Ottawa: King's Printer, 1944), 1.
21 Julia Grace Wales, "Pro, Not Anti: A Principle of Integration," *New Age* 2, no. 31 (8 Aug. 1940): 9-10.
22 J. Richards Petrie, "The Universities and the War," *Brunswickan* 60, no. 7 (8 Nov. 1940): 3, 6. For examples of similar confidence in the university during the 1920s, see Ferguson, *Remaking Liberalism*, 211; Axelrod, *Making a Middle Class*, 12-15.
23 The task of telling the story of Canada's official efforts in postwar reconstruction – a detailed account of the King government's struggle to direct the process of demobilization both before and after victory – has yet to be attempted, although Donaghy, ed., *Uncertain Horizons*, is a promising beginning. See Robert Bothwell, Ian Drummond, and John English, *Canada since 1945: Power, Politics and Provincialism*, rev. ed. (Toronto: University of Toronto Press, 1989), 82, 109-11; Doug Owram, *Born at the Right Time: A History of the Baby Boom Generation* (Toronto: University of Toronto Press, 1996), 24-5.
24 Other major wartime remedies – appearing in a flurry in 1943, close on the heels of Britain's Beveridge Report of December 1942 – were Harry Cassidy's *Social Security and Reconstruction in Canada* (Toronto: Ryerson, 1943), Marsh's *Report on Social Security for Canada* (Ottawa: King's Printer, 1943), and Charlotte Whitton's *The Dawn of Ampler Life*

(Toronto: Macmillan, 1943), "commissioned" by federal Conservative leader John Bracken. Whitton's work "was both a direct attack on Marsh's proposals and an alternative vision of Canada's social welfare future." Brigitte Kitchen, "The Marsh Report Revisited," *Journal of Canadian Studies* 21, no. 2 (summer 1986): 38–40.

25 Canadian Council of Education for Citizenship, "Constitution" [1941], Canadian Citizenship Council Papers, NA, MG 28 I85, vol. 54, Canadian Council of Education for Citizenship.

26 Arthur L. Phelps, "The Canadian Pattern: Problems and Convictions of a Canadian, Part 1," CBC, 19 Dec. 1943, NA, Wartime Information Board (WIB), RG 36/31, vol. 10, file 4–3, Canadian Committee.

27 Albert C. Wakeman, "New Year Thoughts on the War – and After," *Saturday Night* (6 Jan. 1940): 7. W.D. Black, "Industrial Development in Canada to Meet the War Emergency," broadcast on CBC, 13 Nov. 1940, NA, Clarence Decatur Howe Papers, MG 27 III B20, vol. 140, series 89, Articles, Speeches, Books. G.W. Brown to A.R.M. Lower, 31 July 1940, QUA, A.R.M. Lower Papers, Correspondence re: "Social Sciences in Post-war World," box 13, B 142.

28 "A New Approach," *Canadian Forum* 21, no. 248 (Sept. 1941): 166–7.

29 Claris Silcox, *The War and Religion* (Toronto: Macmillan, 1941), 10; Young Men's Christian Associations of Canada, National Council, *We Discuss Canada* (Toronto: Ryerson, 1942), 57; Bruce Hutchison, "Win the Peace NOW!" *Maclean's* (15 April 1943): 18, 44–6.

30 Along with dozens of pamphlets, some of the most prominent books produced on reconstruction themes in the United States were George B. Galloway, *Post-war Planning in the United States* (New York: Twentieth Century Fund, 1942); Fawn M. Brodie, *Peace Aims and Post-war Planning* (Boston: World Peace Foundation, 1942) and *Peace Aims and Post-war Reconstruction* (Princeton, NJ: American Committee for International Studies, 1941); Office of War Information, *Toward New Horizons: The World beyond the War* (Washington, DC: Government Printing Office, 1942); Raoul de Roussy de Sales, *The Making of Tomorrow* (Toronto: McClelland and Stewart, 1942) [a reprint]; and Lewis Corey, *The Unfinished Task: Economic Reconstruction for Democracy* (New York: Viking, 1942). For a more comprehensive listing of reconstruction publications from the United States, Canada and Britain up to 1943, see Ralph Flenley, *Post-war Problems – A Reading List* (Toronto: Canadian Institute of International Affairs, 1943).

31 C.E. Silcox to Abbé Arthur Maheux, 8 July 1942, (UCA), Claris Edwin Silcox Papers, box 11, file 5, Correspondence 1940–1945.

32 John P. Kidd, "Planning the Community," *Food for Thought* 6, no. 3 (Nov. 1945): 24.

33 Print advertising is a rich source on the culture of reconstruction and reflected, as well as helped perpetuate, public awareness of issues such as

planning. Magazine readers could be simultaneously heartened and chastised by ads such as: "The men who are planning the world of tomorrow" (1945); "'Caught Short' through Lack of Planning" (1945) and "Are You a Post-war Planner?" (1945).

34 Watson Kirkconnell, *Seven Pillars of Freedom* (Toronto: Oxford University Press, 1944), vii.

35 These few articles constitute a sampling of *Saturday Night's* treatment of planning: P.M. Richards, "Free Enterprise Must Plan Now" (30 Jan. 1943): 34. Stanley McConnell, "The State: In Theory, Practice, Prospect" (11 Nov. 1944): 20; C.E. Silcox, "Look Out, Leviathan's on the Horizon Again!" (30 Sept. 1944): 16–17; C. Monte Roberts, "*Saturday Night* Presents Its Own Dictionary for Socialists" (28 April 1945): 41; and Wilfrid Eggleston, "Do Most Canadians Really Want More Government Intervention?" (12 April 1947): 8.

36 P.M. Richards, "Principles for the Post-War," *Saturday Night* (7 Nov. 1942): 26.

37 William R. Yendall, *The Common Problem* (Toronto: Ryerson Press, 1942).

38 I.D. Willis to A.D. Dunton, 15 April 1943, NA, Canadian Authors Association Papers, MG 28 I 2, vol. 1, Ontario.

39 Stanley McConnell, "The Menace of Collectivism," *Saturday Night* (19 Sept. 1942): 34 (emphasis added).

40 Examples are "Better Get Ready to Turn Those Theories into Blueprints, Mister," *Saturday Night* (18 Sept. 1943): 33, and "Not So Nice for Him to Come Home to," *Saturday Night* (18 March 1944): 33.

41 C.A. Ashley, "Introduction," in Ashley, ed., *Reconstruction in Canada* (Toronto: University of Toronto Press, 1943), xiii.

42 Bruce Hutchison, "Where Now, Canada?" *Maclean's* (1 July 1942): 7, 38, 50–1. "Planning Our Civilization," *Canadian Forum* 20, no. 234 (July 1940): 100–1; Fergus Glenn, "Anatomy of the Little Man," *Canadian Forum* 25, no. 295 (Aug. 1945): 109–111.

43 On the politics of planning during the Second World War, see chapter 5, "The Coming of the Planners," in Donald Creighton, *The Forked Road: Canada 1939–1957* (Toronto: McClelland and Stewart, 1976).

44 F.R. Scott, "Social Planning and the War," *Canadian Forum* 20, no. 235 (Aug. 1940): 138–9. For a denunciation of the fear and hope that was keeping the ordinary Canadian a part of the harried mass, see Glenn, "Anatomy of the Little Man."

45 The advertising copy is from "Next! Movies that "live and breathe"... the work of men who think of tomorrow!" (June 1944), but Seagram's ran several others in the "Men Who Think of Tomorrow" series.

46 "Post-war Planner" (1943). This advertisement also included a short section entitled "What is Private Enterprise?" "It is the natural desire to make your own way, as far as your ability will take you; an instinct that has

brought to this continent the highest standard of life enjoyed by any people on earth. It is the spirit of democracy on the march."

47 "Young Man With a Plan" (1948).
48 "Moderation promises a glorious future" (1946) featured a new slogan for Seagram's: "Men who Think of Tomorrow ... Practice Moderation Today!"; "We Walk the Middle Road" (1946).
49 John L. McDougall, *The Foundations of National Well-Being – Post-war* (Kingston, 1944), 10.
50 L.C. Marsh, "Is National Planning a Threat to Democracy?" prepared for *Citizens' Forum*, 3 Dec. 1947, UBCSC, Leonard C. Marsh Papers, box 6, Broadcasts.
51 E.A. Corbett "Director's Report" (1946), 7, NA, WIB, RG 36/31, vol. 14, file 8-20-1, CAAE.
52 "Thinking about Canada," *Saturday Night* (2 May 1942): 3.
53 Editorial notice, "'After the War,'" *Saturday Night* (15 Aug. 1942): 3.
54 "A New Approach," *Canadian Forum* 21, no. 248 (Sept. 1941): 166.
55 "Planning Post-war Canada" began its run as a regular section in *Canadian Forum* in April 1943.
56 Association of Canadian Advertisers, *Continuing Study of Trends in Post-war Planning*. Each issue contained a packet of reprints from various sources and an editorial on some aspect of postwar planning. Among the numerous advertising campaigns making use of the idea of reconstruction were: "Two shoulders to the same wheel" (1941); "Canadian Nickel: Serving Today ... Preparing for Tomorrow" (1943); "Post-war Planner" (1943); "What's coming is ... PLENTY!" (1943); "Think Big..." (1944); "Postwarithmetic" (1944); and "The Challenge" (1945).
57 "Canada's Future Possibilities in Post-War Reconstruction As Suggested by an Englishwoman," *Echoes* 161 (Christmas 1940): 8; Velyien E. Henderson, comp., "Reconstruction: Resolutions of National Empire Study Committee," *Echoes* 166 (spring 1942): 24, 167; (summer 1942): 9, 45.
58 Mary Lowrey Ross, "A Reverent Ode to the Great Modern Goddess Panacea," *Saturday Night* (29 Jan. 1944): 29.
59 "Hasty Reformers," *Saturday Night* (21 March 1942): 3.
60 Charles Fraser Comfort, "Art and the Community," Speech at the Opening Ceremonies of the John Gordon McIntosh and Wilhelmina Morris McIntosh Memorial Building, University of Western Ontario, 26 June 1942, 22, NA, Charles Fraser Comfort Papers, MG30 D81, vol. 35, file 1.
61 R.D. Maclennan, "The Continuing Aims of Higher Education," *Culture* 4 (1943): 495.
62 CAAE, "Report of the Proceedings of a Special Programme Committee of the Canadian Association for Adult Education," 27-31 Dec. 1942, 4, Archives of Ontario (AO), CAAE Papers, series B-I, box 3, *Citizens' Forum*, administrative, 1943-1960.

63 Coulter, "Books and Shows," talk number seven, first series, broadcast 28 July 1942, 6, McM, John Coulter Papers, box 36, f. 1.
64 *Transit through Fire*, words by John Coulter and music by Healey Willan (Toronto: Macmillan, 1942), 1. The opera was published in this form, Coulter claimed, "so that they may get into the hands of the young men and women, fighters, workers, students, who may have few pennies in their pockets, but in their hearts and minds have intelligence and will and moral passion to join resolutely in the task which shall await them when the war is won."
65 *Transit through Fire*, 6. Coulter borrowed heavily from the libretto in later critical broadcasts, contending: "In war, we act at last like, or something nearly like, a true community. A Christian community. There's a paradox!" Coulter, "Books and Shows," talk number one, second series, broadcast 24 Nov. 1942, 3–4. McM, John Coulter Papers, vox 36, f. 2, 4–5.
66 "The alternative being / a world-community / ruled by a hierarchy / for whom the State and the Sword / are the avatars of God." *Transit through Fire*, 8; Elizabeth Wyn Wood, "A National Program for the Arts in Canada," *Canadian Art* 1, no. 3 (Feb.–March 1944): 93–4.
67 "Canadian Criticism," *Saturday Night* (27 Nov. 1943): 3.
68 John Coulter, "Books and Shows," talk number seven, second series, broadcast 5 Jan. 1943, 2–3. McM, John Coulter Papers, box 36, f. 2.
69 A.S.P. Woodhouse et al., "Remaining Material," *University of Toronto Quarterly* ("Letters in Canada" 1941 number) 11, nos. 3 and 4 (April and July 1942): 347. The series that Woodhouse enjoyed were *Food for Thought* from the CAAE and *Behind the Headlines* from the Canadian Institute of International Affairs.
70 Baldwin, "Approach to Reconstruction," 28.
71 Father M.M. Coady, "Blueprinting Post-War Canada," *Culture* 4 (1943): 161–71.
72 E.A. Corbett, "Adult Education," typescript (1938), 5, NA, Robert Alexander Sim Papers, MG 30 D 260, vol. 11, file 11, CAAE, correspondence, minutes, pamphlets.
73 See, for instance, number 6 in the CAAE's "Live and Learn" series: John Macdonald, *The Corner Stone of Democracy: The Discussion Group* (Toronto: Ryerson, 1939).
74 David P. Armstrong, "Corbett's House: The Origins of the Canadian Association for Adult Education and its Development during the Directorship of E.A. Corbett, 1936–1951," MA thesis, University of Toronto, 1968, 110–12; "W.E.A. Radio Forum," *Adult Learning* 4 (Nov. 1939): 23–4. See Michael Welton, 'An Authentic Instrument of the Democratic Process': The Itellectual Origins of the Canadian Citizens' Forum," *Studies in the Education of Adults* 18, no. 1 (April 1986): 35–49; Ronald L. Faris, "Adult Education for Social Action or Enlightenment? An Assessment of the Development of the Cana-

dian Association for Adult Education and Its Radio Forums from 1935–1952," PhD, dissertation, University of Toronto, 1971, chaps. 2–5; Gordon Selman, *Adult Education in Canada: Historical Essays* (Toronto: Thompson Educational Publishing, 1995); Gerald Friesen, "Adult Education and Union Education: Aspects of English-Canadian Cultural History in the 20th Century," *Labour/Le Travail* 34 (autumn 1994): 163–88.

75 E.A Corbett, "Education by Radio," *Canadian Forum* 18, no. 218 (March 1939): 374–7.
76 Frank Chamberlain, "The School of the Air," *Saturday Night* (20 Sept. 1941): 16. On the American response to such programs, see Bruce Lenthall, "Critical Reception: Public Intellectuals Decry Depression-era Radio, Mass Culture, and Modern America," in Michelle Hilmes and Jason Loviglio, eds., *Radio Reader: Essays in the Culture History of Radio* (New York: Routledge, 2002), 41–62.
77 Neil M. Morrison, "Community Problems," broadcast on CKUA and CFCN, 20 Nov. 1939, Neil M. Morrison Papers, NA, MG 30 E 273, vol. 28, Public Affairs Scripts Broadcast 1943–51; Armstrong, "Corbett's House," 112. See also "The Common Man in the Post-war World," *New Trail* 1, no. 2 (Jan. 1943): 20–2.
78 John Nicol, Albert Shea, and G.J.P Simmins, *Canada's Farm Radio Forum* (Paris: UNESCO, 1954), 40–6. Marc Raboy, *Missed Opportunities: The Story of Canada's Broadcasting Policy* (Montreal: McGill-Queen's University Press, 1990), 75.
79 Faris, *The Passionate Educators*, 99, 153.
80 Philippe J. Baillargeon, "The CBC and the Cold War Mentality, 1946–1952," MA thesis, Carleton University, 1987, 18–24.
81 Neil Morrison to General Supervisor of Programmes, 22 Feb. 1941, NA, CBC *Citizens' Forum*, MG 28 I 400, vol. 1, file 2, CAAE – CBC co-operation.
82 Program description, "CBC Discussion Club," broadcast 28 Aug. 1942, CBC Radio Archives, Toronto.
83 CAAE Council meeting, Toronto, 16 Nov. 1942, NA, CBC *Citizens's Forum*, MG 28 I 400, vol. 1, file 2, CAAE – CBC co-operation.
84 James S. Thomson to Inch, 16 Dec. 1942, NA, Robert Boyer Inch Papers, MG 30 C 187, vol. 8, file 370, CBC Program, "Of Things to Come."
85 Young Men's Christian Associations of Canada, National Council, *We Discuss Canada* (Toronto: Ryerson, 1942), 57.
86 CAAE, "Report of the Proceedings of a Special Programme Committee of the Canadian Association for Adult Education," Meeting at Macdonald College, 27–31 Dec. 1942, NA, CBC *Citizens' Forum*, MG 28 I 400, vol. 1, file 3, Report of the Special Programme Committee.
87 CAAE, "Proceedings of Special Programme Committee," 15, 28.
88 CAAE, "Proceedings of Special Programme Committee," 27. AO, CAAE Papers, Series B-I, box 3, *Citizens' Forum*, administrative, 1943–1960.

89 These were Father G.-H. Levesque, N.A.M. Mackenzie, and Arthur Surveyer. Other members of the committee were R.E.G. Davis of the Canadian Youth Commission, Mrs G.V. Ferguson, Charles Fraser of the *Halifax Chronicle*, Lomer Gouin, and Robert T. McKenzie of the University of British Columbia's Extension Department.

90 Wells's novel had predicted a world war arising over tension between Germany and Poland by about 1940. Morley Callaghan to Watson Thomson, 5 Feb. 1943; Inch to Hugh Morrison, 11 Feb. 1943; all at NA, CBC, RG 41, vol. 187, file 11–18–5, part 4, CBC broadcasts on *Citizens' Forum*: "Of Things to Come." Wells was active in writing on the theme of reconstruction early in the war, putting out: *The Commonsense of War and Peace* (London: Penguin, 1940); *The New World Order* (London: Secker and Warburg, 1941); *and Guide to the New World* (London: Gollancz, 1941).

91 Claris Silcox to Robert Inch, 23 March 1943, NA, CBC, RG 41, vol. 187, file 11–18–5, part 6, CBC broadcasts on *Citizens' Forum*: "Of Things to Come."

92 "List of Participants in 'Of Things to Come'" Spring Series 1943, NA, CBC *Citizens's Forum*, MG 28 I 400, vol. 1, file 9, "Of Things to Come," Feb. – June 1943.

93 *"Of Things to Come": Inquiry on the Post-war World* (Toronto: CBC, 1943).

94 Morley Callaghan to Watson Thomson, 5 Feb. 1943; Callaghan to Robert T. McKenzie, 12 Feb. 1943, NA, CBC, RG 41, vol. 187, file 11–18–5, part 5.

95 Robert T. McKenzie to Inch, 22 Feb. 1943, NA, CBC, RG 41, vol. 187, file 11–18–5, part 5, CBC broadcasts on *Citizens' Forum*, "Of Things to Come."

96 Responses to Spring Series, "OTT," 1943, NA, CBC, RG 41, vol. 186, file 11–18–5, part 1, CBC broadcasts on *Citizens' Forum*, "Of Things to Come." Kathleen Strange, "Report No. 2," 8 March 1943, NA, Canadian Authors Association Papers, MG 28 I 2, vol. 1, Manitoba.

97 E.A. Corbett to John Grierson, 22 April 1943, NA, WIB, RG 36/31, vol. 14, file 8–20–1, CAAE.

98 H. McDonald, Crossfield, Alberta, to CBC, NA, CBC, RG 41, vol. 186, file 11–18–5, part 1, CBC broadcasts on *Citizens' Forum*: "Of Things to Come."

99 R.B. Inch to Members of the CBC Post-War Committee, 14 July 1943, NA, Canada Foundation, MG 28, I179, vol. 25, file 4a, CBC, 1942–1951.

100 R.B. Inch to E.A. Corbett, 28 July 1943, NA, Robert Boyer Inch Papers, MG30 C 187, vol. 8, file 370, 1, CBC Program, "Of Things to Come." *The Chicago Round Table* and *Town Meeting of the Air* were American radio programs geared towards the discussion of public affairs but did not feature the localized listening groups planned for *Citizens' Forum*. Harry A. and Bonaro W. Overstreet, *Town Meeting Comes to Town* (New York: Harper Brothers, 1938), 57–60.

101 E.A Corbett, "Director's Report," delivered at the CAAE Annual Meeting, 19–22 Aug. 1943, NA, H.R.C. Avison Papers, MG 30 D 102, vol. 5, file 25, C.A.A.E. London Conference, 1943.
102 James S. Thomson, "The New Phase of Adult Education," address delivered at the Macdonald College Conference, 10 Sept. 1943, 12, NA, CBC *Citizens' Forum*, MG 28 I 400, vol. 1, file 8, Macdonald College Conference, Proceedings, Commentary.
103 Thomson, "The New Phase of Adult Education," 14–19.
104 Gregory Vlastos to N.A.M. MacKenzie, 25 Sept. 1943, UBCSC, N.A.M. MacKenzie Papers, box 210, folder 4.
105 Callaghan's instructions to Robert McKenzie seem to confirm the contemporary suspicions that the program exhibited a noticeable CCF slant. For a detailed description of the Liberal government's objections to the program's early format and to some of its panellists, see Marjorie McEnaney, 'Trip to Ottawa in connection with "Of Things to Come"' n.d. [1943], NA, Marjorie McEnaney Papers, MG 30 E342, vol. 1, "Of Things to Come." See also Baillargeon, "The CBC and the Cold War Mentality," 28–32; Ron Faris, *The Passionate Educators*, 104–8; "The Job Ahead," *Canadian Business* 17, no. 1 (Jan. 1944): 17–18; "Radio News and C.C.F.," *Ottawa Citizen*, 28 Feb. 1944, 3.
106 Grant's involvement in the project is best covered in William Christian's *George Grant: A Biography* (Toronto: University of Toronto Press, 1993), 96–102.
107 Canadian Teachers' Federation, "Brief to the House of Commons Special Committee on Reconstruction and Re-establishment." Jan. 1944, NA, RG 14, 1987–88/146 (39) Reconstruction, W-2; Violet Anderson, "Citizens' Forums Breed Democracy in Canada," *Saturday Night* (20 May 1944): 16–17; Toronto's Public Library system issued a reading list to complement forum materials: "Books for Citizens' Forum, Part II," NA, CBC *Citizens' Forum*, MG 28 I 400, vol. 1, file 22, Reading List, 1943–44.
108 Ross, "A Reverent Ode to the Great Modern Goddess Panacea," *Saturday Night* (29 Jan. 1944), 29. Ross might also have adapted her line from the early-seventeenth-century Cornish "Hal-an-Tow." The song's chorus was a particularly optimistic one and told of the excitement building before May Day: "Hal-an-Tow, jolly rumbalo / We were up long before the day-o / To welcome in the summer time / To welcome in the May-o / Summer is a'comin in / And winter's gone away-o."
109 Rev. F.W.L. Brailey, "*Citizens' Forum* in the Churches," [1944], 2, AO, CAAE Papers, series B-I, box 3, *Citizens' Forum*, administrative, 1943–1960; "The Job Ahead," *Canadian Business* 17, no. 1 (Jan. 1944): 17.
110 R.H. Wright to *Citizens' Forum*, 1 April 1944, NA, CBC, RG 41, vol. 188, file 11–18–5, part 9, CBC broadcasts on *Citizens' Forum*, "Of Things to Come."

111 Anne Fromer, "Canada's Rural Movies Building Citizenship," *Saturday Night* (11 March 1944): 19a.
112 Names of forums gleaned from group reports and correspondence in NA, CBC *Citizens' Forum*, MG 28 I 400.
113 E.A Corbett to Col. G.G.D. Kilpatrick, 18 Jan. 1944, NA, CBC, RG 41, vol. 187, file 11-18-5, part 3, CBC broadcasts on *Citizens' Forum*, "Of Things to Come." Kilpatrick was director of education for the Department of National Defence (Army).
114 "He's Ready for the Job Ahead," *Citizens' Forum* pamphlet, 1944, NA, Neil M. Morrison Papers, MG 30 E 273, vol. 11, Brochures 1943–61.
115 Violet Anderson, "Citizens' Forums Breed Democracy in Canada," *Saturday Night* (20 May 1944), 16.
116 George Grant to Harry Avison, 18 Jan. 1944, 3, AO, CAAE Papers, series B-I, box 3, *Citizens' Forum*, administrative, 1943–1960.
117 CAAE, "Proceedings of a Special Programme Committee," 30. *Invitation to Learning* featured American intellectuals Huntington Cairns, Allen Tate, and Mark Van Doren, along with occasional guests, and was a series of debates that incorporated the elements of a Western civilization canon. For transcripts of these programs, see Huntington Cairns, Allen Tate, and Mark Van Doren, *Invitation to Learning* (New York: Random House, 1941).
118 Ernest Bushnell, Memorandum from the General Supervisor of Programmes to the Board of Governors, 8 May 1944. Cited in Faris, "Adult Education for Social Action or Enlightenment?" 293.
119 Jean Hunter Morrison and George Grant, "Who Shapes the Future?" *Citizens' Forum Bulletin* no. 19, 25 April 1944: 2.
120 Jean Hunter Morrison and George Grant, "Action Now," *Citizens' Forum Bulletin* no. 20, 2 May 1944: 4; "'Of Things to Come – A Citizens' Forum' Topics for Discussion – Season 1944–1945" (leaflet) (1944), 1–2.
121 [Martyn Estall], "The War Has Changed Things" [1945], 2, 5, AO, CAAE Papers, series B-I, box 3, *Citizens' Forum*, administrative, 1943–1960.
122 "Comments about "Of Things to Come" from former McGill student, now Lieutenant in the Artillery" (1944), NA, CBC *Citizens' Forum*, MG 28 I 400, vol. 1, file 10, Broadcasts, 1943–44.
123 W.H. Brittain, "The Role of the Canadian Association for Adult Education" (1944), 2–3, 8–9, NA, H.R.C. Avison Papers, MG 30 D 102, vol. 5, file 26, C.A.A.E. 1944.
124 "Comments about 'Of Things to Come' from former McGill student, now Lieutenant in the Artillery" (1944).
125 George Grant, "*Citizens' Forum* – So Far," *Food for Thought* 4, no. 3 (Nov. 1943): 20; "Report to the Executive of the C.A.A.E. on the Progress of Citizens' Forum" (1944), 2, AO, CAAE Papers, series B-I, box 3, *Citizens' Forum*, administrative, 1943–1960.

126 "Submission by the Canadian Council of Education for Citizenship." 16 Nov. 1945, NA, WIB, RG 36/31, vol. 14, file 8–20–3, Canadian Council of Education for Citizenship. Rev. F.W.L. Brailey estimated the number of organized listening groups at 1450 "among civilians" during the first season. "Citizens' Forum in the Churches" (1944), 1.
127 One report listed as members of a BC group a doctor, a principal, a minister, a priest, a postmaster, a rancher, merchants, clerks, and housewives. A group in Ituna, Saskatchewan, included three teachers, two druggists, a municipal secretary, an implement dealer, and two housewives. Anderson, "Citizens' Forums Breed Democracy in Canada," 16–17.
128 N.A.M. MacKenzie, "Canada and the Post War World," address before the Vancouver Canadian Club, 15 Sept. 1944, 3–4, UBCSC, N.A.M. MacKenzie Papers, box 97, folder 1.
129 E.A. Corbett "Director's Report" (1946), 7, NA, WIB, RG 36/31, vol. 14, file 8–20–1, CAAE.
130 Wayne and Shuster's RCA Victor Show, "Story of the CBC," CBC Trans-Canada Network, 24 Oct. 1946, NA, Frank Shuster Papers, MG 31 D 251, vol. 2.
131 J.R. Kidd, "Foreword," in Isabel Wilson, *Citizens' Forum: "Canada's National Platform"* (Toronto: Ontario Institute for Studies in Education, 1980); Faris, "Adult Education for Social Action or Enlightenment?" 336.
132 [Estall], "The War Has Changed Things," 4.
133 "Comments about 'Of Things to Come'" (1944).
134 R.T. McKenzie, "Report on Citizens' Forum 1946–47," NA, CBC *Citizen's Forum*, MG 28 I 400, vol. 1, file 58, National Secretary's Report, 1946–47. (McKenzie was quoting from the local reports that his office received.)
135 McKenzie, "Report on Citizens' Forum 1946–47."
136 E.L. Fortune to Guy Henson, 11 May 1949, AO, CAAE Papers, series B-I, box 1, *Citizen's Forum*, administrative, 1943–1960.
137 Lorne Pierce, *The Beloved Community* (Toronto: Ryerson Press, 1925), 20.
138 "You and Me and Reconstruction," *CBC Discussion Club*, broadcast 28 Aug. 1942, NA, CAVA/AVCA: 1984–0164, reference copy at: 1982–0043/63.
139 *Letter from Home! From a Soldier of 1914–19 to a Soldier of 1939–194?* (1943), University of Saskatchewan Archives (USASK), Pamphlet LX-23.
140 "A Town-Planning Expert," *Saturday Night* (12 July 1941): 1. This piece kicked off a series of articles by Faludi, who also wrote for *Canadian Forum*, *Food for Though*, and *Maclean's* between 1941 and 1950.
141 Dr. E.G. Faludi, "Housing Is Science," *Saturday Night* (15 Aug. 1942): 8.
142 James was responding to an article in which Wells disparaged British architects for mourning the loss of some of Britain's historic buildings. F. Cyril James, "Stained Glass," Address before the Royal Architectural Institute of Canada, 20 Feb. 1943, 5, McG, F. Cyril James Papers, MG 1017, Addresses and Other Papers, 1943.

143 S.K. Jaffary, "The Social Services," in C.A. Ashley, ed., *Reconstruction in Canada* (Toronto: University of Toronto Press, 1943), 111.
144 Richard E. Crouch, "A Community Art Centre in Action," *Canadian Art* 2, no. 1 (Oct.–Nov. 1944): 22.
145 George E. Buckley to Reconstruction Committee, 20 June 1944, NA, RG 14, 1987–88/146 (39) Reconstruction, W-4. Buckley was president of the Theatre Guild of Saint John.
146 Eric R. Arthur, "Town Planning and Tomorrow," *Food for Thought* 3, no. 8 (April 1943): 6–7; Campbell Merrett, "Planning with the People," *Canadian Art* 3, no. 9 (Oct.–Nov. 1945): 18–21.
147 Marcus Adeney, "Community Centres in Canada," *Journal of the Royal Architectural Institute of Canada* 22, no. 2 (Feb. 1945): 22. The power of an anti-modern perspective in a postmodern society is well discussed in Ian McKay's essay on the packaging of history in mid-twentieth-century Nova Scotia. See McKay, "History and the Tourist Gaze: The Politics of Commemoration in Nova Scotia, 1935–1964," *Acadiensis* 22, no. 2 (spring 1993): 102–38.
148 Richard E. Crouch, "A Community Art Centre in Action." *Canadian Art* 2, no. 1 (Oct.–Nov. 1944): 22–8; Paul Duval, "Arthur Lismer, Canadian Artist, Led World in Art Education," *Saturday Night* (13 Oct. 1945): 24–5.
149 NA, Records of the CBC, RG 41, vol. 893, file PG 7, Sports College of the Air, pt. 1, 1944–65.
150 Adeney, "Community Centres in Canada," 23.
151 See especially Jonathan Vance's *Death So Noble: Memory, Meaning and the First World War* (Vancouver: University of British Columbia Press, 1997), chap. 7. Vance notes (204–5) that the impulses to build purely "aesthetic" and to put up utilitarian monuments each had vocal support – a difference of opinion that could in some cases be overcome.
152 Adeney, "Community Centres in Canada," 23. See also Fred Lasserre and Gordon Lunan, "Community Centres," *Canadian Affairs* 2, no. 17 (1945): 3–5. A detailed bibliography of reconstruction-era material on community centres in Canada, the United States, and Britain is James Dahir, comp., *Community Centers as Living War Memorials: A Selected Bibliography with Interpretive Comments* (New York: Russell Sage Foundation, 1946). George Mosse has written on attempts to extract positive motivations from world war experiences in *Fallen Soldiers: Reshaping the Memory of the World Wars* (Oxford: Oxford University Press, 1990). On commemoration, see John E. Bodnar, *Remaking America: Public Memory, Commemoration, and Patriotism in the Twentieth Century* (Princeton, NJ: Princeton University Press, 1992); Michael Kammen, *Mystic Chords of Memory: The Transformation of American Culture* (New York: Knopf, 1991).
153 Librarian Elizabeth Loosley, among others, was still promoting the community centre after the Massey Commission began its hearings in 1949.

She recommended the films *After Six O'Clock* and *When All the People Play* to groups that were planning centres. Loosley, "Solving Community Problems," *Food for Thought* 10, no. 3 (Dec. 1949): 17–21.

154 Martyn Estall, "Proposals for Government Action" (1946), NA, H.R.C. Avison Papers, MG 30 D 102, vol. 5, file 28, C.A.A.E. 1946.

155 E.A. Corbett, "Proposals for Government Action to Assist Community Centres and Leisure-Time Programs in Canada," (1947), 7–8, NA, WIB, RG 36/31, vol. 14, file 8–20–1, CAAE. Lawren Harris et al., "Community Art Centres," *Canadian Art* 2, no. 2 (Dec. 1944–Jan. 1945): 62–3, 77, 85; Anthony Walsh, "Rehabilitation through Art and Handicrafts," *Canadian Art* 2, no. 3 (summer 1945): 3–5, 38; Murray G. Ross, "The Community Centre Movement," *Food for Thought* 6, no. 4 (Jan. 1946): 10–17; Canadian Youth Commission, *Youth and Recreation: New Plans for New Times* (Toronto: Ryerson, 1946); David Murray, "Planned Recreation in Canada," *Canadian Forum* 26, no. 306 (July 1946): 84–5; [H.R.C. Avison], "Memorandum re: Proposed Action by National Organizations in Recreation, Adult Education and the Arts towards a Federal Government Program on Community Centres and Community Leisure-Time Programs" (1946), NA, H.R.C. Avison Papers, MG 30 D 102, vol. 6, file 30, C.A.A.E. 1946; Lionel Scott, "A Community Centre Plan That Works," *Food for Thought* 7, no. 7 (April 1947): 9–13.

156 Corbett, "Proposals for Government Action to Assist Community Centres and Leisure-Time Programs in Canada" (1947), 1–2, 7–8. On recapturing the spirit of fraternity that the Canadian soldier "knew overseas," see the issue on "Community Centres," *Canadian Affairs* 2, no. 17 (1945): 2.

157 Adeney, "Community Centres in Canada," 21.

158 Paul Litt and Maria Tippett both cite the 1944 brief as a prominent wartime declaration of cultural activism. Litt, *The Muses, the Masses, and The Massey Commission* (Toronto: University of Toronto Press, 1992), 23–4; Tippett, *Making Culture: English-Canadian Institutions and the Arts before the Massey Commission* (Toronto: University of Toronto Press, 1990), 171–2. On the artists' brief and on community centres as a source of inspiration for artists and cultural policy makers two generations later, see Dot Tuer, "The Art of Nation Building: Constructing a 'Cultural Identity' for Post-War Canada,'" *Parallelogramme* 17, no. 4 (spring 1992): 24–37.

159 Morley Callaghan, "If Civilization Must Be Saved," *Saturday Night* (16 Dec. 1939): 6.

160 Elizabeth Wyn Wood, "A National Program for the Arts in Canada," *Canadian Art* 1, no. 3 (Feb.–March 1944): 93–4.

161 The draft document was entitled "Suggestions for Increased Government Support of the Arts in Canada" (1944), NA, Canada Foundation, MG 28 I179, vol. 20, file 3b, Arts and Letters Club, Toronto, 1944–1966.

162 [Associated Arts Groups], "Brief Concerning the Cultural Aspects of Canadian Reconstruction," 3, NA, RG 14, 1987–88/146 (39) Reconstruction, W-2; "Canadians Ask Cultural Freedom," *Canadian Author and Bookman* 20, no. 4 (Dec. 1944): 10. Reprinted from *Free World* (1944, issue unknown).

163 [Associated Arts Groups], "Brief Concerning the Cultural Aspects of Canadian Reconstruction," 3.

164 [AAG], "Cultural Aspects of Canadian Reconstruction," 4–5.

165 Walter B. Herbert, "An Acorn of Culture Is Planted on the Hill," *Ottawa Journal*, 29 June 1944, 4.

166 According to Herbert, a Michael Huxley made £10,000 available in 1942 for what became the Canadian Committee, and he noted that "there has been a great deal of discussion and talk among people of a certain type in Canada during the past ten years – all related to a visionary proposal that we should have in our country some organization modelled more or less after the British Council and performing functions more or less similar to those of the British Council. But nothing has ever been done about it." Herbert to Thomas A. Stone, 21 Oct. 1942 NA, Walter B. Herbert Papers, MG 30 D 205, vol. 1, Correspondence, 1942/44.

167 W.B. Herbert to R.B. Inch, 25 March 1943 NA, Canada Foundation, MG 28 I179, vol. 25, file 4c, CBC, 1942–1951. Paul Litt reports that Herbert had been a Liberal Party organizer. Litt, *The Muses, the Masses, and the Massey Commission*, 282, n 18.

168 Walter B. Herbert, "A Ministry of Fine Arts: A Contrary View" (1944), 4, NAC, Walter B. Herbert Papers, MG 30 D 205, vol. 1, Addresses, Articles and Lectures.

169 Stephen Tallents, "The Projection of England." During 1944, Herbert sent a copy of this to A.D. Dunton, then general manager of the WIB, later to head the CBC. NA, WIB, RG 36/31, vol. 10, file 4–3, Canadian Committee.

170 Walter B. Herbert to Paul Martin, 20 May 1944, NA, Canada Foundation, MG 28 I179, vol. 20, file 3b, Arts and Letters Club, Toronto, 1944–1966.

171 Herbert to Mrs John Bracken, 17 April 1946, NA, Canada Foundation, MG 28 I179, vol. 25, file 4b, CBC, 1942–1951.

172 "Project. Publication of a *Canadian Cultural Index*," NA, Canada Foundation, MG 28 I179, vol. 33, file 3, Cultural Index, 1947–1948. *Canadian Cultural Publications* ran to thirteen editions, ceasing publication in 1965.

173 John B. Collins, "'Design in Industry' Exhibition, National Gallery of Canada, 1946: Turning Bombers into Lounge Chairs," *Material History Bulletin* 27 (spring 1988).

174 F.M. Salter, "On the Other Hand," *New Trail* 4, no. 2 (April 1946): 79.

175 For details and statistics on postwar growth, see Kenneth Norrie and Doug Owram, *A History of the Canadian Economy*, 2nd ed. (Toronto: Harcourt Brace, 1996), 408–9 ff.

176 On the difficulty of manipulating tastes via radio, see Kate Whitehead, *The Third Programme: A Literary History* (Oxford: Clarendon, 1989).

CHAPTER THREE

1 Mary Lowrey Ross, "At Least We'll Still Have with Us the Men Who Dream-Up Tomorrow," *Saturday Night* (26 Jan. 1946): 9.
2 Charlotte Whitton, "What Splendour Men Have the Power to Shape," address to the Illinois Welfare Association Convention, Peoria, Ill., 3 Dec. 1945, 6, NA, Charlotte Elizabeth Whitton Papers, vol. 83, Manuscripts.
3 John Grierson, "Education in a Technological Society," address to the National Conference on Adult Education, Winnipeg, 28 May 1945, McG, John Grierson Collection, MG 2067, container 4, file 110; "Genie Out of the Bottle," *Saturday Night* (11 Aug. 1945): 1; "We'd Better Keep Our Scientists," *Maclean's* (1 Oct. 1945): 1; John J. O'Neill, "Freedom in Scientific Research Not Likely for Long Time Yet," *Saturday Night* (20 Oct. 1945): 11.
4 D.R.G. Owen, *Scientism, Man and Religion* (Philadelphia: Westminster, 1952), 13.
5 William H. Whyte, Jr, *The Organization Man* (New York: Simon and Schuster, 1956), 23.
6 University of Montreal Institute of Medieval Studies, "Memorandum to the Royal Commission on National Development in the Arts, Letters and Sciences," Nov. 1949, 4, NA, Royal Commission on National Development in the Arts, Letters and Sciences (RCALS), RG 33/28, vol. 20.
7 C.J. Eustace, "The Role of Religion in Canadian Life, Being an Attempt to Essay the Place of the Church in Our New Changing Society," *Culture* 6 (1945): 147–8.
8 N.A.M. MacKenzie, "V-J Day," radio broadcast, 12 Aug. 1945, 1, UBCSC, N.A.M. MacKenzie Papers, box 103, folder 11.
9 *Citizens' Forum*, "Who Should Go to University?" 3 March 1948, CBC Radio Archives, Toronto, tc on 820219–9(1); Lister Sinclair, "Mankind in the Age of Science," *Maclean's* (1 Jan. 1950): 5–7, 47–8; Doug Owram, *Born at the Right Time: A History of the Baby Boom Generation* (Toronto: University of Toronto Press, 1996). See also T.J. Jackson Lears, "A Matter of Taste," in Lary May, ed., *Recasting America: Culture and Politics in the Age of the Cold War* (Chicago: University of Chicago Press, 1989), 38–57; Owram, *The Government Generation: Canadian Intellectuals and the State, 1910–1945* (Toronto: University of Toronto Press, 1986)
10 "T.M.F" to CBC Talks Department, compiled letters re: "Living in an Atomic Age" (1951), NA, Neil M. Morrison Papers, MG 30 E 273, vol. 6, CBC, Censorship Attempts by Pressure Groups.

11 On "big science" and its cultural impact, see Jon Agar, *Science and Spectacle: The Work of Jodrell Bank in Post-war British Culture* (Amsterdam: Harwood, 1998) Charles E. Rosenberg has revised and expanded his 1976 work *No Other Gods: On Science and American Social Thought* (Baltimore: Johns Hopkins University Press, 1997); Christopher P. Toumey, *Conjuring Science: Scientific Symbols and Cultural Meanings in American Life* (New Brunswick, NJ: Rutgers University Press, 1996); and Peter Galison and Bruce Hevly, eds., *Big Science: The Growth of Large-scale Research* (Stanford, Calif.: Stanford University Press, 1992). On the contingency of the power relationships surrounding research, see Chandra Mukerji, *A Fragile Power: Scientists and the State* (Princeton, NJ: Princeton University Press, 1989).

12 C.D. Howe, "Opportunities for the Young Engineer," address to the graduates of the University of British Columbia, 11 May 1950, NA, Clarence Decatur Howe Papers, MG 27 III B20, vol. 141, series 89, Articles, Speeches, Books, 4. In June 1946, *Toronto Star* cartoonist Les Callan depicted Howe as a waiter serving diners their "atomic age." "Chee! And We Only Ordered Apple Pie!" original at NA, 1990–608–420.

13 I have borrowed this term from James Gilbert. He used it to denote supporters of a religious perspective in his work on two distinctly different contexts: *A Cycle of Outrage: America's Reaction to the Juvenile Delinquent in the 1950s* (New York: Oxford University Press, 1986) and *Redeeming Culture: American Religion in Age of Science* (Chicago: University of Chicago Press, 1997).

14 B.K. Sandwell, "The Science–Faith Borders," *Saturday Night* (28 June 1952): 4.

15 On Canada's late-nineteenth and early-twentieth-century struggles over this question, see David Marshall, *Secularizing the Faith: Canadian Protestant Clergy and the Crisis of Belief, 1850–1940* (Toronto: University of Toronto Press, 1992); Michael Gauvreau, *The Evangelical Century: College and Creed in English Canada from the Great Revival to the Great Depression* (Montreal: McGill-Queen's University Press, 1991); and Ramsay Cook, *The Regenerators: Social Criticism in Late-Victorian English Canada* (Toronto: University of Toronto Press, 1985). Julie A. Reuben's *The Making of the Modern University: Intellectual Transformation and the Marginalization of Morality* (Chicago: University of Chicago Press, 1996) deals with nineteenth-century U.S. developments. For a longer view of the controversy, see John Hedley Brooke, *Science and Religion: Some Historical Perspectives* (Cambridge: Cambridge University Press, 1991).

16 Carl Berger, *Science, God, and Nature in Victorian Canada* (Toronto: University of Toronto Press, 1983); Patricia Jasen, "Romanticism, Modernity, and the Evolution of Tourism on the Niagara Frontier, 1790–1850," *Canadian Historical Review* 72, no. 3 (Sept. 1991): 283–318; Keith Walden, *Be-*

coming Modern in Toronto: The Industrial Exhibition and the Shaping of a Late Victorian Culture (Toronto: University of Toronto Press, 1997). For a compelling introduction to the cultural implications of modernity in the Canadian context, see McKay, "Introduction: All That Is Solid Melts into Air," in McKay, ed., *The Challenge of Modernity: A Reader on Post-Confederation History* (Toronto: McGraw-Hill Ryerson, 1992); ix–xxvi.

17 B.S. Keirstead, "The Boundaries," (1938), University of New Brunswick Archives, Burton Seely Keirstead Papers, UA, RG, 81, 3.1.1, 129.

18 Mary Lowrey Ross, "The Human Equation," *Saturday Night* (13 May 1939): 24.

19 "Design for Canadian Wings," or "Elsie MacGill," n.d. (1941), McM, CBC Scripts Collection, reel 21.

20 A product of the later 1920s, the National Research Council began to pay dividends early in the war. Charles Clay, "Our Headache Headquarters," *Saturday Night* (7 Dec. 1940): 22–3. Blair Fraser, "Hush-Hush Science War," *Maclean's* (15 Jan. 1945): 41–3.

21 George R. Ehrhardt, "Descendants of Prometheus: Popular Science Writing in the United States, 1915–1948," PhD dissertation, Duke University, 1993, iii. Carter was a geologist who wrote science columns for the *Winnipeg Free Press*. He was also a communist and wrote throughout his career for communist periodicals, mostly about Soviet scientific research. When that sort of material began creeping into his national columns, especially following the Soviet Union's alignment with the Allied powers during the Second World War, he found it more difficult to get work. For the perspective of one who oversaw *Scientific American*'s postwar rise to prominence presenting new discoveries to educated lay readers, see Gerard Piel, *What Scientists Learned in the 20th Century* (New York: Basic Books, 2001).

22 Most often relegated to the middle and back pages, these freelance science articles served as commentary on activity behind the lines of battle and did not displace "real" war news from the front pages. Typical items in Maclean's were Creighton Peet, "Your House of Tomorrow" (15 Sept. 1943): 12–13, 43–5; Leonard L. Knott, "Chemistry Fights" (15 May 1942): 24–5, 46–7, 49–51; and Wallace Rayburn, "Medicine Goes to War" (1 Sept. 1943): 18–19, 32, 34–5, 37.

23 Lawrence N. Galton compiled the "Tuning Up for Tomorrow" series beginning in the July 1945 issue of *National Home Monthly*. It is probably best put in John Burnham's category of "Gee Whiz!" science – a pursuit not particularly designed to "disturb one's mysticisms." John C. Burnham, *How Superstition Won and Science Lost: Popularizing Science and Health in the United States* (New Brunswick, NJ: Rutgers University Press, 1987), 5–6.

24 E.L. Harrington, "Physics and Society," *Culture* 5 (1944): 285.

25 Clarie Gillis, M.P. "Letter From Home! From a Soldier of 1914–19 to a Soldier of 1939–194?" (1943), 18 (published by *Canadian Forum*). An early

wartime expression of the notion that ideals must keep pace with material progress appears in: F. Cyril James, "Science and Society," address to the Royal Society of Canada, London, Ont., 21 May 1940, McG, F. Cyril James Papers, MG 1017, Addresses and Other Papers, 1940. C.E. Silcox, "The Consecration of Power and Intelligence," Commencement Address, Andover-Newton Theological School, 19 Sept. 1945, UCA, Claris Edwin Silcox Papers, box 11, file 6, Correspondence, 1946–1949.

26 Watson Kirkconnell, Seven Pillars of Freedom, (1943), AUA, Watson Kirkconnell Papers, P1/12.2; 1. The author's vague reference to religious decay in 1943 became the following indictment by 1948: "Modern science, a sorcerer's apprentice who has summoned up evil powers that he cannot control, exposes our cities to the threat of annihilation by gas, bacteria, and atomic bomb." "The Dykes of Civilization," inaugural address as president of Acadia University, 22 Oct. 1948, 3, AUA, Watson Kirkconnell Papers, P1/18/1.

27 L.A. MacKay, "Functions of a High School," *Saturday Night* (2 Aug. 1941): 15; "Personnel Selection," *Saturday Night* (23 Jan. 1943): 1, 3; William H. Hatcher, "The Future of Chemistry," *Culture* 5 (1944): 258–64. R.C. Wallace, "The Function of Science in the Field of Education," *Culture* 5 (1944): 3–5.

28 B.K. Sandwell, "Religion and Education," *Saturday Night* (16 Aug. 1941): 7.

29 B.K. Sandwell, "Day of Prayer," *Saturday Night* (5 Sept. 1942): 2–3.

30 Silcox, "The Consecration of Power and Intelligence."

31 Harold A. Albert, "Knocking the World About," *National Home Monthly* 46, no. 1 (Jan. 1945): 16.

32 Walter A. McDougall, *The Heavens and the Earth: A Political History of the Space Age* (New York: Basic Books, 1985), 6.

33 C.J. Eustace, "The Role of Religion in Canadian Life, Being an Attempt to Essay the Place of the Church in Our New Changing Society," *Culture* 6 (1945): 151.

34 N.A.M. MacKenzie, "V-J Day," broadcast, 12 Aug. 1945. Lister Sinclair, "You Can't Stop Now," broadcast 11 Nov. 1945, NA, Lister Shedden Sinclair Papers, MG 31 D44, vol. 2, Radio Scripts. A sea change was apparent in popular periodicals as well. See Max Werner, "We Can't Risk War Now," *Maclean's* (1 Oct. 1945): 7, 59–60. John Grierson, "The Political, Economic, and Educational Implications of the Atomic Bomb," address delivered to the International Conference of the Junior League, Quebec, 14 May 1946, McG, John Grierson Collection, MG 2067, container 4, file 108. J.R. Stirrett, "Atomic Admonition," *Canadian Forum* 27, no. 325 (Feb. 1948): 252–3. The sustained influence of atomic weapons on American culture is examined in Margot A. Henriksen, *Dr. Strangelove's America: Society and Culture in the Atomic Age* (Berkeley: University of California Press, 1997), of which part 3, "Is God Dead?" deals more specifically with religion. For a look at the bomb as a "psychic event," see Paul Boyer, *By the*

Bomb's Early Light: American Thought and Culture at the Dawn of the Atomic Age (New York: Pantheon, 1985) and his more recent look at nuclear culture, *Fallout: A Historian Reflects on America's Half-Century Encounter with Nuclear Weapons* (Columbus: Ohio State University Press, 1998). On public and journalistic interest in atomic science at war's end, see Peter B. Hales, "The Atomic Sublime," *American Studies* 32, no. 1 (1991): 5–31; Alice Kimball Smith, *A Peril and a Hope: The Scientists' Movement in America, 1945–1947* (Chicago: University of Chicago Press, 1965).

35 Miriam Chapin, "Psychoanalysis Brings Clearer Understanding of the Child," *Saturday Night* (5 May 1945): 38. The radio series "What's on Your Mind?" featured dramas based on actual case histories from the files of the Canadian National Committee for Mental Hygiene. It debuted with such program titles as "The Crying Wren," broadcast 4, March 1946, and "The Exasperating Electrician," broadcast 11 March 1946; NA, Lister Shedden Sinclair Papers, MG 31 D44, vol. 2, Radio Scripts; Gerald Zoffer, "Psychological Factors In Juvenile Crime," *Saturday Night* (26 Jan. 1946): 18; *Citizens' Forum*, "Psychology Versus the Hairbrush" (1947), NA, Neil M. Morrison Papers, MG 30 E 273, vol. 11, Brochures 1943–61; Northrop Frye, "Dr. Kinsey and the Dream Censor," *Canadian Forum* 28, no. 330 (July 1948): 85–6; W.E. Blatz, "Psychology's No Parlour Game," *Saturday Night* (12 April 1952): 11, 19; John Porter, "Two Cheers for Mental Health," *Canadian Forum* 34, no. 405 (Oct. 1954): 145, 152–3.

36 A.R.M. Lower, "Canada, the Second Great War, and the Future," *International Journal* 1, no. 2 (April 1946): 97–111.

37 C.J. Eustace, "The Future of Religion in the Secular or Neutral Society," *Culture* 7 (1946): 422–3. A similar transition had taken place in the United States, as President Kirtley Mather of the American Association for the Advancement of Science noted in 1951: "Science discloses the imperative need; something that transcends science must assist man to respond to the challenge of our time." Gilbert, *Redeeming Culture*, 38.

38 C.E. Silcox, "Which Way, Canada?" speech to Bathurst Sunday Evening Forum, 20 Jan., 1946, 5, UCA, Claris Edwin Silcox Papers, box 6, file 52.

39 Howard W. Blakeslee, "Atomic World," *Maclean's* (1 Jan. 1947): 18.

40 J.E. Middleton, "Can Science Ever Find the Core of Truth?" *Saturday Night* (18 Jan. 1947): 9. John H. Yocom, "Mankind's Ceaseless Pondering on What Life Is All About," *Saturday Night* (21 Aug. 1948): 19.

41 A.R.M. Lower, "Is the Church Doomed?", [1949–50], QUA, A.R.M. Lower Papers, box 18, B 430.33.6., 15. One observer believed that a link with the infinite was all that the church – especially Protestant churches that held no confession – had to offer. J. Donald L. Howson, "Psychiatry Assumes a Role of the Church," *Saturday Night* (24 Aug. 1946): 14.

42 Marjorie Stella Keirstead, "Skeleton for longer philosophical poem," unpublished, n.d. [1946], 2, UNB, Burton Seely Keirstead Papers, UA RG 81, 3.4.1q.

43 C.R. Tracy, "Education in the Atomic Age," *New Trail* 4, no. 2 (April 1946): 64.
44 "The Mid-Century Appraisal of Man" conference took place in Boston early in 1949 and featured such noted speakers as Winston Churchill and one of Eustace's Catholic heroes, Jacques Maritain.
45 C.J. Eustace, "Science, Materialism, and the Human Spirit: The Religious Implications of Scientific Progress," *Culture* 10 (1949): 120, 124; see also his *An Infinity of Questions: A Study of the Religion of Art, and of the Art of Religion in the Lives of Five Women* (New York: Longmans, 1946) 12–18.
46 Eustace, "Science, Materialism, and the Human Spirit," 125–8.
47 Kirkconnell, "The Dykes of Civilization," 7.
48 Kirkconnell, "Faith and Education," address given on the CBC "Religious Hour" program, 23 Sept. 1951, reprinted in *Maritime Baptist* (3 Oct. 1951): 1. Kirkconnell subscribed to the views of Sir Richard Livingstone, whose *Education for a World Adrift* (1943) spoke of an "age without standards" in need of a "science of good and evil."
49 Kirkconnell emphasized the central place of the spirit for people making their way in the modern world: "Do we accept the fact of God as a supreme reality in human experience? Then at once all values in our philosophy undergo a kaleidoscopic change. Man is no longer a meaningless atom in a universal anarchy. His spiritual destiny becomes a major issue." Kirkconnell, "Faith and Education," 1–4.
50 Julia Grace Wales, "Formula and Faith," *United Church Observer* 13, no. 3 (1 Sept. 1951): 7.
51 On Velikovsky, see chapter 8 of James Gilbert, *Redeeming Culture*.
52 Donald Innis to Harold A. Innis, 27 Jan. 1950, 2, UTA, H.A. Innis Papers, B72-0003, box 5, file 14, Correspondence, 1950.
53 Russell Johnston, "The Early Trials of Protestant Radio," *Canadian Historical Review* 75, no. 3 (Sept. 1994): 376–402. Most of the early broadcasts originated from small evangelical denominations.
54 Parliament of Canada, "Regulations for Broadcasting Stations made under the Canadian Broadcasting Act, 1936 (as revised and amended to 24 March 1941);" CBC Regulations for Broadcasting Stations, revised 1948 edition.
55 These series were broadcast on the following dates and under the following titles: 2 May – 20 June 1951: Fred Hoyle, *The Nature of the Universe*; 5 – 26 Sept. 1951: Brock Chisholm et al., *Man's Last Enemy – Himself*; 28 Sept. – 2 Nov. 1951 – Bertrand Russell, *Living in an Atomic Age*.
56 The BBC, during its early years under Sir John Reith, exercised a similar discipline over agnostic speakers, who were often "well sandwiched into a symposium of 'believers.'" Richard S. Lambert, *Ariel and All His Quality: An Impression of the BBC from Within* (London: Victor Gollancz, 1940), 34–5.
57 Dr Fred Hoyle, "A Personal View," eighth in the series *The Nature of the Universe*, broadcast on the CBC, 20 June 1951, 2–6, Neil M. Morrison Papers, NA, MG 30 E 273, vol. 28, Scripts Reviewed by Parliamentary Committee.

58 "H.K." (Regina, Sask.) to CBC, 1951, compiled letters re: "The Nature of the Universe," NA, Neil M. Morrison Papers, MG 30 E 273, vol. 6, CBC, Censorship Attempts by Pressure Groups.
59 "Report from Ottawa," *Winnipeg Free Press*, 20 June 1951.
60 CBC Talks and Public Affairs, Report on "The Nature of the Universe" (1951), NA, Neil M. Morrison Papers, MG 30 E 273, vol. 6, CBC, Censorship Attempts by Pressure Groups.
61 Dr Ralph Williamson, "Reply to Hoyle," broadcast 27 June 1951, Neil M. Morrison Papers, NA, MG 30 E 273, vol. 28, Scripts Reviewed by Parliamentary Committee, 1–3.
62 Rev. J.M. Kelly, "Reply to Hoyle," broadcast 27 June 1951, Morrison Papers, Scripts Reviewed by Parliamentary Committee, 4–6.
63 N. Alice Frick, *Image in the Mind: CBC Radio Drama 1944 to 1954* (Toronto: Canadian Stage and Arts Publications, 1987), 26. "W.H." (Weston, Ont.) to CBC, 1951, compiled letters re: "The Nature of the Universe," NA, Neil M. Morrison Papers, MG 30 E 273, vol. 6, CBC, Censorship Attempts by Pressure Groups.
64 B.K. Sandwell, "Certain Uncertainties in the Speech of Dr. Chisholm," *Saturday Night* (1 Dec. 1945): 10–11; B.K. Sandwell, "In Chisholm vs. Santa Claus We Are for the Prosecution," *Saturday Night* (22 Dec. 1945): 10; J.E. Middleton, "Wrong Tools," *Saturday Night* (9 Feb. 1946): 3; "See Here Dr. Chisholm!" *Maclean's* (1 March 1946): 62–4.
65 G. Brock Chisholm, MD, "Tell Them the Truth," *Maclean's* (15 Jan. 1946): 9, 42–4. See also E.T. Mitchell, PhD, "You Need a Conscience," *Maclean's* (15 April 1946): 20, 30–2; Major General G.B. Chisholm, "The Reestablishment of Peacetime Society," *Psychiatry* 9, no. 1 (Feb. 1946): 3–20.
66 Brock Chisholm, "The Origins of Hostility," in Chisholm et al., *Man's Last Enemy – Himself!* (Toronto: Canadian Broadcasting Corporation, 1951).
67 "CBC Books Anti-Religious Speakers," *Ensign*, 8 Sept. 1951, 3.
68 Ewen Cameron, "The Nature of Hostility," in G. Brock Chisholm et al., *Man's Last Enemy – Himself!* (Toronto: CBC, 1951): 37. "Complex of the CBC, *Ensign*, 6 oct. 1951. *Relations* piece cited in Miriam Chapin, "Freedom of the Air – For Whom?" unpublished, 1951, 3, NA, Neil M. Morrison Papers, MG 30 E 273, vol. 6, CBC, Censorship Attempts by Pressure Groups. Another account of Cameron's upbraiding appeared in "Church and Psychiatrist," *Saturday Night* (8 May 1951): 5.
69 "The Good in Dr. Chisholm – If" *Prairie Messenger*, 13 Sept. 1951.
70 "Where Science Stops," *Prairie Messenger*, 27 Sept. 1951.
71 In his 1952 book, D.R.G. Owen was careful to differentiate between the "psyche," which was the subject of psychological study, and the "spirit", which was the domain of religion. *Scientism, Man and Religion* (Philadelphia: Westminster, 1952), 14.
72 Marjory Whitelaw to F.P. Whitman, MP, 6 Dec. 1951, 3, NA, Neil M. Morrison Papers, MG 30 E 273, vol. 26, Mass Communications and Freedom, 1950–52.

73 Bertrand Russell, "Perplexities of This Atomic Age," broadcast 28 Sept. 1951, 3; "The Modern Mastery of Nature," broadcast 12 Oct. 1951, 3, Neil M. Morrison Papers, NA, MG 30 E 273, vol. 28, Scripts Reviewed by Parliamentary Committee.

74 "The Achievement of Harmony," broadcast 2 Nov. 1951, 1–3.

75 The United Church of Canada supported the choice of top-flight experts for the psychiatric talks and approved of Bertrand Russell as a suitably well-known figure but urged all the same that air time be allotted for immediate rebuttal. "Propaganda or Discussion," *United Church Observer* 13, no. 15, 1 Oct. 1951, 4. "The CBC under Fire," *United Church Observer* 13, no. 19, 1 Dec. 1951, 4.

76 "Postscript" to Russell's "Living in an Atomic Age" series, broadcast 16 Nov. 1951, CBC Archives, Toronto, tape copy at 820413-9(4).

77 Marc Raboy, *Missed Opportunities: The Story of Canada's Broadcasting Policy* (Montreal: McGill-Queen's University Press, 1990), 109. The Parliamentary Committee on Broadcasting was often active, but it was not a standing committee.

78 Editorial, "Radio and Christianity," *Saturday Night* (10 July 1951): 5–6.

79 Barry MacDonald to Morrison, 11 Oct. 1951, 1, NA, Neil M. Morrison Papers, MG 30 E 273, vol. 6, CBC, Censorship Attempts by Pressure Groups.

80 Morning devotions and other local programs augmented this total. Counting regional and local broadcasts, the CBC carried some, 1220 hours of religious programming during the year ending April 1951. Marjorie McEnaney to Morrison, internal CBC memo, "Recent protests by religious bodies," 23 Oct. 1951, NA, Neil M. Morrison Papers, MG 30 E 273, vol. 6, CBC, Censorship Attempts by Pressure Groups.

81 MacDonald to Morrison, 11 Oct. 1951, 1.

82 Robert W. Keyserlingk, "No Whitewash, Please," *Ensign* (1 Dec. 1951): 1.

83 D.W. Cameron, "Radio Censorship," letter to the editor, *Toronto Star*, 3 Dec. 1951.

84 Chapin, "Freedom of the Air – For Whom?" unpublished, 5.

85 B.K. Sandwell, "Freedom of Speech by Radio," *Saturday Night* (17 Nov. 1951): 5. Sandwell returned to the topic of freedom of speech in the new year, arguing that the small number of radio stations available meant that not everyone had the right to be heard over it. "The Pitches Are Limited," *Saturday Night* (19 Jan. 1952): 4–5.

86 "Religious Censorship and the CBC," *Maclean's* (1 Jan. 1952): 2.

87 D.R.G. Owen, "Science, Scientism and Religion," in *Christianity in an Age of Science* (Toronto: Canadian Broadcasting Corporation, 1952), 5–6.

88 Owen, "Science, Scientism and Religion," 7–8.

89 Owen did not claim to be the first to connect faith in science with communism and was aware of works of fiction making the same connection: "The shape of possible things to come has already been described for us in

George Orwell's *Nineteen Eighty-four* and Virgil Gheorghiu's *The Twenty-fifth Hour.*" Owen, "Science, Scientism and Religion," 9–10.
90 Owen, "Science, Scientism and Religion," 11.
91 Dr. M.M. Coady, "Through the Visible to the Invisible," address to the Rural and Industrial Conference and Convocation celebrating the 25th anniversary of the founding of the Extension Department, St Francis XavierUniversity, 7 July 1953, 1, AO, CAAE Papers, series A-1, box 1, Director's Files, 1935–1943.
92 R.C. Wallace, "Science and Faith," The Haley Lectures, Acadia University, 23–24 Feb. 1953, 5–7, Queen's University Archives, Robert Charles Wallace Papers, coll. 1024, of lectures, box 10, subject files.
93 He continued: "Have the scientists themselves been satisfied with the mechanistic interpretation of the universe? There have been signs in recent years that they are not, and that the newer outlook in science does not bear out the rigid determinism that was prevalent in the last generation. The doubts have come from the investigations into the inner motions of the constituent parts of the atom." Wallace, "Science and Faith," 7–8.
94 "[T]he physicist is prepared to admit today that he has not yet found a complete statement of the laws by which nature operates, more particularly in the sub-atomic realm. Altogether apart from this element of uncertainty, he realizes that there are aspects of life which science has not the tools to deal with; or to be less dogmatic, science has not yet found the tools to deal with them." Wallace, "Science and Faith," 9–10.
95 Wallace, "Science and Faith," 10–11.
96 Wallace, "Science and Faith," 13.
97 Education, religion, and philosophy were all considered contributors to the tradition of looking beyond material life. "Milestone," *Food for Thought* 15, no. 1 (Sept.–Oct. 1954): 1.
98 Wallace, "Science and Faith," 15.
99 Wallace clearly subscribed to the idea that the narrative of human history was more than the story of a species muddling through chaos: "It was asked of old: 'What is man that thou art mindful of him?' Weak though he is, and prone to err, he has got a story behind him that shows that a divine power has indeed been mindful all the way." Wallace, "Science and Faith," 15, 18–21, 27.
100 Lister Sinclair, "Survival: A Study in Technology," [1952], 19, NA, Lister Shedden Sinclair Papers, MG 31 D44, vol. 10, Radio Scripts.
101 N.J. Berrill, "Is There Vital Conflict in Science, Religion?" *Saturday Night* (30 April 1955): 8.
102 Emil L. Fackenheim, "The Current 'Religious Revival': Is It Genuine?" *Canadian Forum* 35, no. 422 (March 1956): 269–70; "Moderation in Suburbia," *Saturday Night* (3 March 1956): 3–4; Alfred Harris, "Religious Revival: Faith or Fear?" *Saturday Night* (10 May 1958): 10–11, 51.

Earlier reports of a revival cited changing community structures and indifference, not rejection, as contributing factors in the revival or abandonment of religion. A.C. Forrest, "Religious Revival in Canadian Suburbia," *Saturday Night* (13 Dec. 1952): 11, 20.; Fred Bodsworth, "Christianity – Revival or Decline?" *Maclean's* (15 Dec. 1953): 9–12. 57, 59–61, 63–5.

103 Berrill, "Is There Vital Conflict in Science, Religion?" 8.

104 Rev. E. Harold Toye, "The Effect of Automation on Religion," in "Report of the Toronto Committee on Automation" (1957), 8–9, Thomas Fisher Rare Book Library, University of Toronto (TFRB), J.A. Irving Papers, col. 132, box 45.

105 "Asking the World," BBC broadcast, 8 Nov. 1959, TFRB, J.A. Irving Papers, col. 132, box 48, file 2.

106 Grant would explore this theme in *Philosophy in the Mass Age* (Toronto: Copp Clark, 1959) and *Lament for a Nation* (Toronto: Gage, 1965); Pierre Berton, *The Comfortable Pew* (Toronto: McClelland and Stewart, 1965), 101, 129.

107 W.L. Morton, "The University As It Is and Is Becoming," address "to University gathering," May 1966. McM, W.L. Morton Papers, box 55, Lectures, No–W. Snow's 1959 book (initially his Rede Lectures at Cambridge), *The Two Cultures* (Cambridge: Cambridge University Press, 1959), approached the divide between the scientific and the literary "communities" as one of the most important problems affecting developed societies.

108 W.L. Morton, "Address to Senior Graduates, University of Manitoba, 26 May 1967," McM, W.L. Morton Papers, box 55, Lectures, No–W. 1–2.

109 "The Christian Pavilion" (1967), NA, Canadian Corporation for the World Exhibition, RG 71, vol. 15, ARC 71/15/37. The pavilion's publication, "The Eighth Day of the Week," suggested that humankind's day of creation is the eighth and emphasized the inability of modern technology to cope with human problems in a climate not informed by true Christian belief and charity. Christian Pavilion, "The Eighth Day of the Week" (1967), NA, Canadian Corporation for the World Exhibition, RG 71, vol. 406, Christian Pavilion.

110 James Gilbert uses this phrase to frame one of the crucial questions in his study of this issue from the American point of view. Gilbert, *Redeeming Culture*, 4.

111 F. Cyril James, "The Renewal of Your Mind," Baccalaureate Sermon, McGill University, 22 May 1955, McG, F. Cyril James Papers, MG 1017, Addresses and Other Papers, 1955, 6.

CHAPTER FOUR

1 In arguing against consumer passivity, Joy Parr raises the important point that critical observers can explain consumption more readily in terms of

exploitation than of consumer agency. Parr, *Domestic Goods: The Material, the Moral and the Economic in the Postwar Years* (Toronto: University of Toronto Press, 1999), 168.

2 Blodwen Davies, *Youth Speaks Its Mind* (Toronto: Ryerson Press, 1948), 152.

3 Promisingly titled, Gary Donaldson's *Abundance and Anxiety: America, 1945–1960* (Westport, Conn.: Praeger, 1997) is a recent survey in which the sole chapter on culture and society alludes only briefly to anxiety. Better examples of generalist work are Loren Baritz, *The Good Life: The Meaning of Success for the American Middle Class* (New York: Knopf, 1989) and William L. O'Neill, *American High: The Years of Confidence, 1945–1960* (New York: Free Press, 1986). The best survey treatment of 1950s' culture, John Patrick Diggins, *The Proud Decades: America in War and Peace, 1941–1960* (New York: Norton, 1988), explicitly questions the interpretation of the decade as "placid." See especially chapters 6 (society and popular culture), and 7 (high culture) which address complexity and anxiety.

4 W.T. Lhamon, Jr, *Deliberate Speed: the Origins of a Cultural Style in the American 1950s*, first pub. Washington, DC: Smithsonian Institution, 1990 (Cambridge, Mass.: Harvard University Press, 2002), 16. Other recent counterpoints to the representation of a placid 1950s include Frances Stonor Saunders, *The Cultural Cold War: The CIA and the World of Arts and Letters* (New York: New Press, 2000); Margot A. Henriksen, *Dr. Strangelove's America: Society and Culture in the Atomic Age* (Berkeley: University of California Press, 1997), James Gilbert, *Redeeming Culture: American Religion in an Age of Science* (Chicago: University of Chicago Press, 1997). In Joel Foreman, ed., *The Other Fifties: Interrogating Midcentury American Icons* (Urbana, IL: University of Illinois Press, 1997), contributors use difference and nonconformity as alternative ways to see American society and culture. Tom Engelhardt notes the "triumphalist despair" of the postwar period in *The End of Victory Culture: Cold War America and the Disillusioning of a Generation* (New York: Basic Books, 1995), 9. In *The Culture of the Cold War* (Baltimore: Johns Hopkins University Press, 1991), Stephen J. Whitfield cites fear of communism as a profound influence on American popular culture. Elaine Tyler May's *Homeward Bound: American Families in the Cold War Era* (New York: Basic Books, 1988) employed the metaphor of "containment" to explore family life during the 1950s and laid the groundwork for other studies such as Stephanie Coontz, *The Way We Never Were: American Families and the Nostalgia Trap* (New York: Basic Books, 1993) and Joanne Meyerowitz, ed., *Not June Cleaver: Women and Gender in Postwar America, 1945–1960* (Philadelphia: Temple University Press, 1994).

5 Alvin Finkel, *Our Lives: Canada after 1945* (Toronto: J. Lorimer, 1997); Robert Bothwell, Ian Drummond, and John English, *Canada since 1945*,

rev. ed. (Toronto: University of Toronto Press, 1989), and Donald Creighton, *The Forked Road: Canada 1939–1957* (Toronto: McClelland and Stewart, 1976).

6 Steve Hewitt, *Spying 101: the RCMP's Secret Activities at Canadian Universities, 1917–1997* (Toronto: University of Toronto Press, 2002); Larry Hannant, *The Infernal Machine: Investigating the Loyalty of Canada's Citizens* (Toronto: University of Toronto Press, 1995); Reg Whitaker and Gary Marcuse, *Cold War Canada: The Making of a National Insecurity State, 1945–1957* (Toronto: University of Toronto Press, 1994). See also Daniel Robinson and David Kimmel, "The Queer Career of Homosexual Security Vetting in Cold War Canada," *Canadian Historical Review* 75 Sept. 1994): 319–45.

7 Valerie Korinek's *Roughing It in the Suburbs: Reading Chatelaine Magazine in the Fifties and Sixties* (Toronto: University of Toronto Press, 2000), examines a magazine's readership as a coherent "community" that was none the less fragmented by class, religious, and other divisions. In *Domestic Goods: The Material, the Moral and the Economic in the Postwar Years* (Toronto: University of Toronto Press, 1999), Joy Parr addresses the design and consumption of furniture and appliances in Canada, portraying the complexity of these acts and their ties to political and ethical choices. Though concerned more specifically with television as a new medium of communications and with its content, Paul Rutherford's *When Television Was Young: Primetime Canada, 1952–1967* (Toronto: University of Toronto Press, 1990) provides a helpful reading of the early-1950s' cultural scene.

8 Owram, *Born at the Right Time: A History of the Baby Boom Generation* (Toronto: University of Toronto Press, 1996). For more of a psychohistorical and literary approach to the same generation, see François Ricard, *The Lyric Generation: The Life and Times of the Baby Boomers,* trans. Donald Winkler (Toronto: Stoddart, 1994), first published as *La generation lyrique: essai sur la vie et l'oeuvre des premiers-nés du baby-boom* (Montreal: Boreal, 1992), in which Ricard also marvels at the extraordinary luck of the "cosseted children of transition" (68). A clearly visible orientation towards family life also helped characterize the decade as sedate. See Veronica Strong-Boag, " 'Their Side of the Story': Women's Voices from Ontario Suburbs, 1945–60," in Joy Parr, ed., *A Diversity of Women: Ontario, 1945–1980* (Toronto: University of Toronto Press, 1995).

9 On the commission from 1943 to 1948, see Linda McGuire Ambrose, "The Canadian Youth Commission: Planning for Youth and Social Welfare in the Postwar Era," PhD dissertation, University of Waterloo, 1992.

10 Vincent Massey headed the commission, and Father Georges-Henri Lévesque took on a leadership role in French-speaking Canada. Paul Litt's 1991 *The Muses, the Masses, and the Massey Commission* (Toronto: University of Toronto Press, 1992), is the definitive study, and the term *creationist myth* first

appears on page 5 of that book. Philip Massolin's recent history of Tory intellectuals, *Canadian Intellectuals, the Tory Tradition, and the Challenge of Modernity* (Toronto, University of Toronto Press, 2001), draws heavily on Litt's work and on Massey's papers in making the commission quite central to his argument. Although Paul Rutherford was not attempting a history of the commission, he portrays it as a "culture probe." Rutherford, *When Television Was Young*, 13–16. George Woodcock wrote of the arts before the Massey Commission: "Canada was a country still emerging from an age of practically minded pioneers; the arts were considered unnecessary luxuries in a life devoted to the conquest of a hostile land." Woodcock, *Strange Bedfellows: The State and the Arts in Canada* (Toronto: Douglas and McIntyre, 1985), 50; see also 12–16 on the need for the state to serve as the agent of the community. Maria Tippett, in *Making Culture: English-Canada Institutions and the Arts before the Massey Commission* (Toronto, University of Toronto Press, 1990), uses the commission as a terminus. While it is an obvious place to end a work dealing with the first half of the twentieth century, her overall argument also suggests that, in creating the commission, Canada's policymakers heralded a new era of cultural awareness. In the same way, Bothwell et al. in the "cultural" chapter of *Canada since 1945* view the commission as a consolidation of cultural policy.

11 "The Donnish Inquisition: The Massey Commission and the Campaign for State-Sponsored Cultural Nationalism in Canada, 1949–1951" is the title of Litt's doctoral dissertation, completed at the University of Toronto in 1990.

12 Arthur Lower, "The Survival Value of a Soft Nation," *Saturday Night* (31 Oct. 1953): 7–8.

13 See Litt, *The Muses, the Masses, and the Massey Commission*, chapter 11 and conclusion, for a catalogue of these recommendations and their fates.

14 Nicholas Brown suggests that in Australia the quick turn from a society characterized during the war by voluntarism and duty towards the "milk bar economy" of the 1950s was particularly jarring for some commentators. Brown, *Governing Prosperity: Social Change and Social Analysis in Australia in the 1950s* (Cambridge: Cambridge University Press, 1995), 99.

15 Arthur L. Phelps, "Community and Culture," Founder's Day Address at the University of New Brunswick, Fredericton, 18 Feb. 1947.

16 Phelps, "Community and Culture," 8.

17 A.J.M. Smith, "Canadian Renaissance," *Canadian Author and Bookman* 22, no. 2 (June 1946): 32.

18 Quotation from United Nations, Constitution of the United Nations Educational, Scientific and Cultural Organization, adopted in London on 16 November 1945, preamble. Walter B. Herbert, "UNECO" [sic] Puts Canada in Humiliating Position," *Saturday Night* (27 Oct. 1945): 22; Walter B. Herbert, "Let's Pull Our Cultural Threads Together," submitted to *Saturday*

Night, 9 Nov. 1945, NA, Walter B. Herbert Papers, MG 30 D 205, vol. 1, Addresses, Articles and Lectures; Blodwen Davies, "The Significance of UNESCO," *Canadian Forum* 26, no. 307 (Aug. 1946): 107–9. Chapter 3 of J.R. Kidd's study of citizenship addresses this new internationalism. Kidd, "A Study to Formulate a Plan for the Work of the Canadian Citizenship Council," EdD project, Columbia University, 1947.

19 B.K. Sandwell, *The Gods in Twilight*, First Hewitt Bostock Memorial Lecture in Canadian Citizenship, Vancouver, 30 Oct. 1947, (Vancouver: University of British Columbia Press, 1948), 17.

20 Sandwell, *The Gods in Twilight*, 17.

21 The *Canadian Forum* certainly took the lead in publishing articles on design early in wartime. Humphrey Carver, "Home-Made Thoughts on Handicrafts" 19, no. 230 (March 1940): 386–7; Douglas MacAgy, "Designers for Living," 20, no. 236 (Sept. 1940): 178–80. Helen Frye, "Design in Industry," 27, no. 315 (April 1947): 12–13. Quotation from Donald W. Buchanan, "Design in Industry – A Misnomer," *Canadian Art* 2, no. 3 (summer 1945): 194–7.

22 Buchanan wrote a rash of articles on design in *Canadian Art,* including, "The Design of Household Goods," 4, no. 2 (Feb.–March 1947): 74–7; "Design Index," 5, no. 2 (Christmas – New Year 1947–48): 86–9; "Take Another Look at Your Kitchen Range," 5, no. 4 (spring-summer 1948): 182–3; and "Completing the Pattern of Modern Living," 6, no. 3 (spring 1949): 111–16. Charles Fraser Comfort, "Living with Design," round-table discussion, during the Ontario Education Association Conference, 8 April 1947, NA, Charles Fraser Comfort Papers, MG30 D81, vol. 35, file 5; H.A. Nieboer, "History and Industrial Design," *Here and Now* 1, no. 3 (Jan. 1949): 79–86. Art Gallery of Toronto, "Submission to the Royal Commission on National Development in the Arts, Letters and Sciences," 21 Oct. 1949, 5, NA, RCALS, RG33/28, vol. 2. For a much more detailed look at design in this period, see Parr, *Domestic Goods*, especially chapter 6, "Inter/national Style."

23 D.B. Cruikshank, "Industrial Design – What Are Canadians Doing about It?" *Industrial Canada* 50, no. 3 (July 1949): 216–19.

24 L.C. Marsh to John Grierson, 25 Feb. 1947. Marsh had taken the job at UBC to hedge his bets and wrote to another famous friend, seeking a job at UNESCO in Paris. Marsh to Julian Huxley, 31 March 1947, UBCSC, Leonard C. Marsh Papers, box 28–26, Correspondence, 1936–1978.

25 This set of Molson's ads ran in national magazines, beginning in summer 1947, "to promote a fuller realization by Canadians of Canada's present greatness."

26 Gerald Anglin, *Canada Unlimited* (Toronto: O'Keefe Foundation, 1948). The book was apparently an adaptation of Eric Johnston's *America Unlimited* (1944). O'Keefe's had been using the slogan "Canada Unlimited" as early as March 1944; *Canadian Business* 17, no. 3 (March 1944): inside

front cover. Carling's countered with its "Nature Unspoiled" series in 1948. For more on Johnston, see Lary May, "Making the American Consensus: The Narrative of Conversion and Subversion in World War II Films," in Lewis A. Erenberg and Susan E. Hirsch, eds., *The War in American Culture: Society and Consciousness during World War II* (Chicago: University of Chicago Press, 1996), 71–102.

27 R.C. Wallace, "Education in Canada," in R.H. Coats, ed., *Features of Present-Day Canada*, in *Annals of the American Academy of Political and Social Science* (Philadelphia: American Academy of Political and Social Science, 1947), 180.

28 "A Canadian," "Christmas – or Paganism?" *Maclean's* (15 Dec. 1945): 5, 45; A. Vibert Douglas, "Growing Materialism Needs Spiritual Aid," *Saturday Night* (24 Nov. 1945): 16. C.E. Silcox, "The Menace of Modernity to Christian Marriage," 1946, UCA, Claris Edwin Silcox Papers, box 9, file 38.

29 C.J. Eustace, "What Is Materialism?" *Culture* 9 (1948): 152. For an example of his early postwar thoughts on materialism, see Eustace, "The Future of Religion in the Secular or Neutral Society," *Culture* 7 (1946): 421–8.

30 Watson Kirkconnell, "Things That Endure," address to the United Baptist Convention of the Maritime Provinces, 28 Aug. 1948, reprinted in *Acadia Bulletin* 34, no. 6 (Sept. 1948): 15–16. Blomidon is the name of the cape near the Minas Basin to the north of Wolfville, Nova Scotia.

31 Dr J.M. Ewing, "Our Changing Society," first in the series *Our Changing Values*, broadcast 11 Aug. 1948, Neil M. Morrison Papers, NA, MG 30 E 273, vol. 28, Public Affairs Scripts Broadcast 1943–51.

32 Ewing, "Our Changing Society," 1–2.

33 Dr J.M. Ewing, "Our New Leisure," seventh in the series *Our Changing Values*, broadcast 22 Sept. 1948, 2–5, quotation from page 5, NA, Neil M. Morrison Papers, MG 30 E 273, vol. 28, Public Affairs Scripts Broadcast 1943–51.

34 Sidney Katz, "What about the Comics?" *Maclean's* (1 Dec. 1948): 7, 71–3, 75. Programs on comics and advertising were the most listened to of *Citizens' Forum's* 1948–49 season. Summary of *Citizens' Forum*, Questionnaires, 1948–49, AO, CAAE Papers, Series B-1, box 1, *Citizens' Forum*, administrative, 1943–1960.

35 CARTB provides a short history of the program as an addendum to its brief to the Royal Commission on Broadcasting in 1956. NA, RCB, RG 33/36, vol. 25, reel C-7019.

36 Mary Lowrey Ross, "The Coming Comic-Strip Age," *Saturday Night* (27 March 1948): 10. Ross later predicted that children would probably grow out of their fascination with them. Ross, "Comics and the Elsie Books," *Saturday Night* (21 Aug. 1948): 9.

37 Canadian Federation of Home and School, brief to the Royal Commission on National Development in the Arts, Letters and Sciences, 29 Aug. 1949, 2, NA, RCALS, RG 33/28, vol. 13.

38 Dora Carney, "What's Wrong with the So-called Comics?" *Saturday Night* (13 Nov. 1948): 32–3. Americans were aware of the comics "problem" at about the same time. See "School for Sadism," *Art Digest* 23, no. 15 (1 May 1949). In response to U.S. psychiatrist Fredric Wertham's long-gestating book on comics, *Seduction of the Innocent* (New York Rinehart, 1954), published about five years after the Canadian controversy, Robertson Davies warned of the dangers of censorship but admitted that comics were proof that "widespread literacy was not inevitably a key to widespread knowledge or improvement; it may equally well be a key to intellectual anarchy and degradation." Robertson Davies, "Greetings, Humanoids! Drag Over a Cyclotron," *Saturday Night* (5 June 1954): 17.

39 "Wayne and Shuster's Toni Show," CBC Trans-Canada Network, 10 Feb. 1949, NA, Frank Shuster Papers, MG 31 D 251, vol. 4.

40 "No Laughing Matter," *Food for Thought* 9, no. 6 (March 1949): 28.

41 T.S. Eliot, *Notes towards the Definition of Culture* (New York: Harcourt, Brace and Company, 1948), 18.

42 See *Royal Commission Studies: A Selection of Essays Prepared for the Royal Commission on National Development in the Arts, Letters and Sciences* (Ottawa: King's Printer, 1951). "Frustrated Artists," *Printed Word* 183 (Dec. 1949): 4; Commission on Culture of the United Church of Canada, "Brief," presented to the Royal Commission on National Development in the Arts, Letters and Sciences, 16 Nov. 1949; *Citizens' Forum*, "Should the Federal Government Support Cultural Activities?" study material to accompany broadcast for 24 Nov. 1949; Walter Herbert, "Who Supports the Arts?" *Food for Thought* 10, no. 8 (May 1950): 49–51; Frank H. Underhill, "Notes on the Massey Report," *Canadian Forum* 31, no. 367 (Aug. 1951): 100–2; John Stewart, "The Massey Report: Ideological Preparation for War," *National Affairs Monthly* 8, no. 1 (Sept. 1951): 34–53; Anne Francis, "Capital Report," broadcast 3 June 1951, NA, CBC, RG 41, vol. 303, file 14–2–2, pt. 2, Massey Commission, Editorial Comment; "Can We Be 'Scared' into Culture?" *Montreal Gazette*, 14 Sept. 1951.

43 Discussion Group of Hamilton, "Brief submitted by the Discussion Group of Hamilton to the Royal Commission on Arts and Science Development" (1949), NA, CBC, vol. 304, file 14–2–2, part 11.

44 Public Affairs Institute [of Vancouver], "Brief," 7.

45 This term, or at least its application to the early-1950s' Canadian cultural and intellectual context, is Paul Litt's. See *The Muses, the Masses, and the Massey Commission*, chap. 4, for a fuller discussion.

46 Federation of Canadian Artists, "Brief submitted in 1949 to the Royal Commission on National Development in the Arts, Letters and Sciences," reprinted April 1951.

47 [Manitoba Citizens], "To the Royal Commission on National Development in the Arts, Letters and Sciences" [1949], ii, 10.

48 Transcript of hearing, University Women's Club, Regina, 3 Nov. 1949, 210, NA, RCALS, RG 33/28, vol. 32, reel C-2016.
49 "Draft and notes for brief on the Visual Arts in Canada" [1950], NA, Charles Fraser Comfort Papers, MG 30 D81, vol. 42, files 8–10, Massey Commission, 1949–1950. Although the draft is not dated, Comfort's notes are dated 19 January 1950. Alternative versions exist in the same volume, files 42–14 and 42–15. Some of this material found its way into Comfort's essay "Painting," in *Royal Commission Studies: A Selection of Essays Prepared for the Royal Commission on National Development in the Arts, Letters and Sciences* (Ottawa: King's Printer, 1951), 407–18.
50 Saskatchewan Arts Board, "Brief to Royal Commission on National Development in the Arts, Letters and Sciences," Oct. 1949, 3, NA, RCALS, RG 33/28, vol. 29, reel C-2014. The board had been established earlier in 1949.
51 Canadian Federation of Home and School, brief to RCALS, 3. NA, RCALS, RG 33/28, vol. 13. One of the Saskatchewan Arts Board's stated objectives was "to make available to the people of Saskatchewan opportunities to engage in any one or more of the following activities: drama, the visual arts, music, literature, handicrafts and the other arts." 1. NA, RCALS, RG 33/28, vol. 29, reel C-2014.
52 Alberta Library Association, "Brief to the Royal Commission on National Development in the Arts, Letters and Sciences," 13 Sept. 1949, 6, NA, RCALS, RG 33/28, vol. 1.
53 Canadian Authors' Association, "Brief," submitted to Royal Commission on National Development in the Arts, Letters and Sciences, 31 Oct. 1949, 3, NA, RCALS, RG 33/28, vol. 9.
54 Blodwen Davies, *Youth Speaks Its Mind* (Toronto: Ryerson Press, 1948), 165.
55 Public Affairs Institute, "Brief," presented to the RCALS, Vancouver, 30 Sept. 1949, 3, NA, RCALS, RG 33/28, vol. 28, reel C-2014.
56 Arts Centre of Greater Victoria, "Supplement to brief to Royal Commission on National Development in the Arts, Letters and Sciences," 29 Oct. 1949, 3, NA, RCALS, RG 33/28, vol. 3.
57 Arts Centre of Greater Victoria, "Supplement to brief to Royal Commission," 2–3.
58 Town Meeting Ltd, "Brief to be presented to the Royal Commission on Arts, Sciences, and Cultural Activities," 1949, 5, NA, RCALS, RG 33/28, vol. 31, reel C-2015.
59 Marius Barbeau, "The Fountain-heads of Canadian Culture," addendum to the brief presented by the National Museum of Canada, 20 July 1949, 3, NA, RCALS, RG 33/28, vol. 25, reel C-2012.
60 Western Stage Society, "A Submission by the Western Stage Society to the Royal Commission on National Development in the Arts, Letters and Sciences," 1949, NA, RCALS, RG 33/28, vol. 32, reel C-2016.
61 The "great tradition" was great and enduring for Williams "[j]ust because it is a mixed inheritance, from many societies and many times as well as from

many kinds of men, it cannot easily be contained within one limited social form." Williams, *Communications*, 3rd ed. (London: Penguin, 1976), 114–15.
62 Frank H. Underhill, "Notes on the Massey Report," 100–2; Robert Ayre, "The Press Debates the Massey Report," *Canadian Art* 9, no. 1 (Oct. 1951): 25–30, 36–8; George Robertson, "A Broader Base of Patronage," *Canadian Art* 9, no. 3 (spring 1952): 107; Gratton O'Leary, "Canada's Political Philosophy," in Lester B. Pearson et al., *Canada: Nation on the March* (Toronto: Clarke, Irwin, 1953), 189; W.M. Haugan, "Cultural Democracy," *Food for Thought* 10, no. 1 (Oct. 1949): 13–16, 50. Haugan conceived of cultural democracy as a state midway between cultural assimilation and cultural pluralism, where the boundaries between ethnic groups were not so rigid.
63 The Periodical Press Association of Canada made one of the clearest cases for such intervention when it showed that under R.B. Bennett's government in the early 1930s import tariffs on American magazines had been beneficial to the Canadian magazine industry. "Brief presented on behalf of Periodical Press Association of Canada," 27 Oct. 1949, 6–7, NA, RCALS, RG 33/28, vol. 27, reel C-2014.
64 On the climate at *Partisan Review*, see Paul Gorman, *Left Intellectuals and Popular Culture in Twentieth-Century America* (Chapel Hill: University of North Carolina Press, 1996), chap. 6, Neil Jumonville, *Critical Crossings: The New York Intellectuals in Postwar America* (Berkeley: University of California Press, 1991).
65 Milton Klonsky, "Along the Midway of Mass Culture," *Partisan Review* 16, no. 4 (April 1949): 349.
66 Russell Lynes, "Highbrow, Lowbrow, Middlebrow," *Harper's* (Feb. 1949): 19–28. For an etymology of these terms, see Joan Shelley Rubin, *The Making of Middlebrow Culture* (Chapel Hill: University of North Carolina Press, 1992), xi–xiv. On the subtlety of such classifications, see Michael Kammen, *The Lively Arts: Gilbert Seldes and the Transformation of Cultural Criticism in the United States* (New York: Oxford University Press, 1996), 89–94.
67 Harold King, "Some Notes for Amateur Artists," *Canadian Art* 7, no. 1 (Oct. 1949): 10–11. Among the passive habits, King placed "possession of pictures for prestige; refined, intellectual hedonism; or the enjoyment of only choice masterpieces in galleries by a respectful, adoring audience," 10.
68 Beatrix Graham, "Planning for Community Welfare," *Food for Thought* 10, no. 3 (Dec. 1949): 12–16. Elizabeth Loosley, "Solving Community Problems," *Food for Thought* 10, no. 3 (Dec. 1949): 17–21; "Community Centres," *New Frontiers* 1, no. 2 (spring 1952): 8.
69 M.B. Mecredy, "Canada's Cultural and Agricultural Outlook," *Culture* 10 (1949): 138.

70 The winning entries, and the *Standard*'s own columns on the subject, originally published during February and March 1946, were eventually put out as a booklet entitled *Into the Atomic Age*. Will F. Jenkins, "Your Great-Great-Great-Grandmother and the Atom Bomb," *National Home Monthly* 47, no. 2 (Feb. 1946): 12, 22–3. E.F. Burton, "Atomic Energy Can Be Power without Tears," *Saturday Night* (24 Aug. 1946): 6–7. Charles Clay, "Atoms or Bacon – It's All in the Day's Work at N.R.C." *Saturday Night* (11 Dec. 1948): 3, 26; Ralph Staples, "Salute to an Atomic Future," *Food for Thought* 10, no. 3 (Dec. 1949): 34–7.

71 C.J. Eustace, "The Price of Time," *Culture* 11 (1950): 369. Lister Sinclair, "You Can't Stop Now," 11 Nov. 1945, NA, Lister Shedden Sinclair Papers, MG 31 D44, vol. 2, Radio Scripts. Max Werner, "We Can't Risk War Now," *Maclean's* (1 Oct. 1945): 7, 59–60. Larry Smith, "We CAN Prepare for Atom-Bombs," *Saturday Night* (26 Sept. 1950): 8, 43.

72 Mary Lowrey Ross, "Miss A. Meets the Atomic World and Puts It in Its Place," *Saturday Night* (1 Sept. 1945): 10. L.E.G. Upper [A.R.M. Lower], "Let's Move Our Mountains," *Saturday Night* (27 Dec. 1949): 25.; Anon., "Death by Atom Light," n.d. [post-1945], McM, CBC Scripts Collection, reel 8.

73 C.R. Tracy, "Education in the Atomic Age," *New Trail* 4, no. 2 (April 1946): 64.; J.R. Stirrett, "Atomic Admonition," *Canadian Forum* 27, no. 325 (Feb. 1948): 252–3. The best historical analysis of "the bomb" as a social and cultural phenomenon is Paul Boyer, *By the Bomb's Early Light: American Thought and Culture at the Dawn of the Atomic Age* (New York: Pantheon, 1985).

74 Dr Aileen Dunham, "A Survey of the First Half of the Twentieth Century," *New Trail* 8, no. 1 (spring 1950): 23–9; C.F. Comfort, "The Artist in Modern Society," address to School of Social Work, University of Toronto, 22 Feb. 1950, NA, Charles Fraser Comfort Papers, MG 30 D81, vol. 35, file 11; A.R.M. Lower, "Canada, 1925–1950," *United Church Observer*, 1 June 1950, 9, 33; Fred Bodsworth, "1900 – How Wrong Can You Be?" *Maclean's* (1 Jan. 1950): 8, 42–3; John Largo, "1950 – Brave New Wacky World," *Maclean's* (1 Jan. 1950): 9, 40–1.

75 George Salverson, "In the Shadow of the Bomb," 1 Jan. 1950, McM, CBC Scripts Collection, reel 98.

76 Salverson, "In the Shadow of the Bomb," 19. In dramatizing this sequence, Salverson borrowed liberally from Gilbert Seldes's article, "Nickleodeon to Television," *Maclean's* (1 Jan. 1950): 12–13, 44.

77 Salverson, "In the Shadow of the Bomb," 20–1.

78 Seldes, "Nickleodeon to Television," 13. Seldes's first influential book, *The Seven Lively Arts*, appeared in 1924. *The Great Audience* came out in 1950, although Seldes may have drawn on its arguments in preparing his piece for *Maclean's*. Adorno and Horkheimer's most influential essay, "The

Culture Industry: Enlightenment as Mass Deception," appeared originally in 1944.
79 Salverson, "In the Shadow of the Bomb," 23–4.
80 Salverson, "In the Shadow of the Bomb," 24–6. Doris Mosdell, "Adults and the Commercial Film," *Food for Thought* 10, no. 6 (March 1950): 15–17.
81 "Television," *Food for Thought* 9, no. 4 (Jan. 1949): 1–3; Blair Fraser, "Why They Won't Let You Have Television," *Maclean's* (15 Jan. 1949): 12–13, 38–9; Morley Callaghan, "Television – the New Monster," *National Home Monthly* 50, no. 3 (March 1949): 16, 38–9; "Warning to Televisionaries," *Saturday Night* (4 July 1950): 6–7; Don Magill, "What TV Will Do to You," *Maclean's* (1 March 1951): 22–4; Nathan Cohen, "TV Will Creep in on Soft-Soled Shoes," *Saturday Night* (26 June 1951): 11, 36; Mavor Moore, "What We'll Do With TV," *Saturday Night* (24 May 1952): 9, 19–20.
82 Still addressing the inadequacies of movies and radio, Salverson had the Showman continue: "and a salesman's job is to lull the critical faculties of whoever's being sold. So, on one side you get mythology. On the other ... flabby minds. Deliberately encouraged. No sir ... you couldn't permit anything to be disturbed, or anything that required hard thinking. The movies make their play frankly for the adolescent, and, except for its factual programs, radio goes ahead promoting immaturity into old age." Salverson, "In the Shadow of the Bomb," 26.
83 Salverson, "In the Shadow of the Bomb," 27.
84 *Report of the Royal Commission on National Development in the Arts, Letters and Sciences 1949–1951* (Ottawa: King's Printer, 1951), 4.
85 Albert A. Shea, "The High Cost of Intellectual Snobbery," *Food for Thought* 11, no. 8 (May 1951): 20–1. Albert A. Shea, *Culture in Canada: A Study of the Findings of the Royal Commission on National Development in the Arts, Letters and Sciences (1949–1951)* (Toronto: Core Press, 1952). Shea had served in the Royal Canadian Air Force, worked for the Wartime Information Board, taught political science at the universities of Toronto and Manitoba, and worked for UNESCO on a survey of mass communications.
86 Walter Herbert, "Who Supports the Arts?" *Food for Thought* 10, no. 8 (May 1950): 49–51.
87 Joseph Pollick to W.B. Herbert, 12 Jan. 1950, NA, Canada Foundation, MG 28 1179, vol. 33, file 4b, Cultural Publications, 1948–1952.
88 Harold A. Innis, *The Strategy of Culture* (Toronto: University of Toronto Press, 1952), 15.
89 Innis, *The Strategy of Culture*, 14.
90 See Margaret Groome, "Canada's Stratford Festival, 1953–1967: Hegemony, Commodity, Institution," PhD dissertation, McGill University, 1988. More general accounts include Tom Patterson with Allan Gould, *First*

Stage: The Making of the Stratford Festival (Toronto: McClelland and Stewart, 1987); John Pettigrew and Jamie Portman, Stratford: The First Thirty Years (Toronto: Macmillan, 1985).

91 Hugh Garner, "Culture and the Privy Purse," Saturday Night (6 March 1954): 9. Although the bulk of his commentary is on matters of church and state, W.L. Smith argued that the state had taken on a greater role as an arbiter of values. "Morals for the Masses," Canadian Forum 31, no. 372 (Jan. 1952): 218.

92 Canadian Federation of Home and School, brief to Royal Commission on National Development in the Arts, Letters and Sciences, 3, NA, RCALS, RG 33/28, RG 33/28 vol. 13.

93 Canadian Association of Consumers, brief to Royal Commission on National Development in the Arts, Letters and Sciences, 7 Nov. 1949, 2, NA, RCALS, RG 33/28, vol. 9.

94 Innis's major works during this period, aside from The Strategy of Culture, were Empire and Communications (Toronto: University of Toronto Press, 1950) and The Bias of Communication (Toronto: University of Toronto Press, 1951). About the same time, McLuhan published The Mechanical Bride: Folklore of Industrial Man (New York: Vanguard, 1951) and began in 1953, with Edmund Carpenter, to edit the journal Explorations. Sandra Campbell, "From Romantic History to Communications Theory: Lorne Pierce as Publisher of C.W. Jefferys and Harold Innis," Journal of Canadian Studies 30, no. 3 (autumn 1995): 91–116; Arthur Kroker, Technology and the Canadian Mind: Innis, Grant, McLuhan (New York: St Martin's, 1985); Joel Persky, "The Media Writings of Harold Adams Innis," Journal of Canadian Culture 2, no. 1 (spring 1985): 79–87; and Persky "The Innescence of Marshall McLuhan," Journal of Canadian Culture 1, no. 2 (autumn 1984): 3–14.

95 Lawren Harris noted this epigram from Alan Valentine's The Age of Conformity in a draft of "Democracy and the Arts" [1954], NA, Lawren Stewart Harris Papers, MG 30 D 208, file 5–15.

96 Rutherford, When Television Was Young: Primetime Canada, 1952–1967 (Toronto: University of Toronto Press, 1989), 21–5.

97 G.P. Gilmour, "Chairman's Message," Canada's Tomorrow Conference, 1953, UBCSC, N.A.M. MacKenzie Papers, box 99, folder 6.

98 Isabel Wilson, "A Report on Citizens' Forum, Canada's National Platform" (1953), AO, CAAE Papers, series B-I, box 1, Citizens' Forum, administrative, 1943–1960.

99 Programs broadcast 17 January 1952, 13 March 1952, 5 November 1953, 7 January 1954, and 21 October 1954, respectively. On these programming decisions and their background, see Isabel Wilson, Citizens' Forum: "Canada's National Platform" (Toronto: Ontario Institute for Studies in Education, 1980).

100 Hilda Neatby, "Education for Democracy," *Dalhousie Review* 24, no. 1 (April 1944): 43–50.
101 Hilda Neatby, *So Little for the Mind* (Toronto: Clarke Irwin, 1953), vi.
102 See, for a concise example, Vernon S. Stevens, "Preface to a Philosophy of Education," *Canadian Forum* 32, no. 376 (May 1952): 33–4.
103 James T. Kloppenberg, *Uncertain Victory: Social Democracy and Progressivism in European and American Thought, 1870–1920* (New York: Oxford University Press, 1986), 374.
104 Neatby, *So Little for the Mind*, 232.
105 Edward A. McCourt, "Schoolhouse in Utopia," *Saturday Night* (12 July 1941): 25.
106 Neatby, *So Little for the Mind*. See especially the opening section of chapter 7, "Comment and Criticism."
107 Catherine Stephen, "Schoolsacross the Sea," *Saturday Night* (23 Nov. 1940): 25.
108 Dr J.M. Ewing, "Our Progressivist Education," sixth in the series *Our Changing Values*, broadcast 15 Sept. 1948, NA, Neil M. Morrison Papers, MG 30 E 273, vol. 28, Public Affairs Scripts Broadcast 1943–51. Neatby herself offered some wartime advice in "Education for Democracy," *Dalhousie Review* 24, no. 1 (April 1944): 43–50. See also William E. Hume, "Are the Schools Ruining Your Child?" *Maclean's* (1 March 1952): 12–13, 37–9.
109 A.R.M. Lower, "Does Our Education Educate?" *Maclean's* (15 Nov. 1948): 9, 72–6.
110 J.J. Brown, "Mr. Brown Looks at Education," *Canadian Business* (Nov. 1951): 48. Neatby also quoted extensively from Toronto sociology professor J.R. Seeley's contribution to the University of London's *Year Book of Education* for 1951. Neatby, *So Little for the Mind*, 264–8.
111 See Stevens, "Preface to a Philosophy of Education," quotation from Jessie Macpherson, "The Ends of Education," *Food for Thought* 14, no. 5 (Feb. 1954): 3–7.
112 Neatby, *So Little for the Mind*, 315, 324–5.
113 Kenneth Patrick Watson, "How Much for the Mind?" *Canadian Forum* 34, no. 399 (April 1954): 7–9.
114 Frank H. Underhill, "So Little for the Mind: Comments and Queries," *Transactions of the Royal Society of Canada* vol. 46, series III (June 1954): 16–17.
115 Robertson Davies, "Dr. Neatby Punches the Pedagogues," *Saturday Night* (14 Nov. 1953): 22–3.
116 Hilda Neatby, "Progressive Education: A Challenge Missed," *Saturday Night* (17 Oct. 1953): 8.
117 Hilda Neatby, *A Temperate Dispute* (Toronto: Clarke Irwin, 1954). The essays "A Temperate Dispute" and "Is Teaching a Learned Profession?" took up directly the educational theme addressed in *So Little for the Mind*.
118 Neatby, "The Debt of Our Reason," in *A Temperate Dispute*, 78–85.

119 Neatby, "The Group and the Herd," in *A Temperate Dispute*, 30–6, 45–9.
120 Ralph Allen, *The Chartered Libertine* (Toronto: Macmillan, 1954). Allen patterned his character Hilary Bonnisteel on Neatby.
121 The most influential of these early community studies were R.S. Lynd and H.M. Lynd, *Middletown: A Study in Contemporary American Culture* (New York: Harcourt, Brace and Company, 1929) and their follow-up study, *Middletown in Transition: A Study in Cultural Conflicts* (New York: Harcourt, Brace and Company, 1937). W. Lloyd Warner and Paul S. Lunt produced the Yankee City series beginning in 1941; it started with *The Social Life of a Modern Community* and *The Status System of a Modern Community* (New Haven, Conn.: Yale University Press, 1941 and 1942).
122 James Gilbert, *A Cycle of Outrage: America's Reaction to the Juvenile Delinquent in the 1950s* (New York: Oxford University Press, 1986), 3.
123 On Riesman, along with other American intellectual notables of the 1950s William Whyte and C. Wright Mills, see Richard Pells, *The Liberal Mind in a Conservative Age: American Intellectuals in the 1940s and 1950s*, 2nd ed.) Middletown, Conn.: Wesleyan University Press, 1989), chap. 4, or Neil Jumonville, *Critical Crossings: The New York Intellectuals in Postwar America* (Berkeley: University of California Press, 1991). On the "Tocqueville revival," see Kammen, *The Lively Arts*, 336.
124 David Riesman, with Reuel Denney and Nathan Glazer, *The Lonely Crowd: A Study of the Changing American Character* (New Haven, Conn.: Yale University Press, 1950). The study also introduced a third category, "tradition-directed," which probably best described intellectuals discontented with the mass society. The same team published a companion volume, *Faces in the Crowd* (New Haven, Conn.: Yale University Press, 1953), which focused on the interviews done for the *Lonely Crowd* project.
125 Riesman, *The Lonely Crowd*, 4. Riesman defined social character as a "product of experience," lending the concept an applicable historical dimension.
126 Murray G. Ross, "Man and His Lack of Community," in R.C. Chalmers and John A. Irving, eds., *The Light and the Flame: Modern Knowledge and Religion* (Toronto: Ryerson, 1956), 66.
127 John R. Seeley, R. Alexander Sim, and E.W. Loosley, *Crestwood Heights: A Study of the Culture of Suburban Life* (Toronto: University of Toronto Press, 1956), 14, 17, 145–6. David Riesman wrote the introduction to *Crestwood Heights*, in which he criticized the authors' lack of a comparative perspective but praised their sensitivity to the "anxiety and other forms of mental suffering among the well-to-do." viii.
128 *Crestwood Heights*, 134.
129 Sandwell, *The Gods in Twilight* (Vancouver: University of British Columbia Press, 1948), 16.
130 Seeley et al., *Crestwood Heights*, 13. The National Committee for Mental Hygiene was a subsidiary of the Canadian Mental Health Association. Under the direction of Dr J.D.M. Griffin, the committee ran a radio

drama/lecture series on the CBC during 1950. Entitled *In Search of Ourselves,* it simplified psychological terms and attempted to remind the average listener of his or her individuality. "In Search of Ourselves," pamphlet [1950], NA, Canada Foundation, MG 28 I179, vol. 25, file 4a, CBC, 1942–1951. See also Harriet Carr, "'In Search of Ourselves,'" *Food for Thought* 10, no. 4 (Jan. 1950): 10–12.

131 David Riesman, "Introduction," *Crestwood Heights,* viii.

132 R. Alex Sim, "Crestwood Heights: An Exploration," address given before the National Council of Jewish Women, Montreal, 16 Jan. 1957, 5–6, NA, Robert Alexander Sim Papers, MG 30 D 260, vol. 5, file 16, Crestwood Heights, An Exploration.

133 See Philip Massolin, *Canadian Intellectuals, the Tory Tradition, and the Challenge of Modernity, 1939–1970* (Toronto: University of Toronto Press, 2001), chap. 3, and A.B. McKillop, *Matters of Mind: The University in Ontario, 1791–1951* (Toronto: University of Toronto Press, 1994).

134 J.L. Synge, "Science and Culture," *University of Toronto Quarterly* 5, no. 3 (April 1936): 349.

135 C.R. Tracy, "Education in the Atomic Age," *New Trail* 4, no. 2 (April 1946): 64–6; J.E. Middleton, "Old Knowledge and New" (poem), *Saturday Night* (1 Feb. 1947): 5; Dennis Healy, letter to the editor, "Overspecialized College Education Promoting a Dangerous Trend," *Saturday Night* (22 Nov. 1947): 4; Watson Kirkconnell, *Liberal Education in the Canadian Democracy,* address at McMaster University, Feb. 1948.

136 A.S.P. Woodhouse, "Research in the Humanities," paper read at the Regional Conference on the Humanities in the Maritime Provinces, 9–10 June 1949, NA, RCALS, 1946–1951, RG 33/28, vol. 45, file 3.9; C.E. Dolman, "Science and the Humanities," address to the British Columbia Academy of Science, University of British Columbia, 14 April 1950; Anne Francis, "Capital Report," CBC broadcast, 3 June 1951, NA, CBC, RG 41, vol. 303, file 14–2–2, pt. 2, Massey Commission, Editorial Comment; F.M. Salter, "The Problem of the Humanities," *New Trail* 9, no. 2 (summer 1951): 79–85.

137 Malcolm W. Wallace, "The Present Status of the Humanities in Canada," Submission to the Royal Commission on National Development in the Arts, Letters and Sciences, 1950, 22, NA, RCALS, 1946–1951, RG 33/28, vol. 54, Special Studies files.

138 A.R.M. Lower, "Uses and Abuses of Universities," *Saturday Night* (25 April 1953): 8.

139 Donald Creighton, "What Can the Humanities Do for Government?" National Conference on the Humanities, 19–20 Nov. 1954, 1, NA, Donald Grant Creighton Papers, MG 31, D77, vol. 10, Humanities Research Council of Canada, 1954–55.

140 E.W.R. Steacie, "The Impact of Society on Science," Purvis Memorial Lecture, Society of Chemical Industry, Montreal, 27 Nov. 1957, in J.D. Bab-

bitt, ed., *Science in Canada: Selections from the Speeches of E.W.R. Steacie* (Toronto: University of Toronto Press, 1965), 97–9. C.D. Howe echoed Steacie's call for a greater scientific awareness among humanists: Howe, "Afternoon Convocation," Address to Convocation of Dalhousie University (1958), NA, Clarence Decatur Howe Papers, MG 27 III B20, vol. 148, series 89-2, Speeches, part 15.

141 A.R.C. Duncan, "An Ideal Programme for the Humanities," speech to Humanities Association of Canada, June 1958, reprinted in *Humanities Association Bulletin* 25 (Jan. 1959): 11–17.

142 "A Summary of the Brief Submitted to the Royal Commission on Broadcasting by Professor A.R.M. Lower of Queen's University" [1956], TFRB, J.A. Irving Papers, col. 132, box 61, CBC 1951–1955.

143 J.B. Priestley and J. Hawkes, *Journey Down a Rainbow* (London: Readers Union, 1957), 43–4, cited in Nick Tiratsoo, "Limits of Americanisation: The United States Productivity Gospel in Britain," in Becky Conekin, Frank Mort, and Chris Waters, eds., *Moments of Modernity: Reconstructing Britain, 1945–1964* (London: Rivers Oram Press, 1999), 96.

144 Saskatchewan Arts Board, "Brief to Royal Commission on National Development in the Arts, Letters and Sciences," Oct. 1949, 3, NA, RCALS, RG 33/28, vol. 29, reel C-2014.

145 Robertson Davies, "The Individual and the Mass," *Saturday Night* (10 May 1958): 26.

CHAPTER FIVE

1 Morley Callaghan, "Canada's Creeping 'Me Too' Sickness," *Saturday Night* (13 April 1957): 18, 38. Callaghan's urge to champion a democratic aristocracy may have been informed by American critic Russell Lynes's *A Surfeit of Honey* (New York: Harper & Brothers, 1953), which was reprinted yearly through at least 1957, see especially chapter 2, "What Became of the Upper Class?"

2 Paul Litt, *The Muses, the Masses, and the Massey Commission* (Toronto: University of Toronto Press, 1992); Andrew Stewart and William Hull, *Canadian Television Policy and the Board of Broadcast Governors* (Edmonton: University of Alberta Press, 1994); Marc Raboy, *Missed Opportunities: The Story of Canada's Broadcasting Policy* (Montreal: McGill-Queen's University Press, 1990); J.L. Granatstein, "Culture and Scholarship: The First Ten Years of the Canada Council," *Canadian Historical Review* 65, no. 4 (Sept. 1984): 441–74; Frank Peers, *The Public Eye: Television and the Politics of Canadian Broadcasting, 1952–1968* (Toronto: University of Toronto Press, 1979).

3 George Salverson, "In the Shadow of the Bomb," 1 Jan. 1950, McM, CBC Scripts Collection, reel 98.

4 Malcolm Ross, *Our Sense of Identity* (Toronto: Ryerson, 1954); W.L. Morton, *The Canadian Identity* (Madison: University of Wisconsin Press, 1961); Blair Fraser, *The Search for Identity: Canada 1945–1967* (Garden City, NY: Doubleday, 1967); Robin Mathews, *Canadian Identity: Major Forces Shaping the Life of a People* (Ottawa: Steel Rail, 1988); Allan Smith, *Canada: An American Nation? Essays on Continentalism, Identity and the Canadian Frame of Mind* (Montreal: McGill-Queen's University Press, 1994).
5 On the anti-modernism of conservative cultural nationalists, see Massolin, *Canadian Intellectuals, the Tory Tradition, and the Challenge of Modernity* (Toronto: University of Toronto Press, 2001), 195–208.
6 Marshall McLuhan, "Why the CBC Must Be Dull," *Saturday Night* (16 Feb. 1957): 14.
7 C.P. Snow, *The Two Cultures,* ed. Stefan Collini (Cambridge: Canto, 1993).
8 Mavor Moore, "What Sputnik Has Done to the Arts," *Canadian Commentator* 2, no. 1 (Jan. 1958): 1–2.
9 Watson Kirkconnell, notes on rock 'n' roll, [1957], AUA, Watson Kirkconnell Papers, P4/36/2. This appears to have been a speech to an Acadia University Student Christian Movement group.
10 F.H. Underhill, "How Good Are Our Universities?" *Canadian Forum* 42, no. 503 (Dec. 1962): 199–201.
11 Canadian Arts Council, "Brief to the Royal Commission on Broadcasting," 22 Aug. 1956, 5, NA, Canadian Conference of the Arts, MG 28 I189, vol. 34, file 20, RCB. An earlier draft (18 May 1956) quoted writer/broadcaster Lister Sinclair: "this is a democracy and one of the principles of a democracy is that everyone should be allowed what they want. Not that everybody should have what most people want."
12 Morley Callaghan, "We're on the Wrong Track in Our Culture Quest," *Maclean's* (25 May 1957): 8, 86–7; Kenneth Forbes, "Don't Fall for the Modern Art Hoax," *Maclean's* (5 July 1958): 8, 50–2; J. Barry Toole, "That Culture Business," *Brunswickan,* 90, no. 26, 31 Jan. 1958, 3; Thelma H. McCormack, "Canada's Royal Commission on Broadcasting," *Public Opinion Quarterly* 23, no. 1 (spring 1959): 92–100.
13 Don Jamieson, address to the Western Association of Broadcasters, June 1957, 6–7, AO, CAAE Papers, series E-I-4, Library, miscellaneous, box 6. Jamieson was vice-president and general manager of CJON-TV in St John's and later president of the Canadian Association of Broadcasters. See especially the chapter "What the Public Wants" of his book on the broadcasting industry in Canada, *The Troubled Air* (Fredericton: Brunswick, 1962).
14 Donald Creighton to W.L. Morton, 29 Oct. 1957, McM, W.L. Morton Papers, box 6, f. 39, Creighton, Donald, 1955–1961.
15 Mavor Moore, "Critic on the Hearth," *Canadian Commentator* 1, no. 3 (March 1957): 13–14; "Snobs at Stratford," *Canadian Commentator* 1, no. 9 (Sept. 1957): 7–8; "Who Killed Agatha Christie? The Snobbery of the Critics," *Canadian Commentator* 1, no. 10 (Oct. 1957): 6–7.

16 The first two years of *Canadian Commentator's* run coincided roughly with the period the saw the formation of the Canada Council and the advent of the Board of Broadcast Governors. Relevant articles included Mavor Moore, "What Will the Council Counsel?" 1, no. 1 (Jan. 1957): 8; Marcus Long, "A Dangerous Proposal," 1, no. 4 (April 1957): 1–2; Pierre Dansereau, "Culture Is What We Are Concerned with," 1, no. 8 (Aug. 1957): 6; Robert Weaver, "What Canada Needs," 1, no. 9 (Sept. 1957): 9; "Bring on the Broadcast Commission," 2, no. 6 (June 1958): 16; and Raymond Varela, "Television and the Majority Rule, " 2, no. 11 (Nov. 1958): 9–10.
17 Watson Kirkconnell, notes on rock 'n' roll, [1957].
18 Ernest van den Haag, "Of Happiness and Despair We Have No Measure," in Bernard Rosenberg and David Manning White, eds., *Mass Culture: The Popular Arts in America* (New York: Macmillan, 1957), 512.
19 Claude T. Bissell, "Sputnik and the Humanities," speech to Humanities Association of Canada, 10 June 1958, Edmonton, reprinted in *Humanities Association Bulletin* 25 (Oct. 1958): 10–16.
20 Humanities Association of Canada, Fredericton Branch, brief submitted to the Royal Commission on Broadcasting, 1956, 1, NA, Royal Commission on Broadcasting (RCB), RG 33/36, vol. 33, reel C-7020.
21 Donald Creighton's presentation to Diefenbaker, 18 July 1958, McM, W.L. Morton Papers, box 3, f. 11, Canadian Broadcasting League.
22 Alan M. Thomas, "Audience, Market and Public – An Evaluation of Canadian Broadcasting," *Canadian Communications Canadiennes* 1, no. 1 (summer 1960): 27.
23 "Forgotten History," *Saturday Night* (29 March 1958): 42; Miriam Chapin, *Contemporary Canada* (New York: Oxford University Press, 1959), 3; Lorne Pierce, *A Canadian Nation* (Toronto: Ryerson, 1960), 36, 38–9.
24 J.A. Irving, "Culture and Society," n.d. [1960?] (typescript), 2–3, TFRB, J.A. Irving Papers, col. 132, box 45.
25 Hugh Garner, "Spoon-Fed Patriotism Won't Work in Canada," *Saturday Night* (29 March 1958): 8. Two years later, Garner recycled the same article in another magazine: "The Phony Cult of Canned Canadianism," *Maclean's* (21 May 1960): 8, 58, 60.
26 John McDade, "So B – – y Grim About Culture," *Canadian Commentator* 4, no. 4 (April 1960): 15–16.
27 *Citizens' Forum*, "Have We a National Identity?" (1963).
28 James R. Edgett, "The United Search of Canada," *Saturday Night* (1 Aug. 1959): 44.
29 Ramsay Cook, "Cultural Nationalism in Canada: An Historical Perspective," in Janice L. Murray, ed., *Canadian Cultural Nationalism: The Fourth Lester B. Pearson Conference on the Canada–U.S. Relationship* (New York: New York University Press, 1977), 15–44. Litt, *The Muses, the Masses, and the Massey Commission*, 4–6.

30 Robert Weaver, "What Canada Needs," *Canadian Commentator* 1, no. 9 (Sept. 1957): 9.
31 Julian Park, ed., *The Culture of Contemporary Canada* (Ithaca, NY: Cornell University Press, 1957), v, ix.
32 Harold A. Innis, *The Strategy of Culture* (Toronto: University of Toronto Press, 1952), 18–20.
33 Frank H. Underhill, "Canadian and American Ties with Europe," *Queen's Quarterly* 66, no. 3 (autumn 1959): 376.
34 Philip Marchand, *Marshall McLuhan: The Medium and the Messenger* (New York: Ticknor and Fields, 1989), especially chap. 7; Lawrence Grossberg, ed., "On Postmodernism and Articulation: An Interview with Stuart Hall," *Journal of Communication Inquiry* 10, no. 2 (1986): 45–60; Arthur Kroker, *Technology and the Canadian Mind: Innis, Grant, McLuhan* (New York: St Martin's, 1985); Joel Persky, "The Innescence of Marshall McLuhan," *Journal of Canadian Culture* 1, no. 2 (autumn 1984): 3–14.
35 Marshall McLuhan, address delivered at the 26th Annual Couchiching Conference, 3–10 Aug. 1957, reprinted in 26th Couchiching Conference, *National Values in a Changing World* (Toronto: CIPA/CAAE, 1957), 31.
36 McLuhan, "Our New Electronic Culture – The Role of Mass Communications in Meeting Today's Problems," *NAEB Journal* (Oct. 1958): 19–20, 24–6.
37 "He was soon to discover the automatism portrayed in *The Mechanical Bride* was yielding to a new tribalism. The study of this new tribalism would strip the last traces of moral earnestness from his prose and immerse him completely in the role of explorer, the relentless seeker of insights unhindered by the striking of moral attitudes." Marchand, *Marshall McLuhan*, 110.
38 McLuhan, "What Canadians Value in Their Reading," 32.
39 Fowler was president of Canadian Pulp and Paper Association. He had served on the Royal Commission on Dominion–Provincial Relations (Rowell–Sirois) and on the Wartime Prices and Trade Board. He was a member of the Canadian Institute for International Affairs and had presented its brief to the Massey Commission.
40 A.D. Dunton, presentation to the Royal Commission on Broadcasting (RCB), Ottawa, 30 April 1956, 22–50, NA, RCB, RG 33/36, reel C-7013.
41 Canadian Association of Radio and Television Broadcasters (CARTB), "Brief of the Canadian Association of Radio and Television Broadcasters," 15 March 1956, 14, NA, RCB, RG 33/36, vol. 25, reel C-7019.
42 CARTB, "Brief of the CARTB," 6–8.
43 CARTB, presentation to the RCB, Hearings, Ottawa, 3 May 1956, 543–610, NA, RCB, RG 33/36, reel C-7013. The CARTB made it clear that its membership opposed regulating the time devoted to certain types of programs, but clause 1 in the *Code of Ethics* (1943) of the Canadian Association of Broadcasters (its original name) committed it to a kind of proportional representation in programming. The 1943 code was included with the CARTB

presentation, having undergone no substantial revisions. NA, RCB, RG 33/36, vol. 25, reel C-7019. Like the CARTB, the directors of the Canadian Marconi Company, which owned CFCF in Montreal, saw broadcasting as little different from publishing and looked at any scheme for assessing the cultural value of a broadcast as silly. Canadian Marconi Company, brief to the RCB, Montreal, 15 April 1956, 7–10, NA, RCB, RG 33/36, vol. 34, reel C-7020.

44 Canadian Association of University Teachers, "Broadcasting in Canada," a brief presented to the RCB by the Canadian Association of University Teachers, (CAUT), 30 April 1956, 4, NA, RCB, RG 33/36, vol. 34, reel C-7020.

45 Humanities Association of Canada, Fredericton Branch, "Brief to Royal Commission on Broadcasting," 1956, 4, NA, RCB, RG 33/36, vol. 33, reel C-7020.

46 RCB, Hearings, Winnipeg, 7 May 1956, 1025, NA, RCB, RG 33/36, reel C-7013.

47 RCB, Hearings, Regina, 11 May 1956, 1417, NA, RCB, RG 33/36, reel C-7013.

48 RCB Hearings, Winnipeg, 7 May 1956, 885–6, 897, NA, RCB, RG 33/36, reel C-7013.

49 RCB, Hearings, Winnipeg, 7 May 1956, 973–1000, NA, RCB, RG 33/36, reel C-7013. The longer quotation comes from p. 979. McNaught does not attribute a source to Priestley's comment. The CAUT shared United College's opinion of the private stations, pointing out that minority tastes were likely to be ignored, especially in peak hours. CAUT, "Broadcasting in Canada," 5.

50 RCB, Hearings, Regina, 11 May 1956, 1400–1, NA, RCB, RG 33/36, reel C-7013.

51 University of Toronto Television Committee, "Educational Television in Canada: The University's Role," brief to RCB, 10 April 1956, 1, NA, RCB, RG 33/36, vol. 32, reel C-7019.

52 Canadian Federation of Newman Clubs, brief presented to the RCB, Halifax, 1956, 2, NA, RCB, RG 33/36, reel C-7020.

53 CAUT, "Broadcasting in Canada," 4. Another organization warned: "The advertising industry itself must take cognizance of the fact that the Canadian public wants quality and variety in its television programming and not meaningless and degrading forms of entertainment." Saskatchewan Arts Board, "Brief to the Royal Commission on Broadcasting, 1956," 3, NA, RCB, RG 33/36, reel C-7019.

54 Canadian Federation of University Women, "Brief to the Fowler Commission on the C.B.C.," Regina, 11 May 1956, 3, NA, RCB, RG 33/36, vol. 30, reel C-7019.

55 Humanities Association of Canada, Fredericton Branch, brief to Royal Commission on Broadcasting, 1956, 6, NA, RCB, RG 33/36, vol. 33, reel C-7020.

56 Canadian Federation of Newman Clubs, brief presented to the RCB, Halifax, 1956, 2–3, NA, RCB, RG 33/36, reel C-7020.

57 RCB, Hearings, Regina, 11 May 1956, 1436, NA, RCB, RG 33/36, reel C-7013.
58 RCB, Hearings, Vancouver, 14 May 1956, 1627, NA, RCB, RG 33/36, vol. 30, reel C-7014.
59 RCB, Hearings, Regina, 11 May 1956, 1502, NA, RCB, RG 33/36, reel C-7013.
60 Paul Rutherford, *When Television Was Young: Primetime Canada 1952–1967* (Toronto: University of Toronto Press, 1990). See especially chapter 8, "Culture on the Small Screen."
61 "Brief of a Group of Regina Housewives," RCB, Hearings, 11 May 1956, 1502–3, NA, RCB, RG 33/36, rell C-7013. Phyllis Levin, Juliet Shapiro, and June Mitchell represented the larger group. The Newman Club Alumni of the University of Manitoba advocated a fairly narrow range of topics for TV: "wholesome matters of scientific, artistic or sporting activities or reporting occasions of State." RCB, Hearings, 7 May 1956, 1009, NA, RCB, RG 33/36, reel C-7013.
62 Humanities Association of Canada, Fredericton Branch, brief to RCB, 1956, 3.
63 Saskatchewan Arts Board, "Brief to the Royal Commission on Broadcasting, 1956," 2, NA, RCB, RG 33/36, reel C-7019.
64 Humanities Association of Canada, Fredericton Branch, brief, 3–4.
65 Canadian Federation of University Women, "Brief," 1.
66 Association of Radio and Television Employees of Canada (NABET–CLC), "Submission to the Royal Commission on Broadcasting," 29 June 1956, 3, NA, RCB, RG 33/36, vol. 35, reel C-7021.
67 On the ambiguity and contention surrounding the idea of the folk, see Ian McKay, *The Quest of the Folk: Antimodernism and Cultural Selection in Twentieth-Century Nova Scotia* (Montreal: McGill-Queen's University Press, 1994).
68 RCB, Hearings, Vancouver, 14 May 1956, 1597–8, NA, RCB, RG 33/36, vol. 30, reel C-7014.
69 RCB, Hearings, Winnipeg, 8 May 1956, 1113, NA, RCB, RG 33/36, reel C-7013.
70 RCB, Hearings, Vancouver, 14 May 1956, 1626–7, NA, RCB, RG 33/36, reel C-7014.
71 Canadian Mental Health Association (CMHA), "Brief to the Royal Commission on Broadcasting," April 1956, 2, NA, RCB, RG 33/36, vol. 32, reel C-7019.
72 CMHA, "Brief," 4–5.
73 A.R.M. Lower, "Brief on the Question of Radio and Television Broadcasting for Submission to the Royal Commission of Inquiry on these Subjects," 1956, 16, NA, RCB, RG 33/36, exhibit 207, reel C-7020.
74 Marchand, *Marshall McLuhan*, 148.
75 A Brief submitted to the Royal Commission on Broadcasting by a number of citizens of Kingston, Ontario, 1956, 5–6, NA, RCB, RG 33/36, vol. 35, reel C-7021.

76 Thelma H. McCormack, "Canada's Royal Commission on Broadcasting," *Public Opinion Quarterly* 23, no. 1 (spring 1959): 96. During the hearings in Vancouver, Geoffrey Andrew (representing the UBC Television Committee), drew the distinction between anti-Americanism and developing "an alert self-consciousness." Brief presented by the University of British Columbia Television Committee, Vancouver, 14 May 1956, RCB, Hearings, 1588, NA, RCB, RG 33/36, reel C-7014.
77 "Memorandum on Broadcasting in Canada," 8 April 1958, NA, Donald Grant Creighton Papers, MG 31 D77, vol. 8, Canadian Broadcasting League, Correspondence and Memoranda.
78 "Bring on the Broadcast Commission," *Canadian Commentator* 2, no. 6 (June 1958): 16.
79 Mary Lowrey Ross, "The Fringe Audiences," *Saturday Night* (3 Jan. 1959): 25.
80 *Citizens' Forum* promotional pamphlet/schedule, 1957, NA, Neil M. Morrison Papers, MG 30 E 273, vol. 11, Brochures 1943–61.
81 Season schedules and individual study bulletins (late 1950s–early 1960s) for *Citizens' Forum*, 1949–63, located in John P. Robarts Library, University of Toronto, and in various archival collections – AO: CAAE Papers; CBC Radio Archives; NA: Canadian Citizenship Council Papers; Canada Foundation, CBC *Citizens' Forum*.
82 CAAE, National Council Meeting, 20 May 1958, Winnipeg, Canadian Citizenship Council Papers, NA, MG 28 I85, vol. 21, CAAE.
83 Peter Siegle, "Kitsch and U," *Food for Thought* 20, no. 3 (Dec. 1959): 107.
84 Geoff Andrew noted while appearing before the Fowler Commission in 1956: "Our national culture, even if not highly developed as yet, is a distinctive culture, and it embraces everything from hockey and lacrosse to the Group of Seven and Andrew Allan's radio drama. It further embraces everything from the Ballads of Newfoundland to the Salmon Derbies of the Pacific Coast." RCB, Hearings, Vancouver, 14 May 1956, 1596, NA, RCB, RG 33/36, vol. 30, reel C-7014.
85 Alphonse Ouimet, "Broadcasting – A Greater Challenge Than Ever," address to the Canadian Club of Toronto, 7 Dec. 1959, 3–4, AO, CAAE Papers, series A-II-2, box 1, Director's Files, 1960.
86 "This *Too* Is Canadian Culture!" CBC magazine advertisement (1961).
87 Bruce Hutchison, *Canada: Tomorrow's Giant* (Toronto: Longmans, Green and Company, 1957); and *The Unknown Country: Canada and Her People* (Toronto: Longmans, Green, 1943).
88 Robertson Davies, "Moderate and Middlebrow," *Saturday Night* (14 April 1956): 26.
89 One submission to the RBC thought very highly of American child expert Frank C. Baxter's assessment of television and its function as an educative medium, quoting him: "Your television set is not a vending machine for higher learning. It can, at best, be an invitation to knowledge. That in itself is very much. God bless TV if it opens our eyes to the hidden treasures that

await, for example, the reading of Robinson Crusoe. But God help us too, if the dramatized smattering on TV is all we ever get." Children's Section, Ontario Library Association, "Brief," NA, RCB, RG 33/36, vol. 32, reel C-7019.

90 Robert Fulford, "Television Notebook," *Canadian Forum* 40, no. 474 (July 1960): 90.

91 See Joan Shelley Rubin, "Self, Culture, and Self Culture in Modern America: The Early History of the Book-of-the-Month Club," *Journal of American History* 71, no. 4 (March 1985): 782–806; and Janice Radway, "The Scandal of the Middlebrow: The Book-of-the-Month Club, Class Fracture, and Cultural Authority," *South Atlantic Quarterly* 89, no. 4 (autumn 1990): 703–36.

92 G.P. Gilmour, ed., *Canada's Tomorrow* (Toronto: Macmillan, 1954); K.R. Swinton, "The Rehabilitation of the Egghead," *Canadian Commentator* 2, no. 5 (May 1958): 9.

93 F. David Hoeniger, "Shakespeare and His Theatre" (CAAE, 1958).

94 Advertisement, "Gems of Wisdom in the Words of the World's Greatest Thinkers," *Canadian Commentator* 3, no. 11 (Nov. 1959): 9–10.

95 "A Bookshelf of Canada," *Citizenship Items* 10, no. 6 (Nov. 1957). Robins was author of *The Incomplete Anglers* (Toronto: Collins, 1943) and editor of the early postwar anthology *A Pocketful of Canada* (Toronto: Collins, 1946).

96 Roy Little, "The Untutored Audience," *Food for Thought* 19, no. 6 (March 1959): 270–80.

97 Rutherford, *When Television Was Young*, 84.

98 Robert Fulford, "What's Behind the New Wave of TV Think Shows," *Maclean's* (5 Oct. 1963): 25–7, 61.

99 Livingston to members of the CBC Science Unit, 27 June 1963, NA, CBC, vol. 203, file 11-18-11-43, Science Programs.

100 See, for example, George Steele and Paul Kircher, *The Crisis We Face: Automation and the Cold War* (New York: McGraw-Hill, 1960).

101 Bernard Rosenberg, "Mass Culture in America," in Bernard Rosenberg and David Manning White, eds., *Mass Culture: The Popular Arts in America* (New York: Free Press, 1957), 11–12.

102 P.M. Richards, "Technology and Jobs," *Saturday Night* (4 May 1940): 11; M.M. Kirkwood, *Women and the Machine Age* Number 7 in The Machine Age Series (Toronto: Social Service Council of Canada, [1940]).

103 Lawren Harris et al., "Community Art Centres," *Canadian Art* 2, no. 2 (Dec. 1944–Jan. 1945): 62.

104 J.E. Middleton, "Are Machines Making Young Canada Soft?" *Saturday Night* (25 Jan. 1947): 11; Dyson Carter, "Speed-Up Brings Killing Diseases," *Canadian Tribune* (7 Dec. 1946): 11.

105 A.W. Blue, "The Machine – Is It Man's Enemy? Technological Unemployment Seen As Society's Most Serious Problem – A Study of Effects and

Possible Remedies," *Saturday Night* (11 July 1931): 21, 28; Eugene A. Forsey, *Unemployment in the Machine Age: Its Causes* no. 5 in The Machine Age Series (Toronto: Social Service Council of Canada, 1940); "Brave New Machine World," *Saturday Night* (20 Sept. 1952): 32; Norman DePoe, "Will a Machine Ever Take Your Job?" *Maclean's* (1 Oct. 1955): 20–1, 62–7; Fred Bodsworth, "What Science Will Do to Us," *Maclean's* (15 Oct. 1955): 16, 102–3, 105; British Columbia Federation of Labour, *What's Happening to Jobs? The Effects of Automation and Related Problems* (Vancouver, 1960).

106 *Oxford English Dictionary*, 2nd ed., J.A. Simpson and E.S.C. Weiner, eds., (Oxford: Clarendon, 1989), vol. I, 805–6. The OED lists 1948 as the term's earliest known appearance. Mary Lowrey Ross, "Miss A. and the Cybernetic Age," *Saturday Night* (11 Jan. 1949): 11; Eric Nicol, "The Machine," Jan. 1953, McM, CBC Scripts Collection, reel 82.

107 See, for example, George Soule, *What Automation Does to Human Beings* (London: Sidgewick and Jackson, 1956); Howard B. Jacobson and Joseph S. Roucek, *Automation and Society* (New York: Philosophical Library, 1959); Walter Buckingham, *Automation: Its Impact on Business and People* (New York: Harper Brothers, 1961), Donald Laird and Eleanor Laird, *How to Get along with Automation* (New York: McGraw-Hill, 1964); Ben Seligman, *A Most Notorious Victory: Man in an Age of Automation* (New York: Free Press/Macmillan, 1966); and George Terborgh, *Automation Hysteria* (New York: Norton, 1966).

108 Kildare R.E. Dobbs, "Automation and Art," *Canadian Forum* 36, no. 423 (April 1956): 8–9.

109 Canadian Institute on Public Affairs Winter Week-End Conference, "Automation – What It Means to You." Upper Canada College, Toronto, 25–26 Feb. 1956.

110 Panel Presentation: "Automation for Canada: Today and To-morrow," 26, in "Automation – What It Means To You." NA, CBC, RG 41, vol. 895, file PG8-1-4-2, pt. 1, Couchiching Conference.

111 Canadian Federation of University Women, "Brief to the Fowler Commission on the C.B.C.," Regina, 11 May 1956, 2, RG 33/36, vol. 30, reel C-7019. Adult education became especially important, since the "intellectual demands" on workers increased apace. University of Toronto Television Committee, "Educational Television in Canada: The University's Role," 1.

112 J.R. Kidd, "The Challenge of Automation," *Food for Thought* 18, no. 5 (Feb. 1958): 214; E.G.D. Murray, ed., Royal Society of Canada, *Our Debt to the Future*, Symposium Presented on the Seventy-fifth Anniversary, 1957 (Toronto: University of Toronto, 1958).

113 United Church of Canada, "Report of the Toronto Committee on Automation," (1957), TFRB, J.A. Irving Papers, col. 132, box 45.

114 John A. Irving, "Can Machines Replace Minds?" *Saturday Night* (8 June 1957): 10–11, 38–9.

115 Geoffrey Vickers, *The Undirected Society: Essays on the Human Implications of Industrialization in Canada* (Toronto: University of Toronto Press, 1959), 39.
116 Bruce Hutchison, "The Coming Revolt against Leisure," *Maclean's* (15 March 1958): 19, 52.
117 Ian Vorres, "Beauty in the Machine Age," *Saturday Night* (1 Aug. 1959): 10–11.
118 Roy Daniells, "Poetry and the Novel," in Julian Park, ed., *The Culture of Contemporary Canada* (Ithaca, NY: Cornell University Press, 1957), 25.
119 William A. Westley, "The Workers Automation Wants," *Executive Decision* (Feb. 1959): 56–7.
120 Alastair W. MacLeod, "Personal Satisfactions," in *Round Table on Man and Industry* (Toronto: University of Toronto, 1958), 15–16.
121 R.S. Hosking, "What's the Matter with Father?" *Toronto Star Weekly Magazine* (21 Nov. 1959): 40–1, 58. Hosking "blamed the changing status of men upon the changing role of women." Christie, "Sacred Sex: The United Church and the Privatization of the Family in Post-war Canada," in Christie, ed., *Households of Faith: Family, Gender and Community in Canada, 1760–1969* (Montreal: McGill-Queen's University Press, 2002).
122 "Toward a Christian Understanding of Sex, Love, Marriage," First Report of the Commission on Christian Marriage and Divorce, (1960), 3, UCA, Commission on Christian Marriage and Divorce, 82.084C, box 1, f. 14; Crossley W. Krug, "The Causes of Divorce" (Aug. 1961), UCCA, Commission on Christian Marriage and Divorce, box 3, f. 28, Briefs 1961.
123 Alf Harris, "The Wonderful Robot," broadcast 8 March 1956. Donald Jack, "The Proof Machine," broadcast 14 April 1956; anon., "Your World on a Plastic Platter," broadcast 19 April 1956; Alf Harris, "The Future of the Past," broadcast on *Prairie Playhouse*, 14 July 1961; Hugh R. Oldham, "The Day the Bomb Went Off," broadcast 29 Nov. 1956; Robert Sherman Townes, "Who Destroyed the Earth?" adapted by George Salverson, broadcast 19 April 1957; Lister Sinclair, "The View From Here Is Yes! – A Nativity Play from the Modern Point of View," broadcast 13 Dec. 1961; Donald Jack, "The Looking Glass World," TV drama, 11 Oct. 1962. McM, CBC Script Collection, various reels.
124 William Paluk, "Let the Machines Do It," 7 April 1961, McM, CBC Scripts Collection, reel 85.
125 "Action to Offset Automation Urged," *Toronto Daily Star*, 19 Aug. 1960, 14; "The Friendly Monster," *Toronto Telegram*, 3 May 1961, 3; "Some Human Consequences of Our Increasing Industrialization," *Royal Bank of Canada Monthly Letter* (Oct. 1961); Sir Geoffrey Vickers, "The Impact of Automation on Society," in *Automation and Social Change* (Toronto: Government of Ontario, 1963), 41–54.
126 "The United Church and the Onrushing Robots," *Maclean's* (19 Sept. 1964): 32.

127 John Maclure, "Are People Obsolete Already?" *Maclean's* (3 Oct. 1964): 20, 36–9; June Callwood, "Tomorrow's Here and We're All Set for Yesterday," *Maclean's* (23 Jan. 1965): 7, 24–8; Harry Bruce, "Can We Stand Life without Work?" *Saturday Night* (April 1965): 22–4.
128 W.L. Morton, "Convocation Address, Brandon College, 1964," McM, W.L. Morton Papers, box 52, Lectures, A–Confederation.
129 J. Franklin Reed, Galt, Ont., letter to the editor, *Maclean's* (28 Sept. 1957): 4.
130 Edmund Carpenter, "The New Languages," *Explorations* 7 (March 1957): 4–21.
131 James S. Thomson, "The Challenge of Existentialism," in Ralph C. Chalmers and John A. Irving, eds., *Challenge and Response: Modern Ideas and Religion* (Toronto: Ryerson, 1959), 73–4.
132 Session: "Values in the Making," 32nd Annual Couchiching Conference, "Values in Conflict," 28 July–1 Aug. 1963, NA, reference copy at: R2818–21, 2822.
133 George Grant, "An Ethic of Community," in Michael Oliver, ed., *Social Purpose for Canada* (Toronto: University of Toronto Press, 1961), 13. The appearance of this collection coincided with the transformation of the CCF into the NDP and with the last years of Grant's affiliation with social-democratic politics.
134 Rosenberg, "Mass Culture in America," 9.
135 "It's the Striving That Matters," *Citizenship Items* 12, no. 1 (Jan.–Feb. 1959): 8.
136 *OED*, 2nd ed., vol. I, 805–6.
137 Cited in Valerie Joyce Korinek, "'Roughing It in Suburbia': Reading *Chatelaine* Magazine, 1950–1969," PhD dissertation, University of Toronto, 1996, 43.
138 Malcolm Ross, "Introduction," in Ross, ed., *The Arts in Canada: A Stocktaking at Mid-century* (Toronto: Ryerson, 1958), 4.
139 "Forgotten History," *Saturday Night* (29 March 1958): 42.
140 Mary Lowrey Ross, "Folk Ways of Television," *Saturday Night* (10 May 1958): 24.

CHAPTER SIX

1 [Peter C. Newman], "1967 Birthday Party," *Maclean's* (7 Dec. 1957): 1. Although Marshall McLuhan had argued earlier in the decade that baseball merited consideration as a cultural activity, his remained a minority viewpoint. McLuhan, "Baseball Is Culture," broadcast on CBC *Wednesday Night*, 24 Sept. 1952.
2 Newman had gathered some more gossip about preparations for the Centennial, including speculation about a new flag and anthem, changes to immigration regulations, and a televised survey of Canada's history. Newman, "Canada's Centennial," *Maclean's* (5 Dec. 1959): 1; "What about

1967?" *Citizenship Items* 12, no. 3 (May–June 1959): 3; "1967: What'll We Do?" *Maclean's* (23 Sept. 1961): 1.

3 The quotation is from Doug Owram's *Born at the Right Time: A History of the Baby-Boom Generation* (Toronto: University of Toronto Press, 1996), in which the author gives an account of 1960s' radicalism in Canada; see especially chapters 8 and 9. Owram considers the development of youth activism a process that took some time: "Between early 1964 and the end of 1966, the youth subcultures merged and became politicized" (190). Massolin, *Canadian Intellectuals, the Tory Tradition, and the Challenge of Modernity* (Toronto: University of Toronto Press, 2001), 270, See also J.L. Granatstein, *Canada 1957–1967: The Years of Uncertainty and Innovation* (Toronto: McClelland and Stewart, 1985); Robert Bothwell, Ian Drummond, and John English, *Canada since 1945: Power, Politics and Provincialism*, rev. ed. (Toronto: University of Toronto Press, 1989); Alvin Finkel, *Our Lives: Canada after 1945* (Toronto: J. Lorimer, 1997). See also Ron Verzuh, *Underground Times: Canada's Flower-Child Revolutionaries* (Toronto: Deneau, 1989), and Myrna Kostash, *Long Way from Home: The Story of the Sixties Generation in Canada* (Toronto: J. Lorimer, 1980)

4 Pierre Berton, *1967: The Last Good Year* (Toronto: Doubleday, 1997); Peter Aykroyd, *The Anniversary Compulsion: Canada's Centennial Celebrations, A Model Mega-Anniversary* (Toronto: Dundurn Press, 1992)

5 For a different perspective on the cultural selectivity of Centennial and Expo authorities, see Richard Gordon Kicksee, " 'Scaled Down to Size': Contested Liberal Commonsense and the Negotiation of 'Indian Participation' in the Canadian Centennial Celebrations and Expo '67, 1963–1967," MA thesis, Queen's University, 1995.

6 On this transition within Canadian public broadcasting, see Marc Raboy, *Missed Opportunities: The Story of Canada's Broadcasting Policy* (Montreal: McGill-Queen's University Press, 1990), 12.

7 Robert Weaver to Bruce Raymond et al., 27 June 1962. National Archives of Canada, Andrew Allan Papers, MG 31 D56, vol. 30, CBC Wednesday Night.

8 Originally a small-scale educational program for Sunday school teachers in upstate New York, the chautauqua movement grew to inspire an independent initiative – the tent shows with which Canadians were familiar. Sheila Jameson, *Chautauqua in Canada* (Calgary: Glenbow/Alberta Institute, 1979). On the original movement, see Theodore Morrison, *Chautauqua: A Center for Education, Religion, and the Arts in America* (Chicago: University of Chicago Press, 1974).

9 See Helen Davies, "The Politics of Participation: A Study of Canada's Centennial Celebration," PhD dissertation, University of Manitoba, 1999. Davies is not actively concerned with the Centennial as contested political territory. Readers interested in that aspect of its history should see Aykroyd, *The Anniversary Compulsion*, and the "Centennial Summer" chapter of

Judy LaMarsh's *Memoirs of a Bird in a Gilded Cage* (Toronto: McClelland and Stewart, 1969), which present sharply conflicting visions of the Centennial Commission.

10 John Fisher, *John Fisher Reports: An Anthology of Radio Scripts* (Hamilton: Niagara Editorial Bureau, 1949); CBC-TV *Newsmagazine*, "A Tale of Two Fairs," 13 July 1965. CBC Radio Archives, Toronto, 850122-9(2); Robert Fulford, *This Was Expo* (Toronto: McClelland and Stewart, 1968), 12.

11 Arthur Marwick, *The Sixties: Cultural Revolution in Britain, France, Italy, and the United States, c.1958–c.1974* (Oxford: Oxford University Press, 1998). On the politicization of American youths in the 1960s, see Rebecca E. Klatch, *A Generation Divided: The New Left, the New Right, and the 1960s* (Berkeley: University of California Press, 1999).

12 Hugh Maclennan, "Two Solitudes Revisited," *Maclean's* (14 Dec. 1964): 27.

13 Norman Creighton, "The Royal Reader," broadcast Sept. 1964, CBC Halifax, 5, Dalhousie University Archives, Norman Creighton Papers, MS-2, 689, G-564.

14 June Callwood, "Is God Obsolete?" *Maclean's* (6 Aug. 1966): 7–9, 31–2. Mary Quayle Innis, "That 'Wild and Wicked' University," *United Church Observer* (1 Sept. 1966): 16–17. Pierre Berton, *The Comfortable Pew: A Critical Look at the Church in the New Age* (Toronto: McClelland and Stewart, 1965), is an extended look at the Anglican church and its apparent inability to make itself relevant to modern Canadian life.

15 Moncrieff Williamson, FRSA, "The New Museums and Art Galleries: 1967 and After," discussion paper at Seminar '65 (1965), D-2, NAC, Records of the Canadian Broadcasting Corporation, RG 41, vol. 853, file PG1–26 pt. 1, Canadian Conference on the Arts, 1962–67.

16 Jacques Ellul, *The Technological Society*, trans: John Wilkinson (New York: Vintage, 1964), from *La technique ou l'enjeu du siècle* (1954).

17 "How to Make the New Canada," *Maclean's* (8 Feb. 1964): 24–6, 36–43.

18 Frank Underhill, "The Scholar: Man Thinking," in George Whalley, ed., *A Place of Liberty: Essays on the Government of Canadian Universities* (Toronto: Clarke Irwin, 1964), 66. On Underhill's affiliations, see R. Douglas Francis, *Frank H. Underhill: Intellectual Provocateur* (Toronto: University of Toronto Press, 1986), chaps. 12 and 13.

19 Paul Rutherford, *When Television was Young: Primetime Canada, 1952–1967* (Toronto: University of Toronto Press, 1990), 110–11.

20 "The Implications of Automation for Leisure, Education, Mental and Physical Health, Law and the Community," panel discussion at conference "The Effects of Changing Technology on Canadian Society," 4–5 Jan. 1965; Robert Fulford, "The Anti-Boredom Riots," *Toronto Daily Star*, 4 March 1965, 37; Abraham Rotstein and Melville H. Watkins, "The Outer Man: Technology and Alienation," *Canadian Forum* 45, no. 535 (Aug. 1965): 105; "Science and the Arts in the Great Society," in John Irwin, ed., *Great*

Societies and Quiet Revolutions, 35th Annual Couchiching Conference, 30–31 July 1966 (Toronto: CBC, 1967), 56–88; Meeting Notice, "Christian Man in an Automated Society," 16 Jan. 1966, United Church of Canada, Commission on Automation, fonds 501, 82.131C (UCC GC 21 C5A8), folders 3 and 4, Background Papers.

21 Robert Fulford, "Starburst at the CBC," *Canadian Forum* 45, no. 536 (Sept. 1965): 124.

22 Frank Peers, "The Nationalist Dilemma in Canadian Broadcasting," in Peter Russell, ed. *Nationalism in Canada* (Toronto: McGraw-Hill, 1966), 252–3.

23 A.R.M. Lower, "Administrators and Scholars," *Queen's Quarterly* 71, no. 2 (Summer 1964): 203–05.

24 H.W. Macdonnell, "Our Universities on a Perilous Road," *Canadian Commentator* 10, no. 3 (March 1966): 4–5; Clifford Solway, "The CBC Is No Longer Important," *Saturday Night* (June 1966): 25–6.

25 James Gonsalves, "CBC Publications," *Canadian Forum* 47, no. 559 (Aug. 1967): 103.

26 Gonsalves, "CBC Publications," 104.

27 Raymond Williams, *Communications,* 3rd ed. (London: Penguin, 1976), 114.

28 Dennis Braithwaite, "Petticoat Perfection," *Toronto Globe and Mail,* 6 Feb. 1964, 23.

29 Alphonse Ouimet, Speech to the Canadian Centenary Council, Charlottetown, 27 May 1964, 9–12, NA, Records of the Centennial Commission, RG 69, vol. 20, file 1–9–29–1, Canadian Broadcasting Corporation.

30 Print ad, "Collect Canada Centennial Picture Cards," *Maclean's* (1 Dec. 1965): 25.

31 R.T. Bowman to A.E. Powley, 8 June 1964, NA, Records of the Canadian Broadcasting Corporation, RG 41, vol. 821, file 43, pt. 1, Centennial of Confederation. Powley was CBC special programs officer for history. Bowman's father, Charles, had also been a member of radio's pioneering Aird Commission, and Bowman himself worked as an assistant to General Manager Ernest Bushnell at the CBC. He left the CBC during the war and became involved in local broadcasting. He presented a brief to the Royal Commission on Broadcasting in 1956 on behalf of station CKLG Vancouver.

32 Memorandum to Cabinet, re: National Centennial Administration, 23 July 1963, NA, Records of the Centennial Commission, RG 69, vol. 384, Background Material, 1962–64.

33 "The Centennial and Sports and Hobbies," speech by H. Veiner, 13 June 1966, NA, Records of the Centennial Commission, RG 69, vol. 387, 7th National Conference, Victoria 1966, Speeches.

34 Transcript of interview with John W. Fisher, 1965, 12. NA, Records of the Centennial Commission, RG 69, vol. 20, file 1–9–29–2, CBC.

35 Canada, Centennial Commission, *The Centennial and Canadians: a Report of Centennial Activities, 1966–1967* (Ottawa: Centennial Commission, 1967), 46–7.

36 Paul Arthur to Peter H. Aykroyd, 13 Nov. 1963; Peter H. Aykroyd to Management Committee, National Centennial Administration, Memo re: Centennial Symbol, 11 Dec. 1963, NA, Records of the Centennial Commission, RG 69, vol. 150, file 4-1-5, sub. 1, vol. 1, Centennial Symbol.
37 Commercial enterprises were able to use the symbol through a licensing agreement which stipulated that products associated with the symbol must be "for the most part" made in Canada and that the design guidelines must be followed. Canada, Centennial Commission, *Centennial Symbol/Graphics Manual* (Ottawa: Queen's Printer, 1965), 1-3.
38 Martine Cardin to Expo 67, 28 Jan. 1965; C.D. Williams to Lester B. Pearson, 6 April 1965, NA, Records of the Centennial Commission, RG 69, vol. 150, file 4-1-5, Centennial Symbol.
39 Canada, Centennial Commission, *Centennial Facts 2: Confederation Train and Caravans* (Ottawa: 1967), 4.
40 F.W. Beal to Robbins Elliott, 30 July 1963; Robbins Elliott to John Fisher, 15 Nov. 1963, NA, Records of the Centennial Commission, RG 69, vol. 157, file 4-1-6, Centennial Train and Caravan. On the Freedom Train as an attempt to package an American national tradition during the early Cold War era, see Michael Kammen, *Mystic Chords of Memory: The Transformation of Tradition in American Culture* (New York: Knopf, 1991), chap. 17.
41 Centennial Commission, Working Paper No. 2, "Confederation Train and Caravans – Comparisons between the relative merits of the two trains," 4 Feb. 1964, NA, Records of the Centennial Commission, RG 69, vol. 5, file 1-2-7-1, Exhibit Sub-Committee.
42 Of the roughly $158 million spent on Centennial projects (excluding buildings), in excess of $47 million went towards the train and caravans, with the remainder distributed for such events and publications as the Voyageur Canoe Pageant and the *Dictionary of Canadian Biography* and towards publicity and smaller projects. Aykroyd, *The Anniversary Compulsion*, Appendix J, 198-9.
43 "The Confederation Caravans," information release from Centennial Commission, May 1967, 5-8, NA, Records of the Centennial Commission, RG 69, vol. 19, file 1-9-27, part 4, National Film Board.
44 Canada, Centennial Commission, "Progress Report on Projects of National Significance for the Celebration of Canada's Centennial of Confederation," 15 Nov. 1965.
45 Centennial poster series, "What Can I Do for Centennial?" (1967).
46 George Grant's *Lament for a Nation* is probably the most familiar here, but he wrote at least three of the essays that became his *Technology and Empire: Perspectives on North America* (Toronto: House of Anansi, 1969) before 1967. See also Philip Stratford, "Two Cults or One Culture?" *Saturday Night* (June 1964): 30-2; John W. Abrams, "The Potential of Technology," National Conference on Canadian Goals, Fredericton, 1964; John Gellner, "Need We Already Lament for Canada?" *Canadian Commentator* 9, no. 5

(May 1965): 3–5; McMaster University Archives, W.L. Morton Papers, box 64, f. 1; Kenneth McNaught, "National Affairs," *Saturday Night* (Aug. 1965): 7–10; Abraham Rotstein and Melville H. Watkins, "The Outer Man: Technology and Alienation," *Canadian Forum* 45, no. 535 (Aug. 1965): 105; John Kettle, "Marshall McLuhan: Prophet and Analyst of the Age of Instant Knowledge: Easing the Technological Burden of Western Man," *Canada Month* (Oct. 1965): 10–12; C.J. Eustace, "Religion, Scientific Revolution, and Social Schizophrenia," *Culture* 26 (1965): 13–31; E.D. Fulton, "Nationalism and North America," Extracts from Opening Remarks, Panel Discussion at the University of Toronto, 12 Feb. 1967, McMaster University Archives, W.L. Morton Papers, box 64, f. 5, Couchiching Conference.

47 Elizabeth Kilbourn, "Toronto's New Airport," *Canadian Forum* 43, no. 517 (Feb. 1964): 257–8.

48 "The New World of Leisure," script, National Film Board exhibit at the C.N.E. Pavilion, 1965, NA, Records of the Centennial Commission, RG 69, vol. 19, file 1-9-27, part 3, National Film Board.

49 Peter Desbarats, "Canada's First World's Fair," *Maclean's* (5 Oct. 1963): 17–21.

50 "What Seattle's 1962 World Fair Will Do for Canada," *Maclean's* (6 Jan. 1962): 1.

51 Robert Metcalfe, "Holiday Weekend at the World's Fair," *Maclean's* (30 June 1962): 20–1. For another perspective on the Seattle fair, see "James Gilbert", *Redeeming Culture: American Religion in an Age of Science* (Chicago: University of Chicago Press, 1997), chap. 13.

52 An alternative or perhaps "sub-theme" of the fair appeared to be "Man in a Shrinking Globe in an Expanding Universe." *Remembering the Future: The New York World's Fair from 1939–1964* (New York: Rizzoli, 1989); Bruce Nicholson, *Hi, Ho, Come to the Fair: Tales of the New York World's Fair of 1964–1965* (Huntington Beach, Calif.: Pelagian Press, 1989). On both New York fairs, see Roland Marchand and Michael L. Smith, "Corporate Science on Display," in Ronald G. Walters, ed., *Scientific Authority and Twentieth Century America* (Baltimore: Johns Hopkins University Press, 1997), 148–82. On the 1939 fair and others held in the United States during the 1930s, see the excellent study by Robert W. Rydell, *World of Fairs: The Century of Progress Expositions* (Chicago: University of Chicago Press, 1993). On the New York fair and the popularization of science, see Peter J. Kuznick, "Losing the World of Tomorrow: The Battle over the Presentation of Science at the 1939 New York World's Fair," *American Quarterly* 46, no. 3 (Sept. 1994): 341–73.

53 Lister Sinclair, "Achievements Section: Preamble and Synopsis of Storyline," n.d., [1964], 1–2, NA, Records of the Centennial Commission, RG 69, vol. 25, file 1-15-1, vol. I, Expo 67.

54 Canadian Corporation for the 1967 World Exhibition, "First Annual Report, for the Year 1963," 2, NA, Canadian Corporation for the World Exhibition, RG 71, vol. 1, ARC 71/1/1, 1st Annual Report.

55 Marshall Delaney [Robert Fulford], "The Corporation Requests General Restraint," *Saturday Night* (May 1967): 20–1, 23, 24–5.
56 Gabrielle Roy, "Introduction: The Theme Unfolded," in *Terre des Hommes – Man and His World* (Ottawa: Canadian Corporation for the 1967 World Exhibition, 1967), 32.
57 Canadian Corporation for the 1967 World Exhibition, *General Report on the 1967 World Exhibition* (Ottawa: Queen's Printer, 1969), 33.
58 Minutes of the Tenth Meeting of the Board of Directors, 7 June 1963, 3. NA, Canadian Corporation for the World Exhibition, RG 71, vol. 152, Board of Directors. The group that gathered at Montebello, Quebec, included A.D. Dunton, co-chair of the Bilingualism and Biculturalism Commission; former member of the Massey Commission N.A.M. Mackenzie; neurologist Wilder Penfield; and F.R. Scott, dean of law at McGill. Lucien Piché to Bienvenu, 31 May 1963, "Le Theme 'Terre des Hommes' et son Developpement à l'Exposition Universelle Canadienne de Montréal en 1967," NA, Canadian Corporation for the World Exhibition, RG 71, vol. 155, Part 10, Notes Sommaires.
59 Irene Howard, "Creative Man and His World: Three Interpretations at EXPO," *Canadian Forum* 47, no. 560 (Sept. 1967): 137.
60 Timothy Raison, "Our Friend Technology," *Expo 67 Newsletter* (25 May 1967).
61 Commissioner General for Government Participation, 1967 Exhibition, "Canadian Government Participation, 1967 Exhibition" [1964], Appendix, NA, Records of the Centennial Commission, RG 69, vol. 25, file 1–15–1, vol. I, Expo 67.
62 Including such distinguished academic and public figures as Gunnar Myrdal and Linus Pauling, this series was notable because people of this stature did not absolutely take it over. A range of noted experts spoke in plain terms about advances in their own fields and often addressed the theme of Expo. The series was published as *Man and His World – Terre des Hommes: The Noranda Lectures, Expo 67* (Toronto: University of Toronto Press, 1968).
63 Eileen Howard, *Expo Summer* (Toronto: Doubleday Canada, 1969).
64 Harvey Cox, "McLuhanite Christianity at Expo 67," *Commonweal* 86, no. 10 (26 May 1967): 277.
65 Robert Fulford, *This Was Expo* (Toronto: McLlelland and Stewart, 1968), 88, 96.
66 Historical work on the 1960s as it unfolded in the English-speaking world outside Canada constitutes a large literature. Some of the more recent and/or comprehensive of these studies include Marwick, *The Sixties: Cultural Revolution in Britain, France, Italy, and the United States, c. 1958–c.1974* (Oxford: Oxford University Press, 1998); David Steigerwald, *The Sixties and the End of Modern America* (New York: St Martin's Press, 1995); David Farber, *The Age of Great Dreams: America in the 1960s* (New York: Hill and Wang, 1994); Elizabeth Nelson, *The British Counter*

Culture, 1966–73: A Study of the Underground Press (Basingstoke: Macmillan, 1989); Todd Gitlin, *The Sixties: Years of Hope, Days of Rage* (New York: Pantheon, 1987); and Robert Hewison, *Too Much: Art and Society in the Sixties 1960–75* (London: Methuen, 1986).
67 The term *counterculture* was first used by Theodore Roszak in his *The Making of a Counter Culture: Reflections on the Technocratic Society and Its Youthful Opposition,* first pub. 1969 (Berkeley, Calif.: University of California Press, 1995).
68 Harold Arthur, "A Modest Centennial Project," *Family Herald* 14 (7 July 1966): 23; see also NA, Records of the Centennial Commission, RG 69, vol. 180, file 4–1–101, Company of Centennial Hitchhikers.
69 W.L. Morton, "Address to Senior Graduates," University of Manitoba, 26 May 1967, McM, W.L. Morton Papers, box 55, Lectures, No–W.
70 Stewart Goodings, "Constructive Dissent and the CYC," *Canadian Forum* 47, no. 561 (Oct. 1967): 160–2.
71 Owram, *Born at the Right Time*, 216.

CONCLUSION

1 E.A. Corbett, *We Have with Us Tonight …* (Toronto: Ryerson, 1957), 222.
2 E.M. Forster, What I Believe," in *Two Cheers for Democracy* (London: Edward Arnold, 1951), 82 (emphasis added).
3 Morley Callaghan, "Canada's Creeping 'Me Too' Sickness," *Saturday Night* (13 April 1957): 38.
4 Adeline Haddow, "A Modern Background for Today's Woman," *Saturday Night* (12 Sept. 1942): 26–8.
5 "The Little King," *Printed Word* 183 (Dec. 1949): 3.
6 Jürgen Habermas, *The Structural Transformation of the Public Sphere: An Inquiry into a Category of Bourgeois Society,* trans. Thomas Burger and Frederick Lawrence (Cambridge, Mass.: MIT Press, 1991).
7 S.K. Jaffary, "The Social Services," in C.A. Ashley, ed., *Reconstruction in Canada* (Toronto: University of Toronto Press, 1943), 111–12.
8 Paul Litt, *The Muses, the Masses, and the Massey Commission* (Toronto: University of Toronto Press, 1992), 18 and 83–120.
9 Editorial from the Orillia Daily Packet, n.d. [Aug. 1964?], cited in "Order and Good Government: A report on the 33rd Annual Couchiching Conference – July 25–31, 1964," NA, RG 41, vol. 895, file PG 8–1–4–2, pt. 2, Couchiching Conference.
10 Owram, *Born at the Right Time A History of the Baby-Boom Generation* (Toronto: University of Toronto Press, 1996), 229–30.
11 Northrop Frye, *The Modern Century: The Whidden Lectures 1967* (Toronto: University of Toronto Press, 1967), 28–9.
12 B.K. Sandwell, "War Gets Things Done," *Saturday Night* (22 March 1941): 14.

Bibliography

PRIMARY SOURCES

Manuscript Collections

ACADIA UNIVERSITY ARCHIVES (AUA), WOLFVILLE, NOVA SCOTIA
Watson Kirkconnell Papers

ARCHIVES OF ONTARIO (AO), TORONTO
Canadian Association for Adult Education

DALHOUSIE UNIVERSITY ARCHIVES (DUA), HALIFAX
W. Graham Allen Papers, MS-2 96
Norman Creighton Papers, MS-2 689
Herbert Leslie Stewart Papers, MS-2 45

MCGILL UNIVERSITY ARCHIVES (MUA), MONTREAL
John Grierson Collection, MG 2067
F. Cyril James Papers, MG 1017

McMASTER UNIVERSITY ARCHIVES (McM), HAMILTON
CBC Script Collection
John Coulter Papers

NATIONAL ARCHIVES OF CANADA (NA), OTTAWA
Manuscript Groups
Andrew Allan, MG 31 D56
H.R.C. Avison, MG 30 D102
Morley Callaghan, MG 30 D365

Canada Foundation, MG 28 I179
Canadian Citizenship Council, MG 28 I85
Canadian Conference of the Arts, MG 28 I189
Canadian Institute on Public Affairs, MG 28 I144
Charles Fraser Comfort, MG30 D81
Donald Creighton, MG 31 D77
Lawren Harris, MG 30 D208
Walter Herbert, MG 30 D205
Clarence Decatur Howe, MG 27 III B20
Arthur Lismer, MG 30 D184
Marshall McLuhan, MG 31 D156
Jean Hunter Morrison, MG 30 D265
Neil Morrison, MG 28 I400
George Raleigh Parkin, MG 30 D77
Frank Shuster, MG 31 D251
Robert Alexander Sim, MG 30 D260
Lister Sinclair, MG 31 D44
Julia Grace Wales, MG 30 D238
Charlotte Elizabeth Whitton, MG 30 E256

Government Record Groups
Canadian Broadcasting Corporation, RG 41
Canadian Corporation for the World Exhibition (Expo '67), RG 71
Centennial Commission, RG 69
National Film Board, RG 53, Part II, 2.1.2 McGill Study of Expo 67, 1967–69
Records of Parliament, RG 14, 1987–88/146 (39), Reconstruction
Royal Commission on Broadcasting, RG 33/36
Royal Commission on National Development in the Arts, Letters and Sciences, RG 33/28
Wartime Information Board, RG 36/31

QUEEN'S UNIVERSITY ARCHIVES (QUA), KINGSTON
Joseph Alexander Gray Papers
A.R.M. Lower Papers, coll. no. 5072
Robert Charles Wallace Papers, coll. 1024

UNITED CHURCH OF CANADA ARCHIVES (UCCA), TORONTO
Board of Information and Stewardship Fonds, 83.001C
Broadcasting Department, 98.030C
Commission on Automation, Fonds 501, 82.131C
Commission on Christian Marriage and Divorce, 82.084C
Commission on Church, Nation and World Order

Ashley W. Lindsay Papers, 86. 304C
Claris Edwin Silcox Papers, 86.208C

UNIVERSITY OF BRITISH COLUMBIA SPECIAL COLLECTIONS AND ARCHIVES, (UBCSCA), VANCOUVER
N.A.M. MacKenzie Papers
Leonard C. Marsh Papers

UNIVERSITY OF NEW BRUNSWICK ARCHIVES (UNBA), FREDERICTON
Alfred Goldsworthy Bailey, UA RG 80
Brunswickan
Burton S. Keirstead Papers, UA RG 81

UNIVERSITY OF SASKATCHEWAN ARCHIVES AND SPECIAL COLLECTIONS (USASK), SASKATOON
George E. Britnell Papers
Vernon C. Fowke Papers
Pamphlet Collection

UNIVERSITY OF TORONTO ARCHIVES (UTA)
Harold Adams Innis Papers, Accessions B72–0003, B72–0025
John A. Irving Papers, MS. col. 132

Periodicals

FULLY CITED IN BIBLIOGRAPHY
- periodicals for which 1939–67 runs exist and which I reviewed in their entirety (*Canadian Forum*, *Maclean's*, and *Saturday Night*)
- periodicals reviewed over a shorter run, or not reviewed in their entirety (for example, *Canadian Commentator, Here and Now*, and *New Frontiers*)
- periodicals with varying publication histories, containing articles retrieved specifically because of topical relevance rather than as the result of an issue-by-issue review (for example, *New Trail* and *Queen's Quarterly*)

FULLY CITED IN NOTES
Canadian Art
Canadian Author (and Bookman)
Canadian Forum
Culture (Revue trimestrielle des sciences religeuses et profanes)
Echoes
Food for Thought

Here and Now
Maclean's
National Home Monthly
New Frontiers
New Trail
Queen's Quarterly
Reading
Saturday Night
United Church Observer
University of Toronto Quarterly

Printed Primary Sources

Advisory Committee on Reconstruction. *Report*. Ottawa, King's Printer, 1944
Allen, Ralph. *The Chartered Libertine*. Toronto: Macmillan, 1954
Anglin, Gerald. *Canada Unlimited*. Toronto: O'Keefe Foundation, 1948
Ashley, C.A., ed. *Reconstruction in Canada*. Toronto: University of Toronto Press, 1943
Bacon, F.L., and E.A. Krug. *Our Life Today*. Boston: Little, Brown, 1939
Barnouw, Erik, ed. *Radio Drama in Action: Twenty-five Plays of a Changing World*. New York: Rinehart & Company, 1945
Berton, Pierre. *The Comfortable Pew: A Critical Look at the Church in the New Age*. Toronto: McClelland and Stewart, 1965
British Columbia Federation of Labour. *What's Happening to Jobs? The Effects of Automation and Related Problems*. Vancouver: 1960
Brodie, Fawn M. *Peace Aims and Post-war Planning*. Boston: World Peace Foundation, 1942
– *Peace Aims and Post-war Reconstruction*. Princeton, NJ: American Committee for International Studies, 1941
Brown, George W. *Canadian Democracy in Action*. Toronto: Ontario Department of Education, 1945
Brown, J.J. "Mr. Brown Looks at Education." *Canadian Business* (Nov. 1951): 48
Buchan, John. *Memory Hold-the-Door*. London: Hodder and Stoughton, 1940
Buckingham, Walter. *Automation: Its Impact on Business and People*. New York: Harper Brothers, 1961
Cairns, Huntington. Allen Tate, and Mark Van Doren. *Invitation to Learning*. New York: Random House, 1941
Canada Council. *The Canada Council and the Arts*. Ottawa, 1959
– "Progress Report on Projects of National Significance for the Celebration of Canada's Centennial of Confederation." Ottawa, 15 Nov. 1965
– *Centennial Facts 2: Confederation Train and Caravans*. Ottawa, 1967
– *Centennial Symbol/Graphics Manual*. Ottawa: Queen's Printer, 1965

Canada, Centennial Commission. *The Centennial and Canadians: A Report of Centennial Activities, 1966–1967*. Ottawa: Centennial Commission, 1967
Canada, Royal Commission on National Development in the Arts, Letters and Sciences. *Report*. Ottawa: King's Printer, 1951
– *Royal Commission Studies: A Selection of Essays Prepared for the Royal Commission on National Development in the Arts, Letters and Sciences*. Ottawa: King's Printer, 1951
Canadian Corporation for the 1967 World Exhibition. *General Report on the 1967 World Exhibition*. Ottawa: Queen's Printer, 1969
– *Terre des Hommes – Man and His World*. Ottawa: Canadian Corporation for the 1967 World Exhibition, 1967
Canadian Hurdles. Canadian Post-war Affairs Discussion Manual No. 4. Ottawa: King's Printer, 1945
Canadian Teachers' Federation. *Freedom of Conscience*. No. 4 in the Democratic Way series, January 1944
– *I'm Free to Choose*. No. 3 in the Democratic Way series, July 1943
Canadian Youth Commission. *Youth and Jobs in Canada*. Toronto: Ryerson Press, 1945
– *Youth and Recreation: New Plans for New Times*. Toronto: Ryerson, 1946
Charlesworth, Hector. *I'm Telling You*. Toronto: Macmillan, 1937
Child, Philip, and John W. Holmes. *Dynamic Democracy: Problem of Strategy in the World War of Morale. Behind the Headlines Series*, vol. 1, no. 9, May 1941. Toronto: CIIA/CAAE, 1941
Chisholm, Major General G.B. "The Reestablishment of Peacetime Society." *Psychiatry* 9, no. 1 (Feb. 1946): 3–20
Cohen, Maxwell. *Governmental Machinery of Wartime Controls and Its Relation to Postwar Problems*. Report to the Advisory Committee on Reconstruction. Ottawa: King's Printer, 1942
Corbett, E.A. *We Have with Us Tonight ...* Toronto: Ryerson, 1957
Corey, Lewis. *The Unfinished Task: Economic Reconstruction for Democracy*. New York: Viking, 1942
Coulter, John, and Healey Willan. *Transit through Fire*. Toronto: Macmillan, 1942
Cox, Harvey. "McLuhanite Christianity at Expo 67." *Commonweal* 86, no. 10 (26 May 1967): 277–9
Cruikshank, D.B. "Industrial Design – What Are Canadians Doing about It?" *Industrial Canada* 50, no. 3 (July 1949): 216–19
Dahir, James, comp. *Community Centers as Living War Memorials: A Selected Bibliography with Interpretive Comments*. New York: Russell Sage Foundation, 1946
Daniells, Roy. "Poetry and the Novel." In Julian Park, ed., *The Culture of Contemporary Canada*. Ithaca, NY: Cornell University Press, 1957
Davies, Blodwen. *Youth Speaks Its Mind*. Toronto: Ryerson Press, 1948
Davis, D.G., *Parents and Democracy*. Toronto: Ryerson, 1941

Dewey, John. *Freedom and Culture*. New York: Putnam, 1939
Eliot, T.S. *Notes towards the Definition of Culture*. New York: Harcourt, Brace and Company, 1948
Ellul, Jacques. *The Technological Society*, trans. John Wilkinson. New York: Vintage, 1964
Elton, Godfrey. *St. George or the Dragon: Towards a Christian Democracy*. London: Collins, 1942
Estall, Martyn. "Learning for Living," *Canadian Affairs* 2, no. 16 (Oct. 1945)
Eustace, C.J. *An Infinity of Questions: A Study of the Religion of Art, and of the Art of Religion in the Lives of Five Women*. New York: Longmans, 1946
Fisher, John. *John Fisher Reports: An Anthology of Radio Scripts*. Hamilton: Niagara Editorial Bureau, 1949
Flenley, Ralph. *Post-war Problems – A Reading List*. Toronto: Canadian Institute of International Affairs, 1943
Forsey, Eugene A. *Unemployment in the Machine Age: Its Causes*. Number 5 in the Machine Age Series. Toronto: Social Service Council of Canada, 1940
Forster, E.M. "What I Believe" (1939) in *Two Cheers for Democracy*. London: Edward Arnold, 1951, 67–76
Fraser, Blair. *The Search for Identity: Canada 1945–1967*. Garden City, NY: Doubleday, 1967
"Frustrated Artists." *Printed Word* 183 (Dec. 1949): 4
Frye, Northrop. *The Modern Century: The Whidden Lectures 1967*. Toronto: University of Toronto Press, 1967
Galloway, George B. *Post-war Planning in the United States*. New York: Twentieth Century Fund, 1942
Gillis, Clarie, MP. *Letter from Home! From a Soldier of 1914–19 to a Soldier of 1939–194?* 1943
Goslin, Ryllis, and Omar Goslin. *Democracy*. New York: Harcourt, Brace, 1940
Government by the People. Canadian Post-war Affairs: Discussion Manual No. 5. Ottawa: King's Printer, 1945
Grant, George. "An Ethic of Community." In Michael Oliver, ed., *Social Purpose for Canada*. Toronto: University of Toronto Press, 1961, 3–26
– *Lament for a Nation*. Toronto: Gage, 1965
– *Philosophy in the Mass Age*. First pub. 1959. Ed. William Christian. Toronto: University of Toronto Press, 1995
– *Technology and Empire: Perspectives on North America*. Toronto: House of Anansi, 1969
Gregory, Sir Richard Arman. *Science in Chains*. No. 12 in the Macmillan War Pamphlets series. London: Macmillan, 1941
Heath, Lilian M., comp. *Platform Pearls for Temperance Workers and Other Reformers*. Toronto, 1896

Howard, Eileen. *Expo Summer*. Toronto: Doubleday Canada, 1969
Hutchison, Bruce. *Canada: Tomorrow's Giant*. Toronto: Longmans, Green and Company, 1957
- *The Unknown Country: Canada and Her People*. Toronto: Longmans, Green, 1943
Huxley, Julian. *Democracy Marches*. New York: Harper and Brothers, 1941
Innis, Harold A. *The Bias of Communication*. Toronto: University of Toronto Press, 1951
- *Empire and Communications*. Toronto: University of Toronto Press, 1950
- *The Strategy of Culture*. Toronto: University of Toronto Press, 1952
Jacobson, Howard B., and Joseph S. Roucek. *Automation and Society*. New York: Philosophical Library, 1959
Jamieson, Don. *The Troubled Air*. Fredericton: Brunswick Press, 1966
Joad, C.E.M. *The Babbitt Warren*. London: Kegan Paul, Trench and Trubner, 1926
"The Job Ahead." *Canadian Business* 17, no. 1 (Jan. 1944): 17–18
Keyserlingk, Robert W. "No Whitewash, Please." *Ensign* (1 Dec. 1951): 1
Kirkconnell, Watson. *Seven Pillars of Freedom*. Toronto: Oxford University Press, 1944
- *Twilight of Liberty*. Toronto: Oxford University Press, 1941
Kirkwood, M.M. *Women and the Machine Age*. No. 7 in the Machine Age Series. Toronto: Social Service Council of Canada, [1940]
Klonsky, Milton. "Along the Midway of Mass Culture," *Partisan Review* 16, no. 4 (April 1949): 348–65
Kristol, Irving. "Democracy and Mass Culture: High, Low, and Modern." *Manchester Guardian* (8 June 1960)
Laird, Donald, and Eleanor Laird. *How to Get Along with Automation*. New York: McGraw-Hill, 1964
Lambert, Richard S. *Ariel and All His Quality: An Impression of the BBC from Within*. London: Victor Gollancz, 1940
Laski, Harold J., et al. *Where Stands Democracy? A Collection of Essays by Members of the Fabian Society*. London: Macmillan, 1940
Lazarsfeld, Paul. "The Effects of Radio on Public Opinion." In Douglas Waples, ed., *Print, Radio and Film in a Democracy: Ten Papers on the Administration of Mass Communications in the Public Interest*. Chicago: University of Chicago Press, 1942, 66–78
Leavis, F.R. *Mass Civilisation and Minority Culture*. Cambridge: Minority Press, 1930
"The Little King," Printed Word 183 (Dec. 1945): 3
Lynd, R.S., and H.M. Lynd. *Middletown: A Study in Contemporary American Culture*. (New York: Harcourt, Brace and Company, 1929
- *Middletown in Transition: A Study in Cultural Conflicts*. (New York: Harcourt, Brace and Company, 1937

Lynes, Russell. "Highbrow, Lowbrow, Middlebrow." *Harper's* (Feb. 1949): 19–28
– *A Surfeit of Honey*. New York: Harper and Brothers, 1953
MacDermot, Terence William Leighton. *Can We Make Good?* No. 4 in the Democracy and Citizenship Series. Toronto: CAAE/CIIA, 1940
Macdonald, John. *The Corner Stone of Democracy: The Discussion Group*. Toronto: Ryerson, 1939
MacFarlane, Ronald Oliver. "Canada Tomorrow: Canada and the Post-war World, Part One," *Behind the Headlines Series*, vol. 2, no. 3, Jan. 1942. Toronto: CIIA/CAAE, 1942
MacLeod, Alastair W. "Personal Satisfactions." in *Round Table on Man and Industry*. University of Toronto, 1958, 12–19
Man and His World – Terre des Hommes: The Noranda Lectures, Expo 67. Toronto: University of Toronto Press, 1968
Martin, Chester. "Trends in Canadian Nationhood." In Chester Martin, ed., *Canada in Peace and War*. Toronto: Oxford University Press, 1941, 3–28
McDougall, John L. *The Foundations of National Well-Being – Post-war*. Kingston, 1944
McLuhan, Marshall. *The Mechanical Bride: Folklore of Industrial Man*. New York: Vanguard, 1951
Milner, Gamaliel. *The Problem of Decadence*. London: Williams and Norgate, 1931
Morton, W.L. *The Canadian Identity*. Madison: University of Wisconsin Press, 1961
Mumford. Lewis. *Faith for Living*. New York: Harcourt, Brace, 1940
Neatby, Hilda. "Education for Democracy." *Dalhousie Review* 24, no. 1 (April 1944): 43–50
– *So Little For the Mind*. Toronto: Clarke Irwin, 1953
– *A Temperate Dispute*. Toronto: Clarke Irwin, 1954
Nicol, John, Albert Shea, and G.J.P Simmins. *Canada's Farm Radio Forum*. Paris: UNESCO, 1954
Ogilvy, Maud. *The Keeper of the Bic Light House: A Canadian Story of Today*. Montreal: E.M. Renouf, 1891
O'Leary, Gratton. "Canada's Political Philosophy." In *Canada: Nation on the March*. Toronto: Clarke, Irwin, 1953
O'Rourke, L.J. *Our Democracy and Its Problems*. Boston: Heath, 1942
Overstreet, Harry A., and Bonaro W. Overstreet. *Town Meeting Comes to Town*. New York: Harper Brothers, 1938
Owen, D.R.G. "Science, Scientism and Religion." In D.R.G. Owen et al., *Christianity in an Age of Science*. Toronto: Canadian Broadcasting Corporation, 1952
– *Scientism, Man and Religion*. Philadelphia: Westminster, 1952
Peers, Frank. "The Nationalist Dilemma in Canadian Broadcasting." In Peter Russell, ed., *Nationalism in Canada*. Toronto: McGraw-Hill, 1966, 252–67

Percival, W.P. "Freedom of Educational Opportunity." *Canadian Geographical Journal* 26, no. 12 (June 1943): 289–96
Phillips, Charles E. *New Schools for Democracy.* Behind the Headlines Series, Vol. 4, no. 6. Toronto: CIIA/CAAE, 1944
Pierce, Lorne. *The Beloved Community.* Toronto: Ryerson Press, 1925
– *A Canadian Nation.* Toronto: Ryerson, 1960
Priestley, J.B. *Out of the People.* New York: Harper, 1941
Riesman, David, Reuel Denney, and Nathan Glazer. *Faces in the Crowd.* New Haven, Conn.: Yale University Press, 1953
– *The Lonely Crowd: A Study of the Changing American Character.* New Haven, Conn.: Yale University Press, 1950
Roberts, Leslie. *We Must Be Free: Reflections of a Democrat.* Toronto: Macmillan, 1939
Robins, G.M. *The Tree of Knowledge.* Montreal: John Lovell and Son, [1890]
Ross, Malcolm. *Our Sense of Identity.* Toronto: Ryerson, 1954
Ross, Murray G. "Man and His Lack of Community." In R.C. Chalmers and John A. Irving, eds., *The Light and the Flame: Modern Knowledge and Religion.* Toronto: Ryerson, 1956, 65–84
Roussy de Sales, Raoul de. *The Making of Tomorrow.* Toronto: McClelland and Stewart, 1942
Sandwell, B.K. *The Canadian Peoples.* London and Toronto: Oxford University Press, 1941
– *You Take Out What You Put In.* No. 3 in the *Democracy and Citizenship Series.* Toronto: CAAE/CIIA, 1940
Saunders, Richard M. "Introduction." In Richard M. Saunders, ed., *Education for Tomorrow.* Toronto: University of Toronto Press, 1946, ix–xiii
"School for Sadism." *Art Digest* 23, no. 15 (1 May 1949)
Seeley, John R., R. Alexander Sim, and E.W. Loosley. *Crestwood Heights: A Study of the Culture of Suburban Life.* Toronto: University of Toronto Press, 1956
Seligman, Ben. *A Most Notorious Victory: Man in an Age of Automation.* New York: Free Press/Macmillan, 1966
Shea, Albert A. *Culture in Canada: A Study of the Findings of the Royal Commission on National Development in the Arts, Letters and Sciences (1949–1951).* Toronto: Core Press, 1952
Silcox, Claris. *The War and Religion.* Toronto: Macmillan, 1941
Smith, Thomas Vernor. *The Democratic Tradition in America.* New York: Farrar and Rinehart, 1941
Smith, Thomas Vernor, Glenn Negley, and Robert Bush. *Democracy vs. Dictatorship.* Washington, DC: National Education Association, 1942
Snow, C.P. *The Two Cultures.* First pub. 1959. Ed. Stefan Collini. Cambridge: Canto, 1993
Soule, George. *What Automation Does to Human Beings.* London: Sidgewick and Jackson, 1956

Steele, George, and Paul Kircher. *The Crisis We Face: Automation and the Cold War*. New York: McGraw-Hill, 1960

Stewart, John. "The Massey Report: Ideological Preparation for War." *National Affairs Monthly* 8, no. 1 (Sept. 1951): 34–53

Stratford, Reginald Killmaster, "The Challenge to Science." In G.P. Gilmour, ed., *Canada's Tomorrow*. Toronto: Macmillan, 1954, 67–90

Terborgh, George. *Automation Hysteria*. New York: Norton, 1966

Thomson, David. *The Democratic Ideal in France and England*. Cambridge: Cambridge University Press, 1940

Thomson, James S. "The Challenge of Existentialism." In Ralph C. Chalmers and John A. Irving, eds., *Challenge and Response: Modern Ideas and Religion*. Toronto: Ryerson, 1959, 73–90

Underhill, Frank. "The Scholar: Man Thinking." In George Whalley, ed., *A Place of Liberty: Essays on the Government of Canadian Universities*. Toronto: Clarke Irwin, 1964, 61–71

United States, Office of War Information. *Toward New Horizons: The World beyond the War*. Washington, DC: Government Printing Office, 1942

Valentine, Alan. *The Age of Conformity*. Chicago: Henry Regnery, 1954

Vickers, Sir Geoffrey. "The Impact of Automation on Society." In *Automation and Social Change*. Toronto: Government of Ontario, 1963, 41–54

– *The Undirected Society: Essays on the Human Implications of Industrialization in Canada*. Toronto: University of Toronto Press, 1959

Wales, Julia Grace. *Democracy Needs Education*. Toronto: Macmillan, 1942

– "Pro, Not Anti: A Principle of Integration." *New Age* 2, no. 31 (8 Aug. 1940): 9–10

Wallace, R.C. "Education in Canada." In R.H. Coats, ed., *Features of Present-Day Canada* in the *Annals of the American Academy of Political and Social Science*. Philadelphia: American Academy of Political and Social Science, 1947

Warner, W. Lloyd, and Paul S. Lunt. *The Social Life of a Modern Community*. New Haven, Conn.: Yale University Press, 1941

– *The Status System of a Modern Community*. New Haven, Conn.: Yale University Press, 1942

Wedgwood, Josiah C. *Testament to Democracy*. London: Hutchinson, [1942]

Wells, H.G. *The Commonsense of War and Peace*. London: Penguin, 1940

– *Guide to the New World*. London: Gollancz, 1941

– *The New World Order*. London: Secker and Warburg, 1941

Westley, William A. "The Workers Automation Wants." *Executive Decision* (Feb. 1959): 56–7

Whyte, William H, Jr. *The Organization Man*. New York: Simon and Schuster, 1956

Willis, I.D. *Democracy: A Tripod*. Port Hope: 1940

– *What Do Canada and Democracy Really Mean to You?* Port Hope, Ont.: 1940

Yendall, William R. *The Common Problem*. Toronto: Ryerson Press, 1942
Young Men's Christian Associations of Canada, National Council. *We Discuss Canada*. Toronto: Ryerson, 1942
Ziemer, Gregor. *Education for Death: The Making of a Nazi*. London: Oxford University Press, 1941

Secondary Sources

Adams, Mary Louise. *The Trouble with Normal: Postwar Youth and the Making of Heterosexuality*. Toronto: University of Toronto Press, 1997
Agar, Jon. *Science and Spectacle: The Work of Jodrell Bank in Post-war British Culture*. Amsterdam: Harwood, 1998
Ambrose, Linda McGuire. "The Canadian Youth Commission: Planning for Youth and Social Welfare in the Postwar Era." PhD dissertation, University of Waterloo, 1992
Armstrong, David P. "Corbett's House: The Origins of the Canadian Association for Adult Education and Its Development during the Directorship of E.A. Corbett, 1936–1951." MA thesis, University of Toronto, 1968
Avery, Donald. *The Science of War: Canadian Scientists and Allied Military Technology during the Second World War*. Toronto: University of Toronto Press, 1998
Axelrod, Paul. *Making a Middle Class: Student Life in English Canada during the Thirties*. Montreal: McGill-Queen's University Press, 1990
Aykroyd, Peter. *The Anniversary Compulsion: Canada's Centennial Celebrations, A Model Mega-Anniversary*. Toronto: Dundurn Press, 1992
Azzi, Stephen. *Walter Gordon and the Rise of Canadian Nationalism*. Montreal: McGill-Queen's University Press, 1999
Baillargeon, Philippe J. "The CBC and the Cold War Mentality, 1946–1952." MA thesis, Carleton University, 1987
Baritz, Loren. *The Good Life: The Meaning of Success for the American Middle Class*. New York: Knopf, 1989
Berger, Carl. *Science, God, and Nature in Victorian Canada*. Toronto: University of Toronto Press, 1983
Berman, Marshall. *All That Is Solid Melts into Air: The Experience of Modernity*. New York: Simon and Schuster, 1982
Berton, Pierre. *1967: The Last Good Year*. Toronto: Doubleday, 1997
Bodnar, John E. *Remaking America: Public Memory, Commemoration, and Patriotism in the Twentieth Century*. Princeton, NJ: Princeton University Press, 1992
Bothwell, Robert, Ian Drummond, and John English. *Canada since 1945: Power, Politics and Provincialism*. Rev. ed. Toronto: University of Toronto Press, 1989
Bothwell, Robert, and William Kilbourn. *C.D. Howe: A Biography*. Toronto: McClelland and Stewart, 1979

Boyer, Paul. *By the Bomb's Early Light: American Thought and Culture at the Dawn of the Atomic Age*. New York: Pantheon, 1985
– *Fallout: A Historian Reflects on America's Half-Century Encounter with Nuclear Weapons*. Columbus: Ohio State University Press, 1998
Brantlinger, Patrick. *Bread and Circuses: Theories of Mass Culture as Social Decay*. Ithaca, NY: Cornell University Press, 1983
Briggs, Asa. *A History of Broadcasting in the United Kingdom*. Oxford: Oxford University Press, 1979
Brooke, John Hedley. *Science and Religion: Some Historical Perspectives*. Cambridge: Cambridge University Press, 1991
Brown, Craig, and Ramsay Cook. *Canada 1896–1921: A Nation Transformed*. Toronto: McClelland and Stewart, 1974
Brown, Nicholas. *Governing Prosperity: Social Change and Social Analysis in Australia in the 1950s*. Cambridge: Cambridge University Press, 1995
Brown, Richard D. *Modernization: The Transformation of American Life, 1600–1865*. New York: Hill and Wang, 1976
Browne, Ray B. "Popular Culture: Notes toward a Definition." In George H. Lewis, ed., *Side-Saddle on the Golden Calf: Social Structure and Popular Culture in America*. Pacific Palisades, Calif: Goodyear, 1972, 5–11
Burnham, John. *How Superstition Won and Science Lost: Popularizing Science and Health in the United States*. New Brunswick, NJ: Rutgers University Press, 1987
Calinescu, Matei. *Faces of Modernity: Avant-Garde, Decadence and Kitsch*. Bloomington: Indiana University Press, 1977
Campbell, Sandra. "From Romantic History to Communications Theory: Lorne Pierce as Publisher of C.W. Jefferys and Harold Innis," *Journal of Canadian Studies* 30, no. 3 (autumn 1995): 91–116
Carey, John. *The Intellectuals and the Masses: Pride and Prejudice among the Literary Intelligentsia, 1880–1939*. London: Faber and Faber, 1992
Carter, Paul. *Another Part of the Fifties*. New York: Columbia University Press, 1983
Cavallo, Dominick. *A Fiction of the Past: The Sixties in American History*. New York: St Martin's Press, 1999
Charney, Leo, and Vanessa R. Schwartz. "Introduction." In Charney and Schwartz, eds., *Cinema and the Invention of Modern Life*. Berkeley: University of California Press, 1995, 1–12
Christian, William. *George Grant: A Biography*. Toronto: University of Toronto Press, 1993
Christie, Nancy. "Sacred Sex: The United Church and the Privatization of the Family in Post-war Canada." In Nancy Christie, ed., *Households of Faith: Family, Gender and Community in Canada, 1760–1969*. Montreal: McGill-Queen's University Press, 2002, 348–76
Christie, Nancy, and Michael Gauvreau. *A Full-orbed Christianity: The Protestant Churches and Social Welfare in Canada, 1900–1940*. Montreal: McGill-Queen's University Press, 1996

Collins, John B. " "Design in Industry" Exhibition, National Gallery of Canada, 1946: Turning Bombers into Lounge Chairs." *Material History Bulletin* 27 (spring 1988): 27–38

Collins, Robert. *You Had to Be There: An Intimate Portrait of the Generation That Survived the Depression, Won the War, and Re-invented Canada.* Toronto: McClelland and Stewart, 1997

Cook, Ramsay. "Cultural Nationalism in Canada: An Historical Perspective." In Janice L. Murray, ed., *Canadian Cultural Nationalism: The Fourth Lester B. Pearson Conference on the Canada–U.S. Relationship.* New York: New York University Press, 1977, 15–44

– *The Regenerators: Social Criticism in Late Victorian English Canada.* Toronto: University of Toronto Press, 1985

Coontz, Stephanie. *The Way We Never Were: American Families and the Nostalgia Trap.* New York: Basic Books, 1993

Creighton, Donald Grant. *The Forked Road: Canada, 1939–1957.* Toronto: McClelland and Stewart, 1976

Cross, Gary, ed. *Worktowners at Blackpool: Mass-Observation and Popular Leisure in the 1930s.* London: Routledge, 1990

Crunden, Robert M. "Introduction." In Robert M. Crunden, ed., *The Superfluous Men: Conservative Critics of American Culture, 1900–1945.* Austin: University of Texas Press, 1977, xi–xx

Davies, Helen. "The Politics of Participation: A Study of Canada's Centennial Celebration." PhD dissertation, University of Manitoba, 1999

Diggins, John Patrick. *The Proud Decades: America in War and Peace, 1941–1960.* New York: Norton, 1988

Donaldson, Gary. *Abundance and Anxiety: America, 1945–1960.* Westport, Conn.: Praeger, 1997

Eagleton, Terry. *The Idea of Culture.* Oxford: Blackwell, 2000

Ehrhardt, George R. "Descendants of Prometheus: Popular Science Writing in the United States, 1915–1948." PhD dissertation, Duke University, 1993

Eaman, Ross A., *Channels of Influence: CBC Audience Research and the Canadian Public.* Toronto: University of Toronto Press, 1994.

Ehrhardt, George R. "Descendants of Prometheus: Popular Science Writing in the United States, 1915–1948." PhD dissertation, Duke University, 1993

Eksteins, Modris. *The Rites of Spring: The Great War and the Birth of the Modern Age.* Toronto: Lester & Orpen Dennys, 1989

Engelhardt, Tom. *The End of Victory Culture: Cold War America and the Disillusioning of a Generation.* New York: Basic Books, 1995

English, John. *Years of Growth, 1948–1967.* Toronto: Grolier, 1986

Evans, Gary. *John Grierson and the National Film Board: The Politics of Wartime Propaganda.* Toronto: University of Toronto Press, 1985

Farber, David. *The Age of Great Dreams: America in the 1960s.* New York: Hill and Wang, 1994

Faris, Ron. *The Passionate Educators: Voluntary Associations and the Struggle for Control of Adult Educational Broadcasting in Canada 1919–1952*. Toronto: Peter Martin Associates, 1975
Faris, Ronald L. "Adult Education for Social Action or Enlightenment? An Assessment of the Development of the Canadian Association for Adult Education and Its Radio Forums from 1935–1952." PhD dissertation, University of Toronto, 1971
Ferguson, Barry. *Remaking Liberalism: The Intellectual Legacy of Adam Shortt, O.D. Skelton, W.C. Clark, and W.A. Mackintosh, 1890–1925*. Montreal: McGill-Queen's University Press, 1993
Finkel, Alvin. *Our Lives: Canada after 1945*. Toronto: J. Lorimer, 1997
Fiske, John. *Understanding Popular Culture*. First pub. 1984. London: Routledge, 1991
Foreman, Joel, ed. *The Other Fifties: Interrogating Midcentury American Icons*. Urbana: University of Illinois Press, 1997
Francis, R. Douglas, *Frank H. Underhill: Intellectual Provocateur*. Toronto: University of Toronto Press, 1986
Frick, N. Alice. *Image in the Mind: CBC Radio Drama 1944 to 1954*. Toronto: Canadian Stage and Arts Publications, 1987
Friesen, Gerald. "Adult Education and Union Education: Aspects of English-Canadian Cultural History in the 20th Century." *Labour/Le Travail* 34 (autumn 1994): 163–88
Friesen, Gerald. *Citizens and Nations: An Essay on History, Comminication, and Canada*. Toronto: University of Toronto Press, 2000
Fulford, Robert. *This Was Expo*. Toronto: McClelland and Stewart, 1968
Galison, Peter, and Bruce Hevly, eds. *Big Science: The Growth of Large-scale Research*. Stanford, Calif.: Stanford University Press, 1992
Gans, Herbert J. *Popular Culture and High Culture*. New York: Basic Books, 1974
Gauvreau, Michael. *The Evangelical Century: College and Creed in English Canada from the Great Revival to the Great Depression* Montreal: McGill-Queen's University Press, 1991
Gilbert, James. *A Cycle of Outrage: America's Reaction to the Juvenile Delinquent in the 1950s*. New York: Oxford University Press, 1986
– *Redeeming Culture: American Religion in Age of Science*. Chicago: University of Chicago Press, 1997
Giner, Salvador. *Mass Society*. London: Martin Robertson, 1976
Gitlin, Todd. *The Sixties: Years of Hope, Days of Rage*. New York: Pantheon, 1987
Goodall, Peter. *High Culture, Popular Culture: The Long Debate*. Sydney: Allen and Unwin, 1995
– *Left Intellectuals and Popular Culture in Twentieth-century America*. Chapel Hill: University of North Carolina Press, 1996
Gramsci, Antonio. *Selections from the Prison Notebooks of Antonio Gramsci*. Ed. and trans. by Quintin Hoare and Geoffrey Nowell Smith. London: Lawrence and Wishart, 1971

Granatstein, J.L. *Canada 1957–1967: The Years of Uncertainty and Innovation*. Toronto: McClelland and Stewart, 1986
– *Canada's War: The Politics of the Mackenzie King Government*. Toronto: University of Toronto Press, 1990
– "Culture and Scholarship: The First Ten Years of the Canada Council," *Canadian Historical Review* 65, no. 4 (Sept. 1984): 441–74
– *The Politics of Survival: The Conservative Party of Canada, 1939–1945*. Toronto: University of Toronto Press, 1967
Greenspan, Louis. "The Unravelling of Liberalism." In Arthur Davis, ed., *George Grant and the Subversion of Modernity: Art, Philosophy, Politics, Religion and Education*. Toronto: University of Toronto Press, 1996, 201–19
Greer, Allan. "Canadian History: Ancient and Modern." *Canadian Historical Review* 77 (Dec. 1996): 575–90
Groome, Margaret. "Canada's Stratford Festival, 1953–1967: Hegemony, Commodity, Institution." PhD dissertation, McGill University, 1988
Grossberg, Lawrence, ed. "On Postmodernism and Articulation: An Interview with Stuart Hall." *Journal of Communication Inquiry* 10, no. 2 (1986): 45–60
Gumbrecht, Hans Ulrich. *In 1926: Living at the Edge of Time*. Cambridge, Mass.: Harvard University Press, 1997
Habermas, Jürgen. *The Structural Transformation of the Public Sphere: An Inquiry into a Category of Bourgeois Society*. Trans. Thomas Burger and Frederick Lawrence. Cambridge, Mass.: MIT Press, 1991
Hales, Peter B. "The Atomic Sublime." *American Studies* 32, no. 1 (1991): 5–31
Hannant, Larry. *The Infernal Machine: Investigating the Loyalty of Canada's Citizens*. Toronto: University of Toronto Press, 1995
Hardy, H. Forsyth. "Democracy as a Fighting Faith." In *John Grierson and the NFB*. Toronto: ECW, 1984, 86–94
Hebdige, Dick. *Subculture: The Meaning of Style*. London: Methuen, 1979
Henriksen, Margot A. *Dr. Strangelove's America: Society and Culture in the Atomic Age*. Berkeley: University of California Press, 1997
Hewison, Robert. *Too Much: Art and Society in the Sixties 1960–75*. London: Methuen, 1986
– *Under Siege: Literary Life in London, 1939–1945*. London: Weidenfeld and Nicolson, 1977
Hewitt, Steve. *Spying 101: The RCMP's Secret Activities at Canadian Universities, 1917–1997*. Toronto: University of Toronto Press, 2002
Hilmes, Michele. *Radio Voices: American Broadcasting, 1922–1952*. Minneapolis: University of Minnesota Press, 1997
Hunt, Leon. *British Low Culture: From Safari Suits to Sexploitation*. London: Routledge, 1998
Jameson, Sheila. *Chautauqua in Canada*. Calgary: Glenbow/Alberta Institute, 1979
Jasen, Patricia. "Romanticism, Modernity, and the Evolution of Tourism on the Niagara Frontier, 1790–1850." *Canadian Historical Review* 72, no. 3 (Sept. 1991): 283–318

Johnson, Paul. *Land Fit for Heroes: The Planning of British Reconstruction, 1916–1919*. Chicago: University of Chicago Press, 1968
Johnston, Russell. "The Early Trials of Protestant Radio." *Canadian Historical Review* 75, no. 3 (Sept. 1994): 376–402
Jumonville, Neil. *Critical Crossings: The New York Intellectuals in Postwar America*. Berkeley: University of California Press, 1991
Kammen, Michael. *American Culture, American Tastes: Social Change and the 20th Century*. New York: Knopf, 1999
– *The Lively Arts: Gilbert Seldes and the Transformation of Cultural Criticism in the United States*. New York: Oxford University Press, 1996
– *Mystic Chords of Memory: The Transformation of American Culture*. New York: Knopf, 1991
Kern, Stephen. *The Culture of Time and Space, 1880–1918*. Cambridge, Mass.: Harvard University Press, 1983
Kettle, John. *The Big Generation*. Toronto: McClelland and Stewart, 1980
Kicksee, Richard Gordon. " 'Scaled Down to Size': Contested Liberal Commonsense and the Negotiation of 'Indian Participation' in the Canadian Centennial Celebrations and Expo '67, 1963–1967." MA thesis, Queen's University, 1995
Kitchen, Brigitte. "The Marsh Report Revisited." *Journal of Canadian Studies* 21, no. 2 (summer 1986): 38–48
Klatch, Rebecca E. *A Generation Divided: The New Left, the New Right, and the 1960s*. Berkeley: University of California Press, 1999
Kloppenberg, James T. *Uncertain Victory: Social Democracy and Progressivism in European and American Thought, 1870–1920*. New York: Oxford University Press, 1986
Korinek, Valerie Joyce. "Roughing It in Suburbia: Reading *Chatelaine* Magazine, 1950–1969." PhD dissertation, University of Toronto, 1996
Kostash, Myrna. *Long Way from Home: The Story of the Sixties Generation in Canada*. Toronto: J. Lorimer, 1980
Kroeber, A.L., and Clyde Kluckhohn. *Culture: A Critical Review of Concepts and Definitions*. New York: Vantage, 1952
Kroker, Arthur. *Technology and the Canadian Mind: Innis/McLuhan/Grant*. Montreal: New World Perspectives, 1984
LaMarsh, Judy. *Memoirs of a Bird in a Gilded Cage*. Toronto: McClelland and Stewart, 1969
Lazarsfeld, Paul. "Introduction." In Bernard Rosenberg and David Manning White, eds., *Mass Culture Revisited*. New York: Van Nostrand Reinhold, 1971; vii–ix
Lears, Jackson. *Fables of Abundance: A Cultural History of Advertising in America*. New York: Basic Books, 1994
– "A Matter of Taste." In Lary May, ed., *Recasting America: Culture and Politics in the Age of the Cold War*. Chicago: University of Chicago Press, 1989, 38–57
– *No Place of Grace: Antimodernism and the Transformation of American Culture, 1880–1920*. New York: Pantheon, 1981

LeMahieu, D.L. *A Culture for Democracy: Mass Communication and the Cultivated Mind in Britain between the Wars.* Oxford: Clarendon Press, 1988

Lenthall, Bruce. "Critical Reception: Public Intellectuals Decry Depression-Era Radio, Mass Culture, and Modern America." In Michele Hilmes and Jason Loviglio, eds., *Radio Reader: Essays in the Culture History of* Radio. New York: Routledge, 2002, 41–62

Levine, Lawrence W. "The Folklore of Industrial Society: Popular Culture and Its Audiences." *American Historical Review* 97, no. 5 (Dec. 1992): 1369–99

– *Highbrow/Lowbrow: The Emergence of Cultural Hierarchy in America.* Cambridge, Mass.: Harvard University Press, 1988

Lhamon, W.T., Jr. *Deliberate Speed: The Origins of a Cultural Style in the American 1950s.* First pub. Washington, DC: Smithsonian Institution, 1990. Cambridge, Mass.: Harvard University Press, 2002

Lindsey, George R., ed. *No Day Long Enough: Canadian Science in World War II.* Toronto: Canadian Institute of Strategic Studies, 1997

Litt, Paul. "The Donnish Inquisition: The Massey Commission and the Campaign for State-Sponsored Cultural Nationalism in Canada, 1949–1951." PhD dissertation, University of Toronto, 1990

– *The Muses, the Masses, and the Massey Commission.* Toronto: University of Toronto Press, 1992

Mackenzie, Hector. "The White Paper on Reconstruction and Canada's Postwar Trade Policy." in Greg Donaghy, ed., *Uncertain Horizons: Canadians and Their World in 1945.* Ottawa: Canadian Committee for the History of the Second World War, 1997

Mackey, Eva. *The House of Difference: Cultural Politics and National Identity in Canada.* London: Routledge, 1999

Marchand, Philip. *Marshall McLuhan: The Medium and the Messenger.* New York: Ticknor and Fields, 1989

Marchand, Roland, and Michael L. Smith. "Corporate Science on Display." In Ronald G. Walters, ed., *Scientific Authority and Twentieth Century America.* Baltimore: Johns Hopkins University Press, 1997, 148–82

Marks, Lynne. *Revivals and Roller Rinks: Religion, Leisure, and Identity in Late-Nineteenth-Century Small Town Ontario.* Toronto: University of Toronto Press, 1996

Marshall, David B. *Secularizing the Faith: Canadian Protestant Clergy and the Crisis of Belief, 1850–1940.* Toronto: University of Toronto Press, 1992

Marshall, Dominique. "Reconstruction Politics, the Canadian Welfare State and the Ambiguity of Children's Rights, 1940–1950." In Greg Donaghy, ed., *Uncertain Horizons: Canadians and Their World in 1945.* Ottawa: Canadian Committee for the History of the Second World War, 1997, 261–83

Marwick, Arthur. *Culture in Britain since 1945.* Oxford: Blackwell, 1991

– *The Sixties: Cultural Revolution in Britain, France, Italy, and the United States, c.1958–c.1974.* Oxford: Oxford University Press, 1998

Mathews, Robin. *Canadian Identity: Major Forces Shaping the Life of a People.* Ottawa: Steel Rail, 1988
May, Elaine Tyler. *Homeward Bound: American Families in the Cold War Era.* New York: Basic Books, 1988
May, Lary. "Making the American Consensus: The Narrative of Conversion and Subversion in World War II Films." In Lewis A. Erenberg and Susan E. Hirsch, eds., *The War in American Culture: Society and Consciousness during World War II.* Chicago: University of Chicago Press, 1996, 71–102
McInnis, Peter S. *Harnessing Labour Confrontation: Shaping the Postwar Settlement in Canada, 1943–1959.* Toronto: University of Toronto Press, 2002
McInnis, Peter S. "Planning Prosperity: Canadians Debate Postwar Reconstruction." In Greg Donaghy, ed., *Uncertain Horizons: Canadians and Their World in 1945.* Ottawa: Canadian Committee for the History of the Second World War, 1997, 231–59
McKay, Ian. "History and the Tourist Gaze: The Politics of Commemoration in Nova Scotia, 1935–1964." *Acadiensis* 22, no. 2 (spring 1993): 102–38
– "Introduction: All That Is Solid Melts into Air." In Ian McKay, ed., *The Challenge of Modernity: A Reader on Post-Confederation History.* Toronto: McGraw-Hill Ryerson, 1992, 9–26
– *The Quest of the Folk: Antimodernism and Cultural Selection in Twentieth-Century Nova Scotia.* Montreal: McGill-Queen's University Press, 1994
McKenzie, Francine. "Canada and the Reconstruction of Postwar Trade, 1943–1945." In Greg Donaghy, ed., *Uncertain Horizons: Canadians and Their World in 1945.* Ottawa: Canadian Committee for the History of the Second World War, 1997, 135–64
McKillop, A.B. "Culture, Intellect, and Context." *Journal of Canadian Studies* 24, no. 3 (autumn 1989): 7–31
– "Nationalism, Identity and Canadian Intellectual History." In McKillop, *Contours of Canadian Thought.* Toronto: University of Toronto Press, 1987, 3–17
Meyerowitz, Joanne, ed. *Not June Cleaver: Women and Gender in Postwar America, 1945–1960.* Philadelphia: Temple University Press, 1994
Miles, Peter, and Malcolm Smith. *Cinema, Literature and Society: Elite and Mass Culture in Interwar Britain.* London: Croom Helm, 1987
Monod, David. *Store Wars: Shopkeepers and The Culture of Mass Marketing, 1890–1939.* Toronto: University of Toronto Press, 1996
Morgan, Kenneth O. *Consensus and Disunity: The Lloyd George Coalition Government, 1918–1922.* Oxford: Clarendon, 1979
Morrison, Theodore. *Chautauqua: A Center for Education, Religion, and the Arts in America.* Chicago: University of Chicago Press, 1974
Morton, Desmond, and Glenn Wright. *Winning the Second Battle: Canadian Veterans and the Return to Civilian Life, 1915–1930.* Toronto: University of Toronto Press, 1987

Mosse, George. *Fallen Soldiers: Reshaping the Memory of the World Wars.* Oxford: Oxford University Press, 1990
Mukerji, Chandra. *A Fragile Power: Scientists and the State.* Princeton, NJ: Princeton University Press, 1989
Mukerji, Chandra, and Michael Schudson. *Rethinking Popular Culture.* Berkeley: University of California Press, 1991
Napoli, Philip Foster. "Empire of the Middle: Radio and the Emergence of an Electronic Society." PhD dissertation, Columbia University, 1998
Nells, H.V. *The Art of Nation-Building: Pageantry and Spectacle at Quebec's Tercentenary.* Toronto: University of Toronto Press, 2000
Nelson, Elizabeth. *The British Counter Culture, 1966–73: A Study of the Underground Press.* Basingstoke: Macmillan, 1989
Nicholson, Bruce. *Hi, Ho, Come to the Fair: Tales of the New York World's Fair of 1964–1965.* Huntington Beach, Calif.: Pelagian Press, 1989
Nolan, Brian. *King's War: Mackenzie King and the Politics of War, 1939–1945.* Toronto: Random House, 1988
Nord, David Paul. "An Economic Perspective on Formula in Popular Culture," *Journal of American Culture* 3 (spring 1980), 17–31
Norris, Ken. "The Beginnings of Canadian Modernism." *Canadian Poetry* 11 (autumn–winter 1982), 56–66
O'Neill, William L. *American High: The Years of Confidence, 1945–1960.* New York: Free Press, 1986
Ostry, Bernard. *The Cultural Connection: An Essay on Culture and Government Policy in Canada.* Toronto: McClelland and Stewart, 1978
Owram, Doug. *Born at the Right Time: A History of the Baby Boom Generation.* Toronto: University of Toronto Press, 1996
– *The Government Generation: Canadian Intellectuals and the State, 1900–1945.* Toronto: University of Toronto Press, 1986
Parr, Joy. *Domestic Goods: The Material, the Moral and the Economic in the Postwar Years.* Toronto: University of Toronto Press, 1999
Patterson, Graeme. *History and Communications: Harold Innis, Marshall McLuhan, the Interpretation of History.* Toronto: University of Toronto Press, 1990
Patterson, Tom, with Allan Gould. *First Stage: the Making of the Stratford Festival.* Toronto: McClelland and Stewart, 1987
Peers, Frank. *The Politics of Canadian Broadcasting, 1920–1951.* Toronto: University of Toronto Press, 1969
– *The Public Eye: Television and the Politics of Canadian Broadcasting, 1952–1968.* Toronto: University of Toronto Press, 1979
Peiss, Kathy. *Cheap Amusements: Working-Class Women and Leisure in Turn-of-the Century New York.* Philadelphia: Temple University Press, 1986
Pells, Richard. *The Liberal Mind in a Conservative Age: American Intellectuals in the 1940s and 1950s.* 2nd ed. Middletown, Conn.: Wesleyan University Press, 1989

- *Not Like Us: How Europeans Have Loved, Hated, and Transformed American Culture since World War II.* New York: Basic Books, 1997
- *Radical Visions and American Dreams: Culture and Social Thought in the Depression Years.* Middletown, Conn.: Wesleyan University Press, 1984
Persky, Joel. "The Innescence of Marshall McLuhan," *Journal of Canadian Culture* 1, no. 2 (autumn 1984): 3–14
- "The Media Writings of Harold Adams Innis." *Journal of Canadian Culture* 2, no. 1 (spring 1985): 79–87
Pettigrew, John, and Jamie Portman. *Stratford: The First Thirty Years.* Toronto: MacMillan, 1985
Raboy, Marc. *Missed Opportunities: The Story of Canada's Broadcasting Policy.* Montreal: McGill-Queen's University Press, 1990
Radway, Janice, *Reading the Romance: Women, Patriarchy, and Popular Literature.* Chapel Hill: University of North Carolina Press, 1984
- "The Scandal of the Middlebrow: The Book-of-the-Month Club, Class Fracture, and Cultural Authority." *South Atlantic Quarterly* 89, no. 4 (autumn 1990): 703–36
Remembering the Future: The New York World's Fair from 1939–1964. New York: Rizzoli, 1989
Reuben, Julie A. *The Making of the Modern University: Intellectual Transformation and the Marginalization of Morality.* Chicago: University of Chicago Press, 1996
Ricard, François. *The Lyric Generation: The Life and Times of the Baby Boomers.* Trans. Donald Winkler. Toronto: Stoddart, 1994. First pub. as *La generation lyrique: essai sur la vie et l'oeuvre des premiers-nés du baby-boom.* Montreal: Boreal, 1992
Robinson, Daniel, and David Kimmel. "The Queer Career of Homosexual Security Vetting in Cold War Canada," *Canadian Historical Review* 75 (Sept. 1994): 319–45
Rosenberg, Charles E. *No Other Gods: On Science and American Social Thought.* First pub. 1976. Baltimore: Johns Hopkins University Press, 1997
Rosenzweig, Roy. *Eight Hours for What We Will: Workers and Leisure in an Industrial City 1870–1920.* New York: Cambridge University Press, 1983
Ross, Andrew. *No Respect: Intellectuals and Popular Culture.* New York: Routledge, 1989
Roszak, Theodore. *The Making of a Counter Culture: Reflections on the Technocratic Society and Its Youthful Opposition.* First pub. 1969 Berkeley: University of California Press, 1995
Rubin, Joan Shelley. *The Making of Middlebrow Culture.* Chapel Hill: University of North Carolina Press, 1992
- "Self, Culture, and Self Culture in Modern America: The Early History of the Book-of-the-Month Club," *Journal of American History* 71, no. 4 (March 1985): 782–806

Rutherford, Paul. "Made in America: The Problem of Mass Culture in Canada." In David H. Flaherty and Frank E. Manning, eds., *The Beaver Bites Back? American Popular Culture in Canada*. Montreal: McGill-Queen's University, 1993: 260–80
- *When Television Was Young: Primetime Canada, 1952–1967*. Toronto: University of Toronto Press, 1990
Rydell, Robert W. *World of Fairs: The Century of Progress Expositions*. Chicago: University of Chicago Press, 1993
Saunders, Frances Stonor. *The Cultural Cold War: The CIA and the World of Arts and Letters*. New York: New Press, 2000
Scannell, Paddy. *Radio, Television and Modern Life: A Phenomenological Approach*. Oxford: Blackwell, 1996
- *A Social History of British Broadcasting, 1922–1939: Serving the Nation*. Oxford: Blackwell, 1991
Schorske, Carl E. *Fin-de-siècle Vienna: Politics and Culture*. New York: Vintage Books, 1981
Scotchie, Joseph. *Barbarians in the Saddle: An Intellectual Biography of Richard M. Weaver*. New Brunswick, NJ: Transaction, 1997
Selman, Gordon. *Adult Education in Canada: Historical Essays*. Toronto: Thompson Educational Publishing, 1995
Siomopoulous, Anna. "Entertaining Ethics: Technology, Mass Culture and American Intellectuals of the 1930s." *Film History* 11, no. 1 (1999): 45–54
Skinner, David. "A System Divided: A Political Economy of Canadian Broadcasting." PhD dissertation, Simon Fraser University, 1997
Slater, David. "Colour the Future Bright: The *White Paper*, the Green Book and the 1945–1946 Dominion–Provincial Conference on Reconstruction." In Greg Donaghy, ed., *Uncertain Horizons: Canadians and Their World in 1945*. Ottawa: Canadian Committee for the History of the Second World War, 1997, 191–208
- *War, Finance and Reconstruction: The Role of Canada's Department of Finance 1939–1946*. Ottawa: Department of Finance, 1995
Smith, Alice Kimball. *A Peril and a Hope: The Scientists' Movement in America, 1945–1947*. Chicago: University of Chicago Press, 1965
Smith, Allan. *Canada: An American Nation? Essays on Continentalism, Identity and the Canadian Frame of Mind*. Montreal: McGill-Queen's University Press, 1994
Smulyan, Susan. *Selling Radio: The Commercialization of American Broadcasting, 1920–1934*. Washington, DC: Smithsonian Institution Press, 1994
Steigerwald, David. *The Sixties and the End of Modern America*. New York: St Martin's Press, 1995
Stewart, Andrew, and William Hull. *Canadian Television Policy and the Board of Broadcast Governors*. Edmonton: University of Alberta Press, 1994
Strong-Boag, Veronica. "'Their Side of the Story': Women's Voices from Ontario Suburbs, 1945–60." In Joy Parr, ed., *A Diversity of Women: Ontario, 1945–1980*. Toronto: University of Toronto Press, 1995

Struthers, James. *No Fault of Their Own: Unemployment and the Canadian Welfare State, 1914–1941*. Toronto: University of Toronto Press, 1983

Susman, Warren I. "Culture and Commitment." In Susman, *Culture History: The Transformation of American Society in the Twentieth Century*. New York: Pantheon, 1984, 184–210

Taylor, Charles. *The Malaise of Modernity*. Toronto: CBC/Anansi, 1991

Tippett, Maria. *Art at the Service of War: Canada, Art, and the Great War*. Toronto: University of Toronto Press, 1984

– *Making Culture: English-Canadian Institutions and the Arts before the Massey Commission*. Toronto: University of Toronto Press, 1990

– "The Making of English-Canadian Culture, 1900–1939: The External Influences." Paper delivered 28 April 1987, York University. Toronto: ECW Press, 1988

Tiratsoo, Nick. "Limits of Americanisation: The United States Productivity Gospel in Britain." In Becky Conekin, Frank Mort, and Chris Waters, eds., *Moments of Modernity: Reconstructing Britain, 1945–1964*. London: Rivers Oram Press, 1999, 96–113

Toumey, Christopher P. *Conjuring Science: Scientific Symbols and Cultural Meanings in American Life*. New Brunswick, NJ: Rutgers University Press, 1996

Tuer, Dot. "The Art of Nation Building: Constructiong a 'Cultural Identity' for Post-War Canada." *Parallelogramme* 17, no. 4 (spring 1992): 24–37

Vance, Jonathan F. *Death So Noble: Memory, Meaning, and the First World War*. Vancouver: University of British Columbia Press, 1997

Verzuh, Ron. *Underground Times: Canada's Flower-Child Revolutionaries*. Toronto: Deneau, 1989

Vipond, Mary. *Listening In: The First Decade of Canadian Broadcasting, 1922–1932*. Montreal: McGill-Queen's University Press, 1992

– "The Nationalist Network: English Canada's Intellectuals and Artists in the 1920s." *Canadian Review of Studies in Nationalism* 5 (spring 1980): 32–52

Walden, Keith. *Becoming Modern in Toronto: The Industrial Exhibition and the Shaping of a Late Victorian Culture*. Toronto: University of Toronto Press, 1997

Weir, E. Austin. *The Struggle for National Broadcasting in Canada*. Toronto: McClelland and Stewart, 1965

Welton, Michael. 'An Authentic Instrument of the Democratic Process': The Intellectual Origins of the Canadian Citizens' Forum." *Studies in the Education of Adults* 18, no. 1 (April 1986): 35–49

Westbrook, Robert B. "Fighting for the American Family: Private Interests and Political Obligation in World War II." In Jackson Lears and Richard W. Fox, eds., *The Power of Culture: Critical Essays in American History*. Chicago: University of Chicago Press, 1993, 195–221

Whisnant, David E. *All That Is Native and Fine: The Politics of Culture in an American Region*. Chapel Hill: University of North Carolina Press, 1983

Whitaker, Reg, and Gary Marcuse. *Cold War Canada: The Making of a National Insecurity State, 1945–1957*. Toronto: University of Toronto Press, 1994

Whitaker, Reginald. *The Government Party: Organizing and Financing the Liberal Party of Canada, 1930–1958*. Toronto: University of Toronto Press, 1977

Whitehead, Kate, *The Third Programme: A Literary History*. Oxford: Clarendon, 1989

Whitfield, Stephen J. *The Culture of the Cold War*. Baltimore: Johns Hopkins University Press, 1991

Williams, Raymond. *Communications*. 3rd ed. London: Penguin, 1976

– *Culture and Society, 1780–1950*. London: Chatto and Windus, 1958

– *Keywords: A Vocabulary of Culture and Society*. London: Fontana/Croom Helm, 1976

Wilson, Isabel. *Citizens' Forum: 'Canada's National Platform'*. Toronto: Ontario Institute for Studies in Education, 1980

Wilson, Jeremy. "The Impact of Communications Developments on British Columbia Electoral Patterns, 1903–1975." *Canadian Journal of Political Science* 13, no. 3 (Sept. 1980): 509–35

Woodcock, George. *Strange Bedfellows: The State and the Arts in Canada*. Vancouver: Douglas & McIntyre, 1985

Young, Walter. *Anatomy of a Party: The National CCF, 1932–1961*. Toronto: University of Toronto Press, 1969

Young, William R. "Making the Truth Graphic: The Canadian Government's Home Front Information Structure and Programmes." PhD dissertation, University of British Columbia, 1978

Index

Aberhart, William, 120
active citizenship, 90–2, 103, 173, 217, 233
Adeney, Marcus, 97–9
Adorno, Theodor, 157
advertising, 142, 150, 193; criticism of, 87, 98, 168, 190–1, 234; in wartime, 37, 42, 76–7
Alexander, William Hardy, 49
Allen, Ralph, 167
American. *See* United States
Anderson, Violet, 90
Anthology, 196
Arnold, Matthew, 21, 237
Ash, Stuart, 226–7
Ashley, C.A., 75
atomic bomb. *See* nuclear weapons
authority, 73, 133, 237–8
automation, 132, 178, 203–10, 214, 313n20
Ayre, Robert, 38

Baldwin, John, 82
Barbeau, Marius, 152
Barnard, Leslie, 35
Baxter Dictionary of Dates and Events, 202
Beaubien, Phillipe de Gaspé, 219
The Beloved Community, 95

Bennett, Albert, 191
Berger, Carl, 110
Berman, Marshall, 15
Berrill, N.J., 132
Berton, Pierre, 218
The Best Years of Our Lives, 147
Binger, Carl, 123
Bissell, Claude, 184
Board of Broadcast Governors (BBG), 178
Books and Shows, 62
Bowman, R.T., 224–5
Brailey, F.W.L., 89
Braithwaite, Dennis, 224
Britain, cultural influence of, 21–3
British Columbia Parent-Teacher Federation, 197
Brittain, W.H., 92
"brow" theory (highbrow/middlebrow/lowbrow), 19, 22, 24, 57, 70, 99, 137, 144, 151, 154, 158, 177, 180, 182, 186, 189, 196, 198, 201, 215–16, 221–2, 225–6, 247n56
Brown, H. Leslie, 231
Brown, J.J., 165
Brown, Nicholas, 12
Buchan, John (Lord Tweedsmuir), 54
Buchanan, Donald, 141
Buddhism, 133

Bureau of Public Information (BPI), 36
Bushnell, Ernest, 91

Callaghan, Morley, 14, 21, 51, 86–7, 92, 99, 177
Cameron, Ewen, 123
Canada Council, 102, 152, 178, 181–2
Canada Foundation, 70, 159
Canada: Tomorrow's Giant, 201
Canadian Arts Council, 182
Canadian Association for Adult Education (CAAE), 11, 20, 42, 44–5, 50, 53–4, 69, 72, 80–1, 97, 113, 118, 151; as force behind *Citizens' Forum*, 83–90
Canadian Association of Consumers, 161
Canadian Association of Radio and Television Broadcasters (CARTB), 145, 189–91
Canadian Association of University Teachers (CAUT), 190, 193
Canadian Broadcasting Corporation (CBC), 11, 84, 116, 120–3, 125, 145, 147–8, 150–1, 186,

189–98, 200–2, 216, 218–19, 222–3, 236, 239n3; and *Citizens' Forum*, 83–94
Canadian Commentator, 183, 202
Canadian Council of Education for Citizenship (CCEC), 72
Canadian Federation of Home and School, 145, 150
Canadian Federation of University Women, 192
Canadian Forum, 20, 79
Canadian Institute of Public Affairs (CIPA), 11
Canadian Life, 159
Canadian Mental Health Association (CMHA), 197
Canadian National Exhibition (CNE), 141, 219, 229
Canadian Radio League, 83–4
Canadian Television network (CTV), 222
Canadian Youth Commission (CYC), 54, 138
Carpenter, Edmund, 124, 211
Carter, Dyson, 111
Carver, Humphrey, 51–2
CBC Discussion Club, 85
Centennial, 1967, 217–20, 224–9, 231; Centennial Commission, 225–9; symbol, 226–7
Chapin, Miriam, 126
Chaplin, Charlie, 204
Chardin, Teilhard de, 133
The Chartered Libertine, 167
Chicago Round Table, 88
Child, Philip, 55
Chisholm, Brock, 116, 123–5, 134, 140
Christianity, 108, 110, 114, 121, 123–7, 181, 193
Christianity in an Age of Science, 127–8

Christie, Agatha, 183
Churchill, Winston, 42
Citizens' Forum, 69–70, 92, 102–3, 146, 151, 162, 168, 199–200, 213; genesis of, 83–8; listening groups, 87–9; membership decline, 92–4, 199
Clark, (Sir) Kenneth, 64
class, 144, 153, 182, 248n62
Claxton, Brooke, 146
Clay, Charles, 145
Coady, M.M., 56, 82–3, 128–9
Cold War, 135–6, 159, 178, 183, 203, 211, 233–4
Columbia School of the Air, 84
Comfort, Charles, 63–4, 80, 149
comic magazines, 139–40, 145–6
commercialization, 139, 146–7, 149–51, 155, 157, 178, 180–3, 187, 190–2, 197–8, 201–2, 211–12, 219, 228, 231–2, 236
community centre(s), 94–9, 100, 150, 168; as war memorials, 98
Company of Young Canadians (CYC), 233–4
Confederation Train and Caravans, 227
conformity, 160, 167, 169, 172, 204
Conservative Party. *See* Progressive Conservative Party
consumerism, 135, 137, 141, 143, 161, 171, 207, 211, 236–7
Co-operative Commonwealth Federation (CCF), 19, 36
Corbett, Edward Anand (Ned), 15, 78, 83, 87–8, 90, 93, 98–9, 235
Corwin, Norman, 58, 150

Couchiching Conference, 206, 212, 237
Coulter, John, 9, 62–3, 81–2, 244n39
counterculture, 232
Creighton, Donald, 33, 171, 183–4
Creighton, Norman, 220
Crestwood Heights, 3, 168–9, 204
Critically Speaking, 183
Crouch, Richard, 96
cultural critics: defined, 12–15; variety of political outlooks/affiliations, 20
cultural democracy, 3, 62, 152, 157, 174, 182, 232, 237–8, 239n3
culture. *See* high culture; mass culture; popular culture

Dafoe, John, 87
Daniells, Roy, 207
Davies, Raymond, 31
Davies, Robertson, 166, 174, 201
Deacon, William, 21
Death of a Salesman, 158
democracy, 19–20, 31–2, 102, 126, 135, 148–51, 158, 160, 167, 171, 177, 184, 193, 199, 213, 222, 232, 235–8; relationship to mass culture, 53–64, 152, 193, 213, 236
Denison, Merrill, 58
design, 141–2
Dewey, John, 35, 50–1, 53; Hilda Neatby on, 163–4
Diefenbaker, John, 178, 217, 221
Dobbs, Kildare, 205–6
Dominion Advisory Committee on Reconstruction (James Committee), 68–9, 71
Dominion Drama Festival, 97
Dominion of the North, 183

Dumbrille, Dorothy, 30-1
Duncan, A.R.C., 172

Eagleton, Terry, 16
Ed Sullivan Show, 197
education, 153, 160-1, 181, 188, 192, 213, 222-3; as defence against propaganda, 43-4; Hilda Neatby on progressive, 163-7
Einstein, Albert: relativity theory, 130
Eisenhower, Dwight, 203
Eliot, T.S., 60, 146, 164, 201, 231
elitism, 141, 148, 151, 157, 180, 191, 215, 232-3, 237
Ellul, Jacques, 221
enemy culture, 38-46, 64, 229, 255n57; as antidemocratic, 55-7
The Ensign, 123
Estall, Martyn, 61, 93, 98
Eustace, C.J., 114-15, 117-8, 121, 124, 128, 143, 155
Ewing, J.M., 19, 143-5
expertise, 48, 68, 72, 74, 81, 108, 148, 163-5
Exploring Minds, 196
Expo 67, 133, 217-19, 229-32; pavilions at, 230-2
Expo Summer, 231

Fairbanks, Douglas, Jr, 58
Faludi, Eugenio, 95-6
La Famille Plouffe, 196
family, 143, 194, 208-9
Farm Forum. *See* National Farm Radio Forum
Fighting Words, 199
Fisher, John, 219, 226, 233
folk culture, 7, 66, 93, 94, 97, 137, 152, 159, 161, 173, 182, 196, 202, 215, 218
Food for Thought, 42
Ford, Henry, 156
Forsey, Eugene, 206

Forster, E.M., 11, 13, 54, 235
Fowler, R.M., 173, 188
Fowler Commission. *See* Royal Commission on Broadcasting
Fraser, Blair, 48, 214-15
Fraser, Peter, 33-4
Freud, Anna, 123
Freud, Sigmund, 21
Friesen, Gerald, 8
Frye, Northrop, 12, 42, 53, 57, 60, 237-8
Fulford, Robert, 201, 222, 231
Fulton, Davie, 145

Garner, Hugh, 161, 185
Gillis, Clarie, 112-13
Gilmour, G.P., 162
Gilroy, Marion, 192
Gonsalves, James, 223
Goodings, Stewart, 233-4
Gorman, Paul, 14
Gramsci, Antonio, 13-14
Grant, George, 19, 20, 89-92, 94, 213, 218, 221
Greene, Lorne, 156
Greer, Allan, 5
Gregory, Sir Richard, 47
Grierson, John, 37, 62
Guthrie, Tyrone, 161

Haddow, Adeline, 52, 236
Hamilton, Alvin, 217
Harrington, E.L., 48, 112
Harris, Lawren, 52, 162, 204
Hatcher, William, 113
Havelock, Eric, 50-1
Healy, W.J., 40, 49
Heisenberg, Werner: uncertainty principle, 130
Herbert, Walter, 101-2, 159-60
Here and Now, 159
Hexicon, 202
high culture, 7, 22, 66, 93-4, 97, 160, 173, 182, 189, 194, 202, 234, 247n56

Hilton, James, 48
Hitler, Adolf, 41, 43-6
Holmes, John, 55
Horkheimer, Max, 157
Hosking, R.S., 208
House of Commons Special Committee on Reconstruction and Re-establishment (Turgeon Committee), 68, 70-1, 99-100
Howe, C.D., 63, 109
Hoyle, Fred, 116, 120-3, 125, 134
humanities, 44, 107; as opposed to sciences, 170-2, 179
Humanities Association of Canada, 191
Hutchins, Robert, 155, 164
Hutchison, Bruce, 201, 207

identity, 12, 24, 67, 147, 174, 178-9, 188, 195, 210, 212, 214, 226
Ilsley, J.L., 145
Imperial Order Daughters of the Empire (IODE), 79
In the Shadow of the Bomb, 155-8
Inch, Robert Boyer, 86, 88
Innis, Donald, 119-20
Innis, Harold, 8, 119-20, 160-2, 187
Invitation to Learning, 91
Irving, John A., 124, 133, 185, 206

Jaffary, Stuart, 56, 96
Jake and the Kid, 196
James, F.C. (Cyril), 46, 62, 68-9, 96, 134
Jamieson, Don, 182-3
Jasen, Patricia, 110
Jefferson, Thomas, 177
Joad, C.E.M., 23
Johnson, Lyndon, 223
Jones, Emrys, 152
Jung, Carl Gustav, 174

Kafka, Franz, 191

346 INDEX

Kammen, Michael, 8
Katimavik, 231
Keirstead, Burton, 23, 110
Keirstead, Stella, 116
Keirstead, W.C., 49–50
Keith, C.I., 191
Kelly, J.M., 122–3
Kidd, J.R., 206
King, William Lyon Mackenzie, 41
Kipling, Rudyard, 64
Kirkconnell, Watson, 40–1, 58–9, 74, 143, 181, 183; attitude towards science, 113, 118–19, 131
kitsch, 200, 202, 214, 246n51
Klonsky, Milton, 153
Kloppenberg, James, 164

Labour Forum, 83
Labour-Progressive Party, 20, 196–7
Lambert, R.S., 42–3, 44–5, 55
Lament for a Nation, 218, 221
Lanchester, Elsa, 58
Laughton, Charles, 58
Lazarsfeld, Paul, 39
Le Bon, Gustav, 21
Leacock, Stephen, 33
Lears, Jackson, 12, 15
Leavis, F.R., 22
leisure, 52, 61, 95–6, 98, 139, 143–5, 157–8, 160, 162, 166, 203, 207, 212–13, 235–6, 238
LeMahieu, Daniel, 8, 13, 54
Levine, Lawrence, 18
Lhamon, W.T., 136
Liberal Party, 36, 75, 136, 159
liberalism, 19–20
libraries, 96
literature, 140, 145–6, 186, 205, 210–11, 234
Litt, Paul, 7–8, 138
Living in the Atomic Age, 124–5
Livingstone, Sir Richard, 164
Lockhart, W.C., 191–2

The Lonely Crowd, 168
Loosley, Elizabeth, 168
Lost Weekend, 158
Low, David, 75
low culture. See mass culture
Lower, A.R.M., 22, 32–3, 42, 116, 165, 171, 173, 197, 222–3
Luke, Gospel of, 42
Lynes, Russell, 154

McArthur, Duncan, 59
McCarthy, Joseph, 136
McClelland and Stewart, 185, 224
McCourt, Edward, 164
McDade, John, 185
MacDonald, Barry, 125–6
Macdonald, Dwight, 186
McDougall, John L., 77
MacFarlane, Ronald, 61, 71
MacGill, Elsie, 111
MacGillivray, J.R., 38–9
McKay, Ian, 8
Mackay, L.A., 59
MacKenzie, N.A.M. (Larry), 44, 50, 93, 108
McKenzie, Robert T., 87, 94
McKillop, Brian, 8
Maclean's, 155, 215
Maclennan, Hugh, 220
MacLeod, Alastair, 208
McLuhan, Marshall, 3, 162, 180, 187–8, 198, 212
McNaught, Kenneth, 191–2
Man's Last Enemy – Himself!, 123
Marsh, Leonard, 72, 77–8, 142
Martin, Chester, 35–6
mass culture: defined, 16–17, 246n49; as destructive force, 81, 108, 126, 133–4, 135, 138, 140, 144, 146, 150–1, 153, 155–8, 162, 168, 173–4, 177, 180–8, 194–5, 198–9, 201, 214, 218, 222–3, 229, 235–8;

Nazi tendency to exploit, 41–6, 50; relationship to popular culture, 17, 151, 153, 172, 200, 221–2, 246n50–2
mass production, 30, 52, 141, 155–8, 204, 223
mass society, 128, 135, 141, 160, 166–7, 173
Massey, Raymond, 58
Massey, Vincent, 147, 149
Massey (or Massey–Lévesque) Commission. See Royal Commission on National Development in the Arts, Letters and Sciences
Massolin, Philip, 7
materialism, 129, 142–3, 160, 165–6, 173, 185, 209
Matthew, Gospel of, 124
The Mechanical Bride, 188
Mecredy, M.B., 154
middlebrow culture, 10, 19, 22, 70, 93, 144, 155, 157, 159, 163, 178, 185, 195–8, 201–3, 207, 210, 212, 220, 237, 242n19, 249n74
Miles, Peter, 36
Milner, Gamaliel, 23
Ministry of Information (Britain), 36
Moberly, Sir Walter, 164
modern life, 4–5, 37, 49, 54, 97; defined, 15–16; effects of, 130–1, 137, 139, 152, 162, 168, 174, 194, 205, 211, 218, 228, 233, 237–8, 244n44, 245n46
Moore, Mavor, 180, 183
Morris, William, 51–2
Morrison, Jean Hunter, 91
Morrison, Neil, 84–5, 125–6
Morton, W.L., 20, 133, 183, 209–10, 233
movies: criticism of, 77, 96, 147; Hollywood as source of popular and/or bad, 62–3, 88, 97, 137, 158, 201
Murray, Gladstone (W.E.G.), 84–5

Mussolini, Benito, 42

National Committee for Mental Hygiene, 169
National Farm Radio Forum (Farm Forum), 84–5, 87, 92, 94
National Film Board (NFB), 37, 62, 89, 148, 229
National Religious Advisory Council, 120
nationalism, 173–4, 179, 200, 206, 211–12, 215, 219, 224; cultural, 154, 159, 178–9, 184, 186–7, 193, 195, 197–8, 202, 217, 225–6, 234, 236
Neatby, Hilda, 53, 137, 163–7
New Democratic Party (NDP), 19
New Frontiers, 20
Newman, Peter C., 217
Nicol, Eric, 205
North Atlantic Treaty Organization (NATO), 215
Northcliffe, Lord (Alfred Harmsworth), 43, 47
nuclear weapons, 107–9, 113–16, 126, 129, 136, 139, 155, 170, 210, 232, 280n34

Of Things to Come, 86–7
Office of War Information (U.S.), 36
The Organization Man, 173, 204
Ortega y Gasset, José, 21
Orwell, George (Eric Blair), 36
Ouimet, Alphonse, 200
Our Changing Values, 143–5
Owen, D.R.G., 124, 127–9, 131, 134
Owram, Doug, 8–9, 136, 237

Paluk, William, 209
Park, Julian, 186–7, 207, 215
Parliamentary Committee on Broadcasting, 125
Partisan Review, 153
Pearson, Lester, 221
Pells, Richard, 14
Percival, Lloyd, 97
Petrie, J.R., 72
Petticoat Junction, 224
Phelps, Arthur, 24, 72–3, 139–40
Phillips, Charles, 59
Piché, Lucien, 230
Pierce, Lorne, 95, 97
planning, 73–8; as antithesis of free enterprise, 75
A Play on Words, 155
poetry: modern, 31; patriotic, 30–1
Pollick, Joseph, 159–60
popular culture, 136, 144, 147, 169, 227, 232, 246n50–2, 247n56; relationship to mass culture, 17, 169, 173, 246n49
Pratt, E.J., 31
Priestley, J.B., 41, 174, 192
Progressive Conservative Party, 101, 136, 178
propaganda, 39–44
psychology, 123–4, 130, 163, 167, 180, 197, 212
public intellectuals, 7, 159, 243n29

Quebec, 221, 224

Raboy, Marc, 125
radio: criticism of programs, 48, 57, 87, 119–27, 191; power of, 83–4, 88, 91, 93, 121–2, 192–4; in United States, 84, 125, 150–1
Rawhide, 196
Reading, 159
reconstruction: culture of, 68–9, 72–3, 102, 112, 173; planning for, begins early in wartime, 68, 71–3
regimentation, 31–2, 44, 45, 50, 74–5, 78
Reid, Stewart, 191–2
Relations, 123
religion, 108–10; as opposed to science, 109–19, 124–5, 127–34; religious minorities, 126
Richards, P.M., 75
Riesman, David, 167–8, 172, 207
Robins, John D., 202
rock and roll, 181
Roosevelt, Franklin Delano, 32, 42, 59
Rosenberg, Bernard, 203–4
Ross, Andrew, 12
Ross, Malcolm, 215
Ross, Mary Lowrey, 79, 89, 107, 111, 145, 199, 205, 215
Ross, Murray, 168
Roy, Gabrielle, 210, 230
Royal Commission on Bilingualism and Biculturalism, 221, 224
Royal Commission on Broadcasting (Fowler Commission), 138–9, 173, 182, 188–98, 206
Royal Commission on National Development in the Arts, Letters and Sciences, 7, 36, 69, 137–8, 146–53, 157, 161, 170–1, 212, 237; members of, 44, 86; recommendations of, 138–9, 147; submissions to, 100, 138, 147, 149, 151
Rubin, Joan Shelley, 8
Rue Deschambault, 210
rural life, idealized, 33–5, 89, 154–5
Ruskin, John, 51, 81
Russell, Bertrand, 116, 120, 124–5
Rutherford, Paul, 16, 162, 194

Saint-Exupéry, Antoine de, 230
Salter, F.M., 102–3
Salverson, George, 155, 157–9, 173–4, 178
Sandwell, B.K., 35, 39, 45, 57, 60, 66, 78, 80, 82, 110, 113, 125–6, 132, 140–1, 168

348 INDEX

satire, 79, 93, 164, 167, 185, 196, 204, 218
Saturday Night, 20, 47, 78
Saunders, Richard, 64–5
Schrecker, Paul, 52
science: during Cold War, 155; enemy uses of, 47–50, 113, 171; as opposed to humanities, 50, 170–2, 179; as opposed to religion, 109–19, 124–5, 127–34, 171; reputation of, 47–9, 111, 131, 171–2, 229–30; on television, 203
The Science Front, 47
scientism, 107–8, 117, 127–8, 133, 160, 209
Scientism, Man and Religion, 127
Scott, F.R., 75–6
Seeley, John, 3, 168
Seldes, Gilbert, 155–6, 160
Shea, Albert, 159
Shoub, Mac, 45
Silcox, Claris, 39, 64, 73, 86, 115
Sim, R. Alex, 168–9
Sinclair, Lister, 131, 155, 230
Siomopoulous, Anna, 14
Smith, A.J.M., 31, 140
Smith, Malcolm, 36
Smythe, Dallas, 188
Snow, C.P., 133, 170, 179
So Little For the Mind, 163–6
Social Credit, 83
Spengler, Oswald, 21
Sports College of the Air, 97
Steacie, E.W.R., 171–2
Stratford Festival, 161, 215
Susman, Warren, 16.
Synge, J.L., 170

Tallents, Stephen, 101
taste, 52, 99, 141–3, 154, 172, 174, 177, 182, 185, 190, 195, 212, 237
Technocracy movement, 83

technology, 46–53, 111–12, 114, 131–4, 171–2, 179, 204–6, 208, 212–13, 219–21, 228–31, 235
television, 156, 158, 162, 186, 194–5, 199, 201–2, 222, 228
A Temperate Dispute, 166
Terre des Hommes (Man and His World), 219, 230
Theatre of Freedom, 58
Third Programme (BBC), 121, 196
Thomas, Alan, 184
Thomson, James S., 85, 88
Thomson, Watson, 30, 85, 87
Tippett, Maria, 7
Toqueville, Alexis de, 167, 174
Town Meeting (Canada), 151
Town Meeting of the Air (United States), 88, 151
Toye, Harold, 132–3
Tracy, C.R., 155
Transit through Fire, 62, 81
The Trial, 191
Trueman, A.W., 39
Tuning Up for Tomorrow, 47
Twain, Mark, 201
The Two Cultures, 170

Underhill, Frank, 40–1, 60, 166, 168, 181, 187, 222
The Undiscovered Self, 174
United Church of Canada, 115, 132, 206, 208; Commission on Automation, 209; Commission on Christian Marriage and Divorce, 208
United Nations (UN), 215
United Nations Educational, Scientific and Cultural Organization (UNESCO), 140, 192
United States: Canada's relationship with, 178–9, 233–4; cultural influences from, 21–3, 147, 173, 186, 189, 194, 197–8, 211–12, 216, 222, 228
The Unknown Country, 201
utilitarianism, 50–2, 64, 108, 135, 171

Valentine, Alan, 162
van den Haag, Ernest, 183–4
Vance, Jonathan, 10, 30
Velikovsky, Immanuel, 119
Vipond, Mary, 14
Vlastos, Gregory, 89

Wakeman, Albert, 51
Walden, Keith, 110
Wales, Julia Grace, 72, 119
Wallace, Malcolm, 170
Wallace, R.C., 129–31, 134, 142
Wartime Information Board (WIB), 36, 43
Watson, Patrick, 203
Wayne and Shuster, 93, 146
We Discuss Canada, 85
Weaver, Richard, 3
Welles, Orson, 58
Wells, H.G., 86, 96
Westley, William, 207–8
Whitton, Charlotte, 107
Whyte, William, 133, 173, 204, 208
Willan, Healey, 62, 81
Williams, Raymond, 17, 152, 224, 246n52
Williamson, Ralph, 122
Willis, I.D., 32, 54, 56
Wilson, Isabel, 163, 199
Woodhouse, A.S.P., 82
Woodside, Willson, 3
Workers' Educational Association (WEA), 83
World's Fairs, 219
Wyn Wood, Elizabeth, 81–2, 99

Young Men's Christian Association (YMCA), 85, 97

Ziemer, Gregor, 44